W9-BYK-807

Teaching
Student-Centered
MATHEMATICS
Grades K–3

JOHN A. VAN DE WALLE
Virginia Commonwealth University

LOUANN H. LOVIN
James Madison University

PEARSON

Boston | New York | San Francisco
Mexico City | Montreal | Toronto | London | Madrid | Munich | Paris
Hong Kong | Singapore | Tokyo | Cape Town | Sydney

Series Editor: Traci Mueller
Development Editor: Sonny Regelman
Editorial Assistant: James P. Neal, III
Marketing Manager: Jen Armstrong
Senior Editorial-Production Administrator: Donna Simons
Composition and Prepress Buyer: Linda Cox
Manufacturing Buyer: Andrew Turso

Cover Designer: Kristina Mose-Libon
Permissions Coordinator: William Walsh
Permissions Researcher: Renee Nicholls
Editorial-Production Service: Omegatype Typography, Inc.
Interior Designer: The Davis Group, Inc.
Illustrations: Omegatype Typography, Inc.
Electronic Composition: Omegatype Typography, Inc.

For related titles and support materials, visit our online catalog at www.abprofessionaled.com.

Between the time website information is gathered and published, some sites may have closed. Also, the transcription of URLs can result in typographical errors. The publisher would appreciate notification where these errors occur so that they may be corrected in subsequent editions.

Many of the designations used by manufacturers and sellers to distinguish their products are claimed as trademarks. Where those designations appear in this book, and Allyn and Bacon was aware of a trademark claim, the designations have been printed in initial or all caps.

Library of Congress Cataloging-in-Publication Data

Van de Walle, John A.
    Teaching student-centered mathematics : Grades K–3 / John A. Van de Walle, LouAnn H. Lovin.
        p. cm. — (The Van de Walle professional mathematics series ; v. 1)
    Includes bibliographical references and index.
    ISBN 0-205-40843-5
    1. Mathematics—Study and teaching—United States.   I. Lovin, LouAnn H.   II. Title.   III. Series.

QA13.V36 2006
372.7–dc22

2005043008

Printed in the United States of America

24 25 26 27 28 29 EBM 13 12

BRIEF CONTENTS

CONTENTS

PREFACE

And once I had a teacher who understood. He brought with him the beauty
of mathematics. He made me create it for myself. He gave me nothing,
and it was more than any other teacher has ever dared to give me.

—Cochran (1991, pp. 213–214)

Math makes sense! This is the most fundamental idea that an elementary teacher of
mathematics needs to believe and act on. It is through the teacher's actions that every
child in his or her own way can come to believe this simple truth and more important,
believe that he or she is capable of making sense of mathematics. Helping students
come to this belief should be a goal of every teacher.

The title of this book, *Teaching Student-Centered Mathematics,* reflects our belief in
the best way for students to develop this confidence and understanding of mathematics.
We believe that teachers must create an environment where students are trusted to solve
problems and work together using their ideas to do so. Instruction involves posing tasks
that will engage students in the mathematics they are expected to learn. Then, by allowing students to interact with and struggle with the mathematics using *their* ideas and
their strategies—a student-centered approach—the mathematics they learn will be integrated with their ideas; it will make sense to them, be understood, and be enjoyed.

Our Goals for the Book

For many teachers, the idea of allowing students to struggle with mathematics is
sometimes difficult to accept. "How and why should I allow students to wrestle with
problems and not show them the solutions? Where can the right kinds of tasks be
found? Where can I learn the mathematics content information I really need in order

to be able to teach in this way?" With these and other questions firmly in mind, we have three main objectives for this book:

1. To help teachers understand what it means to teach in a student-centered, problem-based manner. This is a theme that runs throughout the book. We have also tried to help you understand why this is the best method available for helping students understand mathematics.
2. To provide a reference book for all of the mathematics content found in kindergarten to third grade and the best information available concerning how children learn this mathematics. We have tried to provide this information in a readable, useful manner, completely integrated with instructional strategies.
3. To provide a resource of simple, problem-based activities and tasks that can engage students in the mathematics that is important for them to learn.

These are also goals of my larger book, *Elementary and Middle School Mathematics: Teaching Developmentally.* Written primarily as a textbook for college courses about teaching mathematics, *EMSM* has, over the years, also become popular as a resource book for classroom teachers. Therefore, it made sense to use that larger text as the basis for this series of books.

My first decision was to ask Dr. LouAnn Lovin to assist me in adapting *EMSM.* Together, we decided to use it as the foundation for each of the books in this series of three grade-banded books. In many instances we have used both text and activities exactly as they appear in the college text. Those of you familiar with that book will undoubtedly see overlap, as we included much of the material, both text and activities, from *EMSM.* However, we also quickly found that in order for the books to be more useful for the classroom teacher at the prescribed grade level, there were gaps to be filled, material to be rearranged, and language to be focused. As a result, we wrote new activities, expanded the mathematics, and in a few cases wrote almost completely new chapters. Unlike *EMSM,* this book is designed expressly for the classroom teacher at the kindergarten to third-grade level. We hope you will find that this is a better resource for your purposes.

What You Will Find in This Book

We view this book as a primary resource for teachers. It is not simply a book of activities, although it has well over 150 good, practical activities. It is not a book about content, although it addresses a deep understanding of mathematics and how children learn it. Nor is it a book about constructivist views of teaching, although it is firmly based on a constructivist view of how children learn. Rather, we have attempted to bring together all of these aspects of teaching student-centered, problem-based mathematics and integrate them in a manner that we hope is most helpful to you, the classroom teacher.

Foundations of Student-Centered Instruction

Chapter 1 is the only "general" chapter in the book. It describes four core ideas for effective mathematics teaching: knowledge of how children learn, an explanation of teaching mathematics through problem solving, suggestions for planning student-centered lessons, and strategies for assessment in a student-centered environment. We strongly believe that this is the most important chapter of the book. The remaining 11 chapters are based on these core ideas. We encourage you to read this chapter thoughtfully.

Big Ideas in Mathematics

Much of the literature espousing a student-centered approach suggests that teachers plan their instruction around "big ideas" rather than individual skills or concepts. At the start of every chapter after the first one, you will find a list of the key mathematical ideas associated with the chapter. Teachers find these lists beneficial because they focus thinking on the broader goals of a mathematics unit and thus keep both instruction and assessment on target.

Activities

Throughout Chapters 2 to 12, you will find numerous activities that can be directly adapted to lessons in your classroom. Most of the time you will find these set off from the text with a number and a title. Many additional ideas are described directly in the text or in the illustrations. Each of these is a problem-based task as described in Chapter 1.

It is important that you see these activities as an integral part of the text that surrounds them. The activities are inserted as examples to support the development of the mathematics being discussed and how children can be helped to learn that content. Therefore, we hope that you will not take any activity as a suggestion for instruction without reading carefully the full text in which it is embedded.

Following this Preface, you will find the Activities at a Glance chart, a list of all the named and numbered activities with a short statement of the mathematical goal for each. You may occasionally find that a topic you are teaching is not in the list. Whole-number computation is an example, even though all of Chapter 6 is devoted to this large curricular area. The format of a boxed activity did not lend itself to the topic. Keep in mind that although this book addresses all of the big ideas in K–3 mathematics, it is not an activity book in the traditional sense.

Assessment Notes

We believe that in a student-centered environment, assessment should be integral to instruction rather than an interruption or a test at the end of a unit. To teach in a student-centered manner demands "listening" carefully to the thinking of students (including paying attention to what they do and write) so that you can plan tomorrow's lesson, assist students, and communicate with parents. To aid in your listening, you will find assessment ideas located throughout Chapters 2 to 12.

Stop and Reflect

Reflective thinking is the key to effective learning. This is true not only for students but also for all learners. Throughout the book you will run across stop signs with questions that ask you to pause in your reading and reflect on some aspect of what you have read. These "stop and reflect" sections do not signal every important idea, but we have tried to place them where it seemed natural and helpful for you to slow down a bit and think.

Expanded Lessons

The activities in the book are written in a brief format so as not to detract from the flow of ideas. Details of how an activity should be implemented in the classroom are generally left to you, with the assumption that your class is unique. The process of designing a good student-centered, problem-based lesson requires careful thought regardless of where the idea for the lesson comes from. By way of example, we selected one activity in each chapter and expanded it into a complete lesson plan, following the structure described in Chapter 1. We included lesson elements such as mathematical goals, notes on preparation, specific expectations for the students, and notes on assessment. Clearly, any lesson should be modified to suit the special needs of your class. We offer these examples as suggestions for making the many decisions involved in lesson planning. These Expanded Lessons are located at the end of Chapters 2 to 12.

NCTM Standards Appendix

NCTM's *Principles and Standards for School Mathematics* (2000) has been a guiding force for the reform in school mathematics and we feel that this book is reflective of that document. In Appendix A, you will find a copy of the appendix to the *Standards,* listing all of the content standards and goals for each of the four grade bands: pre-K–2, 3–5, 6–8, and 9–12.

Blackline Masters

Throughout the book there are references to Blackline Masters that are useful for conducting the activities being discussed. In Appendix B, you will find a thumbnail version of all of the Blackline Masters so that you will be able to see what they look like. A PDF version of each Master is available on the website for the book: www.ablongman. com/vandewalleseries. We have found that this method of providing the masters is actually much more useful to teachers than having to copy pages from the book. Each time you download a master, remember to keep a copy on your computer. That way they will always be at your fingertips. You may copy these masters freely for use in your classroom.

Acknowledgments

This series of books began as a straightforward and seemingly simple project: adapt *Elementary and Middle School Mathematics* to suit the needs of classroom teachers in three grade bands, K–3, 3–5, and 5–8. It was not nearly as simple as it initially seemed. I am indebted to a number of people who have helped to make the books a reality.

Two people at Allyn & Bacon have been truly indispensable. Our editor, Traci Mueller, has offered encouragement from start to finish. She has answered questions and helped with many big decisions. Our development editor, Sonny Regelman, is a master of detail and a font of good judgment. Her constant prodding and careful editing have become my safety net. Throughout the development of these books, and also *EMSM*, we have become close professional friends. It has been a pleasure to continue my association with these and all of the people at Allyn & Bacon.

I would especially like to take this opportunity to offer a huge thank you to my coauthor, Dr. LouAnn Lovin. In addition to contributing manuscript, LouAnn brought to this project a valuable second viewpoint on issues of mathematics and how best to help students learn. Without LouAnn's able collaboration, this series would probably not exist. More important, the books are significantly better for her efforts. Thanks, LouAnn!

To all of the teachers throughout the United States and Canada who have encouraged me and expressed their appreciation of the *EMSM* book, a special thanks. We hope that this book will be of even more help to you as you work with your students. Remember always to believe in kids. Allow them to think and to make sense of mathematics daily.

—John Van de Walle

ACTIVITIES AT A GLANCE

This table lists all of the named and numbered activities in the book. In addition to providing an easy way to find an activity, the table provides the main mathematical goal or objective for each activity, stated as succinctly as possible. We hope this will be useful.

Rather than a book of activities, this is a book about teaching mathematics. Many practical and effective activities are used as examples. Every activity should be seen as an integral part of the text that surrounds it. Therefore, it is extremely important not to take any activity as a suggestion for instruction without reading carefully the full text in which it is embedded.

In addition to containing the named and numbered activities, the book is also full of ideas for problem-based instruction that are found within the text and in the illustrations but without an activity name and number. Although we know you will find the activities in this table useful, you should see the table only as a listing of the named activities, and not as an index to instructional ideas.

Chapter 3 Developing Meaning for the Operations and Solving Story Problems

Chapter 4 Helping Children Master the Basic Facts

Chapter 5   Base-Ten Concepts and Place Value

ACTIVITIES AT A GLANCE

Chapter 6 Strategies for Whole-Number Computation

Chapter 7 Geometric Thinking and Geometric Concepts

Chapter 8 Developing Measurement Concepts

ACTIVITIES AT A GLANCE

Chapter 9　Early Fraction Concepts

	Activity	Mathematical Goal	page number
9.1	Correct Shares	Develop understanding of fractional parts	257
9.2	Finding Fair Shares	Develop understanding of fractional parts	257
9.3	More, Less, or Equal to One Whole	Develop understanding of fractional parts	258
9.4	Mixed-Number Names	Develop understanding of mixed numbers	260
9.5	Zero, One-Half, or One	Develop benchmarks of 0, $\frac{1}{2}$, and 1 for fractions	263
9.6	Close Fractions	Develop benchmarks of 0, $\frac{1}{2}$, and 1 for fractions	263
9.7	About How Much	Develop an understanding of the size of fractions	263
9.8	Ordering Unit Fractions	Develop an understanding of the size of unit fractions	264
9.9	Choose, Explain, Test	Develop an understanding of the relative size of fractions	266
9.10	Line 'Em Up	Develop an understanding of the relative size of fractions	266
9.11	First Estimates	Develop an understanding of the relative size of fractions through estimation	267
9.12	Different Fillers	Develop an understanding of the concept of equivalent fractions	269
9.13	Dot Paper Equivalencies	Develop an understanding of the concept of equivalent fractions	269
9.14	Group the Counters, Find the Names	Develop an understanding of the concept of equivalent fractions	270
9.15	Missing-Number Equivalencies	Use equivalent fraction concepts to find specific equivalent fractions	271

Chapter 10　Algebraic Reasoning

	Activity	Mathematical Goal	page number
10.1	Pattern Strips	Explore repeating patterns	276
10.2	Pattern Match	Distinguish between the structure of a repeat pattern and its representation	277
10.3	Same Pattern, Different Stuff	Distinguish between the structure of a repeat pattern and its representation	278
10.4	Predict Down the Line	Explore the structure of repeating patterns analytically	279
10.5	Grid Patterns	Explore how repeat patterns create new patterns when modeled in an array	280
10.6	Extend and Explain	Explore growing patterns	281
10.7	Predict How Many	Develop functional relationships in growing patterns	282
10.8	What's Next and Why?	Explore relationships in number patterns	285
10.9	Calculator Skip Counting	Explore patterns in skip counts	285
10.10	Start and Jump Numbers	Develop the ability to analyze numeric patterns	286
10.11	Start and Jump on the Hundreds Chart	Explore skip-count patterns on the hundreds chart	287
10.12	Fractured Chart Pieces	Explore number relationships on the hundreds chart	288
10.13	How Many Ways?	Develop a pattern in combinations for a given whole number	289
10.14	One Up and One Down: Addition	Develop an understanding of how complimentary changes in two addends leaves the sum unchanged	289

ACTIVITIES AT A GLANCE

ABOUT THE AUTHORS

John A. Van de Walle is Professor Emeritus at Virginia Commonwealth University. After 30 years with his university, Dr. Van de Walle continues to work with teachers at the K–8 level as a mathematics education consultant. He has taught mathematics to children at all levels, K–8. He is a coauthor of a mathematics series for K–6 (Scott Foresman) and the author of *Elementary and Middle School Mathematics: Teaching Developmentally,* the market-leading text and resource book on which this series is based.

LouAnn Lovin is a former classroom teacher and is currently an assistant professor in mathematics education at James Madison University, where she teaches mathematics methods and mathematics content courses for Pre-K–8 prospective teachers and has been involved in the mathematical professional development of teachers in grades 4–8. She is actively involved with NCTM and is also President of the Valley of Virginia Council of Teachers of Mathematics (V²CTM). Her research interests are in the area of teacher knowledge, in particular, exploring the nature of the mathematical knowledge needed for effective teaching.

FOUNDATIONS OF STUDENT-CENTERED INSTRUCTION

What is basic in mathematics is as simple as this: *Math makes sense!* Every child in his or her own way can come to believe this. More important, every child can come to believe that he or she is capable of making sense of mathematics.

Students have to develop this understanding themselves. Their understanding and, thus, their confidence grow as a result of being engaged in doing mathematics. To teach effectively means to engage students at their level so they can create or develop new ideas to use and understand so they can make sense of mathematics.

The fundamental core of effective teaching of mathematics combines an understanding of how children learn, how to promote that learning through problem solving, and how to plan for and assess that learning on a daily basis. Information to help you with these four foundational components—children learning constructively, teaching with problems, planning lessons, and assessing where students are—are discussed in the next four sections of this chapter.

This book is designed to help you apply these core ideas to the content that you teach.

HOW CHILDREN LEARN AND UNDERSTAND MATHEMATICS

To put it simply, *children construct their own knowledge*. This is the basic tenet of the theory of learning called *constructivism*. In fact, not just children, but all people, all of the time construct or give meaning to things they perceive or think about. As you read these words, you are giving meaning to them. You are constructing ideas.

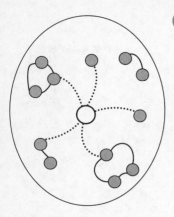

FIGURE 1.1 • • • • • • • • • • •

We use the ideas we already have (gray dots) to construct a new idea (white dot), developing in the process a network of connections between ideas. The more ideas used and the more connections made, the better we understand.

Constructing Ideas

To construct or build something in the physical world requires tools, materials, and effort. Constructing ideas can be viewed similarly. The tools we use to build understanding are our existing ideas, the knowledge that we already possess. The materials may be things we see, hear, or touch—elements of our physical surroundings. Sometimes the materials are our own thoughts and ideas—existing ideas and thoughts used to modify other ideas. The effort that must be supplied is active and reflective thought. If minds are not actively engaged in thought, no effective learning occurs.

To get a notion of what it means to construct an idea, consider the diagram in Figure 1.1. Imagine that it represents a small portion of a student's knowledge concerning a collection of related ideas. The gray dots represent ideas that the student already has developed. The lines joining these dots represent connections between and among the ideas. Every idea or bit of knowledge that a person has is connected in at least some way to some other idea. No idea exists in complete isolation.

Now suppose that this person is trying to understand, learn, or give meaning to a new idea, the one represented by the white dot in the diagram. The tools that are available to construct this idea are precisely the related ideas that the person already owns. As the existing ideas give meaning to the new idea, new connections are formed—the dotted lines in the diagram—between the new idea and the existing ones. The more existing ideas that are used to give meaning to the new one, the more connections will be made. The more connections made, the better the new idea is understood.

Understanding

It is possible to say that we know something or we do not. That is, knowledge is something that we either have or don't have. In contrast, *understanding* can be defined as a measure of the quality and quantity of connections that an idea has with existing ideas. Understanding is never an all-or-nothing proposition. It depends on the existence of appropriate ideas and on the creation of new connections (Backhouse, Haggarty, Pirie, & Stratton, 1992; Davis, 1986; Hiebert & Carpenter, 1992; Janvier, 1987; Schroeder & Lester, 1989). For example, consider first-grade children working through a page of addition facts. Each child may be said to know his or her facts, but their understanding is quite different. Some use their fingers and count each addend, beginning with the one on the top. Others begin with the larger number and use their fingers to count on from the smaller number. Still others seem to be able to write the answer without counting. These latter children may be using a variety of thought strategies, most without consciously thinking about what they are doing. They often say something like, "I just know it in my head." Clearly, each child brings a different set of "dots" to this task. Each "understands" addition in a different way.

Another way to think about an individual's understanding is that it exists along a continuum (see Figure 1.2). At one extreme is a very rich set of connections. The understood idea is associated with many other existing ideas in a meaningful network of concepts and procedures. Hiebert and Carpenter (1992) refer to "webs" of interrelated ideas. Clearly, our goal for children is that each new mathematical idea be well understood—that it be imbedded in as rich a web of related mathematical ideas as is possible.

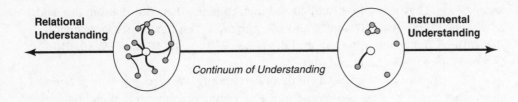

Relational Understanding

Instrumental Understanding

Continuum of Understanding

FIGURE 1.2 • • • • • • • • • •

Understanding is a measure of the quality and quantity of connections that a new idea has with existing ideas. The greater the number of connections to a network of ideas, the better the understanding.

At the other end of the continuum, ideas are completely isolated or nearly so. Here we find ideas that have been rotely learned. Due to their isolation, poorly understood ideas are easily forgotten and are unlikely to be useful for constructing new ideas.

For instance, consider the concept of "seven" as constructed by a child in the first grade. Seven for a first grader is most likely connected to counting, to the construct of "more than," and is probably understood as less than 10 and more than 2. What else would we want this child to eventually connect to the concept of seven? Seven is 1 more than 6; it is 2 less than 9; it is the combination of 3 and 4, or 2 and 5; it is odd; it is small compared to 73 and large compared to one-tenth; it is the number of days in a week; it is "lucky"; it is prime; and on and on. The web of potential ideas connected to a number can grow large and involved. Children who possess only a few of these ideas understand seven less well than children who possess a lot of these ideas. And understanding is not only a matter of quantity but also of quality. We want the things that students relate to an idea to be those that are most helpful and useful. For first-grade students the concept of prime is not significantly useful. But knowing that seven is three away from 10 is very useful.

Computational procedures also provide a good opportunity to see how understanding can differ from one child to another. For addition and subtraction with two- or three-digit numbers, a flexible and rich understanding of numbers and place value is very helpful. How might different children approach the task of finding the sum of 37 and 28? For children whose understanding of 37 is based only on counting, the use of counters and a count-all procedure is likely. (See Figure 1.3(a).) A student who has learned something about tens and ones but with limited understanding may use the traditional algorithm, lining up the digits and beginning by adding 7 and 8. Some may write a 15 for this sum and end up with an answer of 515. (See Figure 1.3(b).) The understanding of place value these children possess is limited. It allows them to name the digit in the tens place, but this knowledge is not related to the actual size of the numbers, or the result would most likely be startling.

Now consider children who understand that numbers can be broken apart in many different ways, who realize that from 38 to 40 is the same as from 8 to 10, or who notice that the sum of two numbers remains the same if you add something to one and subtract it from the other. These students can add in

(a)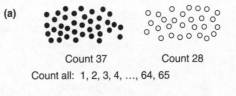

Count 37   Count 28

Count all: 1, 2, 3, 4, ..., 64, 65

(b)

$$\begin{array}{r} 1 \\ 37 \\ + 28 \\ \hline 65 \end{array} \qquad \begin{array}{r} 37 \\ + 28 \\ \hline 515 \end{array}$$

Traditional algorithm. Errors are often made.

(c) Take 2 from the 37 and put it with the 28 to make 30. 30 and 35 is 65.

37 and 30 is 67, but you have to take 2 away—65.

(d) 37 and 20 more—47, 57, 58, 59, 60, 61, 62, 63, 64, 65

(counting on fingers)

FIGURE 1.3 •

A range of computational examples showing different levels of understanding.

flexible ways. They may add 30 and 20 and then combine that with the sum of 8 and 7. They may think about 37 and 30 and take two away. Less flexible students might start with 38 and count on by tens and then ones: 38 then 48, 58 then 59, 60, 61, 62, 63, 64, 65. (See Figure 1.3(c) and (d).)

Of course, we cannot "see" a child's understanding. We can only make inferences about what it may be. The assumption in the preceding examples is that children use the ideas that they have in order to solve the tasks they are given. In the case of traditional computational rules, the risk is that some students actually learn the rules correctly but have very limited or no understanding of why these rules work.

Classroom Influences on Learning

The theory of constructivism suggests that we cannot teach students by telling. Rather, we must help them construct their own ideas using the ideas that they already own. This does not mean that we simply let students play around and hope that they will magically discover new mathematical ideas. On the contrary the manner in which you conduct your class plays an enormous role in what is learned and how well it is understood. Let's examine three factors that influence learning:

- student reflective thinking
- social interaction with other students in the classroom
- use of models or tools for learning (manipulatives, symbolism, computer tools, drawings, and even oral language)

Each factor impacts what and how well students learn. Each one is significantly influenced by you, the classroom teacher.

Reflective Thought

 Stop for a moment and see if you can come up with a good definition of reflective thinking. What does that phrase mean to you?

Whatever your description of reflective thinking, it almost certainly involves some form of mental activity. It is an active, not a passive, endeavor. You may have said that it involves figuring something out or trying to connect ideas in your head. You may have used the words *ponder* or *consider*. What you just did to try to come up with a definition of reflective thinking almost certainly involved reflective thinking.

If we assume that constructivist theory is correct, then we want students to be reflective about the ideas they need to learn. For a new idea you are teaching to be interconnected in a rich web of interrelated ideas, children must be mentally engaged. They must find the relevant ideas they possess and bring them to bear on the development of the new idea. In terms of the dots in Figure 1.1, we want to activate every gray dot a student has that is related to the new white dot we want them to learn. The more relevant gray dots used—the more reflective thinking—the better the new ideas will be constructed and understood.

But we can't just hold up a big THINK sign and expect children to ponder the new thought. The challenge is to get them mentally engaged. As you will see later in this chapter and throughout this book, the key to getting students to be reflective is to engage them in problems that force them to use their ideas as they search for solutions and create new ideas in the process. Two other related activities are also encouraged: writing about solutions to problems and discussions with the rest of the class. Each is a method of promoting reflective thinking. Each should be built into most of your lessons.

Children Learning from Others

Reflective thought and, hence, learning are enhanced when the learner is engaged with others working on the same ideas. Students reside in classrooms. An interactive, thoughtful atmosphere in a classroom can provide some of the best opportunities for learning.

A worthwhile goal is to transform your classroom into what might be termed a "mathematical community of learners," or an environment in which students interact with each other and with the teacher. In such an environment students share ideas and results, compare and evaluate strategies, challenge results, determine the validity of answers, and negotiate ideas on which all can agree. The rich interaction in such a classroom significantly raises the chances that productive reflective thinking about relevant mathematical ideas will happen.

The Interaction of Students' Ideas with the Ideas of Others

Piaget helped us to focus on the cognitive activity of the child and to begin to understand how an individual uses ideas in a reflective manner to construct new knowledge and understanding. Vygotsky focused on social interaction as a key component in the development of knowledge. Vygotsky viewed the ideas that exist in the classroom and in books and those shared by teachers and other authorities as distinct from the ideas constructed by the child. The well-formulated ideas that are external to the child he called *scientific concepts,* whereas those developed by the child (in the manner described by Piaget) he called *spontaneous concepts.*

Vygotsky talked about these two types of concepts as working in opposite directions as shown in Figure 1.4. The scientific concepts work downward from external authority. As such, they impose their logic on the child. The spontaneous concepts bubble upward as a result of reflective activity. In Vygotsky's *zone of proximal development,* the child is able to meaningfully work with the scientific concepts from outside. Here, the child's own conceptual understanding is sufficiently advanced to begin to take in the ideas from "above."

It is not necessary to choose between a social constructivist theory that favors the views of Vygotsky and a cognitive constructivism that is built on the theories of Piaget (Cobb, 1996). In a classroom mathematical community of learners, students' learning is enhanced by the reflective thought that social interaction promotes. At the same time, the value of the interaction for individual students is determined to a large extent by the ideas that each individual brings to the discussions. When, for any given child, the conversation of the classroom is within his or her zone of proximal development, the best social learning will occur. Classroom discussion based on students' own ideas and solutions to problems is absolutely "foundational to children's learning" (Wood & Turner-Vorbeck, 2001, p. 186).

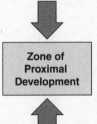

Scientific Concepts
(external to the learner)

Zone of Proximal Development

Spontaneous Concepts
(developed from within)

FIGURE 1.4 • • • • • • • • •

Vygotsky's zone of proximal development is the place where new external ideas are accessible to the learner with those ideas already developed.

Mathematical Communities of Learners

In the wonderful book *Making Sense* (Hiebert et al., 1997), the authors describe four features of a productive classroom culture for mathematics, in which students can learn from each other as well as from their own reflective activity.

1. Ideas are important, no matter whose ideas they are. Students can have their own ideas and share them with others. Similarly, they need to understand that they can also learn from the ideas that others have formulated. Learning mathematics is about coming to understand the ideas of the mathematical community.
2. Ideas must be shared with others in the class. Correspondingly, each student must respect the ideas of others and try to evaluate and make sense of them. Respect for the ideas shared by others is critical if real discussion is to take place.
3. Trust must be established with an understanding that it is okay to make mistakes. Students must come to realize that errors are an opportunity for growth as they are uncovered and explained. All students must trust that their ideas will be met with the same level of respect whether they are right or wrong. Without this trust, many ideas will never be shared.
4. Students must come to understand that mathematics makes sense. As a result of this simple truth, the correctness or validity of results resides in the mathematics itself. There is no need for the teacher or other authority to provide judgment of student answers. In fact, when teachers routinely respond with "Yes, that's correct," or "No, that's wrong," students will stop trying to make sense of ideas in the classroom and discussion and learning will be curtailed.

Classrooms with these characteristics do not just happen. The teacher is responsible for creating this climate. It happens over time in two ways. First, there must be some direct discussion of the ground rules for classroom discussions. Second, teachers can model the type of questioning and interaction that they would like to see from their students.

Tools for Learning

It would be difficult for you to have become a teacher and not at least heard that the use of manipulatives, or a "hands-on approach," is the recommended way to teach mathematics. There is no doubt that these materials can and should play a significant role in your classroom. Used correctly they can be a positive factor in children's learning. But they are not the cure-all that some educators seem to believe them to be. It is important that you have a good perspective on how manipulatives can help or fail to help children construct ideas.

Models Are Not the Same as Concepts

Conceptual knowledge of mathematics consists of logical relationships constructed internally and existing in the mind as a part of a network of ideas. It is the type of knowledge Piaget referred to as *logico-mathematical knowledge* (Kamii, 1985, 1989; Labinowicz, 1985). By its very nature, conceptual knowledge is knowledge that is understood (Hiebert & Carpenter, 1992). Ideas such as seven, rectangle, ones/tens/hundreds, sum, and product are all examples of mathematical relationships or concepts.

Figure 1.5 shows the three blocks commonly used to represent ones, tens, and hundreds. By the middle of second grade, most children have seen pictures of these or have used the actual blocks. Most second-grade children are able to identify the rod as the "ten" piece and the large square block as the "hundred" piece. Does this mean that they have constructed the concepts of ten and hundred? All that is known for sure is that they have learned the usual names typically assigned to them. The mathematical concept of a ten is that *a ten is the same as ten ones*. Ten is not a rod. The concept is the relationship between the rod and the small cube. It is not the rod or a bundle of ten sticks or any other model of a ten. This relationship called "ten" must be created by children in their own minds. The blocks can help students "see" the relationships and talk about them, but what they see are blocks, not concepts.

With this understanding we can define a model as follows: A *model* for a mathematical concept refers to any object, picture, or drawing that represents the concept and onto which the relationship for that concept can be imposed. In this sense, any group of 100 objects can be a model of the concept "hundred" because we can impose the 100-to-1 relationship on the group and a single element of the group.

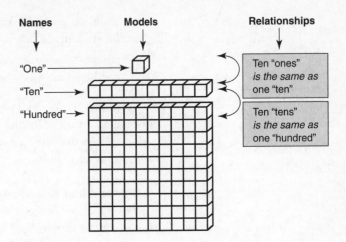

FIGURE 1.5 ●

Objects and names of objects are not the same as relationships between objects.

It is incorrect to say that a model "illustrates" a concept. To illustrate implies showing. That would mean that when you looked at the model, you would see an example of the concept. Technically, all that you actually see with your eyes is the physical object; only your mind can impose the mathematical relationship on the object (Thompson, 1994). For a person who does not yet have the relationship, the model does not illustrate the concept *for that person*. In contrast, when you see a bicycle, what you see is in fact an example of the physical concept of *bicycle*. But unlike physical concepts, there are no physical examples of mathematical concepts. Mathematical concepts are relationships constructed in a person's mind.

Models and Other Tools for Learning

Hiebert and his colleagues (1997) argue that the concept of model should be expanded to include oral language, written symbols for mathematics, and any other tools that can help students think about mathematics. Certainly, calculators can and should be included in this broad definition of mathematical tools. For example, the automatic constant feature of a calculator can assist students in the development of skip counting and pattern recognition. By pressing ⓪ ➕ ④ ⁼ ⁼ . . . a child can skip count by four and observe the 0, 4, 8, 2, 6 pattern repeat in the ones digit. Using the same feature to count by ones to 100 can help students understand both the patterns in numbers as well as develop some sense of how large 100 really is.

Although children do not see concepts by seeing mathematical models or by handling manipulative materials, these various tools can help children learn important mathematical ideas in several important ways:

- Ideas that students are in the process of developing can be tested to see if they "fit" or work correctly when applied to a model that the teacher or other students have suggested represents that idea.

- It is often easier for students to think through a problem or task by use of an appropriate model or tool.

- Tools are especially helpful in communicating ideas that are otherwise difficult for students to talk about or write about.

- Simple drawings of counters, base-ten blocks, number lines, or fraction pieces can help students who are trying to record their ideas.

As children use a tool to represent an idea, their work or reflective activity can help develop meaning for the tool in their own minds. As these meanings for tools are developed, they also become more useful as a tool for further learning. That is, children must both develop meanings *for* tools and meaning can be developed *with* tools.

Procedural Knowledge as a Tool

Procedural knowledge of mathematics is knowledge of the rules and the procedures that one uses in carrying out routine mathematical tasks and also of the symbolism that is used to represent mathematics. Procedural knowledge of mathematics plays a very important role both in learning and in doing mathematics. For example, algorithmic procedures help do routine tasks easily and, thus, free children's minds to concentrate on more important tasks. Symbolism is a powerful mechanism for conveying mathematical ideas to others and for "doodling around" with an idea as students do mathematics. But even the most skillful use of a procedure will not help develop conceptual knowledge that is related to that procedure (Hiebert, 1990). Doing endless column additions with regrouping will not help students understand why regrouping works or what the carried 1 represents. In fact, students who are skillful with a particular procedure are very reluctant to attach meanings to it after the fact. It is generally accepted that procedural rules should never be learned in the absence of a concept, although, unfortunately, that happens far too often.

Using Models in the Classroom

Mathematical concepts that children are in the process of constructing are formulated little by little over time. As children actively reflect on their new ideas, they test them out through as many different avenues as we might provide. This is where the value of student discussions and a mathematical environment comes in. Talking through an idea, arguing for a viewpoint, listening to others, and describing and explaining are all mentally active ways of testing an emerging idea against external reality. As this testing process goes on, the developing idea gets modified, elaborated, and further integrated with existing ideas. When there is a good fit with external reality, the likelihood of a correct concept being formed is good.

Models and mathematical tools in the more general sense can play this same role, that of a testing ground for emerging ideas. Tools can be thought of as "thinker toys," "tester toys," and "talker toys." It is difficult for students (of all ages) to talk about and test out abstract relationships using words alone. Models give learners something to think about, explore with, talk about, and reason with.

Introducing Models and Making Them Available

We can't just give students a ten-frame or bars of Unifix cubes and expect them to develop the mathematical ideas that these materials can potentially represent. When a new model or new use of a familiar model is introduced into the classroom, it is generally a good idea to explain how the model is used and perhaps conduct a simple activity that illustrates this use.

For example, suppose that you have been doing activities in the first or second grade in which large quantities are counted by grouping objects into sets and counting accordingly. As a class, children are coming around to the idea that groups of ten are especially useful in the counting tasks. You might decide to have the students make a model for tens and ones by having them fill small portion cups with ten lima beans each and putting a lid on each cup. The cups and loose limas are a nice model for representing tens and ones. After ample cups of ten have been capped and put into a storage bin, you ask the children for some ways that they can show you 84 things. Some, but not all, children will think to use the cups and beans. When someone does, you can comment on how the model seems to work well. In a similar manner you might introduce bundles of coffee stirs or bars of snap cubes. However, once you are comfortable that the models have been explained, you should not force their use on students. Rather, students should feel free to select and use models that make sense to them. In most instances, not using a model at all should also be an option. The choice a student makes can provide you with valuable information about the level of sophistication of the student's reasoning.

Whereas the free choice of models should generally be the norm in the classroom, you can often ask students to use a model to show their thinking. This will help you find out about a child's understanding of the idea and also his or her understanding of the models that have been used in the classroom.

The following are simple rules of thumb for using models:

- Introduce new models by showing how they can represent the ideas for which they are intended.

- Allow students (in most instances) to select freely from available models to use in solving problems.

- Encourage the use of a model when you believe it would be helpful to a student having difficulty.

Assessment Note

Lesh, Post, and Behr (1987) talk about five representations for concepts, two of which are manipulative models and pictures. (See Figure 1.6.)

Their research has found that children who have difficulty translating a concept from one representation to another are the same children who have difficulty solving problems and understanding computations. As children move between and among these representations for concepts, there is a better chance of a concept being formed correctly and integrated into a rich web of ideas.

Translation activities can be used for lessons or for diagnosis. For example, students may be given blocks that show three hundred forty-seven. Their task may be to write the number (symbols), get that many counters (a different manipulative), and write a story in which that number is used and makes sense (real-world situation).

Think about translation tasks when you want to do a short interview with a child to find out more about his or her thinking. How a child represents ideas in

(continued)

various forms and explains why these representations are similar can often provide you with valuable information about what misconceptions he or she may have and what type of activity to use to help.

Incorrect Use of Models

The most widespread error that teachers make with manipulative materials is to structure lessons in such a manner that students are being directed in exactly how to use a model, usually as a means of getting answers. There is a natural temptation to get out the materials and show children exactly how to use them. Children will blindly follow the teacher's directions, and it may even look as if they understand. A rote procedure with a model is still just that, a rote procedure (Ball, 1992; Clements & Battista, 1990).

A natural result of overly directing the use of models is that children begin to use them as answer-getting devices rather than as thinker toys. When getting answers rather than solving problems becomes the focus of a lesson, children will gravitate to the easiest method available to get the answers. For example, if you have carefully shown and explained to children how to get an answer with a number line, then an imitation of that method is the procedure they will most likely select. Little or no reflective thought will go into exploring the concepts involved with the result that little understanding will be constructed.

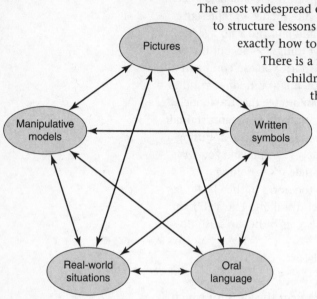

FIGURE 1.6

Five different representations of mathematical ideas. Translations between and within each can help develop new concepts.

TEACHING WITH PROBLEMS

Understanding should be a goal for all of the mathematics we teach. This message of NCTM's *Principles and Standards for School Mathematics* (2000) is a goal with which it is difficult to argue. For many years and continuing today, didactic, top-down, do-as-I-show-you instruction has been the norm in the United States. The results have not been positive except for our brightest students and those who memorize rules well. There must be a better method of teaching.

The single most important principle for improving the teaching of mathematics is to *allow the subject of mathematics to be problematic for students* (Hiebert et al., 1996). That is, students solve problems not to apply mathematics but to learn new mathematics. When students engage in well-chosen problem-based tasks and focus on the solution methods, what results is new understanding of the mathematics embedded in the task. When students are actively looking for relationships, analyzing patterns, finding out which methods work and which don't, justifying results, or evaluating and challenging the thoughts of others, they are necessarily and optimally engaging in reflective thought about the ideas involved. The appropriate dots in their cognitive structure are acting to give meaning to new ideas. *Most, if not all, important mathematics concepts and procedures can best be taught through problem solving.*

Problem-Based Tasks

A *problem* is defined here as any task or activity for which the students have no prescribed or memorized rules or methods, nor is there a perception by students that there is a specific correct solution method (Hiebert et al., 1997).

A problem for learning mathematics also has these features:

- *The problem must begin where the students are.* The design or selection of the task should take into consideration the current understanding of the students. They should have the appropriate ideas to engage and solve the problem and yet still find it challenging and interesting. In other words, it should be within their zone of proximal development.

- *The problematic or engaging aspect of the problem must be due to the mathematics that the students are to learn.* In solving the problem or doing the activity, students should be concerned primarily with making sense of the mathematics involved and thereby developing their understanding of those ideas. Although it is acceptable and even desirable to have contexts or external conditions for problems that make them interesting, these aspects should not overshadow the mathematics to be learned.

- *The problem must require justifications and explanations for answers and methods.* Students should understand that the responsibility for determining if answers are correct and why rests with them. Students should also expect to explain their solution methods as a natural part of solving problems.

It is important to understand that mathematics is to be taught *through* problem solving. That is, problem-based tasks or activities are the vehicle through which your curriculum can be developed. Student learning is an outcome of the problem-solving process.

Teaching with problem-based tasks is student centered rather than teacher centered. It begins with and builds on the ideas that children have available—their dots, their understandings. It is a process that requires faith in children, a belief that all children can create meaningful ideas about mathematics.

Learning Through Problem Solving: A Student-Centered Approach

Let's look into a hypothetical second-grade classroom near the middle of the year. The children have done lots of activities with the hundreds chart. They have counted collections of objects and made many measurements of things in the room. In their counting and measuring, they often use groups of objects instead of counting by ones.

Counting by tens has become a popular method for most but not all children. The class has taken big numbers apart to show different ways that can be done. In many of these activities, the children have used combinations of tens to make numbers.

All of these experiences have helped students develop ideas about numbers using a system of tens. These are their gray dots—their ideas about place value. Each child's unique collection of ideas is connected in different ways. Some ideas are well understood, others less so; some are well formed, others still emerging.

The students in the class have not been taught the typical algorithms for addition or subtraction. As is often the case, this class begins with a story problem and students are set to work.

> *When Carla was at the zoo, she saw the monkeys eating bananas. She asked the zookeeper how many bananas the monkeys usually ate in one day. The zookeeper said that yesterday they ate 36 bananas but today they only ate 25. How many bananas did the monkeys eat in those two days?*

Some children use counters and count by ones. Some use the hundreds chart or base-ten models and others use mental strategies. All are required to use words and numbers and, if they wish, drawings to show what they did and how they thought about the problem. After about 20 minutes the teacher begins a discussion by having students share their ideas and answers. As the students report, the teacher records their ideas on the board so all can see. Sometimes the teacher asks questions to help clarify ideas for others. She makes no evaluative comments, even when a student is in error. Although this is a hypothetical class, the following solutions are not unusual for classes such as this.

 Before reading further, see how many different ways you can think of to solve this problem (36 + 25). Then check to see if your ways are alike or different from those that follow.

Mathematical task: 36 + 25

Student 1:   *I know that 25 and 25 is 50—like two quarters. And 35 is ten more so that is 60. And then one more is 61.*

Teacher: What do you mean when you say '35 is ten more'?

Student 1:   *Well, I used 25 of the 36 and 25 and ten more is 35.*

Student 2:   *Thirty and twenty is 50 and then 5 + 6 more. Five and five is ten and so that's 11. And then 50 and 11 is 61.*

Student 3:   *I counted on using the hundreds chart. I started at 36 and then I had to go 20 from there and so that was 46 and then 56. And then I went 57, 58, 59, 60, 61.*

The teacher's objectives were the development of place-value concepts and flexible methods of addition that utilize these ideas. These were the white dots that the class has been constructing, with each student developing his or her own ideas. By allowing children to solve the problem in their own way, each child is essentially required to use his or her own particular set of gray dots to give meaning to the solution strategy.

What ideas did you learn from those shared in this example? Try using some of these new ideas to find the sum of 64 and 27.

During the discussion periods of classes such as this one, ideas continue to grow. Students may hear and understand a clever idea that they could have used but that did not occur to them. Other students actually begin to create new ideas to use as they hear (usually after numerous lessons) the strategies used by their classmates. Perhaps earlier they had not been able to use or understand these ideas. Some in the class may hear excellent ideas from their peers that do not make sense to them. These students are simply not ready or do not have the prerequisite concepts to construct these new ideas. On subsequent days there will be similar opportunities for all students to grow at their own pace based on their own understandings.

In classrooms such as the one just described, teachers begin *where the children are*—with *their* ideas. They do this by allowing children to solve problems or approach tasks in ways that make sense to them. The children have no other place to turn except to their own ideas.

Show and Tell: A Teacher-Directed Approach

In contrast to the student-centered class just described, let's consider how a lesson with the same basic objective might look using a teacher-directed approach.

The teacher distributes base-ten blocks so that pairs of students have enough materials to solve any problem. She reads to the class the same monkeys and bananas problem that was used earlier. The class quickly agrees that they need to add the two numbers in the problem. Using the overhead, the teacher directs students to make the two numbers on their place-value mats. Care is taken that the 25 is shown with the blocks beneath the 36. Students are directed to begin with the ones place. A series of easily answered questions guides students through each step in the traditional algorithm.

- How many ones are there all together?
- What do we need to do with the 11 ones? (regroup, make a ten)
- Where do we put the ten?
- How many tens are there?
- What is the answer?

Next, students are given five similar problems to do with the models. Students work in pairs and record answers on their papers. The teacher circulates and helps students having difficulty by guiding the students through the same steps indicated by her earlier questions.

 Think about what you like and do not like about this lesson. How is it different from the earlier example? What ideas will the students be focusing on?

In this lesson the teacher and students are using manipulatives in a very conceptual manner. The process of regrouping is "seen" as children trade ten ones for a ten and place the ten at the top of the tens column, a process that will later be connected to recording a one at the top of the tens column. After several lessons similar to this one, most of the class will learn how to add with regrouping. This is a typical example of what often is viewed as an excellent lesson.

But let's examine this lesson more closely. The entire focus of the lesson is on the steps and procedures that the teacher has delineated. She receives no information about the ideas that individual students may have. She can only find out who has and who has not been able to follow the directions. The assumption is that those students who solve the problems correctly also understand. However, many students (including some of those who do the problems correctly) will not understand and will be reinforced in their belief that mathematics is a collection of rules to be learned. Everyone in the class must do the problem the way that makes sense to the teacher rather than the way that makes sense to him or her. No student is given the opportunity to find out that his or her own personal ideas count or that there are numerous good ways to solve the problem. This disenfranchises the student who needs to continue working on the development of basic ideas of tens and ones and the student who could easily find one or more ways to do the problem mentally if only asked to do so. Rather, students are likely to use the same tedious method to add 29 + 29 instead of thinking 30 and 30 then take away 2.

The Value of Teaching with Problems

There is no doubt that teaching with problems is difficult. Tasks must be designed or selected each day, taking into consideration the current understanding of your students and the needs of your curriculum. It is hard to plan more than a few days in advance. If you are using a traditional textbook, modifications will need to be made. However, there are excellent reasons for making the effort.

- *Problem solving focuses students' attention on ideas and sense making.* When solving problems, students must necessarily reflect on the mathematics inherent in the problems. Emerging ideas are more likely to be integrated with existing ones, thereby improving understanding. In contrast, no matter how skillfully you explain ideas and offer directions, students will attend to the directions but rarely to the ideas.

- *Problem solving develops the belief in students that they are capable of doing mathematics and that mathematics makes sense.* Every time you pose a problem-based task and expect a solution, you say to students, "I believe you can do this." Every time the class solves a problem and students develop their understanding, confidence and self-esteem are enhanced.

- *Problem solving provides ongoing assessment data.* As students discuss ideas, draw pictures or use manipulatives, defend their solutions and evaluate those of others, and write reports or explanations, they provide a steady stream of valuable information. That information can be used for planning the next lesson, helping individual students, evaluating their progress, and communicating with parents.

- *Problem solving is an excellent method for attending to a breadth of abilities.* Good problem-based tasks have multiple paths to the solution, from simple or inefficient to clever or insightful. Each student gets to make sense of the task using his or her own ideas. Furthermore, students expand on these ideas and grow in their understanding as they hear and reflect on the solution strategies of others. A teacher-directed approach ignores diversity to the detriment of most students.

- *Problem solving engages students so that there are fewer discipline problems.* For most students, the process of solving problems in ways that make sense to them is intrinsically rewarding. There is less reason to act out or to cause trouble. Real learning is engaging, while following directions is often boring.

- *Problem solving develops "mathematical power."* Students solving problems will be engaged in all five of the process standards described in the NCTM *Principles and Standards* document: problem solving, reasoning, communication, connections, and representation. These are the processes of doing mathematics.

- *It is a lot of fun!* After experiencing teaching in this manner, very few teachers return to a teach-by-telling mode. The excitement of students developing understanding through their own reasoning is worth all the effort. And, of course, it is fun for the students.

A Three-Part Format for Problem-Based Lessons

It is useful to think of problem-based lessons as consisting of three main parts: *before, during,* and *after.* (See Figure 1.7.)

If you allot time for each before, during, and after segment, it is quite easy to devote a full period to one seemingly simple problem. The same three-part structure can be applied to small tasks, resulting in a 10- to 20-minute mini-lesson (common in kindergarten). As you will see, the same structure applies to station or center activities.

The Before Phase

You have three tasks to accomplish here: get students mentally prepared for the task, be sure the task is understood, and be certain that you have clearly established your expectations beyond simply getting an answer.

Get Students Mentally Prepared
You want to be sure that whatever ideas students have about the mathematics in the task for the day are "up and running" in their heads. There are several possible strategies you might consider.

- Begin with a simple version of the task you intend to pose. For example, if the task will involve working on strategies for solving "doubles-plus-one" facts (e.g., 5 + 6 or 8 + 7), you might begin with a discussion of doubles.

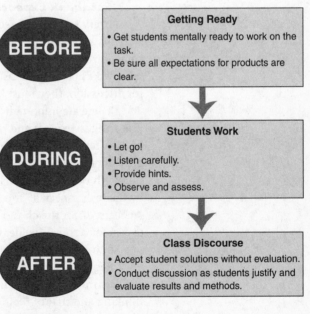

BEFORE

Getting Ready
- Get students mentally ready to work on the task.
- Be sure all expectations for products are clear.

DURING

Students Work
- Let go!
- Listen carefully.
- Provide hints.
- Observe and assess.

AFTER

Class Discourse
- Accept student solutions without evaluation.
- Conduct discussion as students justify and evaluate results and methods.

FIGURE 1.7

Teaching through problem solving suggests a simple three-part structure for lessons.

If you want students to explore area and perimeter of rectangles on a geoboard, you might have them make a specific rectangle and discuss how many squares are inside and also the distance around the outside.

- You might begin a lesson by posing the task right away and then brainstorming solution strategies. For example, if the task involves gathering data, you might ask students to think about the graphing techniques that they have learned recently and briefly discuss the pros and cons of each for the task at hand. Brainstorming works best when the task has multiple solution paths that students may not necessarily think of without some prompting.

- For tasks involving a single computation, you can have students think about the size of the answer—is it more than 30? Less than 100? You may even have students tell what they think the answer is because many will be able to compute mentally. This does not spoil the task for others or "give away the answer." Remember, students must explain the reasoning they use to get the answer. It is helpful for students to hear ideas before they are left completely on their own.

Be Sure the Task Is Understood

You must always be sure that students understand the problem or task before setting them to work. Remember that their perspective is different from yours.

For simple story problems, for example, it is useful in the early grades to ask a series of direct questions that can be answered just by looking at the problem. Go over vocabulary that may be troubling. You might have students explain to you what the problem is asking. Having students restate the problem in their own words forces them to think about what the problem is asking.

For games or stations, you might play a demonstration game or have students role play how the activity is to be done.

Establish Expectations

Every task should require more of students than simply the answer. Minimally, students should be prepared to explain their thinking to the class. Whenever possible, some form of writing that shows how students have solved the problem should be included as part of the task. Whatever the expectations, written work, or preparation for discussion, they must be made clear at the outset.

There are important reasons for requiring more than just answers. Students preparing to explain and defend their answers will spend time reflecting on the validity of their results and will often make revisions even before sharing them. They will have a greater interest in the class discussion because they will want to compare their solution with others' solutions. When an explanation is included as part of what is required by the task, especially if it is in the form of writing and drawings, students will have "rehearsed" for the class discussion and be ready to participate. Students should be expected to show the ideas and the work that they have considered even when they are unable to fully solve a problem.

Requesting students to use words, pictures, and numbers to explain their thinking also has the effect of placing an emphasis on process. Students need to know that their thinking and that of their classmates are at least as important as the answers.

It is never too early to begin written explanations, even in kindergarten. There, the writing may be in the form of drawings and numbers, but this early form of written communication is just as important. Figure 1.8 shows one student's solution for ways to make 5. One or possibly two students working together might prepare an explanation of their work on a large sheet of newsprint. It may contain only crude drawings. However, in the sharing portion of the lesson, if the page is taped temporarily to the board, the students can use what they drew to explain orally to their classmates how they solved the problem.

By second or third grade, consider replacing the instruction "Show how you got your answer" with "Explain why you think your answer is correct." With the former direction, students may simply record their steps ("First we did, and then we . . ."). The focus needs to shift to justification and reasoning rather than simply a record of what was done.

For some tasks you may decide to forgo written work. If so, strongly consider using a "think-pair-share" approach, requiring students to reflect on results before sharing. This causes students to defend their ideas to a peer and prepares them to talk to the class.

FIGURE 1.8

A kindergarten student shows her thinking about ways to make 5.

The During Phase

The most important thing for you to do here is to *let go!* Give students a chance to work without your guidance. Give them the opportunity to use *their* ideas and not simply follow directions. Your second task is to *listen*. Find out how different children or groups are thinking, what ideas they are using, and how they are approaching the problem.

You must demonstrate confidence and respect for your students' abilities. Set them to work with the expectation that they will solve the problem. Students must deeply believe that the teacher does not have a predetermined or preferred method for solving the problem. If they suspect otherwise, there is no reason for them to take risks with their own ideas and methods.

Provide Hints but Not Solutions

How much help to give students is always an issue. Should you let them stumble down the wrong path? Do you correct errors you see? Always keep in mind that as soon as students sense that you have a method of solving the problem, they will almost certainly stop searching for their own methods because they are convinced that your way must be best.

Before being tempted to help or provide a suggestion, first find out what ideas the student or group has. Try to construct any hints on ideas that you hear them considering. "If you think finding the difference in those numbers might help, then go ahead and try it and see how that turns out." Notice that a phrase like this does not suggest that the student's idea is right or wrong, only that she needs to continue with it rather than wait for sanction from you.

You might suggest that the students try using a particular manipulative or draw a picture if that seems appropriate. For example, if a student cannot decide whether to add or subtract, a suggestion to see how it would work out in a picture or with counters can give the student some confidence.

Encourage Testing of Ideas

Students will look to you for approval of their results or ideas. Consistently avoid being the source of "truth" or of right and wrong. When asked if a result or method is correct, ask students "How can you decide?" or "Why do you think that might be right?" or "I see what you have done. How can you check that somehow?" Even if not asked for an opinion, asking "How can we tell if that makes sense?" reminds students that answers without reasons are not acceptable.

Listen Actively

This is one of two opportunities you will get in the lesson (the other is in the discussion period) to find out what your students know, how they think, and how they are approaching the task you have given them. You might sit down with a group and simply listen for a while, have the students explain what they are doing, or take notes. If you want further information, try saying, "Tell me what you are doing," or "I see you are using Unifix cubes. Can you tell me what they stand for in your problem?" You want to convey a genuine interest in what students are doing and thinking. This is *not* the time to evaluate or to tell students how to solve the problem.

The After Phase

Plan ample time for this portion of the lesson and then be certain to *save* the time. It is not necessary to wait for every student to finish. Often this is when the best learning will take place. Twenty minutes or more is not at all unreasonable for a good class discussion and sharing of ideas. This is not a time to check answers but for the class to share ideas. Over time, you will develop your class into a community of learners who together are involved in making sense of mathematics. This atmosphere will not develop easily or quickly. You must teach your students about your expectations for this time and how to interact with their peers.

Engage the Full Class in Discussion

You may want simply to list answers from all of the groups and put them on the board without comment. Following that, you can return to one or more students to get explanations for their solutions or to explain their processes.

When there are different answers, the full class should be involved in the discourse concerning which answers are correct. Allow those responsible for the answers to defend them, and then open the discussion to the class. "Who has an idea about this? George, I noticed that you got a different answer than Tomeka. What do you think of her explanation?"

One of your functions is to make sure that all students participate, that all listen, and that all understand what is being said. Encourage students to ask questions. "Pete, did you understand how they did that? Do you want to ask Mary a question?"

A second suggestion is to begin discussions by calling first on the children who tend to be shy or lack the ability to express themselves well. Rowan and Bourne (1994) note that the more obvious ideas are generally given at the outset of a discussion. When asked to participate early and given sufficient time to formulate their thoughts, these reticent children can more easily participate and, thus, be valued.

Make it a habit to ask for explanations to accompany *all* answers. Soon the request for an explanation will not signal an incorrect response, as children initially believe. Many incorrect answers are the result of small errors in otherwise excellent thinking. Likewise, many correct answers may not represent the insightful thinking you might have assumed. A child who has given an incorrect answer is very likely to see the error and correct it during the explanation. Try to support children's thinking without evaluating responses. "Does someone have a different idea or want to comment on what Daniel just said?" All children should hear the same teacher reactions that only the so-called "smart kids" used to hear.

Use Praise Cautiously

Be an attentive listener to all ideas, both good and not so good. Praise offered for a correct solution or excitement over an interesting idea suggests that the student did something unusual or unexpected. This can be negative feedback for those who do not get praise.

In place of praise that is judgmental, Schwartz (1996) suggests comments of interest and extension: "I wonder what would happen if you tried" or "Please tell me how you figured that out." Notice that these phrases express interest and value the child's thinking. They also can and should be used regardless of the validity of the responses.

Teachers' Questions about Problem-Based Teaching

A problem-based approach to teaching is a new idea to many teachers. Even for those who have been working at it for some time, there are stumbling blocks and doubts that arise. Here are a few questions that are often raised by teachers and our answers to them.

> **STOP** After reading each of the following questions, pause first to consider your personal response. Then compare your thoughts with the ideas suggested.

What Can I Tell Them? Should I Tell Them Anything?

When teaching through problem solving, one of the most perplexing dilemmas is how much to tell or not to tell. To tell too little can sometimes leave students floundering and waste precious class time. A good rule of thumb is that you should feel free to share relevant information as long as the mathematics in the task remains problematic for the students (Hiebert et al., 1997). That is, "information can and should be shared as long as it does not solve the problem [and] does not take away the need for students to reflect on the situation and develop solution methods they understand" (p. 36).

According to Hiebert et al. (1997), three specific types of information can and should be shared:

1. *Mathematical conventions.* Students must be told about the social conventions of symbolism and terminology that are important in mathematics. For example, representing "three and five equals eight" as "3 + 5 = 8" is a convention. Definitions and labels are also conventions.

2. *Clarification of students' methods.* You should help students clarify or interpret their ideas and perhaps point out related ideas. Discussion or clarification of students' processes focuses attention on ideas you want the class to learn. Care must be taken that attention to one student's ideas does not diminish those of other students or suggest that one method is the preferred approach.

3. *Alternative methods.* You can, with considerable care, suggest to students an alternative method or approach for consideration. You must be very cautious in not conveying to students that their ideas are second best. Nor should students ever be forced to adopt your suggestion over their own approach. In contrast, try this: "The other day I saw some students in another class solve a problem this way. (Show the method.) What do you think of that idea?"

How Will I Be Able to Teach All of the Basic Skills?

There is a tendency to believe that mastery of the basics is incompatible with a problem-based approach or that drill is essential for basic skills. However, the evidence strongly suggests otherwise. First, drill-oriented approaches in U.S. classrooms have consistently produced poor results (Battista, 1999; Kamii & Dominick, 1998; O'Brien, 1999). Short-term gains on low-level skills may possibly result from drill, but even state testing programs require more.

Second, research data indicate that students in constructivist programs based on a problem-solving approach do as well or nearly as well as students in traditional programs on basic skills as measured by standardized tests (Campbell, 1995; Carpenter, Franke, Jacobs, Fennema, & Empson, 1998; Hiebert & Wearne, 1996; Silver & Stein, 1996). Any deficit in skill development is more than outweighed by strength in concepts and problem solving.

Finally, traditional skills such as basic fact mastery and computation can be effectively taught in a problem-solving approach (for example, see Campbell, Rowan, & Suarez, 1998; Huinker, 1998).

Why Is It Okay for a Student to "Tell" or "Explain" but Not for Me?

There are three answers to this question. First, students will question their peers when an explanation does not make sense to them, whereas explanations from the teacher are nearly always accepted without scrutiny—even when they are not understood. Second, when students are responsible for explaining, class members develop a sense of pride and confidence that *they* can figure things out and make sense of mathematics. Third, having to explain forces the student who is doing the explaining to clarify his or her thoughts.

This Approach Takes More Time. How Will I Have Time to Cover Everything?

The first suggestion is to teach with a goal of developing the "big ideas," the main concepts in a unit or chapter. Most of the skills and ideas on your list of objectives will be addressed as you progress. If you focus separately on each item on the list, big ideas

and connections—the essence of understanding—are unlikely to develop. Second, with a traditional approach far too much time is spent reteaching because students don't retain ideas. Time spent up front to help students develop meaningful networks of ideas drastically reduces the need for reteaching, thus creating time in the long term. You must have faith that time invested in concept development will create time later.

Do I Need to Use a Problem-Based Approach Every Day?

Yes! Any attempt to mix problem-based methods with traditional teaching by telling will cause difficulties. Consider the response of Mokros, Russell, and Economopoulos (1995):

> In classrooms where both approaches are used to teach a skill, children become confused about when they are supposed to use their own strategies for figuring out a problem and when they are supposed to use the officially sanctioned approach. Children get the sense that:
> - Their own approach to problem-solving is merely "exploration," and they will later learn the "right way."
> - Their own approach isn't as good as the one the teacher shows.
> - The teacher didn't really mean it when he or she said there were lots of good strategies for solving problems like 34 × 68. (p. 79)

Is There Any Place for Drill and Practice?

Yes! However, the tragic error is to believe that drill is a method of developing ideas. Drill is only appropriate when (a) the desired concepts have been meaningfully developed, (b) students already have developed (not mastered) flexible and useful procedures, *and* (c) speed and accuracy are needed. Watch children drilling basic facts who are counting on their fingers or using some other inefficient method. What they may be improving is their ability to count quickly. They are not learning their facts.

If you consider carefully these three criteria for drill, you will likely do much less of it than in the past.

My Textbook Is a Traditional Basal. How Can I Use It?

Traditional textbooks are designed to be teacher directed, a contrast to the approach you have been reading about. But they should not be discarded. Much thought went into the content and the pedagogical ideas. Your book can still be used as a prime resource if you think about translating units and lessons to a problem-oriented approach.

Adopt a *unit perspective*. Avoid the idea that every lesson and idea in the unit require attention. Examine a chapter or unit from beginning to end, and identify the two or three *big ideas*, the essential mathematics in the chapter. (Big ideas are listed at the start of each of the remaining chapters in this book. These may be helpful as a reference.) Temporarily ignore the smaller subideas that often take up a full lesson.

With the big ideas of the unit in mind, you can now do two things: (1) adapt the best or most important lessons in the chapter to a problem-solving format and

(2) create or find tasks in the text's teacher notes and other resources that address the big ideas. The combination will almost certainly provide you with an ample supply of tasks.

What Do I Do When a Task Bombs or Students Don't "Get It"?

There may be times when your class simply does not solve the problem during the class period, but not as often as you might suspect. When it does happen, do not give in to the temptation to "show 'em." Set the task aside for the moment. Ask yourself why it bombed. Did the students have the ideas they needed? How did students attempt the task? Occasionally we need to regroup and offer students a simpler related problem that gets them prepared for the one that proved difficult. When you sense that a task is not going anywhere, listen to your students and you will know where to go next. Don't spend days just hoping that something wonderful might happen.

PLANNING IN A PROBLEM-BASED CLASSROOM

Teaching with a problem-based approach requires more time for planning lessons than simply following the pages in a traditional text. Every group of students is different and each day is best built on the actual growth of the previous day. Choices of tasks must be made daily to best fit the needs of your students.

Planning Problem-Based Lessons

The outline in Figure 1.9 illustrates suggested steps for planning a lesson. The first four steps involve the most thought and are the most crucial. The next four steps follow from these initial decisions and will assure that your lesson runs smoothly. Finally, you can write a concise lesson plan that will be easy to follow.

Step 1: **Begin with the Math!** Articulate clearly the ideas you want students to learn as a result of the lesson. Think in terms of mathematical concepts, not skills. Describe the mathematics, not the student behavior.

But what if a skill is the intended outcome? Often state or local objectives are written in procedural terms, for example, "The student will be able to . . . ." Perhaps you want students to master their subtraction facts. Rather than drill facts, work on number relationships or use story problems that lead to strategies. Instead of a page of computation following your rules, have students develop their own method of subtracting two-digit numbers. For every skill there are underlying concepts and relationships. Identify these concepts at this step of your planning. The best tasks will get at skills through concepts.

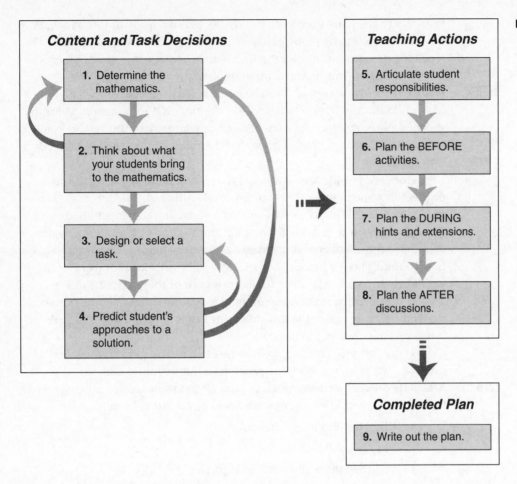

Content and Task Decisions

1. Determine the mathematics.

2. Think about what your students bring to the mathematics.

3. Design or select a task.

4. Predict student's approaches to a solution.

Teaching Actions

5. Articulate student responsibilities.

6. Plan the BEFORE activities.

7. Plan the DURING hints and extensions.

8. Plan the AFTER discussions.

Completed Plan

9. Write out the plan.

FIGURE 1.9 • • • • • • • • •

Planning steps for thinking through a problem-based lesson.

Step 2: **Think About Your Students.** What do your students know or understand about this topic? Are they ready to tackle this bit of mathematics or are there some background ideas that they have not yet developed?

Be sure that the mathematics you identified in step 1 includes something new or at least slightly unfamiliar to your students. At the same time, be certain that your objectives are not out of reach. For real learning to take place, there must be some challenge, some new ideas—even if it is simply seeing an old idea in a new format or with a different model. If necessary, now is the time to revisit step 1 and make adjustments in your goals.

Step 3: **Decide on a Task.** Keep it simple! Good tasks need not be elaborate. Often a simple story problem is all that is necessary as long as the solution involves children in the intended mathematics. Do not feel compelled to search through books for clever or elaborate tasks.

Keep the content foremost in mind. Frantically searching through books for a problem can be a waste of time due to the difficulty of finding a task that meets your needs. Teachers frequently realize the task that looked so good in the resource did not exactly get at the intended mathematics.

Good tasks can often come directly from your text. Modify a direct-instruction lesson to allow students to wrestle with the main idea. This book is full of tasks and is intended as a resource for you. NCTM has numerous publications with excellent ideas. Children's literature can often inspire great tasks. There are many excellent resource books but stick with those that allow the mathematics to be problem based. The longer you have had to build a repertoire of task ideas from journals, resource books, conferences, and in-service, the easier this important step in planning will become.

Step 4: ***Predict What Will Happen.*** You have made hypotheses about what your students know and have selected a task. Now use that information and think about all of the things your students are likely to do with this task. If you catch yourself saying, "Well, I hope that they will . . . ," then *stop*. Predict! Don't hope!

Does every student in your class have a chance of engaging in this problem in some manner that is meaningful? Although students may each tackle the task differently, don't leave your struggling students to flounder. Perhaps you want to provide for modifications in the task for different students. (See the discussion of diversity later in this chapter.) This is also a good time to think about whether your students will work alone, in pairs, or in groups. Group work may assist students in need of some extra help.

If your predictions are beginning to make you uneasy about your task, this is the time to revisit the task. Maybe it needs to be modified, or perhaps it is simply too easy or too difficult.

These first four decisions define the heart of your lesson. The next four decisions define how you will carry the plan out in your classroom.

Step 5: ***Articulate Student Responsibilities.*** You always want more than answers. For nearly every task, you want students to be able to tell you

- What they did to get the answer
- Why they did it that way
- Why they think the solution is correct

Decide how you want students to supply this information. If responding in writing, will students write individually or prepare a group presentation? Will they write in their journals, on paper to be turned in, on a page you prepare that includes the problem, or perhaps on chart paper that can be used for sharing with the class?

You may choose to have students simply report or discuss their ideas without writing. Although this option may occasionally be adequate, it should not be used often, especially in the early grades. Young children will not be able to explain their thinking well if they do not have something prepared to talk from. Writing is a form of rehearsal for discussions.

Step 6: ***Plan the Before Portion of the Lesson.*** Sometimes you can simply begin a lesson with the task and articulation of students' responsibilities. But, in many instances, you will want to orient students' thinking with a related task or warm-up exercise. After presenting the task, will you "let go" or do you want students to brainstorm solutions or estimate answers? (See the earlier discussion of the "before phase" of a lesson on pp. 15–17.)

Consider how you will present the task. Options include having it written on paper, taken from students' texts, shown on the overhead, or written on the board or on chart paper.

Step 7: ***Think About the During Portion of the Lesson.*** Look back at your predictions. What hints or assists can you plan in advance for students who may be stuck? Are there particular groups or individual students you wish to specially observe or assess in this lesson? Make a note to do so. Think of extensions or challenges you can pose to students who finish quickly.

Estimate how much time you think students should be given for the task. It is useful to tell students in advance. Some teachers set a timer that all students can see. Plan to be flexible, but do not use up your discussion period.

Step 8: **_Think About the After Portion of the Lesson._** How will you begin your discussion? One option is to simply list all of the different answers from groups or individuals, doing so without comment, and then returning to students or groups to explain their solutions and justify their answers. You may also begin with full explanations from each group or student before you get all the answers. Will you record on the board what is being said or have students write on the board or show their work in other ways?

Plan an adequate amount of time for your discussion. A good average is about 15 to 20 minutes.

Step 9: **_Write Your Lesson Plan._** If you have thought through these steps, a plan is simply a listing of the critical decisions you have already made. The outline shown here is a possible format:

- The mathematics or goals
- The task and expectations
- The *before* activities
- The *during* hints and extensions for early finishers
- The *after*-lesson discussion format
- Assessment notes (what to be looking for, students to watch)

Note that at the end of each of the remaining chapters of this book, we have selected an activity from the chapter and expanded it into a complete lesson plan utilizing this structure.

Variations of the Three-Part Lesson

Certainly, not every lesson is developed around a task given to a full class. This is especially true in kindergarten and first grade. However, the basic concept of tasks and discussions can be adapted to most any problem-based lesson.

Mini-Lessons

Many tasks do not require the full period. The three-part format can be compressed to as little as 10 minutes. You might plan two or three cycles in a single lesson. For example, consider these tasks:

Grades K–1: Make up two questions that we can answer using the information in our graph.

Grades 1–3: Pose a simple story problem structured to evoke possible strategies for basic facts. For example: *At the Zoo, Molly saw 6 polar bears and 7 brown bears. How many bears did she see in all?* (Possible strategy: double 6 and one more.) "Solve this problem in your head. Discuss your method with your partner and then we'll listen to your ideas."

These are worthwhile tasks that do not require a full period to do and discuss. A think-pair-share strategy is useful for these shorter tasks.

Workstations and Games

There is no reason to abandon stations or learning centers in a problem-based classroom. The before portion of a lesson adapted for stations, games, and computer activities generally happens with the whole class when you explain the activity.

Many station activities can be profitably repeated several times and still retain a problem-based flavor. For example, students might be replacing missing numbers on a hundreds chart or playing a "game" in which one student covers part of a known number of counters and the other student names the covered part. In the pre-K–3 section of the NCTM e-Standards are several computer-based activities that are worth revisiting more than once. Whereas the format of an activity can remain constant, the specific task for the day can change and advance with the children's growth.

A game or other repeatable activity may not look like a problem, but it can nonetheless be problem based. The determining factor is this: Does the activity cause students to be reflective about new or developing mathematical relationships? If the activity merely has students repeating a procedure without wrestling with an emerging idea, then it is not a problem-based experience. However, the few examples just mentioned and many others do have children thinking through ideas that are not easily developed in one or two lessons. In this sense, they fit the definition of a problem-based task.

The time during which students are working at stations is analogous to the during phase of a lesson. A discussion with students who have been working on a task, the after phase, is just as important for games and stations. However, these discussions will generally take place in small groups. You might sit down with students at a station and ask about what they have been doing, what strategies they have discovered, or how they have been going about the activity in general. Try to get at the reasoning behind what they are doing. Another possibility is to wait until all in the class have worked at the same game or station and have a full group discussion about the learning that came from that activity.

Just as with any task, some form of recording or writing should be included with stations whenever possible. Students solving a problem on a computer can write up what they did and explain what they learned. Students playing a game can keep records and then tell about how they played the game—what thinking or strategies they used.

Diversity in the Classroom

Perhaps one of the most difficult challenges for teachers today is to reach all of the students in their increasingly diverse classrooms. Every teacher faces this dilemma because every classroom contains a range of student abilities and backgrounds.

Interestingly, a problem-based approach can be the best way to attend to the range of students. In the problem-based classroom, children make sense of the mathematics in their own way, bringing to the problems only the skills and ideas that they own. The sophistication of the methods and approaches used will vary in accord with the range of ideas found within the class. In contrast, in a traditional, highly directed lesson, it is assumed that all students will understand and use the same approach and the same ideas. Students not ready to understand the ideas presented by the teacher must focus their attention on following the rules or directions in a mindless manner. This, of course, leads to endless difficulties and leaves many students behind or in need of serious remediation and reteaching.

In addition to using a problem-based approach, specific things you can do to help attend to the diversity of learners in your classroom include:

- Making sure that problems have multiple entry points.
- Plan differentiated tasks.
- Use heterogeneous groupings.

Plan for Multiple Entry Points

Step 4 in the planning guidelines suggests that you predict how all of the students in the class are likely to approach the task you've selected. Many tasks can be solved with a range of strategies. This is especially true of computational tasks in classes where student-invented methods are encouraged and valued. (See the example of 36 + 25 earlier in this chapter.) For many tasks, the use or nonuse of manipulative models is all that is necessary to vary the entry point. Other students can be challenged to devise rules or to use methods that are less dependent on manipulatives or drawings. When considering a task, think of the least sophisticated method of solution you can imagine. Will this method provide an entry for your struggling students? Is there a clever method or extension you can imagine that will challenge your more able students?

Plan Differentiated Tasks

The idea here is to plan a task with multiple versions; some less difficult, others more so. For many problems involving computations, you can insert multiple sets of numbers. In the following problem students are permitted to select the first, second, or third number in each bracket.

· ·

Eduardo had {12, 60, 121} marbles. He gave Erica {5, 15, 46} marbles. How many marbles does Eduardo have now?

· ·

Students tend to select the numbers that provide them with the greatest challenge without being too difficult. For this example, consider the differences in the three problems: 12 – 5, 60 – 15, and 121 – 46. In the discussions, all children benefit and feel as though they worked on the same task. Games and station activities can be modified in a similar manner.

Another way to differentiate a task is to present a simple situation with related but different questions that can be asked. The situation might be data in a chart or graph, a measurement to be made, or a set of geometric shapes or geoboard. Here is a measurement example:

- -

Students are given a large, informal unit of length, perhaps a "giant's footprint" cut from poster board. These questions can be posed:

- How long is our classroom in giant footprints?
- How much longer is the classroom front to back than side to side? Use your giant footprints.
- The giant's daughter has a footprint that is only half as long as his. First measure the classroom with the giant's footprint. Then explain what the answer would be if you used the daughter's footprint.

- -

Workstations and games also provide some method of task differentiation. Two similar stations can vary simply by the materials that are provided or the numbers that are involved. Stations can be assigned to students to best fit their needs and yet all will be working on the same concept.

Use Heterogeneous Groupings

Avoid ability grouping! Trying to split a class into ability groups is futile; every group still has diversity. It is demeaning to those students not in the top group. Students in the lower group will not experience the thinking and language of the top group, and top students will not hear the often unconventional but interesting approaches to tasks in the lower group. Furthermore, having two or more groups means that you must diminish the time you can spend with each group.

It is much more profitable to capitalize on the diversity in your room by using pairs or cooperative groups that are heterogeneous. Try to pair students in need of help with capable students but also students who will be compatible and willing to assist. Students will find that everyone has ideas to contribute. This does not mean that every cooperative group need be of mixed ability. Some teachers find it useful to vary this approach, sometimes grouping children more homogeneously and other times heterogeneously.

ASSESSMENT IN A PROBLEM-BASED CLASSROOM

In a problem-based approach, teachers often ask, "How do I assess?" The question stems from the realization and acceptance of the fact that the traditional skill-oriented testing fails to adequately tell what students know. Both the *Assessment Standards for School Mathematics* (1995) and *Principles and Standards for School Mathematics* (2000) stress that the line between assessment and instruction should be blurred. Teaching with problems allows us to blur that line. Assessment need not look different from instruction. The typical approach of an end-of-chapter test of skills may have some value but it is not appropriate as the main method of assessment. Assessment can and should happen every day as an integral part of instruction. If you restrict your view of assessment to tests and quizzes, you will miss seeing how assessment can help students grow and inform instruction. "Assessment should focus on what students *do know* instead of what they *do not know*" (NCTM, 1989).

Appropriate Assessment

An *appropriate assessment task* refers to a task or problem that allows students to demonstrate what they know. Both you and your students must see it as an integral part of the learning process.

If you take a problem-based approach to instruction but most of your assessments focus on recall and closed response items, you are sending mixed messages to your students. Recall and skill assessments tell students that what is valued is getting answers. Soon they will not be willing to solve problems or engage in class discussions but rather will insist that you simply "show them how to get the answers."

Assessment Tasks

Recall that a problem was any task or activity for which the students have no prescribed or memorized rules or specific correct solution method. The same definition should be used for assessment tasks. Perhaps you have heard about *performance assessment tasks* or *alternative assessments*. These terms seem to refer to tasks that are in some way different from those used in instruction. They should not be different! An assessment task should be a performance task as should problem-based tasks for learning.

 Do you think that you can or should use problem-based tasks such as those that have been described to assess your students? What are the pros and cons of such an approach?

Good tasks—for either instruction and/or assessment purposes—should permit every student in the class, regardless of mathematical prowess, to demonstrate his or her knowledge, skill, or understanding. Lower-ability students should be encouraged to use the best ideas they possess to work on a problem, even if these are not the same skills or strategies used by others in the room. When problem-based tasks are used for assessment and evaluation, then rather than find out what students *do not know* (e.g., they can't add with regrouping), you will have a broad description of the ideas and skills students possess—what they *do know* (e.g., counts up using tens, then counts on; often makes counting errors; needs a recording mechanism).

Tasks used in this way focus attention on the thinking and processes that students use in solving tasks. The percentage of correct answers is a very incomplete picture of what a student knows. However, the potential data about your students can and should come daily as you "listen" in as many ways as possible to the methods that your students use to grapple with the tasks you give them.

Collecting Assessment Data

In some instances, the real value of a task or what can be learned about students will come primarily during the discussion in the after phase of your lesson. At other times, the best assessment data will be in the written work that students do. To consistently receive valid data, it is important that you develop in your students the habit of adding justifications to their answers and listening to and evaluating the explanations of others.

Many activities have no written component and no "answer" or result. This is especially true of games and station activities. For example, students may be playing a comparison game in which dice or dominoes are being used. A teacher who sits in on the game will see great differences in how children use numbers. Some will count every dot on the card or domino. Others will use a counting-on strategy. Some will recognize the dot patterns without counting. Others may be unsure if 13 beats 11. This information significantly differentiates students relative to their understanding of number concepts. Data gathered from observing a pair of children work on a simple activity or an extended project provides significantly greater insight into students' thinking than almost any written test we could devise. Data from student conversations and observations of student behavior can be recorded and used for the same purposes that written data can, including evaluation and grading.

The amount of information available from students, both from their written work and their discussions, is voluminous. However, you must find ways to record it so that you have the data when you need it. Your memory of what transpired today may be sufficient for planning tomorrow's lesson. However, to help with grades and parent conferences, you need records. Here are some ideas:

- Make a habit of recording quick observational data. There are lots of options. A full class checklist with space for comments is one method. Another is to write anecdotal notes on address labels and stick them into binders.

- Focus on big ideas rather than small skills. For example, "Uses number relationships to answer basic facts" is more helpful than "Has mastered more than half of addition facts."

- You need not assess every child on every task. By focusing on big ideas, you will not feel required to check on every student on any given day. Make a habit of selecting a small number of students to focus on during a lesson. Gather data on a big idea over a week or so.

- Save or make copies of student work that indicates well the thinking of a child. There may be days when you announce to students that you are going to keep their written work in their folders. However, some children may produce better work the next day or will have done better thinking the day before. Use written work to show what students know.

- Use traditional tests for skills that you feel are essential. Use this technique sparingly.

Rubrics and Their Uses

Appropriate assessment tasks yield an enormous amount of information that cannot be evaluated by simply counting correct answers. We need to find ways to manage this information and make it useful. One important tool is a rubric.

A *rubric* consists of a scale of three to six points that is used as a rating of performance rather than a count of how many items are correct or incorrect. The rating is applied by examining total performance on a single task as opposed to counting the number of correct items.

Simple Rubrics

The following simple four-point rubric was developed by the New Standards Project and is used by many teachers and some school districts:

4   Excellent: Full Accomplishment

3   Proficient: Substantial Accomplishment

2   Marginal: Partial Accomplishment

1   Unsatisfactory: Little Accomplishment

This four-point rubric allows a teacher to rate performances using a double-sort technique as illustrated in Figure 1.10. The broad categories of the first sort (*Got It* or

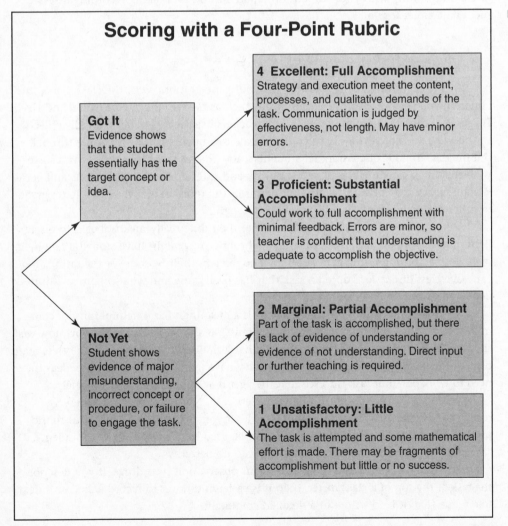

Scoring with a Four-Point Rubric

Got It
Evidence shows that the student essentially has the target concept or idea.

4 Excellent: Full Accomplishment
Strategy and execution meet the content, processes, and qualitative demands of the task. Communication is judged by effectiveness, not length. May have minor errors.

3 Proficient: Substantial Accomplishment
Could work to full accomplishment with minimal feedback. Errors are minor, so teacher is confident that understanding is adequate to accomplish the objective.

Not Yet
Student shows evidence of major misunderstanding, incorrect concept or procedure, or failure to engage the task.

2 Marginal: Partial Accomplishment
Part of the task is accomplished, but there is lack of evidence of understanding or evidence of not understanding. Direct input or further teaching is required.

1 Unsatisfactory: Little Accomplishment
The task is attempted and some mathematical effort is made. There may be fragments of accomplishment but little or no success.

FIGURE 1.10 ● ● ● ● ● ● ● ●

With a four-point rubric, performances are first sorted into two categories. Each performance is then considered again and assigned to a point on the scale.

RUBRICS AND THEIR USES

Not Yet) are relatively easy to discern. The scale then allows you to separate each category into two levels as shown. Some teachers use a 4+ rating to note truly exceptional performance. A rating of 0 can be given for no response or effort or for responses that are completely off-task.

The advantage of the four-point scale is the relatively easy double sort that can be made. The first sort, between those who have basically developed the idea from those students who need further experiences or instruction, is most important for judging how to pace your lessons and identifying students in need of additional instruction.

Other teachers prefer a three-point rubric such as the following example:

3   Above and beyond—uses exemplary methods, shows creativity, goes beyond the requirements of the problem

2   On target—completes the task with no more than minor errors, uses expected approaches

1   Not there yet—makes significant errors or omissions, uses inappropriate approaches

The exact rubric you use is less important than having a well-understood method of communicating with your students and parents and for making recording assessment data easier for you.

Involve Students with Rubrics

In the beginning of the year, discuss your general rubric with the class. For K to 3 children, you will want to use simple words such as "Wow, Got It, Not Quite, and Need Help." Post the rubric prominently. Many teachers use the same rubric for all subjects. In this way, the words you use to communicate to students will be the same throughout the day. In your discussion, let students know that as they do activities and solve problems in class, you will look at their work and listen to their explanations and occasionally provide them with feedback in terms of the rubric rather than as a letter grade or other evaluative mark.

When students start to understand what the rubric really means, begin to discuss performance on tasks in terms of the general rubric. You might have students rate their own work according to the general rubric and explain their reasons for the rating. You can have class discussions about a task that has been done and what might constitute good and exceptional performance.

A rubric is much more than a grade. It is a meaningful and helpful form of communication with your students (and their parents). It should let students know how well they are doing and encourage them to work harder. When their performance is less than okay, students should understand not that they have failed but that there are ideas they need to work on. Your task is to see that they get that opportunity and your help.

You do not need to use rubrics with every task. Nor is it necessary to reserve rubrics for assessments that you want to grade. If you are using the four-point rubric just described, the language of the rubric can be used informally with your students. "Maggie, that paper is only a 2. I know you can do better."

The rubric scale can also be used in your observation recordings. If you describe the task at the top of a class roster, then it is easier and faster to record a 2, 3, or 4 next to a name than it is to write out a detailed comment.

Diagnostic Interviews

An interview is simply a one-on-one discussion with a child to help you see how she is thinking about a particular subject, what processes she uses in solving problems, or what attitudes and beliefs she may have. It may be as short as 5 to 10 minutes.

Many teachers avoid interviews because of time constraints. This is unfortunate because interviews have the potential to give you information that you simply cannot get in any other way. Think of interviews as a method to be used for only a few students at a time—not for every student in the class. You can interview a single student while the rest of the class is working on a task.

The most obvious reason to consider an interview is that you need more information concerning a particular child and how he or she is constructing concepts or using a procedure. Remediation will almost always be more successful if you can pinpoint *why* a student is having difficulty before you try to fix the problem.

A second reason is to get information either to plan your instruction or to assess the effectiveness of your instruction. For example, are you sure that your students have a good understanding of equivalent fractions, or are they just doing the exercises according to rote rules?

Planning an Interview

There is no magic right way to plan or structure an interview. In fact, flexibility is a key ingredient. You should, however, have some overall game plan before you begin, and be prepared with key questions and materials. Begin an interview with questions that are easy or closest to what the child is likely to be able to do, usually some form of procedural exercise. For numeration or computation topics, for example, begin with a pencil-and-paper task such as a computation, writing or comparing numerals. When the opening task has been completed, ask the child to explain what was done. "How would you explain this to a second grader (or your younger sister)?" "What does this (point to something on the paper) stand for?" "Tell me about why you do it that way." At this point, you may try a similar task but with a different feature; for example, after doing 372 – 54, try 403 – 37. The second problem has a zero in the tens place, a possible source of difficulty.

The next phase in the interview might involve models or drawings that the child can use to demonstrate understanding of the earlier procedural task. Computations can be done with base-ten materials, blocks or counters can be used, number lines explored, grid paper used for drawing, and so on. Be careful not to interject or teach. The temptation to do so is sometimes overwhelming. Watch and listen. Next, explore connections between what was done with models and what was done with pencil and paper. Many children will do the very same task and get two different answers. Does it matter to the child? How is the discrepancy explained? Can the student connect actions using models to what he or she wrote or explained earlier?

Alternative beginnings to an interview include making an estimate of the answer to either a computation or a word problem, doing a computation mentally, or trying to predict the solution to a given task. Your goal is not to use the interview to teach but to find out where the child is in terms of concepts and procedures at this time.

Suggestions for Effective Interviews

The following suggestions have been adapted from excellent discussions of interviewing children by Labinowicz (1985, 1987), Liedtke (1988), and Scheer (1980).

- *Be accepting and neutral as you listen to the child.* Smiles, frowns, or other body language can make the child think that the answer he or she gave is right or wrong. Develop neutral responses such as "Uh-huh," "I see," or even a silent nod of the head.

- *Avoid cuing or leading the child.* "Are you sure about that?" "Now look again closely at what you just did." "Wait. Is that what you mean?" These responses will indicate to children that they have made some mistake and cause them to change their responses. This can mask what they really think and understand. A similar form of leading is a series of easily answered questions that direct the student to a correct response. That is teaching, not interviewing.

- *Wait silently.* Give the student plenty of time before you ask a different question or probe. After the child makes a response, wait again! This second wait time is even more important because it allows and encourages the child to elaborate on the initial thought and provide you with more information. Wait even when the response is correct. Waiting can also give you a bit more time to think about the direction you want the interview to take. Your wait time will almost never be as long as you imagine it is.

- *Do not interrupt.* Let children's thoughts flow freely. Encourage children to use their own words and ways of writing things down. Interjecting questions or correcting language can be distracting to the child's thinking.

- *Use imperatives rather than questions.* Say, "show me," "tell me," "do," or "try," rather than "can you?" or "will you?" In response to a question, the child can simply say no, leaving you without information.

- *Avoid confirming a request for validation.* Students frequently follow answers or actions with, "Is that right?" This query can easily be answered with a neutral, "That's fine," or "You're doing okay," regardless of whether the answer is right or wrong.

Interviewing is not an easy thing to do well. Many teachers are timid about it and fail to take the time. But not much damage is possible, and the rewards of listening to children, both for you and your students, are so great that you really do not want to pass it up.

Grading

Myth: A grade is an average of a series of scores on tests and quizzes. The accuracy of the grade depends primarily on the accuracy of the computational technique used to calculate the final numeric grade.

Reality: A grade is a statistic that is used to communicate to others the achievement level that a student has attained in a particular area of study. The accuracy or validity of the grade depends on the information that is used in preparing the grade, the professional judgment of the teacher, and the alignment of the assessments with the true goals and objectives of the course.

Confronting the Myth

Most experienced teachers will say that they know a great deal about their students in terms of what the students know, how they perform in different situations, their attitudes and beliefs, and their various levels of skill attainment. Unfortunately, when it comes to grades, they often ignore this rich storehouse of information and rely on test scores and rigid averages that tell only a small fraction of the story.

The myth of grading by statistical number crunching is so firmly ingrained in schooling at all levels that you may find it hard to abandon. But it is unfair to students, to parents, and to you as the teacher to ignore all of the information you get almost daily from a problem-based approach in favor of a handful of numbers based on tests that usually focus on low-level skills.

Grading Issues

Some hard decisions are inevitable for effective use of the assessment information gathered from problems, tasks, and other appropriate methods to assign grades. Some decisions are philosophical, some require school or district agreements about grades, and all require us to examine what we value and the objectives we communicate to students and parents.

In contrast to the myth of grading, one thing is undeniably true: *What gets graded is what gets valued.* Using rubric scales to provide feedback and to encourage a pursuit of excellence must also relate to grades. However, "converting four out of five to 80 percent or three out of four to a grade of C can destroy the entire purpose of alternative assessment and the use of scoring rubrics" (Kulm, 1994, p. 99). Kulm explains that directly translating rubrics to grades focuses attention on grades and away from the purpose of every good problem-solving activity, to strive for an excellent performance. When papers are returned with less than top ratings, the purpose is to help students know what is necessary to achieve at a higher level. This purpose must be explicitly communicated to students and parents. Early on, there should be opportunities to improve based on feedback. When a grade of 75 percent or a C– is returned, all the student knows is that he or she did poorly. If, for example, a student's ability to justify his or her own answers and solutions has improved, should the student be penalized in the averaging of numbers that includes a weaker performance early in the marking period?

What this means is that grading must be based on the performance tasks and other activities for which you assigned rubric ratings; otherwise, students will soon realize that these are not important scores. At the same time, they need not be added or averaged in any numeric manner. The grade at the end of a unit or chapter should reflect a holistic view of where the student is now relative to your goals for that unit.

The grades you assign should reflect all of your objectives. Procedural skills remain important but should be weighted in proportion to other goals in keeping with your value system. If you are restricted to assigning a single grade for mathematics, different factors probably have different weights or values in making up the grade. There are no simple answers to how you balance all of your objectives—concepts, skills, problem solving, communication, and so on. However, these questions should be addressed at the beginning of the grading period and not the night you set out to assign grades.

A multidimensional reporting system is a big help. If you can assign several grades for mathematics and not just one, your report to parents is more meaningful. Even if the school's report card does not permit multiple grades, you can devise a supplement indicating several ratings for different objectives. A place for comments is also helpful. This form can be shared with students periodically during a grading period and can easily accompany a report card.

GET STARTED

In this chapter we have briefly touched on the foundational ideas of how children learn, teaching through problem solving, planning problem-based lessons, and assessment. It may take some time for you to completely adopt these ideas and approaches. Some things may make more sense to you than others. It may be discomforting to give up methods with which you've become familiar. It is hard to think of allowing—even planning for—the students in your room to struggle. Most people get into teaching because they want to help students learn. To not show them a solution when they are experiencing difficulty seems almost counterintuitive.

It is unrealistic to think you could simply read this chapter and then turn around and become a problem-based teacher. However, if you give this approach a fair chance and try to apply your understanding of how children learn to your daily teaching, your students will reward you with their performance, enthusiasm, and understanding. No, it will not happen overnight. But now is the time to begin—so get started!

As reflective thinking is the key ingredient in student learning, so also is reflection necessary to improve as a teacher. Do not be discouraged by lessons that did not go as you planned. Rather, ask yourself what happened and why. How could you have changed the lesson to make it better? How will you apply what you learned to the next lesson?

Social learning is also an important tool for teachers. Get other teachers on your grade level or in your school to try new ideas together. Talk informally about what seems to make a good lesson and what gets in the way. Use the planning guide discussed in this chapter to create lessons together. Don't try to jointly plan every lesson— just one every two or three weeks. Then have everyone teach the same lesson and compare notes. Make revisions based on your experiences. File these "special" lessons away and use them next year.

In addition to simply getting started and trying these ideas, the most important ingredient is to *believe in your kids!* Your students can think and can make sense of mathematics—*all of your students*. Some may learn more slowly or create different approaches that have never occurred to you, but they all can think and they all can learn. By allowing the mathematics to be problematic for students every day, we demonstrate to students every day our belief in their abilities to do and learn mathematics. Just give them the chance and let them amaze you.

DEVELOPING EARLY NUMBER CONCEPTS AND NUMBER SENSE

Number is a complex and multifaceted concept. A complete and rich understanding of number involves many different ideas, relationships, and skills. Children come to school with many ideas about number. These ideas should be built upon as we work with children and help them develop new relationships. It takes time and lots of experiences for children to develop a full understanding of number that will grow and enhance all of the further number-related concepts of the school years.

This chapter looks at the development of number ideas for numbers up to about 20. These foundational ideas can all be extended to larger numbers, operations, basic facts, and computation.

big ideas

1 Counting tells how many things are in a set. When counting a set of objects, the last word in the counting sequence names the quantity for that set.

2 Numbers are related to each other through a variety of number relationships. The number 7, for example, is more than 4, two less than 9, composed of 3 and 4 as well as 2 and 5, is three away from 10, and can be quickly recognized in several patterned arrangements of dots. These ideas further extend to an understanding of 17, 57, and 370.

3 Number concepts are intimately tied to the world around us. Application of number relationships to the real world marks the beginning of making sense of the world in a mathematical manner.

Early Counting and Number

Parents help children count their fingers, toys, people at the table, and other small sets of objects. Questions concerning "who has more?" or "are there enough?" are part of the daily lives of children as young as 2 or 3 years of age. Considerable evidence indicates that these children have some understanding of the concepts of number and counting.

The Relationships of More, Less, and Same

The concepts of "more," "less," and "same" are basic relationships contributing to the overall concept of number. Children begin to develop these ideas before they begin school. An entering kindergarten child can almost always choose the set that is *more* if presented with two sets that are quite obviously different in number. Classroom activities should help children build on this basic notion and refine it.

Though the concept of less is logically equivalent to the concept of more (selecting the set with more is the same as *not* selecting the set with less), the word *less* proves to be more difficult for children than *more*. A possible explanation is that children have many opportunities to use the word *more* but have limited exposure to the word *less*. To help children with the concept of less, frequently pair it with the word *more* and make a conscious effort to ask "which is less?" questions as well as "which is more?" questions. For example, suppose that your class has correctly selected the set that has more from two that are given. Immediately follow with the question "Which is less?" In this way, the less familiar term and concept can be connected with the better-known idea.

For all three concepts (more, less, and same), children should construct sets using counters as well as make comparisons or choices between two given sets. The activities described here include both types. These activities should be conducted in a spirit of inquiry followed whenever possible with requests for explanations. "Why do you think this set has less?"

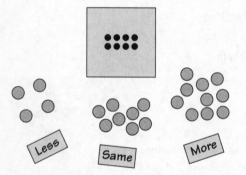

FIGURE 2.1 • • • • • • • • • • • • • • • • •

Making sets that are more, less, and the same.

ACTIVITY 2.1

Make Sets of More/Less/Same

At a workstation or table, provide about eight cards with sets of 4 to 12 objects, a set of small counters or blocks, and some word cards labeled *More*, *Less,* and *Same*. Next to each card have students make three collections of counters: a set that is more, one that is less, and one that is the same. The appropriate labels are placed on the sets (see Figure 2.1).

In Activity 2.1, students create a set with counters, which gives them the opportunity to reflect on the sets and adjust them as they work. The next activity is done without counters. Although it addresses the same basic ideas, it provides a different problem situation.

ACTIVITY 2.2

Find the Same Amount

Give children a collection of cards with sets on them. Dot cards are one possibility (see the Blackline Masters). Have the children pick up any card in the collection and then find another card with the same amount to form a pair. Continue to find other pairs.

BLMs 3–8

Activity 2.2 can be altered to have children find dot cards that are "less" or "more."

Assessment Note

Observe children as they do this task. Children whose number ideas are completely tied to counting and nothing more will select cards at random and count each dot. Others will begin by selecting a card that appears to have about the same number of dots. This is a significantly higher level of understanding. Also observe how the dots are counted. Are the counts made accurately? Is each counted only once? A significant milestone for children occurs when they begin recognizing small patterned sets without counting.

Early Counting

Meaningful counting activities can begin in preschool. Generally, children at midyear in kindergarten should have a fair understanding of counting, but children must construct this idea. It cannot be forced. Only the counting sequence is a rote procedure. The *meaning* attached to counting is the key conceptual idea on which all other number concepts are developed.

Meaning Attached to Counting

Fosnot and Dolk (2001) make it very clear that an understanding of cardinality and the connection to counting is not a simple matter for 4-year-olds. Children will learn *how* to count (matching counting words with objects) before they understand that the last count word indicates the *amount* of the set or the *cardinality* of the set. Children who have made this connection are said to have the *cardinality principle,* which is a refinement of their early ideas about quantity. Most, but certainly not all, children by age $4\frac{1}{2}$ have made this connection (Fosnot & Dolk, 2001; Fuson & Hall, 1983).

Assessment Note

To determine if young children have the cardinality rule, listen to how they respond when you discuss counting tasks with them. You ask, "How many are here?" The child counts correctly, and says, "Nine." Ask, "Are there nine?" Before developing cardinality, children may count again or will hesitate. Children with cardinality are apt to emphasize the last count, will explain that there are nine "Because I just counted them," and can use counting to find a matching set. Fosnot and Dolk discuss a class of 4-year-olds in which children who knew there were 17 children in the class were unsure how many milk cartons they should get so that each could have one.

To develop their understanding of counting, engage children in almost any game or activity that involves counts and comparisons. The following is a simple suggestion.

ACTIVITY 2.3

Fill the Chutes

Create a simple game board with four "chutes." Each consists of a column of about twelve 1-inch squares with a star at the top. Children take turns rolling a die and collecting the indicated number of counters. They then place these counters in one of the chutes. The object is to fill all of the chutes with counters. As an option, require that the chutes be filled exactly. A roll of 5 cannot be used to fill a chute with four spaces.

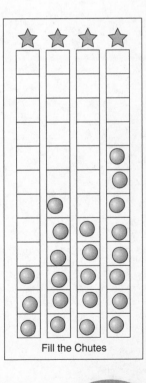

Fill the Chutes

This "game" provides opportunities for you to talk with children about number and assess their thinking. Watch how the children count the dots on the die. Ask, "How do you know you have the right number of counters?" and "How many counters did you put in the chute? How many more do you need to fill the chute?"

Technology Note

Computer software that allows children to create sets on the screen with the click of a mouse is quite common. *Unifix Software* (Hickey, 1996) is an electronic version of the popular Unifix cubes, plastic cubes that snap together to make bars. The software allows the teacher to add features to counting activities that are not available with the cubes alone. In its most basic form, children can click to create as many single cubes as they wish. They can link cubes to make bars of cubes, break the bars, move them around, add sounds to each cube, and more. The teacher can choose to have a numeral appear on each bar showing the total. From one to four loops can be created, with the loop total another option. Not only can students count to specified numbers and have the numerals appear for reinforcement, but also they can informally begin to explore the idea that two quantities can form a larger amount.

Do not let these computer tools become toys. It is important to keep the task problem based. For example, in early kindergarten, students could make a set of single blocks in one loop that is just as many as (or more or less than) a bar the teacher has made in the first loop. (Files can be prepared ahead of time.) Later students can explore different combinations of two bars that would equal a third bar.

Counting On and Counting Back

Although the forward sequence of numbers is relatively familiar to most young children, counting on and counting back are difficult skills for many. Frequent short practice drills are recommended.

ACTIVITY 2.4

Up and Back Counting

Counting up to and back from a target number in a rhythmic fashion is an important counting exercise. For example, line up five children and five chairs in front of the class. As the whole class counts from 1 to 5, the children sit down one at a time. When the target number, 5, is reached, it is repeated; the child who sat on 5 now stands, and the count goes back to 1. As the count goes back, the children stand up one at a time, and so on, "1, 2, 3, 4, 5, 5, 4, 3, 2, 1, 1, 2, ..." Kindergarten and first-grade children find exercises such as this both fun and challenging. Any movement (clapping, turning around, doing jumping jacks) can be used as the count goes up and back in a rhythmic manner.

The calculator provides an excellent counting exercise for young children because they see the numerals as they count.

ACTIVITY 2.5

Calculator Up and Back

Have each child press $[+]\,[1]\,[=]\,[=]\,[=]\,[=]\,[=]$. The display will go from 1 to 5 with each $[=]$ press. The count should also be made out loud in a rhythm as in the other exercises. To start over, press the clear key and repeat. Counting up and back is also possible, but the end numbers will not be repeated. The following illustrates the key presses and what the children would say in rhythm:

$[+]\,1\,[=]\,[=]\,[=]\,[=]\quad[-]\quad1\,[=]\,[=]\,[=]\,[=]\quad[+]\quad1\,[=]\,[=]\,\ldots$

"1, 2, 3, 4, 5, minus 1, 4, 3, 2, 1, plus 1, 2, 3, . . ."

The last two activities are designed only to help students become fluent with the number words in both forward and reverse order and to begin counts with numbers other than 1. Although not at all easy for young students, these activities do not address counting on or counting back in a meaningful manner. Fosnot and Dolk (2001) describe the ability to count on as a "landmark" on the path to number sense. The next two activities are designed for that purpose.

ACTIVITY 2.6

Counting On with Counters

Give each child a collection of 10 or 12 small counters that the children line up left to right on their desks. Tell them to count four counters and push them under their left hands (see Figure 2.2). Then say, "Point to your hand. How many are there?" (Four.) "So let's count like this: f-o-u-r (pointing to their hand), five, six, ..." Repeat with other numbers under the hand.

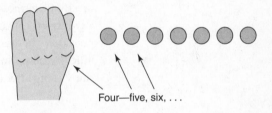

Four—five, six, . . .

FIGURE 2.2 • • • • • • • • • • • • • • • • •

Counting on: "Hide four. Count, starting from the number of counters hidden."

The following activity addresses the same concept in a bit more problem-based manner.

ACTIVITY 2.7

Real Counting On

This "game" for two children requires a deck of cards with numbers 1 to 7, a die, a paper cup, and some counters. The first player turns over the top number card and places the indicated number of counters in the cup. The card is placed next to the cup as a reminder of how many are there. The second child rolls the die and places that many counters next to the cup. (See Figure 2.3.) Together they decide how many counters in all. A record sheet with columns for "In the Cup," "On the Side," and "In All" is an option. The largest number in the card deck can be adjusted if needed.

FIGURE 2.3 • • • • • • • •

How many in all? How do children count to tell the total? Dump the counters? Count up from 1 without dumping the counters? Count on?

Watch how children determine the total amounts in this last activity. Children who are not yet counting on may want to dump the counters from the cup or will count up from one without dumping out the counters. Be sure to permit these strategies. As children continue to play, they will eventually count on as that strategy becomes meaningful and useful.

Early Number Sense

Number sense was a term that became popular in the late 1980s, although it continues to have somewhat vague definitions. Howden (1989) described number sense as a "good intuition about numbers and their relationships. It develops gradually as a result of exploring numbers, visualizing them in a variety of contexts, and relating them in ways that are not limited by traditional algorithms" (p. 11). This may still be the best definition.

The discussion of number sense begins in this book with the remainder of this chapter as we look at the kinds of relationships and connections children should be making about smaller numbers up to about 20. But "good intuition about numbers" does not end with these smaller whole numbers. Children continue to develop number sense as they begin to use numbers in operations, build an understanding of place value, and devise flexible methods of computing and making estimates involving large numbers. Flexible, intuitive thinking with numbers—number sense—should continue to be developed throughout the school years as fractions, decimals, and percents are added to students' repertoire of number ideas.

The early number ideas that have been discussed to this point in the chapter are the rudimentary aspects of number. Unfortunately, too many traditional programs move directly from these beginning ideas to addition and subtraction, leaving students with a very limited collection of ideas about number to bring to these new topics. The result is often that children continue to count by ones to solve simple story problems and have difficulty mastering basic facts. Early number sense development should demand significantly more attention than it is given in most traditional K–2 programs.

Relationships Among Numbers 1 Through 10

Once children have acquired a concept of cardinality and can meaningfully use their counting skills, little more is to be gained from the kinds of counting activities described so far. More relationships must be created for children to develop number sense, a flexible concept of number not completely tied to counting.

A Collection of Number Relationships

Figure 2.4 illustrates the four different types of relationships that children can and should develop with numbers:

- *Spatial relationships:* Children can learn to recognize sets of objects in patterned arrangements and tell how many without counting. For most numbers, there are several common patterns. Patterns can also be made up of two or more easier patterns for smaller numbers.

- *One and two more, one and two less:* The two-more-than and two-less-than relationships involve more than just the ability to count on two or count back two. Children should know that 7, for example, is 1 more than 6 and also 2 less than 9.

- *Anchors or "benchmarks" of 5 and 10:* Since 10 plays such a large role in our numeration system and because two fives make up 10, it is very useful to develop relationships for the numbers 1 to 10 to the important anchors of 5 and 10.

- *Part-part-whole relationships:* To conceptualize a number as being made up of two or more parts is the most important relationship that can be developed about numbers. For example, 7 can be thought of as a set of 3 and a set of 4 or a set of 2 and a set of 5.

The principal tool that children will use as they construct these relationships is the one number tool they possess: counting. Initially, then, you will notice a lot of counting, and you may wonder if you are making progress. Have patience! Counting will become less and less necessary as children construct these new relationships and begin to use the more powerful ideas.

Spatial Relationships: Patterned Set Recognition

Many children learn to recognize the dot arrangements on standard dice due to the many games they have played that use dice. Similar instant recognition can be developed for other patterns as well. The activities suggested here encourage reflective thinking about the patterns so that the relationships will be constructed. Quantities up to 10 can be known and named without the routine of counting. This can then aid in counting on (from a known patterned set) or learning combinations of numbers (seeing a pattern of two known smaller patterns).

A good set of materials to use in pattern recognition activities is a set of dot plates. These can be made using small paper plates and the peel-off dots commonly available in office supply stores. A reasonable collection of patterns is shown in Figure 2.5. Note that some patterns are combinations of two smaller patterns or a pattern with one or two additional dots. These should be made in two colors. Keep the patterns compact. If the dots are spread out, the patterns are hard to see.

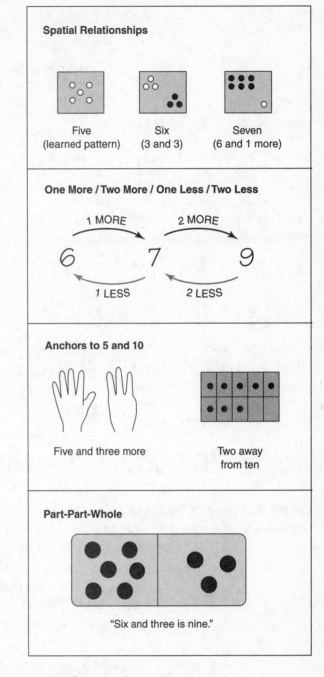

FIGURE 2.4

Four relationships to be developed involving small numbers.

ACTIVITY 2.8

Learning Patterns

To introduce the patterns, provide each student with about ten counters and a piece of construction paper as a mat. Hold up a dot plate for about 3 seconds. "Make the pattern you saw using the counters on the mat. How many dots did you see? How did you see them?" Spend some time discussing the configuration of the pattern and how many dots. Do this with a few new patterns each day.

RELATIONSHIPS AMONG NUMBERS 1 THROUGH 10

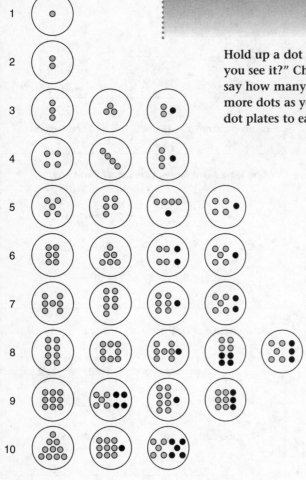

FIGURE 2.5 •

A useful collection of dot patterns for "dot plates."

Dot Plate Flash

Hold up a dot plate for only 1 to 3 seconds. "How many? How did you see it?" Children like to see how quickly they can recognize and say how many dots. Include lots of easy patterns and a few with more dots as you build their confidence. Students can also flash the dot plates to each other as a workstation activity.

The instant recognition activities with the plates are exciting and can be done in 5 minutes at any time of day or between lessons. There is value in using them at any primary grade level and at any time of year.

In addition to dot plates, a good set of materials is a set of dot-pattern dominoes. Make a set of dominoes out of poster board and put a dot pattern on each end. The dominoes can be about 2 inches by 4 inches. The same patterns can appear on lots of dominoes with different pairs of patterns making up each one. Let the children play dominoes in the regular way, matching up the ends. As a speed activity, spread out all of the dominoes and see how fast the children play all of the dominoes or play until no more can be played. Regular dominoes could also be used, but there are not as many patterns.

One and Two More, One and Two Less

When children count, they have no reason to reflect on the way one number is related to another. The goal is only to match number words with objects until they reach the end of the count. To learn that 6 and 8 are related by the twin relationships of "two more than" and "two less than" requires reflection on these ideas within tasks that permit counting. Counting on (or back) one or two counts is a useful tool in constructing these ideas.

One-Less-Than Dominoes

Use the dot-pattern dominoes or a standard set to play "one-less-than" dominoes. Play in the usual way, but instead of matching ends, a new domino can be added if it has an end that is one less than the end on the board. A similar game can be played for two less, one more, or two more.

The following activities can be done for any of the four relationships; each will be described for only one.

ACTIVITY 2.11

Make a Two-More-Than Set

Provide students with about six dot cards. Their task is to construct a set of counters that is two more than the set shown on the card. Similarly, spread out eight to ten dot cards, and find another card for each that is two less than the card shown. (Omit the 1 and 2 cards for two less than, and so on.)

EXPANDED LESSON

(pages 63–64)

A complete lesson plan based on "Make a Two-More-Than Set" can be found at the end of this chapter.

In activities where children find a set or make a set, they can add a numeral card (a small card with a number written on it) to all of the sets involved. They can also be encouraged to take turns reading a number sentence to their partner. If, for example, a set has been made that is two more than a set of four, the child can read this by saying the number sentence, "Two more than four is six."

The calculator can be an exciting device to practice the relationships of one more than, two more than, one less than, and two less than.

ACTIVITY 2.12

A Calculator Two-More-Than Machine

Teach children how to make a two-more-than machine. Press 0 ⊞ 2 ⊟. This makes the calculator a two-more-than machine. Now press any number—for example, 5. Children hold their finger over the ⊟ key and predict the number that is two more than 5. Then they press ⊟ to confirm. If they do not press any of the operation keys (+, –, ×, ÷) the "machine" will continue to perform in this way.

What is really happening in the two-more-than machine is that the calculator "remembers" or stores the last operation, in this case "+2," and adds that to whatever number is in the window when the ⊟ key is pressed. If the child continues to press ⊟, the calculator will count by twos. At any time, a new number can be pressed followed by the equal key. To make a two-less-than machine, press 2 ⊟ 2 ⊟. (The first press of 2 is to avoid a negative number.) In the beginning, students forget and press operation keys, which change what their calculator is doing. Soon, however, they get the hang of using the calculator as a machine.

Anchoring Numbers to 5 and 10

Here again, we want to help children relate a given number to other numbers, specifically 5 and 10. These relationships are especially useful in thinking about various combinations of numbers. For example, in each of the following, consider how the knowledge of 8 as "5 and 3 more" and as "2 away from 10" can play a role: 5 + 3, 8 + 6, 8 – 2, 8 – 3, 8 – 4, 13 – 8. (It may be worth stopping here to consider the role of 5 and 10 in each of these examples.) Later similar relationships can be used in the development of mental computation skills on larger numbers such as 68 + 7.

The most common and perhaps most important model for this relationship is the ten-frame. The ten-frame is simply a 2 × 5 array in which counters or dots are placed to illustrate numbers (see Figure 2.6). Ten-frames can be simply drawn on a full sheet of

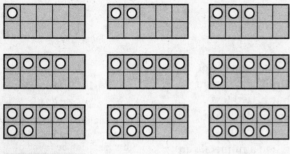

FIGURE 2.6 • • • • • • • • • • • • • • • • • • •

Ten-frames.

BLMs 1–2

FIGURE 2.7 • • • • • • • • • • •

A five-frame focuses on the 5 anchor. Counters are placed one to a section, and students tell how they see their number in the frame.

construction paper (or use the Blackline Master). Nothing fancy is required, and each child can have one. The ten-frame has been incorporated into a variety of activities in this book and is now popular in standard textbooks for children.

For children in kindergarten or early first grade who have not yet explored a ten-frame, it is a good idea to begin with a five-frame. This row of five sections is also drawn on a sheet of construction paper (or use the Blackline Master). Provide children with about ten counters that will fit in the five-frame sections, and conduct the following activity.

ACTIVITY 2.13

Five-Frame Tell-About

Explain that only one counter is permitted in each section of the five-frame. No other counters are allowed on the five-frame mat. Have the children show 3 on their five-frame. "What can you tell us about 3 from looking at your mat?" After hearing from several children, try other numbers from 0 to 5. Children may place their counters on the five-frame in any manner. What they observe will differ a great deal from child to child. For example, with four counters, a child with two on each end may say, "It has a space in the middle" or "It's two and two." There are no wrong answers. Focus attention on how many more counters are needed to make 5 or how far away from 5 a number is. Next try numbers between 5 and 10. The rule of one counter per section still holds. As shown in Figure 2.7, numbers greater than 5 are shown with a full five-frame and additional counters on the mat but not in the frame. In discussion, focus attention on these larger numbers as 5 and some more: "Eight is five and three more."

Notice that the five-frame really focuses on the relationship to 5 as an anchor for numbers but does not anchor numbers to 10. When five-frames have been used for a week or so, introduce ten-frames. You may want to play a ten-frame version of a "Five-Frame Tell-About" but soon introduce the following rule for showing numbers on the ten-frame: *Always fill the top row first, starting on the left, the same way you read. When the top row is full, counters can be placed in the bottom row, also from the left.* This will produce the "standard" way to show numbers on the ten-frame as in Figure 2.6.

For a while, many children will count every counter on their ten-frame. Some will take all counters off and begin each number from a blank frame. Others will soon learn to adjust numbers by adding on or taking off only what is required, often capitalizing on a row of five without counting. Do not pressure students. With continued practice, all students will grow. How they are using the ten-frame provides insight into students' current number concept development.

ACTIVITY 2.14

Crazy Mixed-Up Numbers

This activity is adapted from *Mathematics Their Way* (Baratta-Lorton, 1976). All children make their ten-frame show the same number. The teacher then calls out random numbers between 0 and 10. After each number, the children change their ten-frames to show the new number. Children can play this game independently by preparing lists of about 15 "crazy mixed-up numbers." One child plays "teacher," and the rest use the ten-frames. Children like to make up their own number lists.

"Crazy Mixed-Up Numbers" is much more of a problem than it first appears. How do you decide how to change your ten-frame? Some children will wipe off the entire frame and start over with each number. Others will have learned what each number looks like. To add another dimension, have the children tell, *before changing their ten-frames,* how many more counters need to be added ("plus") or removed ("minus"). They then call out plus or minus whatever amount is appropriate. If, for example, the frames showed 6, and the teacher called out "four," the children would respond, "Minus two!" and then change their ten-frames accordingly. A discussion of how they know what to do is valuable.

Ten-frame flash cards are an important variation of ten-frames. Make cards from poster board about the size of a small index card, with a ten-frame on each and dots drawn in the frames. A set of 20 cards consists of a 0 card, a 10 card, and two each of the numbers 1 to 9. The cards allow for simple drill activities to reinforce the 5 and 10 anchors.

ACTIVITY 2.15

Ten-Frame Flash Cards

Flash ten-frame cards to the class or group, and see how fast the children can tell how many dots are shown. This activity is fast-paced, takes only a few minutes, can be done at any time, and is a lot of fun if you encourage speed.

Important variations of "Ten-Frame Flash Cards" include

- Saying the number of spaces on the card instead of the number of dots
- Saying one more than the number of dots (or two more, and also less than)
- Saying the "ten fact"—for example, "Six and four make ten"

Ten-frame tasks are surprisingly problematic for students. Students must reflect on the two rows of five, the spaces remaining, and how a particular number is more or less than 5 and how far away from 10. The early discussions of how numbers are seen on the five-frames or ten-frames are examples of brief "after" activities in which students learn from one another.

Part–Part–Whole Relationships

STOP Before reading on, get some counters or coins. Count out a set of eight counters in front of you as if you were a first- or second-grade child counting them.

Any child who has learned how to count meaningfully can count out eight objects as you just did. What is significant about the experience is what it did *not* cause you to think about. Nothing in counting a set of eight objects will cause a child to focus on the fact that it could be made of two parts. For example, separate the counters you just set out into two piles and reflect on the combination. It might be 2 and 6 or 7 and 1 or 4 and 4. Make a change in your two piles of counters and say the new combination to yourself. Focusing on a quantity in terms of its parts has important implications for developing number sense. The ability to think about a number in terms of parts is a major milestone in the development of number. Of the four number relationships we have discussed, part-whole ideas are easily the most important.

Basic Ingredients of Part-Part-Whole Activities

Most part-part-whole activities focus on a single number for the entire activity. Thus, a child or group of children working together might work on the number 7 throughout the activity. Either children build the designated quantity in two or more parts, using a wide variety of materials and formats, or else they start with the full amount and separate it into two or more parts. A group of two or three children may work on one number in one activity for 5 to 20 minutes. Kindergarten children will usually begin these activities working on the number 4 or 5. As concepts develop, the children can extend their work to numbers 6 to 12. It is not unusual to find children in the second grade who have not developed firm part-part-whole constructs for numbers in the 7-to-12 range.

When children do these activities, have them say or "read" the parts aloud or write them down on some form of recording sheet (or do both). Reading or writing the combinations serves as a means of encouraging reflective thought focused on the part-whole relationship. Writing can be in the form of drawings, numbers written in blanks (_____ and_____), or addition equations if these have been introduced ($3 + 5 = 8$). There is a clear connection between part-part-whole concepts and addition and subtraction ideas.

A special and important variation of part-part-whole activities is referred to as *missing-part* activities. In a missing-part activity, children know the whole amount and use their already developed knowledge of the parts of that whole to try to tell what the covered or hidden part is. If they do not know or are unsure, they simply uncover the unknown part and say the full combination as they would normally. Missing-part activities provide maximum reflection on the combinations for a number. They also serve as the forerunner to subtraction concepts. With a whole of 8 but with only 3 showing, the child can later learn to write "$8 - 3 = 5$."

Part-Part-Whole Activities

The following activity and its variations may be considered the "basic" part-part-whole activity.

ACTIVITY 2.16

Build It in Parts

Provide children with one type of material, such as connecting cubes or squares of colored paper. The task is to see how many different combinations for a particular number they can make using two parts. (If you wish, you can allow for more than two parts.) Each different combination can be displayed on a small mat, such as a quarter-sheet of construction paper. Here are just a few ideas, each of which is illustrated in Figure 2.8.

- Use two-color counters such as lima beans spray painted on one side (also available in plastic).
- Make bars of connecting cubes. Make each bar with two colors. Keep the colors together.
- Color rows of squares on 1-inch grid paper.
- Make combinations using two dot strips—strips of poster board about 1 inch wide with stick-on dots. (Make lots of strips with from one to four dots and fewer strips with from five to ten dots.)
- Make combinations of "two-column strips." These are cut from tagboard ruled in 1-inch squares. All pieces except the single squares are cut from two columns of the tagboard.

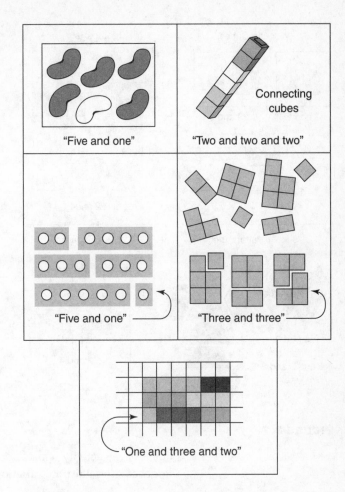

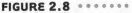

FIGURE 2.8 •

Assorted materials for building parts of 6.

As you observe children working on the "Build It in Parts" activity, ask them to "read" a number sentence to go with each of their designs. Encourage children to read their designs to each other. Two or three children working together with the same materials may have quite a large number of combinations including lots of repeats.

In the "Build It in Parts" activity, the children are focusing on the combinations. To add some interest, vary the activity by adding a design component. Rather than create a two-part illustration for a number, they create an interesting design with an assigned number of elements. For each design, they are then challenged to see and read the design in two parts. Here are some ideas.

- Make arrangements of wooden cubes.
- Make designs with pattern blocks. It is a good idea to use only one or two shapes at a time.
- Make designs with flat toothpicks. These can be dipped in white glue and placed on small squares of construction paper to create a permanent record.
- Make designs with touching squares or triangles. Cut a large supply of small squares or triangles out of construction paper. These can also be pasted down.

It is both fun and useful to challenge children to see their designs in different ways, producing different number combinations. In Figure 2.9, decide how children look at the designs to get the combinations listed under each.

The following activity is strictly symbolic. However, children should use counters if they feel they need to.

Wooden Cubes

4 and 2

3 and 3

1 and 2 and 3
or 3 and 3

Toothpicks

4 and 2
or
3 and 3

5 and 1

2 and 2 and 2

Pattern Blocks

4 and 2
or
2 and 2 and 2

1 and 3 and 2
or
1 and 5

Squares

3 and 3

2 and 4
or
3 and 3

FIGURE 2.9 •

Designs for 6.

ACTIVITY 2.17

Two out of Three

Make lists of three numbers, two of which total the whole that children are focusing on. Here is an example list for the number 5:

$$2—3—4$$
$$5—0—2$$
$$1—3—2$$
$$3—1—4$$
$$2—2—3$$
$$4—3—1$$

With the list on the board, overhead, or work-sheet, children can take turns selecting the two numbers that make the whole. As with all problem-solving activities, children should be challenged to justify their answers.

Missing-Part Activities

Missing-part activities require some way for a part to be hidden or unknown. Usually this is done with two children working together or else in a teacher-directed manner with the class. Again, the focus of the activity remains on a single designated quantity as the whole. The next four activities illustrate variations of this important idea.

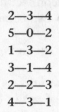

ACTIVITY 2.18

Covered Parts

A set of counters equal to the target amount is counted out, and the rest are put aside. One child places the counters under a margarine tub or piece of tagboard. The child then pulls some out into view. (This amount could be none, all, or any amount in between.) For example, if 6 is the whole and 4 are showing, the other child says, "Four and *two* is six." If there is hesitation or if the hidden part is unknown, the hidden part is immediately shown (see Figure 2.10).

ACTIVITY 2.19

Missing-Part Cards

For each number 4 to 10, make missing-part cards on strips of 3-by-9-inch tagboard. Each card has a numeral for the whole and two dot sets with one set covered by a flap. For the number 8, you need nine cards with the visible part ranging from 0 to 8 dots. Students use the cards as in "Covered Parts," saying, "Four and two is six" for a card showing four dots and hiding two (see Figure 2.10).

Counters under tub

"Four and two is six."

ACTIVITY 2.20

I Wish I Had

Hold out a bar of connecting cubes, a dot strip, a two-column strip, or a dot plate showing 6 or less. Say, "I wish I had six." The children respond with the part that is needed to make 6. Counting on can be used to check. The game can focus on a single whole, or the "I wish I had" number can change each time.

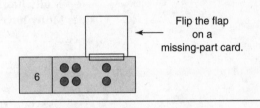

"Six minus four is two" or "Four and two is six."

The following activity is completely symbolic.

Flip the flap on a missing-part card.

ACTIVITY 2.21

Calculator Parts of 8 Machine

Make a parts of 8 machine by pressing 8 ⊟ 8 ⊜. Now if any number from 0 to 8 is pressed followed by ⊜, the display shows the other part. (The second part shows as a negative number. Tell students that is how they can tell it is the second part.) Children should try to say the other part before they press ⊜. Though this is basically a drill activity, a discussion with any child concerning his or her reasoning returns it to a problem orientation. Machines can be made for any number in the same way.

"I WISH I HAD 6."

I have

(You need 3 more.)

I have

(You need 1 more.)

FIGURE 2.10 •

Missing-part activities.

Here is a possible list of the kinds of things that children should know about the number 8 (or any number up to about 12) by the end of the first grade.

Skills

- Count to eight (know the number words).
- Count eight objects and know that the last number word tells how many.
- Write the numeral 8.
- Recognize the numeral 8.

Relationships

- More and less by 1 and 2: 8 is one more than 7, one less than 9, two more than 6, and two less than 10.
- Spatial patterns for 8 such as

- Anchors to 5 and 10: 8 is 5 and 3 more and 2 away from 10.
- Part-whole relationships: 8 is 5 and 3, 2 and 6, 7 and 1, and so on.

- Other relationships such as

    Doubles: double 4 is 8.

    Relationships to the real world: 8 is one more than the days of the week, my brother is 8 years old, my reading book is 8 inches wide.

Children often construct number relationships as they work to solve simple story problems prior to their mastery of basic facts. Consider the following problem:

Molly has 2 more toy cars than Jack has. Jack has 5 cars. How many does Molly have?

In solving this problem, children might

- Use counters for each set.
- Use counters for Molly's cars starting with 5 and adding 2 more.
- Counting on from 5

BLMs 3–8

Each of these possibilities can contribute to the development of the two-more-than relationship between 5 and 7. Problems that involve 5 and 10 as one of the numbers are useful for developing those numbers as reference points. It is easy to think of problems that involve separation of a number into two parts. The following problem might promote missing-part thinking:

Doug has a pocketful of pennies and nickels. He has 9 coins in all. He has 3 pennies. How many nickels does Doug have?

Research has demonstrated that when kindergarten and first-grade children are regularly asked to solve problems, not only do they develop a collection of number relationships, but they also learn addition and subtraction facts based on these relationships.

Dot Card Activities

Many good number development activities involve more than one of the relationships discussed so far. As children learn about ten-frames, patterned sets, and other relationships, the dot cards in the Blackline Masters provide a wealth of activities (see Figure 2.11). The cards contain dot patterns, patterns that require counting, combinations of two and three simple patterns, and ten-frames with "standard" as well as unusual placements of dots. When children use these cards for almost any activity that involves num-

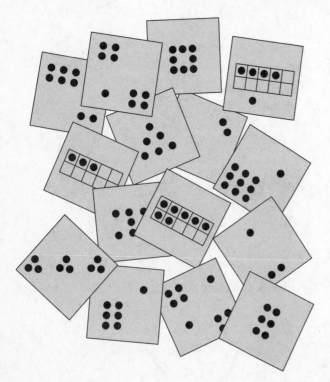

FIGURE 2.11

Dot cards can be made using the Blackline Masters.

ber concepts, the cards make them think about numbers in many different ways. The dot cards add another dimension to many of the activities already described and can be used effectively in the following activities.

ACTIVITY 2.22

Double War

The game of "Double War" (Kamii, 1985) is played like war, but on each play, both players turn up two cards instead of one. The winner is the one with the larger total number. Children playing the game can use many different number relationships to determine the winner without actually finding the total number of dots.

ACTIVITY 2.23

Dot-Card Trains

Make a long row of dot cards from 0 up to 9, then go back again to 1, then up, and so on. Alternatively, begin with 0 or 1 and make a two-more/two-less train.

ACTIVITY 2.24

Difference War

Besides dealing out the cards to the two players as in regular "War," prepare a pile of about 50 counters. On each play, the players turn over their cards as usual. The player with the greater number of dots wins as many counters from the pile as the difference between the two cards. The players keep their cards. The game is over when the counter pile runs out. The player with the most counters wins the game.

ACTIVITY 2.25

Number Sandwiches

Select a number between 5 and 12, and find combinations of two cards that total that number. With the two cards students make a "sandwich" with the dot sides out. When they have found at least ten sandwiches, the next challenge is to name the number on the other "slice" of the sandwich. The sandwich is turned over to confirm. The same pairs can then be used again to name the hidden part.

Assessment Note

The four types of number relationships (spatial representations, one and two more or less than, 5 and 10 anchors, and part-whole relationships) provide an excellent reference for assessing where your students are relative to number concepts. If you have station activities for these relationships, careful observations alone will tell a lot about students' number concepts. For a

(continued)

FIGURE 2.12 • • • • • • •

A missing-part number assessment. Eight in all. "How many are hidden?"

more careful assessment, each relationship can be assessed separately in a one-on-one setting, taking only a few minutes.

With a set of dot plates and a set of ten-frame cards you can quickly check which dot patterns children recognize without counting and whether they recognize quantities on ten-frames. To check the one- and two-more or less-than relationships, simply write a few numbers on a sheet of paper. Point to a number and have the child tell you the number that is *"two less than* this number," varying the specific request with different numbers. It is not necessary to check every possibility.

For part-whole relationships, use a missing-part assessment similar to Activity 2.18 ("Covered Parts") on p. 50. Begin with a number you believe the child has "mastered," say, 5. Have the child count out that many counters into your open hand. Close your hand around the counters and confirm that she knows how many are hidden there. Then remove some and show them in the palm of your other hand. (See Figure 2.12.) Ask the child, "How many are hidden?" Repeat with different amounts removed, although it is only necessary to check three or four missing parts for each number. If the child responds quickly and correctly and is clearly not counting in any way, call that a "mastered number." If a number is mastered, repeat the entire process with the next higher number. Continue until the child begins to stumble. In early first grade you will find a range of mastered numbers from 4 to 7 or 8. By spring of the first grade, most children should have mastered numbers to 10.

Relationships for Numbers 10 to 20

Even though kindergarten, first-, and second-grade children daily experience numbers up to 20 and beyond, it should not be assumed that they will automatically extend the set of relationships they have developed on smaller numbers to the numbers beyond 10. And yet these numbers play a big part in many simple counting activities, in basic facts, and in much of what we do with mental computation. Relationships with these numbers are just as important as relationships involving the numbers through 10.

A Pre–Place-Value Relationship with 10

A set of ten should play a major role in children's initial understanding of numbers between 10 and 20. When children see a set of six with a set of ten, they should know without counting that the total is 16. However, the numbers between 10 and 20 are not an appropriate place to discuss place-value concepts. That is, prior to a much more complete development of place-value concepts (appropriate for second grade and beyond), children should not be asked to explain the 1 in 16 as representing "one ten."

STOP Say to yourself, "One ten." Now think about that from the perspective of a child just learning to count to 20! What could *one* ten possibly mean when *ten* tells me how many fingers I have and is the number that comes after nine? How can it be one?

The concept of a single ten is just too strange for a kindergarten or early first-grade child to grasp. Some would say that it is not appropriate for grade 1 at all. The inappropriateness of discussing "one ten and six ones" (what's a one?) does not mean that a set of ten should not figure prominently in the discussion of the teen numbers. The following activity illustrates this idea.

Activity 2.26 is designed to teach new number names and, thus, requires a certain amount of directed teaching. Following this activity, explore numbers to 20 in a more open-ended manner. Provide each child with two ten-frames drawn one under the other on a construction paper mat or use the Blackline Master provided. In random order, have children show numbers to 20 on their mats. There is no preferred way to do this as long as there are the correct number of counters.

Assessment Note

What is interesting is to discuss how the counters can be placed on the mat so that it is easy to see how many are there. Have children share their ideas. Not every child will use a full set of ten, but as this idea becomes more popular, the notion that ten and some more is a teen amount will soon be developed. Do not forget to include numbers less than ten as well. As you listen to your children, you may want to begin challenging them to find ways to show 26 counters or even more.

Extending More and Less Relationships

The relationships of one more than, two more than, one less than, and two less than are important for all numbers. However, these ideas are built on or connected to the same concepts for numbers less than 10. The fact that 17 is one less than 18 is connected to the idea that 7 is one less than 8. Children may need help in making this connection.

How many?
What is one more?
Two less?

How many?
What is one more?
Two less?

FIGURE 2.13 • • • • • • • • • • • • • • • • • • •

Extending relationships to the teens.

Double and Near-Double Relationships

The use of doubles (double 6 is 12) and near-doubles (13 is double 6 and 1 more) is generally considered a strategy for memorizing basic addition facts. There is no reason why children should not begin to develop these relationships long before they are concerned with memorizing basic facts. Doubles and near-doubles are simply special cases of the general part-part-whole construct.

Relate the doubles to special images. Thornton (1982) helped first graders connect doubles to these visual ideas:

Double 3 is the bug double: three legs on each side.

Double 4 is the spider double: four legs on each side.

Double 5 is the hand double: two hands.

Double 6 is the egg carton double: two rows of six eggs.

Double 7 is the two-week double: two weeks on the calendar.

Double 8 is the crayon double: two rows of eight crayons in a box.

Double 9 is the 18-wheeler double: two sides, nine wheels on each side.

Children can draw pictures or make posters that illustrate the doubles for each number. There is no reason that the images need be restricted to those listed here. Any images that are strong ideas for your children will be good for them.

Periodically conduct oral exercises in which students double the number you say. Ask children to explain how they knew a particular double. Many will not use the pictures.

ACTIVITY 2.28

The Double Maker

Make the calculator into a "double maker" by pressing 2 ☒ ☐. Now a press of any digit followed by ☐ will produce the double of that number. Children can work in pairs or individually to try to beat the calculator.

As a related oral task, say a number, and ask students to tell what double it is. "What is fourteen?" (Double 7!) When students can do this well, use any number up to 20. "What is seventeen?" (Double 8 and 1 more.)

Numbers to 100: Early Introductions

An early exposure to numbers to 100 is important even at the K–1 level. Although it is extremely unlikely that students in kindergarten or first grade will have an understanding of tens and ones or place value, they can learn much about the sequence of numbers to 100 if not beyond. Most important at this early level is for students to become familiar with the counting patterns to 100.

The hundreds chart (Figure 2.14) is an essential tool for every classroom K to 3.

An extremely useful version of the chart is made of transparent pockets into which each of the 100 numeral cards can be inserted. You can hide a number by inserting a blank card in front of a number in the pocket. You can insert colored pieces of paper in the slots to highlight various number patterns. And you can remove some or all of the number cards and have students replace them in their correct slots.

An overhead transparency of a hundreds chart is almost as flexible as the pocket chart version. Numbers can be hidden by placing opaque counters on them. Patterns can be marked with a pen or with transparent counters. A transparency of a blank 10 × 10 grid serves as an empty hundreds chart on which you can write numbers. These transparencies can be made from the Blackline Masters and are also available commercially.

1	2	3	4	5	6	7	8	9	10
11	12	13	14	15	16	17	18	19	20
21	22	23	24	25	26	27	28	29	30
31	32	33	34	35	36	37	38	39	40
41	42	43	44	45	46	47	48	49	50
51	52	53	54	55	56	57	58	59	60
61	62	63	64	65	66	67	68	69	70
71	72	73	74	75	76	77	78	79	80
81	82	83	84	85	86	87	88	89	90
91	92	93	94	95	96	97	98	99	100

FIGURE 2.14 •

A hundreds chart.

There are many useful hundreds-chart activities for the K–2 level. If nothing else, students should orally count to 100 as you or a student points to each number on the chart. Whenever collections of things are counted, a good idea is to pause long enough to find the number on the chart. This can help put numbers for large quantities in perspective. Point out, for example, that 87 is a big number that is close to 100. The number 35 is also big but is closer to 20 than 100 and is far away from 87. Consider the following activities.

BLMs 9–10

ACTIVITY 2.29

Patterns on the Hundreds Chart

Have children work in pairs to find patterns on the hundreds chart. Solicit ideas orally from the class. Have children explain patterns found by others to be sure that all understand the ideas that are being suggested.

There are many different patterns on the hundreds chart. In a discussion, different children will describe the same pattern in several ways. Accept all ideas. Here are some of the patterns they may point out:

- The numbers in a column all end with the same number, which is the same as the number at the top.
- In a row, one number "counts" (the ones digit goes 1, 2, 3, . . . , 9, 0); the "second" number goes up by ones, but the first number (tens digit) stays the same.
- In a column, the first number (tens digit) "counts" or goes up by ones.

- You can count by tens going down the right-hand column.
- If you count by fives, you get two columns, the last column and the 5 column.

For children, these patterns are not at all obvious or trivial. For example, one child may notice the pattern in the column under the 4—every number ends in a 4. Two minutes later another child will "discover" the parallel pattern in the column headed by 7. That there is a pattern like this in every column may not be completely obvious.

Although not essential, skip-count patterns can also be explored at an early level. Skip counts by twos, fives, and tens are the easiest and the most important. Help children see the column patterns that these counts make.

ACTIVITY 2.30

Missing Numbers

Provide students with a hundreds chart on which some of the number cards have been removed. (Use the classroom pocket chart.) The students' task is to replace the missing numbers in the chart. Beginning versions of this activity have only a random selection of individual numbers removed. Later, remove sequences of several numbers from three or four different rows. Finally, remove all but one or two rows or columns. Eventually, challenge children to replace all of the numbers in a blank chart.

The "Missing Numbers" activity can also be done with the full class. Use construction paper tabs to cover numbers on the chart. Have students write the missing numbers as you point to them. You may think that the adjacent numbers are too much of a clue, but the clue is itself a help in learning the number sequence.

Other activities for the hundreds chart are discussed in Chapter 5.

Assessment Note

Replacing the number cards or tiles from a blank chart is a good station activity for two students to work on together. By listening to how students go about finding the correct places for numbers, you can learn a lot about how well they have constructed an understanding of the 1-to-100 sequence.

Number Sense and the Real World

Here we examine ways to broaden the early knowledge of numbers in a different way. Relationships of numbers to real-world quantities and measures and the use of numbers in simple estimations can help children develop the flexible, intuitive ideas about numbers that are most desired.

Estimation and Measurement

One of the best ways for children to think of real quantities is to associate numbers with measures of things. In the early grades, measures of length, weight, and time are good places to begin. Just measuring and recording results will not be very effective, however, since there is no reason for children to be interested in or think about the result. To help children think or reflect a bit on what number might tell how long the desk is or how heavy the book is, it would be good if they could first write down or tell you an estimate. To produce an estimate is, however, a very difficult task for young children. They do not understand the concept of "estimate" or "about." For example, suppose that you have cut out of poster board an ample supply of very large footprints, say, about 18 inches long. All are exactly the same size. You would like to ask the class, "About how many footprints will it take to measure across the rug in our reading corner?" The key word here is *about,* and it is one that you will need to spend a lot of time helping children understand. To this end, the request of an estimate can be made in ways that help with the concept of "about" yet not require students to give a specific number.

The following estimation questions can be used with most early estimation activities:

- *More or less than _____?* Will it be more or less than 10 footprints? Will the apple weigh more or less than 20 wooden blocks? Are there more or less than 15 connecting cubes in this long bar?

- *Closer to _____ or to _____?* Will it be closer to 5 footprints or closer to 20 footprints? Will the apple weigh closer to 10 blocks or closer to 30 blocks? Does this bar have closer to 10 cubes or closer to 50 cubes?

- *About _____.* Use one of these numbers: 5, 10, 15, 20, 25, 30, 35, 40, ... About how many footprints? About how many blocks will the apple weigh? About how many cubes are in this bar?

Asking for estimates using these formats helps children learn what you mean by "about." Every child can make an estimate without having to pull a number out of the air.

To help with numbers and measures, estimate several things in succession using the same unit. For example, suppose that you are estimating and measuring "around things" using a string. To measure, the string is wrapped around the object and then measured in some unit such as craft sticks. After measuring the distance around Demetria's head, estimate the distance around the wastebasket or around the globe or around George's wrist. Each successive measure helps children with the new estimates. See Chapter 8 for a complete discussion of measurement.

More Connections

Here are some additional activities that can help children connect numbers to real situations.

ACTIVITY 2.31

Add a Unit to Your Number

Write a number on the board. Now suggest some units to go with it, and ask the children what they can think of that fits. For example, suppose the number is 9. "What do you think of when I say 9 *dollars? 9 hours? 9 cars? 9 kids? 9 meters? 9 o'clock? 9 hand spans? 9 gallons?*" Spend some time in discussion of each. Let children suggest units as well. Be prepared to explore some of the ideas either immediately or as projects or tasks to share with parents at home.

Is It Reasonable?

Select a number and a unit—for example, 15 feet. Could the teacher be 15 feet tall? Could your living room be 15 feet wide? Can a man jump 15 feet high? Could three children stretch their arms 15 feet? Pick any number, large or small, and a unit with which children are familiar. Then make up a series of these questions.

Once children are familiar with Activity 2.32, have them select the number and the unit or things (10 kids, 20 bananas, . . .), and see what kinds of questions children make up. When a difference of opinion develops, capitalize on the opportunity to explore and find out. Resist the temptation to supply your adult-level knowledge. Rather, say, "Well, how can we find out if it is or is not reasonable? Who has an idea about what we could do?"

These activities are problem-based in the truest sense. Not only are there no clear answers, but children can easily begin to pose their own questions and explore number in the part of the environment most interesting to them. Children will not have these real-world connections when you begin, and you may be disappointed in their limited ideas about number. Howden (1989) writes about a first-grade teacher of children from very impoverished backgrounds who told her, "They all have fingers, the school grounds are strewn with lots of pebbles and leaves, and pinto beans are cheap. So we count, sort, compare, and talk about such objects. We've measured and weighed almost everything in this room and almost everything the children can drag in" (p. 6). This teacher's children had produced a wonderfully rich and long list of responses to the question "What comes to your mind when I say twenty-four?" In another school in a professional community where test scores are high, the same question brought almost no response from a class of third graders. It can be a very rewarding effort to help children connect their number ideas to the real world.

Graphs

Graphing activities are another good way to connect children's worlds with numbers. Chapter 11 discusses ways to make graphs with children in grades K–2. Graphs can be quickly made of almost any data that can be gathered from the students: favorite ice cream, color, sports team, pet; number of sisters and brothers; kids who ride different buses; types of shoes; number of pets; and so on. Graphs can be connected to content in other areas. A unit on sea life might lead to a graph of favorite sea animals.

Once a simple bar graph is made, it is very important to take a few minutes to ask as many number questions as is appropriate for the graph. In the early stages of number development (grades K–1), the use of graphs for number relationships and for connecting numbers to real quantities in the children's environment is a more important reason for building graphs than the graphs themselves. The graphs focus attention on counts of realistic things. Equally important, bar graphs clearly exhibit comparisons between and among numbers that are rarely made when only one number or quantity is considered at a time. See Figure 2.15 for an example of a graph and questions that can be asked. At first, children will have trouble with the questions involving differences, but repeated exposure to these ideas in a bar graph format will improve their understanding. These comparison concepts add considerably to children's understanding of number.

Literature Connections

Children's literature abounds with wonderful counting books. Involving children with books in a variety of ways can serve to connect number to reality, make it a personal experience, and provide ample opportunities for problem solving. Be sure to go beyond simply reading a counting book or a number-related book and looking at the pictures. Find a way to extend the book into the children's world. Create problems related to the story. Have children write a similar story. Extend the numbers and see what happens. Create a mural, graphs, or posters. The ideas are as plentiful as the books. Here are a few ideas for making literature connections to number concepts and number sense.

Anno's Counting House (Anno, 1982)

In the beautiful style of Anno, this book shows ten children in various parts of a house. As the pages are turned, the house front covers the children, and a few are visible through cutout windows. A second house is on the opposite page. As you move through the book, the children move one at a time to the second house, creating the potential for a 10–0, 9–1, 8–2, . . . , 0–10 pattern of pairs. But as each page shows part of the children through the window, there is an opportunity to discuss how many in the missing part. Have children use counters to model the story as you "read" it the second or third time.

What if the children moved in pairs instead of one at a time? What if there were three houses? What if there were more children? What else could be in the house to count? How many rooms, pictures, windows? What about your house? What about two classrooms or two buses instead of houses?

The Very Hungry Caterpillar (Carle, 1969)

This is a predictable-progression counting book about a caterpillar who eats first one thing, then two, and so on. Children can create their own eating stories and illustrate them. What if more than one type of thing were eaten at each stop? What combinations for each number are there? Are seven little things more or less than three very large things? What does all of this stuff weigh? How many things are eaten altogether?

Two Ways to Count to Ten (Dee, 1988)

This Liberian folktale is about King Leopard in search of the best animal to marry his daughter. The task devised involves throwing a spear and counting to 10 before the spear lands. Many animals try and fail. Counting by ones proves too lengthy. Finally, the antelope succeeds by counting "2, 4, 6, 8, 10."

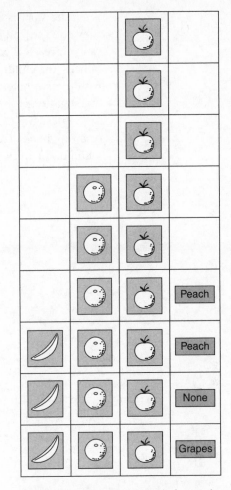

Class graph showing fruit brought for snack. Paper cutouts for bananas, oranges, apples, and cards for "others."

- — Which bar (or refer to what the graph represents) is most, least?
- — Which are more (less) than 7 (or some other number)?
- — Which is one less (more) than this bar?
- — How much more is _____ than _____? (Follow this question immediately by reversing the order and asking how much less.)
- — How much less is _____ than _____? (Reverse this question after receiving an answer.)
- — How much difference is there between _____ and _____ ?
- — Which two bars together are the same as _____ ?

FIGURE 2.15 • • • • • • • • • • • • • • •

Relationships and number sense in a bar graph.

The story is a perfect lead-in to skip counting. Can you count to 10 by threes? How else can you count to 10? How many ways can you count to 48? What numbers can you reach if you count by fives? The size of the numbers you investigate is limited only by the children. A hundreds board or counters are useful thinker toys to help with these problems. Be sure to have children write about what they discover in their investigations.

These two examples are here primarily to encourage your use of number and counting books. Good counting books can always be the springboard for a good exploration of quantity in the real world.

EXPANDED LESSON

Two-More-Than/Two-Less-Than

Based on: Activity 2.11, p. 45

GRADE LEVEL: Late kindergarten or early first grade.

MATHEMATICS GOALS

- To help students develop the paired relationships of two-more-than and two-less-than for numbers to 12.
- To provide continued exposure to patterned sets with the goal of instant recognition.

THINKING ABOUT THE STUDENTS

Students must be able to count a set accurately and understand that counting tells how many. They may or may not be able to recognize patterned sets or be able to count on and count back from a given number. For those students still having difficulty matching the correct numeral and set, the written component of the activity can be omitted.

MATERIALS AND PREPARATION

- This will be a station activity. (Alternatively, students can do the activity at their seats.) Each student doing the activity at the same time will need the materials described.
- Place four dot cards, showing 3 to 10 dots each, in a plastic bag.
- Each bag should also have at least 12 counters and a crayon or pencil.
- Make one two-sided recording sheet for each student. The backside of the sheet is the same as the front except that it says "2 LESS THAN" at the top. (See the Blackline Masters L-1 and L-2.)

- -

lesson

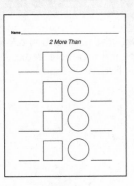

BLM L-1

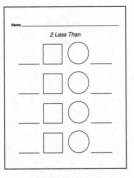

BLM L-2

BEFORE

The Task

- For each dot card, the task is to make a set that has two more counters than dots on the card. Similarly, students will make sets that have two fewer counters than dots on the card. The task is completed with the counters.

Establish Expectations

- Show the class (or a small group) a bag of cards and counters. Empty the counters and select one card. Have a student count the dots on the card. Have a second student use counters on the overhead (or on the carpet, if in a circle setting). Say: *Make a set that has two more counters than dots on this card.*
- Discuss with the students how they can decide if the set is actually two more. Accept students' ideas and try them. For example, they might say: *Count each set. Set a counter aside for each dot. Make the counters into a pattern that is the same as on the dot card.*
- Show students the recording sheet. Point out the words "2 MORE THAN" and "2 LESS THAN" on the top. Explain that they will record their two-more-than sets on the 2 MORE THAN side. Demonstrate how to first draw the same number of dots as are on the dot card. Next show how to draw dots in the oval to show the number of counters that they made for their two-more-than set. Beside each set they should write the corresponding number.
- If students are ready, have them tell how they think the 2 LESS THAN side should be completed. (You may choose to do only one side of the sheet at a time.)
- Explain that bags with counters and dots will be at stations. (Or pass out bags at this time to each student.) Bags will be different, so each student's paper will also be different.

DURING

- Observe the methods that students use to count the dots on the cards and to create their sets.

- Challenge students to explain how they know their set is correct. Focus on the actual counters and dot cards rather than on the record sheet because that is less important.
- Challenge task for capable students: Make sets and record numbers for sets that are 10-more-than the given sets. Look for understanding of the teen numbers.

AFTER (WHEN ALL STUDENTS HAVE COMPLETED THE STATION)

- Show students a sheet of paper with 6 dots in a patterned arrangement. Ask: *How many dots? How can we tell how many are two more than this?* Students' suggestions should be tied to the methods they used in the activity. Some students may know immediately that 8 is two-more-than 6. Begin with students who are likely to be still developing this idea. Have different students explain how they did the activity.

ASSESSMENT NOTES

- How do students count or know how many dots are on the cards? Do they recognize patterned sets or do they count each dot? Which patterns do they know?
- How do students create their two-more-than sets? Is there indication of the two-more-than relationship developing or being already developed? If students are working on both sides of the paper, look for similar two-less-than concepts.
- Look for ease or difficulty in recording. Do students correctly write numerals with sets?

- Students who experience difficulty with this activity should do similar tasks using the one-more-than relationship and possibly smaller numbers on the dot cards.
- "Real Counting On" (Activity 2.7) may be a useful companion to this activity.
- For students who are successful with this activity, test their understanding with an activity involving only numerals. For example, prepare a worksheet with random numbers written down a center column. Have students write the number that tells two-less to the left of the number and two-more to the right. Activity 2.12, "A Calculator Two-More-Than Machine," is also appropriate.

next steps

DEVELOPING MEANING FOR THE OPERATIONS AND SOLVING STORY PROBLEMS

This chapter is about helping children connect different meanings, interpretations, and relationships to the four operations of addition, subtraction, multiplication, and division so that they can effectively use these operations in real-world settings.

The main thrust of this chapter is helping children develop what might be termed *operation sense,* a highly integrated understanding of the four operations and the many different but related meanings these operations take on in real contexts.

big ideas

1 Addition and subtraction are connected. Addition names the whole in terms of the parts, and subtraction names a missing part.

2 Multiplication involves counting groups of like size and determining how many are in all (multiplicative thinking).

3 Multiplication and division are related. Division names a missing factor in terms of the known factor and the product.

4 Models can be used to solve contextual problems for all operations and to figure out what operation is involved in a problem regardless of the size of the numbers. Models also can be used to give meaning to number sentences.

Addition and Subtraction

Consider each of the following two problems.

Aidan had 7 marbles in her marble bag. After school, she found some more marbles that she had misplaced and put them in her bag. When she counted all of her marbles there were 15 in all. How many extra marbles did Aidan find and put in her bag?

Maggie had a large collection of stuffed animals. She gave away 6 of her favorite animals to her little sister, Grace. Maggie still has 15 stuffed animals left in her collection. How many did she have before she gave the animals to Grace?

Each of these problems involves an action. One is a joining, or put-together, action and the other is a separate, or take-away, action. Which is which? Now suppose that you had to solve each problem using a calculator and the two numbers in the problem. What operation would you use for each problem? Do this now before reading further.

Were you surprised that the problem with the take-away action (Maggie's animals) was the one that you had to use addition to solve? And, similarly, the problem that sounded like addition (Aidan's marbles) was the one that you used subtraction for? Also, note that if you were looking for a key word or words to decide on an operation, the one with the words "in all" was the subtraction problem. The problem with the word "left" was the addition problem.

Are these just trick problems? Doesn't addition mean "join" or "put together" and subtraction mean "take away"? It is true that these are the typical definitions for addition and subtraction found in the first and second grades. However, these are unfortunately narrow, if not actually incorrect, definitions. In fact, *addition* is used to name the whole when the parts of the whole are known. In connection with this definition, *subtraction* is used to name a part when the whole and the remaining part are known. As you will see, in the case of comparison situations, these definitions require some adaptation but the basic ideas need not be changed.

 Go back to the two problems you just solved and identify the parts and wholes in each.

Had these problems involved two-digit numbers or decimals or fractions, many students in the third, fourth, and fifth grades would have added for the first problem and subtracted in the second.

The perspective on addition and subtraction taken in this chapter is based on what has been learned from numerous research studies and not on the typical approach to addition and subtraction found in textbooks. It assumes that children can solve verbal problems with appropriate numbers by thinking through the structure of the problems rather than by identifying the type of action or key words, two strategies that invariably will lead to failure.

Structures for Addition and Subtraction Problems

Researchers have separated addition and subtraction problems into categories based on the kinds of relationships involved. These include *join* problems, *separate* problems, *part-part-whole* problems, and *compare* problems (Carpenter & Moser, 1983; Gutstein & Romberg, 1995; Carpenter, Fennema, Franke, Levi, & Empson, 1999). The basic structure for each of these four types of problems is illustrated in Figure 3.1. Each structure involves a number "family" such as 3, 5, 8. A different problem results depending on which of the three quantities in the structure is unknown.

Examples of Problems for Each Structure

The number family 4, 8, 12 is used in each of the story problems that follows and can be connected to the structure in Figure 3.1. These drawings are not intended for

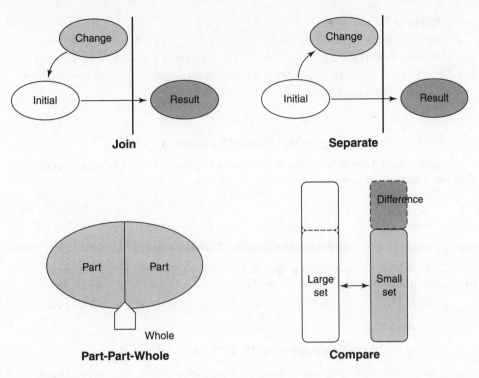

FIGURE 3.1 • • • • • • • • • • • •

Four basic structures for addition and subtraction story problems. Each structure has three numbers. Any one of the three numbers can be the unknown in a story problem.

children but to help you as a teacher consider the different structures. Also note that the problems are described in terms of their structure and not as addition or subtraction problems.

Join Problems

For the action of joining, there are three quantities involved: an initial amount, a change amount (the part being added or joined), and the resulting amount (the amount after the action is over).

Join: Result Unknown

Sandra had 8 pennies. George gave her 4 more. How many pennies does Sandra have altogether?

Join: Change Unknown

Sandra had 8 pennies. George gave her some more. Now Sandra has 12 pennies. How many did George give her?

Join: Initial Unknown

Sandra had some pennies. George gave her 4 more. Now Sandra has 12 pennies. How many pennies did Sandra have to begin with?

Separate Problems

Notice that in the separate problems, the initial amount is the whole or the largest amount, whereas in the join problems, the result was the whole. Again, refer to Figure 3.1 as you consider these problems. Be sure you can identify what quantities are the initial, change, and result amounts.

Separate: Result Unknown

Sandra had 12 pennies. She gave 4 pennies to George. How many pennies does Sandra have now?

Separate: Change Unknown

Sandra had 12 pennies. She gave some to George. Now she has 8 pennies. How many did she give to George?

Separate: Initial Unknown

Sandra had some pennies. She gave 4 to George. Now Sandra has 8 pennies left. How many pennies did Sandra have to begin with?

Part–Part–Whole Problems

Part-part-whole problems involve two parts that are combined into one whole. The combining may be a physical action, or it may be a mental combination where the parts are not physically combined.

There is no meaningful distinction between the two parts in a part-part-whole situation, so there is no need to have a different problem for each part as the unknown. For each possibility (whole unknown and part unknown), two problems are given here. The first is a mental combination where there is no action. The second problem involves a physical action.

Part-Part-Whole: Whole Unknown

George has 4 pennies and 8 nickels. How many coins does he have?

George has 4 pennies and Sandra has 8 pennies. They put their pennies into a piggy bank. How many pennies did they put into the bank?

Part-Part-Whole: Part Unknown

George has 12 coins. Eight of his coins are pennies, and the rest are nickels. How many nickels does George have?

George and Sandra put 12 pennies into the piggy bank. George put in 4 pennies. How many pennies did Sandra put in?

Compare Problems

Compare problems involve the comparison of two quantities. The third amount does not actually exist but is the difference between the two amounts. There are three types of compare problems, corresponding to which quantity is unknown (smaller, larger, or difference). For each of these, two examples are given: one problem where the difference is stated in terms of more and another in terms of less.

Compare: Difference Unknown

George has 12 pennies and Sandra has 8 pennies. How many more pennies does George have than Sandra?

George has 12 pennies. Sandra has 8 pennies. How many fewer pennies does Sandra have than George?

Compare: Larger Unknown

George has 4 more pennies than Sandra. Sandra has 8 pennies. How many pennies does George have?

Sandra has 4 fewer pennies than George. Sandra has 8 pennies. How many pennies does George have?

Compare: Smaller Unknown

George has 4 more pennies than Sandra. George has 12 pennies. How many pennies does Sandra have?

Sandra has 4 fewer pennies than George. George has 12 pennies. How many pennies does Sandra have?

 Go back through all of these problems and match the numbers in the problems with the components of the structures in Figure 3.1. For each problem, do two additional things. First, use a set of counters to model (solve) the problem as you think children in the primary grades might do. Second, for each problem, write either an addition or subtraction equation that you think best represents the problem as you did it with counters.

Reflections on the Four Structures

In most curricula, the overwhelming emphasis is on the easier join and separate problems with the result unknown. These become the de facto definitions of addition and subtraction: Addition is "put together" and subtraction is "take away." As already noted, these are *not* the definitions of addition and subtraction.

When students develop these limited put-together and take-away definitions for addition and subtraction, they often have difficulty later when addition or subtraction is called for but the structure is other than put together or take away. It is important that children be exposed to all forms within these structures.

Computational and Semantic Forms of Equations

If you wrote an equation for each of the problems as just suggested, you may have some equations where the unknown quantity is not isolated on one side of the equal sign. For example, a likely equation for the join problem with initial part unknown is $\boxed{8} + 4 = 12$. This is referred to as the *semantic* equation for the problem since the numbers are listed in the order that follows the meaning of the problem. When the semantic form does not isolate the unknown, an equivalent equation can be written for the same problem. In this case, the equation $12 - 4 = \boxed{8}$ is referred to as the *computational* form of the equation; it isolates the unknown. When the two forms are not the same, children must eventually come to see the equivalence of these equations.

Problem Difficulty

The various types of problems are not at all equal in difficulty for children. The change problems where the initial part is unknown are among the most difficult, probably because children modeling the problems directly do not know how many counters to put down to begin with. Problems where the change amounts are unknown are also difficult. How problems are worded, whether the action sequence matches the way the numbers appear in the story, and other subtle changes can each cause problems to be more or less difficult. The size of the numbers is generally not a factor as long as they are within reach of the child's number understanding.

Many children will solve compare problems as part-part-whole problems without making separate sets of counters for the two amounts. The whole is used as the large amount, one part for the small amount and the second part for the difference. This actually models how part-whole ideas can be used even for comparison problems. There is absolutely no reason this should be discouraged as long as children are clear about what they are doing.

Teaching Addition and Subtraction

So far you have seen a variety of types of story problems for addition and subtraction and you may have used some counters to help you understand how these problems can be solved by children. These two methods, contextual problems and models (counters, drawings, number lines), are the main teaching tools that you have to help students construct a rich understanding of these two operations. Let's examine how each approach can be used in the classroom.

Using Contextual Problems

There is more to think about than simply giving students problems to solve.

Context or Story Problems

In contrast with the rather sterile story problems in the previous section, consider the following problem.

> Yesterday we were measuring how tall we were. You remember that we used the connecting cubes to make a big train that was as long as we were when we were lying down. Susan and Marcy were wondering how many cubes long they would be if they lay down head to foot. Susan had measured Marcy and she was 84 cubes long. Marcy measured Susan and she was 102 cubes long. Let's see if we can figure out how long they will be end to end, and then we can check by actually measuring them.

Fosnot and Dolk (2001) point out that in story problems children tend to focus on getting the answer, probably in the way that the teacher wants. "Context problems, on the other hand, are connected as closely as possible to children's lives, rather than to 'school mathematics.' They are designed to anticipate and to develop children's mathematical modeling of the real world" (p. 24). Contextual problems might derive from recent experiences in the classroom, a field trip, a discussion you have been having in art or social studies, or from children's literature.

Lessons Built on Context or Story Problems

The tendency in the United States is to have students solve a lot of problems in a single class period. The focus of these lessons seems to be on how to get answers. In Japan, however, a complete lesson will often revolve around one or two problems and the related discussion (Reys & Reys, 1995).

What might a good lesson look like for second grade that is built around word problems? The answer comes more naturally if you think about students not just solving the problems but also using words, pictures, and numbers to explain how they went about solving the problem and why they think they are correct. Children should be allowed to use whatever physical materials they feel they need to help them, or they can simply draw pictures. Whatever they put on their paper should explain what they did well enough to allow someone else to understand it. Allow at least a half page of space for a problem.

Choosing Numbers for Problems

Even kindergarten children should be expected to solve story problems. Their methods of solution will typically involve using counters in a very direct modeling of the problems. This is what makes the join and separate problems with the initial parts unknown so difficult. For these problems, children initially use a trial-and-error approach (Carpenter, Fennema, Franke, Levi, & Empson, 1999).

Although the structure of the problems will cause the difficulty to vary, the numbers in the problems should be in accord with the number development of the children. Kindergarten children can use numbers as large as they can count meaningfully, which is usually to about 10 or 12.

Second-grade children are also learning about two-digit numbers and are beginning to understand how our base-ten system works. Rather than wait until students have learned about place value and have developed techniques for computing numbers, word problems are a problem-based opportunity to learn about number and computation at the same time. For example, a problem involving the combination of 30 and 42 has the potential to help students focus on the sets of ten. As they begin to think of 42 as 40 and 2, it is not at all unreasonable to think that they will add 30 and

40 and then add 2 more. The structure of a word problem can strongly influence the type of invented strategy a student uses to solve a multidigit problem. This is especially true with addition and subtraction for students who have not been taught the standard algorithms for these operations. For example, consider the following problem.

> A school of fish was swimming together in the ocean. There were 28 fish in all. Another school of fish decided to join them, making a larger school of fish. The new larger school had 64 fish. How many fish were in the school that joined the first group of fish?

Because this is a join action, the problem increases the probability that students will use an add-on approach to solve the problem. One such approach is to add on 40 to 28 making 68 and then taking off the 4 extra—4 from 40 is 36. However, if the problem had been a take-away, result unknown problem (64 fish and 28 swam away), the tendency might be to use a take-away approach, which is generally more difficult. You can learn more about invented strategies for computation in Chapter 6.

Introducing Symbolism

Very young children have no need for the symbols +, −, and =. However, these symbolic conventions are important. When you feel your students are ready to use these symbols, introduce them in the discussion portion of a lesson where students have solved story problems. Say, "You had the whole number of 12 in your problem and the number 8 was one of the parts of 12. You found out that the part you did not know was 4. Here is a way we can write that: 12 − 8 = 4." The minus sign should be read as "minus" or "subtract" but not as "take away." The plus sign is easier since it is typically a substitute for "and."

Some care should be taken with the equal sign. The equal sign means "is the same as." However, most children come to think of it as a symbol that tells you that the "answer is coming up." It is interpreted in much the same way as the ⊟ on a calculator. That is, it is the key you press to get the answer. An equation such as 4 + 8 = 3 + 9 has no "answer" and is still true because both sides stand for the same quantity. A good idea is to often use the phrase "is the same as" in place of or in conjunction with "equals" as you read equations with students.

Using Model-Based Problems

Many children will use counters or number lines (models) to solve story problems. The model is a thinking tool to help them both understand what is happening in the problem and a means of keeping track of the numbers and solving the problem. Problems can also be posed using models when there is no context involved. The part-part-whole concept as discussed in Chapter 2 is a good way to help students think about addition and subtraction when they are focused on models.

Addition

When the parts of a set are known, addition is used to name the whole in terms of the parts. This simple, albeit sterile, definition of addition serves both action situations (join and separate) and static or no-action situations.

Each of the part-part-whole models shown in Figure 3.2 is a model for 5 + 3 = 8. Some of these are the result of a definite put-together or joining action, and some are not. Notice that in every example, both of the parts are distinct, even after the parts are joined. If counters are used, the two parts should be kept in separate piles or in separate sections of a mat or should be two distinct colors. For children to see a relationship between the two parts and the whole, the image of the 5 and 3 must be kept as two separate sets. This helps children reflect on the action after it has taken place. "These red chips are the ones I started with. Then I added these five blue ones, and now I have eight altogether."

A number line presents some real conceptual difficulties for first and second graders. Its use as a model at that level is generally not recommended. A number line measures distances from zero the same way a ruler does. In the early grades, children focus on the dots or numerals on a number line instead of the spaces. However, if arrows (hops) are drawn for each number in an exercise, the length concept is more clearly illustrated. To model the part-part-whole concept of 5 + 3, start by drawing an arrow from 0 to 5, indicating, "This much is five." Do not point to the dot for 5, saying "This is five."

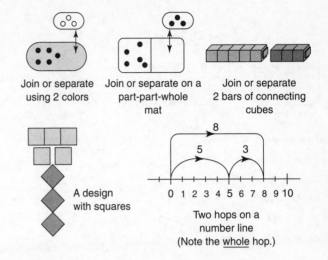

Join or separate using 2 colors

Join or separate on a part-part-whole mat

Join or separate 2 bars of connecting cubes

A design with squares

Two hops on a number line (Note the whole hop.)

FIGURE 3.2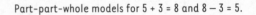

Part-part-whole models for 5 + 3 = 8 and 8 − 3 = 5.

ACTIVITY 3.1

Equations with Number Patterns

Recall Activity 2.16 (p. 48) called "Build It in Parts" and its variations, in which children made designs or built sets for a specific number. When children seem ready to deal with written symbolism, simply show them how to write a plus or addition number sentence (equation) for each design. In those initial activities, children said a combination, such as "Four and five is nine." Now they have a new symbolic way to match what they say.

Two children can work together, do something with a model, say the combination, and together write the equation. The children can vary the total amounts they construct each time—within appropriate limits, of course. Remember that what makes "Equations with Number Patterns" problem based is the challenge to find different combinations for a number.

Subtraction

In a part-part-whole model, when the whole and one of the parts are known, subtraction names the other part. This definition is in agreement with the drastically overused language of "take away." If you start with a whole set of 8 and remove a set of 3, the two sets that you know are the sets of 8 and 3. The expression 8 − 3, read "eight minus three," names the five remaining. Therefore, eight minus three is five. Notice that the models in Figure 3.2 are models for subtraction as well as addition (except for the action). Helping children see that they are using the same models or pictures aids in connecting the two operations.

TEACHING ADDITION AND SUBTRACTION

Start with 9 in all.
Remove some.
How many covered?

?

No action

Start with a bar of 9.
Break some off.
How many hidden?

The other part of
the bar is hidden.

FIGURE 3.3 •

Models for 9 − 4 as a missing-part problem.

ACTIVITY 3.2

Missing-Part Subtraction

A fixed number of counters is placed on a mat. One child separates the counters into two parts while the other child hides his or her eyes. The first child covers one of the two parts with a sheet of tagboard, revealing only the other part (see Figure 3.3). The second child says the subtraction sentence. For example, "Nine minus four [the visible part] is five [the covered part]." The covered part can be revealed if necessary for the child to say how many are there. Both the subtraction equation and the addition equation can then be written.

Subtraction as Think-Addition

Note that in Activity 3.2, the situation ends with two parts clearly distinct, even when there is a remove action. The removed part remains in the activity or on the mat as a model for an addition equation to be written after writing the subtraction equation. A discussion of how these two equations can be written for the same model situation is an important opportunity to connect addition and subtraction. This is significantly better than the traditional worksheet activity of "fact families" in which children are given a family of numbers such as 3, 5, and 8 and are told to write two plus equations and two minus equations. Very quickly this becomes a matter of dropping the numbers in the various slots.

Subtraction as "think-addition" is extremely significant for mastering subtraction facts. Because the counters for the remaining or unknown part are left hidden under the cover, when children do these activities, they are encouraged to think about the hidden part: "What goes with the part I see to make the whole?" For example, if the total or whole number of counters is 9, and 6 are removed from under the cover, the child is likely to think in terms of "6 and what makes 9?" or "What goes with 6 to make 9?" The mental activity is "think-addition" instead of a "count what's left" approach. Later, when working on subtraction facts, a subtraction fact such as 9 − 6 = ☐ should trigger the same thought pattern: "6 and what makes 9?"

Assessment Note ⎯⎯⎯⎯⎯⎯⎯⎯⎯⎯⎯⎯

The techniques that children use to solve problems provide you with important information concerning their number development, strategies that they may be using to answer basic facts, and methods that they are using for multidigit computation. Therefore, it is essential that you look at more than the answers students get. These methods can give you clues as to what numbers to use in problems for the next day. The information can also be used to give special number or computation development work to students in need of it. Key papers can be saved in folders and used in conferences to show parents how their child is working and progressing.

For example, a student who counts out counters for each of two addends and then counts all of the counters might be encouraged to count on by posing a problem involving adding 14 + 3, a large number and a small one. If you have been working on the meaning of the teens or other ideas about tens, you can be sure the problems you pose involve opportunities for students to use these ideas. For example, pose problems for 14 – 10 or 10 + 10 + 10 + 6. Then you can observe students' use of the ideas you have been working on.

Similarly, you can pose problems involving number concepts or computations that you have not yet explored with your students. How they approach the problems will give you clues as to where that portion of your number program can best begin.

The point is to use story problems to assess more than problem solving. Number and computation skills are often much more clearly visible in students' work with story problems than on the exercises often found at the end of numeration lessons.

Comparison Models

Comparison situations involve two distinct sets or quantities and the difference between them. Several ways of modeling the difference relationship are shown in Figure 3.4. The same kind of model can be used whether the difference or one of the two quantities is unknown.

Note that it is not immediately clear how you would associate either the addition or subtraction operations with a comparison situation. From an adult vantage point, you can see that if you match part of the larger amount with the smaller amount, the large set is now a part-part-whole model that can solve the problem. In fact, many children do model compare problems in just this manner. But that is a very difficult idea to show children if they do not construct the idea themselves.

Have children make two amounts, perhaps with two bars of connecting cubes. Discuss the difference between the two bars to generate the third number. For example, if the children make a bar of 10 and a bar of 6, the difference is 4. "What equations can we make with these three numbers?" Have children make up story problems that involve two amounts of 10 and 6. Discuss which equations go with the problems that are created.

The Order Property and the Zero Property

The *order* property (or *commutative* property) for addition says that it makes no difference in which order two numbers are added. Most children find little difficulty with this idea. Since it is quite useful in problem solving, mastering basic facts, and mental mathematics, there is value in spending some time helping children construct the relationship. The name of the property is not important, but the idea is.

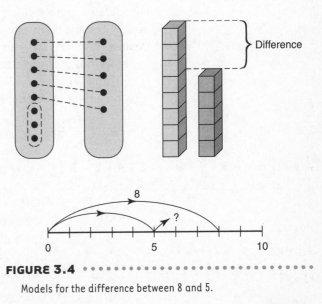

FIGURE 3.4

Models for the difference between 8 and 5.

TEACHING ADDITION AND SUBTRACTION

To help children focus on the order property, pair problems that have the same addends but in different orders. The context for each problem should be different. For example:

> Tania is on page 32 in her book. Tomorrow she hopes to read 15 more pages. What page will she be on if she reads that many pages?

> The milk tray in the cafeteria was down to only 15 cartons. Before lunch, the delivery person brought in some more milk. She filled up the tray with 32 more cartons. How many cartons does the milk tray hold?

Ask if anyone notices how these problems are alike. If done as a pair, some (not all) students will see that having solved one they have essentially solved the other. The following activity is also important and helps with the same idea.

ACTIVITY 3.3

More Than Two Addends

Give students six sums to find involving three or four addends. Prepare these on one page divided into six sections so that there is space to write beneath each sum. Within each, include at least one pair with a sum of ten or perhaps a double: $4 + 7 + 6$, $5 + 9 + 9$, or $3 + 4 + 3 + 7$. Students should show how they added the numbers. Allow students to find the sums without any other directions.

Figure 3.5 illustrates how students might show what they did. As they share their solutions, almost certainly there will be students who added in different orders but got the same result. From this discussion you can help them conclude that you can add numbers in any order. You are also using the associative property but it is the order or commutative property that is more important. This is also an excellent number sense activity because many students will find combinations of ten in these sums or will use doubles (easy facts for many students). Learning to adjust strategies to fit the numbers is the beginning of the road to computational fluency.

Using story problems involving zero or with zeros in the three-addend sums is also a good method of helping students understand zero in addition or subtraction. Occasionally students feel that $6 + 0$ must be more than 6 or that $12 - 0$ must be 11 since "plus makes numbers bigger" or "minus makes numbers smaller." Instead of making arbitrary-sounding rules about adding and subtracting zero, build opportunities for discussing zero into the problem-solving routine.

The *Investigations in Number, Data, and Space* curriculum uses a story problem technique that can be adapted to any program to help connect the ideas of addition and subtraction and also attend to individual differences. Six story problems are typed up on a single sheet—three addition and three subtraction problems. Students cut apart the problems, which are then placed in six envelopes.

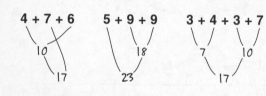

FIGURE 3.5

Students show how they added.

Students may select any envelope, take a problem, and paste it on their paper to solve. As a result, no hints are available concerning which operation is to be used or how much space is required for showing work. When students complete one problem, they can select another and paste it on the page. The envelope technique allows students to solve problems at their own pace without having to turn in unsolved problems. Because the problems are mixed, it is possible to discuss all of the problems as a class and make connections between addition and subtraction concepts.

Problem Structures for Multiplication and Division

Like addition and subtraction, there are problem structures that will help you in formulating and assigning multiplication and division tasks. As with the additive structures, these are for you, not for students.

Most researchers identify four different classes of multiplicative structures (Greer, 1992). Of these, the two described in Figure 3.6, *equal groups* (*repeated addition, rates*) and *multiplicative comparison,* are by far the most prevalent in the elementary school. Problems matching these structures can be modeled with sets of counters, number lines, or arrays. They represent a large percentage of the multiplicative problems in the real world. (The term *multiplicative* is used here to describe all problems that involve multiplication and division structure.)

Examples of Problems for Each Structure

In multiplicative problems one number or *factor* counts how many sets, groups, or parts of equal size are involved. The other factor tells the size of each set or part. These two factors have traditionally been referred to as the *multiplier* (number of parts) and the *multiplicand* (size of each part). These terms are not particularly useful to

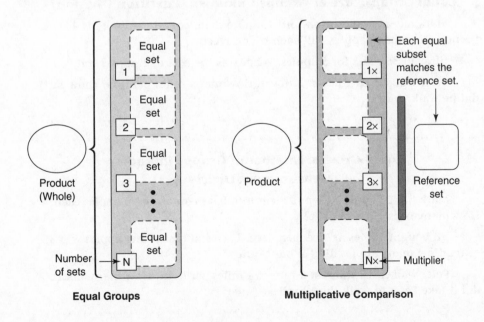

Equal Groups   **Multiplicative Comparison**

FIGURE 3.6

Two of the four basic structures for multiplication and division story problems. Each structure has three numbers. Any one of the three numbers can be the unknown in a story problem.

children and will not be used here. The third number in each of these two structures is the *whole* or *product* and is the total of all of the parts. The parts and wholes terminology is useful in making the connection to addition.

Equal-Group Problems

When the number and size of groups are known, the problem is a multiplication situation. When either the number of sets or the size of sets is unknown, division results. But note that these latter two situations are not alike. Problems where the size of the sets is unknown are called *fair-sharing* or *partition* problems. The whole is shared or distributed among a known number of sets to determine the size of each. If the number of sets is unknown but the size of the equal sets is known, the problems are called *measurement* or sometimes *repeated-subtraction* problems. The whole is "measured off" in sets of the given size. These terms are used with the examples to follow. Keep in mind the structure in Figure 3.6 to see which numbers are given and which are unknown.

There is also a subtle difference between problems that might be termed *repeated-addition* problems (If 3 children have 4 apples each, how many apples are there?) and those that might be termed *rate* problems (If there are 4 apples per child, how many apples would 3 children have?). For each category, two examples of rate problems are provided.

···

Equal Groups: Whole Unknown (Multiplication)

Mark has 4 bags of apples. There are 6 apples in each bag. How many apples does Mark have altogether?

If apples cost 7 cents each, how much did Jill have to pay for 5 apples? (*rate*)

Peter walked for 3 hours at 4 miles per hour. How far did he walk? (*rate*)

···
···

Equal Groups: Size of Groups Unknown (Partition Division)

Mark has 24 apples. He wants to share them equally among his 4 friends. How many apples will each friend receive?

Jill paid 35 cents for 5 apples. What was the cost of 1 apple? (*rate*)

Peter walked 12 miles in 3 hours. How many miles per hour (how fast) did he walk? (*rate*)

···
···

Equal Groups: Number of Groups Unknown (Measurement Division)

Mark has 24 apples. He put them into bags containing 6 apples each. How many bags did Mark use?

Jill bought apples at 7 cents apiece. The total cost of her apples was 35 cents. How many apples did Jill buy? (*rate*)

Peter walked 12 miles at a rate of 4 miles per hour. How many hours did it take Peter to walk the 12 miles? (*rate*)

···

Multiplicative Comparison Problems

In multiplicative comparison problems, there are really two different sets, as there were with comparison situations for addition and subtraction. One set consists of multiple copies of the other. Two examples of each possibility are provided here. In multiplicative situations, the comparison is based on one set's being a particular multiple of the other.

Comparison: Product Unknown (Multiplication)

Jill picked 6 apples. Mark picked 4 times as many apples as Jill. How many apples did Mark pick?

This month Mark saved 5 times as much money as last month. Last month he saved $7. How much money did Mark save this month?

Comparison: Set Size Unknown (Partition Division)

Mark picked 24 apples. He picked 4 times as many apples as Jill. How many apples did Jill pick?

This month Mark saved 5 times as much money as he did last month. If he saved $35 this month, how much did he save last month?

Comparison: Multiplier Unknown (Measurement Division)

Mark picked 24 apples, and Jill picked only 6. How many times as many apples did Mark pick as Jill did?

This month Mark saved $35. Last month he saved $7. How many times as much money did he save this month as last?

What you just read is a lot to take in without reflection. Stop now and get a collection of counters—at least 35. Use the counters to solve each of the problems. Look first at the equal-group problems and do the "Mark problems" or the first problem in each set. Match the numbers with the structure model in Figure 3.6. How are these problems alike and how are they different, especially the two division problems? Repeat the exercise with the "Jill problems" and then the "Peter problems." Can you see how the problems in each group are alike and how the problems across groups are related?

When you are comfortable with the equal-group problems, repeat the same process with the multiplicative comparison problems. Again, start with the first problem in all three sets and then the second problem in all three sets. Reflect on the same questions posed earlier.

Reflections on the Multiplicative Structures

Kindergarten and first-grade children are quite successful at solving multiplication and division problems, even division involving remainders (Carpenter, Ansell, Franke,

PROBLEM STRUCTURES FOR MULTIPLICATION AND DIVISION

Fennema, & Weisbeck, 1993; Carpenter, Carey, & Kouba, 1990; Fennema et al., 1997). A strong argument can be made that students should be exposed to all four operations from the first year of school and that multiplication and division should be much more closely linked in the curriculum.

Teaching Multiplication and Division

Multiplication and division are taught separately in most traditional programs, with multiplication preceding division. It is important, however, to combine multiplication and division soon after multiplication has been introduced in order to help students see how they are related. In most curricula, these topics are a main focus of the third grade with continued development in the fourth and fifth grades.

One of the major conceptual hurdles of working with multiplicative structures is that of understanding groups of things as single entities while also understanding that a group contains a given number of objects. Children can solve the problem *How many apples in 4 baskets of 8 apples each?* by counting out 4 sets of 8 counters and then counting all. To think multiplicatively about this problem as *4 sets of eight* requires children to conceptualize each group of eight as a single item to be counted. Experiences with making and counting groups, especially in contextual situations, are extremely useful.

Using Contextual Problems

Many of the issues surrounding addition and subtraction also apply to multiplication and need not be discussed in depth again. It remains important to use contextual problems whenever reasonable instead of more sterile story problems. Just as with additive structures, it is a good idea to build lessons around only two or three problems. Students should solve problems using whatever techniques they wish. What is important is that they explain—preferably in writing—what they did and why it makes sense. Words, pictures, and numbers remain important.

Symbolism for Multiplication and Division

When students solve simple multiplication story problems before learning about multiplication symbolism, they will most likely write repeated-addition equations to represent what they did as an equation. This is your opportunity to introduce the multiplication sign and explain what the two factors mean.

The usual convention is that 4×8 refers to four sets of eight, not eight sets of four. There is absolutely no reason to be rigid about this convention. The important thing is that the students can tell you what each factor in *their* equations represents. In vertical form, it is usually the bottom factor that indicates the number of sets. Again, this distinction is not terribly important.

The quotient 24 divided by 6 is represented in three different ways: $24 \div 6$, $6\overline{)24}$, and $\frac{24}{6}$. The fraction notation becomes important at the middle school level. The computational form $6\overline{)24}$ would probably not exist if it were not for the standard pencil-and-paper procedure that utilizes it. Children have a tendency to read this as "6 divided by 24" due to the left-right order of the numerals. Generally this error does not match what they are thinking.

Compounding the difficulty of division notation is the unfortunate phrase, "six goes into twenty-four." This phrase carries little meaning about division, especially in connection with a fair-sharing or partitioning context. The "goes into" (or "guzinta") terminology is simply engrained in adult parlance and has not been in textbooks for years. If you tend to use that phrase, it is probably a good time to consciously abandon it.

Choosing Numbers for Problems

When selecting numbers for multiplicative story problems or activities, there is a tendency to think that large numbers pose a burden to students or that 3 × 4 is somehow easier to understand than 4 × 17. Conceptually, products or quotients are not affected by the size of numbers as long as the numbers are within the grasp of the students. Little is gained by restricting early explorations of multiplication to small numbers. Even in early third grade, students can work with larger numbers using whatever counting strategies they have at their disposal. A contextual problem involving 14 × 8 is not at all too large for third graders even before they have learned a computation technique. When given these challenges, children are likely to invent computational strategies.

Remainders

More often than not, division does not result in a simple whole number. For example, problems with 6 as a divisor will "come out even" only one time out of six. In the absence of a context, a remainder can be dealt with in only two ways: It can either remain a quantity left over or be partitioned into fractions. In Figure 3.7, the problem 11 ÷ 4 is modeled to show fractions.

In real contexts, remainders sometimes have three additional effects on answers:

The remainder is discarded, leaving a smaller whole-number answer.

The remainder can "force" the answer to the next highest whole number.

The answer is rounded to the nearest whole number for an approximate result.

The following problems illustrate all five possibilities.

· ·

You have 30 pieces of candy to share fairly with 7 children. How many pieces of candy will each child receive?

Answer: 4 pieces of candy and 2 left over. (*left over*)

Each jar holds 8 ounces of liquid. If there are 46 ounces in the pitcher, how many jars will that be?

Answer: 5 and $\frac{6}{8}$ jars. (*partitioned as a fraction*)

The rope is 25 feet long. How many 7-foot jump ropes can be made?

Answer: 3 jump ropes. (*discarded*)

Partition $11 \div 4 = 2\frac{3}{4}$
$2\frac{3}{4}$ in each of the 4 sets
(each leftover divided in fourths)

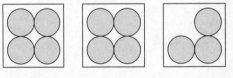

Measurement $11 \div 4 = 2\frac{3}{4}$
$2\frac{3}{4}$ sets of 4
(2 full sets and $\frac{3}{4}$ of a set)

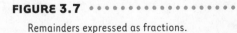

FIGURE 3.7 · · · · · · · · · · · · · · · · ·

Remainders expressed as fractions.

TEACHING MULTIPLICATION AND DIVISION

The ferry can hold 8 cars. How many trips will it have to make to carry 25 cars across the river?

Answer: 4 trips. (*forced to next whole number*)

Six children are planning to share a bag of 50 pieces of bubble gum. About how many pieces will each child get?

Answer: About 8 pieces for each child. (*rounded, approximate result*)

In the early grades, it is a mistake to always have students write remainders as "R3" and/or to only pose problems without remainders. Rather, it is useful to include story problems with remainders and explore the different ways that students handle these in context. There is no reason to make a rule about remainders. For students beginning to talk about fractions, include partition problems in which items can be subdivided into fractional parts (brownies, pies, cups of milk, etc.). Some children will handle these as in Figure 3.7. It is a bit more difficult to conceptualize a measurement problem with a fractional remainder. Consider the following problems:

Tania was filling crates with special oranges. Each crate holds 4 oranges. If Tania has 11 oranges, how many crates will her 11 oranges fill?

Toby has 11 cups of milk in a pitcher. If he pours all 11 cups into jars that hold 4 cups each. How many jars will Toby fill?

The first problem can be modeled exactly as in Figure 3.7 as 2 full crates and $\frac{3}{4}$ of a crate. This requires thinking of each crate as a whole and assumes that the student will think about a partial crate as part of the answer. In the milk problem, there may be a greater chance of thinking about a jar being $\frac{3}{4}$ full. If you want to introduce these fractional ideas and no one in the class suggests them, offer them yourself. You can say, "If someone said that Toby filled two and three-fourths jars with milk, would that make sense? Do you think that could be a correct answer?" There is no need to be afraid of these ideas even if they do not appear in your curriculum.

Using Models-Based Problems

In the beginning, children will be able to use the same models—sets and number lines—for all four operations. A model not generally used for addition but extremely important and widely used for multiplication and division is the array. An *array* is any arrangement of things in rows and columns, such as a rectangle of square tiles or blocks.

To make clear the connection to addition, early multiplication activities should also include writing an addition sentence for the same model. A variety of models is shown in Figure 3.8. Notice that the products are not included—only addition and multiplication "names" are written. This is another way to avoid the tedious counting of large sets. A similar approach is to write one sentence that expresses both concepts at once, for example, $9 + 9 + 9 + 9 = 4 \times 9$.

Multiplication and Division Activities

As with additive problems, children can benefit from a few activities with models and no context. The purpose of such activities is to focus on the meaning of the opera-

FIGURE 3.8 • • • • • • • • • • • •

Models for equal-group multiplication.

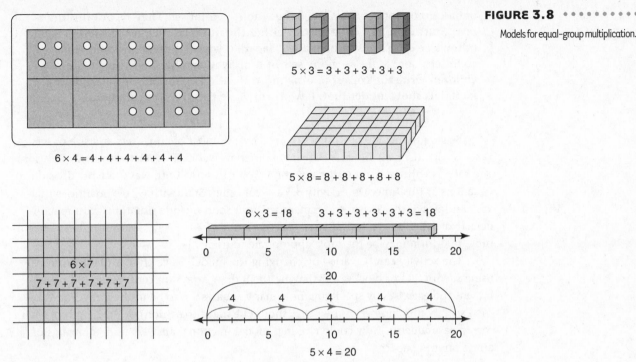

$5 \times 3 = 3 + 3 + 3 + 3 + 3$

$6 \times 4 = 4 + 4 + 4 + 4 + 4 + 4$

$5 \times 8 = 8 + 8 + 8 + 8 + 8$

6×7

$7 + 7 + 7 + 7 + 7 + 7$

$6 \times 3 = 18$ $3 + 3 + 3 + 3 + 3 + 3 = 18$

$5 \times 4 = 20$

$4 + 4 + 4 + 4 + 4 = 20$

tion and the associated symbolism. Activity 3.4 has a good problem-solving spirit. The language you use depends on what you have used with your children in the past.

ACTIVITY 3.4

Finding Factors

Start by assigning a number that has several factors—for example, 12, 18, 24, 30, or 36. Have students find multiplication expressions for their assigned number. With counters, students attempt to find a way to separate the counters into equal subsets. With arrays (perhaps made from square tiles or cubes or drawn on grid paper), students try to build rectangles that have the given number of squares. For each such arrangement of sets or appropriate rectangles, both an addition and a multiplication equation should be written.

Activity 3.4 can also include division concepts. When children have learned that 3 and 6 are factors of 18, they can write the equations $18 \div 3 = 6$ and $18 \div 6 = 3$ along with $3 \times 6 = 18$ and $6 + 6 + 6 = 18$ (assuming that three sets of six were modeled). The following variation of the same activity focuses on division. Having children create word problems is another excellent elaboration of this activity. Require children to explain how their story problems fit with what they did with the counters.

ACTIVITY 3.5

Learning About Division

Provide children with an ample supply of counters and some way to place them into small groups. Small paper cups work well. Have children count

EXPANDED LESSON

(pages 92–93)
A complete lesson plan based on "Learning About Division" can be found at the end of this chapter.

(continued)

out a number of counters to be the whole or total set. They record this number: "Start with 31." Next specify either the number of equal sets to be made or the size of the sets to be made: "Separate your counters into four equal-sized sets," or "Make as many sets of four as is possible." Next have the children write the corresponding multiplication equation for what their materials show; under that, have them write the division equation.

Be sure to include both types of exercises: number of equal sets and size of sets. Discuss with the class how these two are different, yet each is related to multiplication and each is written as a division equation. You can show both ways to write division equations at this time. Do Activity 3.5 several times. Start with whole quantities that are multiples of the divisor (no remainders) but soon include situations with remainders. (Note that it is technically incorrect to write 31 ÷ 4 = 7 R 3. However, in the beginning, that form may be the most appropriate to use.)

The activity can be varied by changing the model. Have children build arrays using square tiles or blocks or by having them draw arrays on centimeter grid paper. Present the exercises by specifying how many squares are to be in the array. You can then specify the number of rows that should be made (partition) or the length of each row (measurement). How could children model fractional answers using drawings of arrays on grid paper?

ACTIVITY 3.6

The Broken Multiplication Key

The calculator is a good way to relate multiplication to addition. Students can be told to find various products on the calculator without using the × key. For example, 6 × 4 can be found by pressing + 4 = = = = = =. (Successive presses of = add 4 to the display each time. You began with zero and added 4 six times.) Students can be challenged to demonstrate their result with sets of counters. But note that this same technique can be used to determine products such as 23 × 459 (+ 459 and then 23 presses of =). Students will want to compare to the same product using the × key.

"The Broken Multiplication Key" can profitably be followed by "The Broken Division Key."

ACTIVITY 3.7

The Broken Division Key

Have children work in groups to find methods of using the calculator to solve division exercises without using the divide key. The problems can be posed without a story context. "Find at least two ways to figure out 61 ÷ 14 without pressing the divide key." If the problem is put in a story context, one method may actually match the problem better than another. Good discussions may follow different solutions with the same answers. Are they both correct? Why or why not?

Assessment Note

A good way to check on students' understanding of the operations is to provide several story problems with different operations. It is not necessary to do this all in one day. Have students work on two or three problems a day over the course of a week. If your objective is to find out about their understanding of the operations, you can do this by not having them actually do the computations. Rather, have them indicate what operation they would use and with what numbers. To avoid guessing, you can have students draw a picture to explain why they chose the operation that they did.

Useful Multiplication and Division Properties

As with addition and subtraction, there are some multiplicative properties that are useful and, thus, worthy of attention. The emphasis should be on the ideas and not terminology or definitions.

The Order Property in Multiplication

It is not intuitively obvious that 3×8 is the same as 8×3 or that, in general, the order of the numbers makes no difference (the *order* or *commutative* property). A picture of 3 sets of 8 objects cannot immediately be seen as 8 piles of 3 objects. Eight hops of 3 land at 24, but it is not clear that 3 hops of 8 will land at the same point.

The array, by contrast, is quite powerful in illustrating the order property, as is shown in Figure 3.9. Children should draw or build arrays and use them to demonstrate why each array represents two different multiplications with the same product.

The Role of Zero and One in Multiplication

Zero and, to a lesser extent, 1 as factors often cause difficulty for children. Children can use a calculator to explore products involving factors of 0 or 1 (423×0, 0×28, 1536×1, etc.) and look for patterns. The patterns will suggest the rules for factors of 0 and 1 but not reasons. Have students make up story problems that will go with their results. This approach is far preferable to an arbitrary rule, since it asks students to reason. Problems with 0 as a first factor are really strange. Note that on a number line, 5 hops of 0 land at 0 (5×0). What would 0 hops of 5 be? Another fun activity

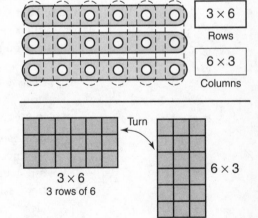

FIGURE 3.9 • • • • • • • • • • • • • • • • • •

Two ways an array can be used to illustrate the order (commutative) property for multiplication.

---

*There are two measurement approaches or two ways to find out how many 14s are in 61. A third way is essentially related to partitioning or finding 14 times what number is close to 61.

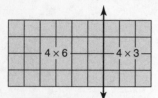

$4 \times 9 = (4 \times 6) + (4 \times 3)$

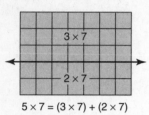

$5 \times 7 = (3 \times 7) + (2 \times 7)$

FIGURE 3.10 • • • • • • •

Models for the distributive property.

is to try to model 6×0 or 0×8 with an array. (Try it!) Arrays for factors of 1 are also worth investigating.

The Distributive Property

It may not be essential for young children to know the *distributive* property in the form $a \times (b + c) = (a \times b) + (a \times c)$. But the concept involved is very useful in relating one basic fact to another, and it is also involved in the development of two-digit computation. Figure 3.10 illustrates how the array model can be used to illustrate that a product can be broken up into two parts. Third grade is not too soon to explore this concept.

The next activity is designed to help children discover how to partition factors or, in other words, learn about the distributive property.

ACTIVITY 3.8

Slice It Up

Supply students with several sheets of centimeter grid paper. Assign each pair of students a product such as 6×8. (Products can vary across the class or all be the same.) The task is to find all of the different ways to make a single slice through the rectangle. For each slice students write an equation. For a slice of one row of 8, students would write $6 \times 8 = 5 \times 8 + 1 \times 8$. The individual products can be written in the arrays as was done in Figure 3.10.

More Thoughts About Children Solving Story Problems

Solving word problems of all sorts on a regular basis can be a significant tool in your number and computation curriculum. Your goals for students should go beyond being able to solve story problems. In fact, problem solving per se should not be a strand in your curriculum. Rather, solving problems is a means of helping students learn. At the K–3 level, there are many interrelated objectives that you should have in mind when you pose story problems:

- *Understanding the various meanings of the four operations.* It is primarily through story problems that children will gain a full understanding of which operation to use in any given situation.

- *Development of number skills and concepts.* As students solve problems, they are forced to deal with the numbers involved. Initially, they will use immature counting techniques. Later these techniques will give rise to more efficient skills and eventually will provide the foundations for mastery of basic facts.

- *Computational fluency.* Related to their number skills are the many different methods that students will develop for computing. Place-value ideas will be enhanced and utilized as students find new and better ways to break numbers apart and combine them. The structure of the problem can significantly influence the way students compute.

This broad array of goals suggests that there is much more to story problems than simply having students get answers. We want them to develop number skills and computational techniques as well as to have a rich understanding of the operations. To attend to these goals requires that we think carefully about the problems we pose. What operation structures do students need to work on? What numbers will challenge students but not overwhelm them? In other words, think of story problems as a means to an end rather than an end in themselves.

Caution: Avoid Key Words!

It is often suggested that students should be taught to find "key words" in story problems. Some teachers even post lists of key words with their corresponding meanings. For example, "altogether" and "in all" mean you should add and "left" and "fewer" indicate you should subtract. The word "each" suggests multiplication. To some extent, teachers have been reinforced by the overly simple and formulaic story problems often found in textbooks. When problems are written in this way, it may appear that the key word strategy is effective.

In contrast with this belief, researchers and mathematics educators have long cautioned against the strategy of key words. Here are three arguments against the key word approach.

1. Key words are misleading. Often the key word or phrase in a problem suggests an operation that is incorrect. For example:

    Maxine took the 28 stickers she no longer wanted and gave them to Zandra. Now Maxine has 73 stickers *left*. How many stickers did Maxine have to begin with?

    If you look through the story problems in this chapter, you will find other examples of misleading key words.
2. Many problems have no key words. Especially when you get away from the overly simple problems found in primary textbooks, you will find that a large percentage of problems have no key words. A child who has been taught to rely on key words is left with no strategy. In both the additive and the multiplicative problems in this chapter, you will find numerous examples of problems with no key words. And this is from a collection of overly simple problems designed to help you with structure.
3. The key word strategy sends a terribly wrong message about doing mathematics. The most important approach to solving any contextual problem is to analyze its structure—to make sense of it. The key word approach encourages students to ignore the meaning and structure of the problem and look for an easy way out. Mathematics is about reasoning and making sense of situations. A sense-making strategy will *always* work.

Encourage Problem Analysis

Many children in kindergarten and first grade will do better at solving problems than will students in the upper grades. Once children have learned computational techniques, they often think that is what solving story problems means—grab the numbers and compute. These are the children that ignore problem context and often use extraneous numbers in their computations. In contrast, kindergarten and first-grade children have little or no means of computing. They pay attention to the problem, often use counters or other models, and figure out the solution based on the meaning in the story. Regardless of what grade you are teaching, it is important to always have children think through the problem before they get started. For example, let's consider the following problem:

> Luke is saving up to buy a new model boat that costs $33. Each week his dad agrees to put $6 in a savings account if Luke cuts the back grass. How many weeks will Luke have to work before he has enough money to buy the model boat?

Here are some questions that you might have the class discuss or answer on paper. Similar questions can be used for most any problem:

What is happening in this problem? Luke is cutting grass to save money to buy a boat.

What will the answer tell us? How many weeks Luke will have to cut grass in order to have enough money.

Do you think it will be a big number or a small number? Well, each week he gets $6. If he works 10 weeks he would have $60. He only needs $33. So it must be less than 10.

About how many weeks do you think he will have to work? [Some children may be able to compute the answer mentally. Others may not even be able to make a good guess.]

In these questions students are asked to focus on the problem and the meaning of the answer instead of on numbers. The thinking leads to an idea of the size of the answer or a rough estimate of the answer. Knowing about how big the answer might be—even knowing if it will be more or less than one of the numbers in the problem— is a big first step in solving the problem. It is also a useful bit of information to use in judging the answer when the problem is solved.

Require Explanations

Chapter 1 stressed the importance of having students write. In the early years, story problems provide an excellent place to begin this habit. This is especially true before students have developed methods of computation. You may find that students who know their basic facts or have learned traditional methods of computing will write little more than the computations they used. It is important to show them that you want explanations, nearly always using words and numbers and often using pictures as well.

The solutions shown in Figure 3.11 are offered by children in a mixed K–1 classroom. Reginald, a first grader, at first offered only the numbers at the top of the page.

I went to visit Mrs. Sato's farm last week.

- On Monday, I found 1 egg.
- On Tuesday, I found 2 eggs.
- On Wednesday, I found 3 eggs.
- On Thursday, I found 4 eggs.
- On Friday, I found 5 eggs.

How many eggs did I find last week?

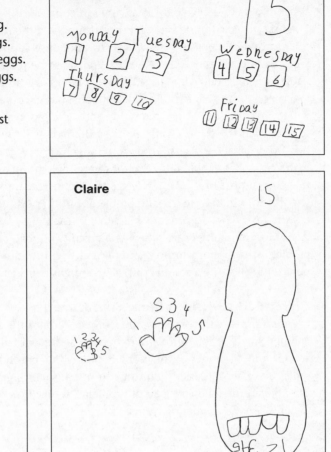

FIGURE 3.11 ● ● ● ● ● ● ● ●

Three K–1 students solve a complex problem using different types of drawings and explanations for their work.

Ms. S. asked him to write down where the numbers had come from. Notice that he has no need for an equal sign. Amanda is also in the first grade. She first solved the problem with Unifix cubes and then made a picture showing each cube. Ms. S. suggested that if she labeled the days it would make it easier to explain her thinking to the class. Claire, a kindergarten child, drew this picture on her own. When asked to explain, she showed how she had counted on her fingers and "then I had to go to my feet." She traced her shoe and showed the toes inside. This was the first time that Ms. S. had asked the kindergartners to show their thinking with a picture.

As students continue to attempt to show their thinking, they will improve both from practice and from seeing the methods used by others. For the examples in Figure 3.11, the students are showing *how* they solved the problem. It is quite clear that they knew to add. To ask them to explain why they added in this example would be overly abstract. For some problems it may also be useful to ask students *why* they used a particular operation or some other question that shifts the explanation away from simply the steps of computation. For second- and third-grade students, you might ask questions such as, "Why do you think your answer is correct?" or "Why did you decide that multiplication was the right thing to do in this problem?"

MORE THOUGHTS ABOUT CHILDREN SOLVING STORY PROBLEMS

Assessment Note

What do you do if a student is having difficulty solving word problems? The first thing is to find out what is causing the difficulty. If you can't tell from the student's written efforts or from observation, a short interview session is highly recommended. Prepare some problems written out on paper, one problem to the page. To avoid issues of reading, read the problem together with the student. Provide counters, but encourage the student to use whatever he or she wishes in order to solve the problem. Explain that you want to hear what the student is thinking so that you will know how to help him or her. Do not make the session too long. If you cannot get a clue to the difficulty with one or two problems, use additional problems on another day. Remember that the purpose of your interview is to gain insight into the student's difficulties. Use this information to prepare problems or other tasks for a later lesson. Do not use the interview as a time to intervene or teach!

Most difficulties can be separated into two broad categories: difficulty with problem structure or wording, and difficulty with number concepts and/or computation. Following are some things you might consider within each category.

Difficulties with Problem Structure

Examine the way the problems are worded. Perhaps the semantics of the problem have made it too difficult. Problems that are worded in such a way that the actions and quantities in the problem follow in a chronological or natural story order are generally easier than those in which the problem order is inverted. For example, in the following pair of problems, notice how the second problem matches a natural order of events:

Mike's grandpa gave him some money for his birthday. Mike already had 6 dollars. Now Mike has 9 dollars. How much did Mike's grandpa give him?

Mike had 6 dollars. His grandpa gave him some money for his birthday. Now he has 9 dollars. How much did Mike's grandpa give him?

Join problems in which the change is unknown can be structured in terms of "how much more is needed" or in terms of "how much was added." Some students find actions that happened in the past more difficult to grasp. These students would find the first of the following two problems easier:

Joyce has 3 eggs in her basket. How many more eggs does she need to find to have 8 eggs?

Joyce has 3 eggs in her basket. She found some more eggs for her basket in the chicken coop. Now she has 8 eggs. How many more eggs did Joyce find in the chicken coop?

When you think that problems with wording are the cause of student difficulty, pose problems with similar structure but with the wording of the problem made as clear and as straightforward as possible.

- When students do not seem to know what to do with a problem, a simple yet effective suggestion is to have students use counters to act out the problem. Have students say out loud what each set of counters stands for and explain with the counters what is happening in the problem. This can help students with similar analyses when you are not there to make these suggestions.
- Many students have difficulty with problems in which the initial part is unknown. These students are trying to model the problem in chronological order and they can't make the set that represents the beginning of the problem. Write a question mark on an index card and have students use the card to represent the unknown amount.
- Have students talk about what is happening in the problem. (See the suggestions in the earlier section, "Encourage Problem Analysis.")

Difficulties with Number or Computation

There are many reasons why students may have difficulties with number or computation that have nothing to do with understanding the problem. The challenge is to help students with these difficulties.

- Encourage students to use counters to model the numbers in the problem. Many students simply do not have computational skills and yet try to use abstract counting or other techniques for which they are not ready. If appropriate, have students use base-ten models for numbers involving two or three digits.
- Have students work on similar computations without story problems. Make the use of models completely optional. Be sure to have students use drawings to show what they did.
- Provide appropriate conceptual development with number concepts and relationships. Be certain that you have enough information to know what number concepts are the source of the difficulty.
- Adjust the numbers in the problems so that the numbers are within the student's comfort range. Avoid making them so easy that they are insulting.

EXPANDED LESSON

Learning About Division

Based on: Activity 3.5, p. 83

GRADE LEVEL: Late third grade, early fourth grade.

MATHEMATICS GOALS

- To develop the measurement (repeated subtraction) concept of division.
- To connect this concept of division to multiplication and addition.

THINKING ABOUT THE STUDENTS

Students have explored multiplication concepts, but it is not necessary that they have mastered multiplication facts.

This lesson could be used as an introduction to division. For students who have been exposed to division, the lesson can further develop early ideas and help connect the ideas to contextual situations.

MATERIALS AND PREPARATION

- Students will each need about 35 counters.
- If possible, provide students with small paper cups or portion cups that will hold at least 6 counters. Alternatively, students can stack counters in piles.

lesson

BEFORE

Begin with a Simpler Version of the Task

- Draw 13 dots on the board. Ask: *How many sets of 3 dots can we make if we have 13 to work with? How many will be left over?* Most students should be able to answer this question mentally. After receiving several answers, have a student come to the board and demonstrate how to verify the answer of 4 sets of 3 and 1 left.

- Ask: *What equation could we write for what we have on the board?* Accept students' ideas. Correct ideas include:
  - $3 + 3 + 3 + 3 + 1 = 13$
  - $4 \times 3 + 1 = 13$ ($3 \times 4 + 1$ technically represents 3 sets of 4 and 1 more.)
  - $13 \div 3 = 4 \text{ R } 1$

  Note: If this is the introduction to division symbolism, you may want to use 12 instead of 13 so that there are no remainders. However, it is also okay to begin this way.

- Say: *Think of a situation in which someone might have 13 things and wants to find out how many sets of 3. Make up a story problem about your situation.* Have several students share their story problem.

The Task

- Begin with a set of 31 counters. Use the counters to see how many sets of 4 you can make. Repeat with a set of 27 counters and find out how many sets of 6 you can make.

Establish Expectations

- Write the directions on the board:
  - 31 counters—how many sets of 4?
  - 27 counters—how many sets of 6?
- Explain (and record on the board) that for each of these tasks students are to:
  - Write three equations: one addition, one multiplication, and one division.
  - Write a story problem to go with their division equation.

DURING

- Ask students to explain why their equations go with what they did with the counters. Do not correct incorrect equations or story problems. You only want to be sure students are attempting to connect the activity with the symbolism and the stories.
- Challenge early finishers to see if they can do the same thing for a set of 125 things in piles of 20. However, they will have to figure it out without using counters.

AFTER

- For 31 counters in sets of 4, ask how many sets and how many are left over. Most students should agree that there are 7 sets and 3 left over. Draw a picture that looks similar to those you have seen on students' papers.
- Have a number of students share their equations. After several equations are on the board, ask those who have different equations to share theirs as well.
- Have students explain how their equations match what was done with the counters. If students disagree, have them politely explain their reasoning. Students should be comfortable with their ideas about the multiplication and addition equations. For an introductory lesson on division, you should correct any misunderstandings about the division equation and what it means.
- Have several students share their story problems. Students should explain how the story situation matches the action of finding how many sets of 4 in 31. For example: "There were 31 apples in the basket. If each apple tart requires 4 apples, how many tarts can be made?"
- If time permits, repeat with the $27 \div 6$ situation.

ASSESSMENT NOTES

- The key idea in this lesson is the connection between the action of finding how many equal sets in a given quantity, and the manner in which a multiplication equation and a division equation are connected to this action. Look for evidence that this idea is clear to students. Do not be overly concerned about the use of 4×7 instead of 7×4.
- Story problems should indicate the action of measuring sets of 4 rather than creating four sets, a sharing or partition concept. If students make this error, simply have them discuss whether or not the story fits well with the action. Do not indicate that the story is incorrect. It is also possible that students will create multiplication stories (31 being the unknown amount). Here ask students which equation best represents the problem.

- This activity or a variation of it should also be done in which students explore the *size* of the set when the number of sets is given (partition or fair-sharing concept).
- Rather than begin with a model, such as in this lesson, have students solve division story problems using coun-

ters or drawings if necessary. Always be sure that equations are included with the story problems.

next steps

HELPING CHILDREN MASTER THE BASIC FACTS

Chapter

4

Basic facts for addition and multiplication refer to combinations where both addends or both factors are less than 10. Subtraction and division facts correspond to addition and multiplication facts. Thus, $15 - 8 = 7$ is a subtraction fact because both parts are less than 10.

Mastery of a basic fact means that a child can give a quick response (in about 3 seconds) without resorting to nonefficient means, such as counting.

All children are able to master the basic facts—including children with learning disabilities. Children simply need to construct efficient mental tools that will help them. This chapter is about helping children develop those tools.

big ideas

1 Number relationships provide the foundation for strategies that help students remember basic facts. For example, knowing how numbers are related to 5 and 10 helps students master facts such as 3 + 5 (think of a ten-frame) and 8 + 6 (since 8 is 2 away from 10, take 2 from 6 to make 10 + 4 = 14).

2 "Think addition" is the most powerful way to think of subtraction facts. Rather than 13 "take away 6," which requires counting backward while simultaneously keeping track of the number of counts, students can think 6 and what makes 13. They might add up to 10 or they may think double 6 is 12 so it must be 13.

3 All of the facts are conceptually related. You can figure out new or unknown facts from those you already know. For example, 6 × 8 can be thought of as five 8s (40) and one more 8. It might also be three 8s doubled.

From Concepts and Strategies to Fact Mastery

Fortunately, we know quite a bit about helping children develop fact mastery, and it has little to do with quantity of drill or drill techniques. If appropriate development is undertaken in the primary grades, there is no reason that all children cannot master their facts by the end of grade 3. Three components or steps to this end can be identified:

1. Help children develop a strong understanding of number relationships and of the operations.
2. Develop efficient strategies for fact retrieval through practice.
3. Provide drill in the use and selection of those strategies once they have been developed.

The Role of Number and Operation Concepts

Number relationships play a significant role in fact mastery. The 8 + 6 example in the first Big Idea requires the relationship between 8 and 10 (8 is 2 away from 10), the part-part-whole knowledge of 6 (2 and 4 more makes 6), and the fact that 10 and 4 is 14. For 6 × 7, it is efficient to think "5 times 7 and 7 more." For many children, the efficiency of this approach is lost because they need to count on 7 to get from 35 to 42. With an extension of the number relationships just noted, it is possible to think "35 and 5 more is 40, and 2 more is 42." Every relationship discussed in Chapter 2 can contribute to fact mastery.

The meanings of the operations also play a role in the construction of efficient strategies. The ability to relate 6 × 7 to "5 times 7 and 7 more" is based on an understanding of the meanings of the first and second factors. To relate 13 – 7 to "7 and what makes 13" requires an understanding of how addition and subtraction are related. The commutative or "turnaround" properties for addition and multiplication reduce the number of addition and multiplication facts from 100 each to 55 each.

Teachers in grade 3 with students who have not mastered basic addition and subtraction facts will do well to investigate what command of number relationships the students have. Without these relationships, the strategies discussed throughout this chapter will be difficult.

Development of Efficient Strategies

An efficient strategy is one that can be done mentally and quickly. The emphasis is on *efficient*. Counting is not efficient. If drill is undertaken when counting is the only strategy available, all you get is faster counting.

What Is a Strategy?

We have already seen some efficient strategies: the use of building up through 10 in adding 8 + 6 and the use of the related fact 5 × 7 to help with 6 × 7.

 Consider for a moment how you think about 6 + 6. What about 9 + 5?

You may think that you just "know" these. What is more likely is that you used some ideas similar to double six (for 6 + 6) and 10 and 4 more (for 9 + 5). Your response may be so automatic by now that you are not reflecting on the use of these relationships or ideas. That is one of the features of efficient mental processes—they become automatic with use.

Many children have learned basic facts without being taught efficient strategies. They develop or learn many of these methods in spite of the drill they may have endured. The trouble is that far too many students do not develop strategies without

FROM CONCEPTS AND STRATEGIES TO FACT MASTERY

instruction and far too many students in middle school continue to count on their fingers. The challenge for teachers is to devise lessons in which all children will develop strategies that are useful. A strategy is most useful to students when it is theirs, built on and connected to concepts and relationships they already own.

Two Approaches to Fact Strategies

You need to plan lessons or short activities in which specific strategies are likely to be developed. There are two basic types of lessons suggested for this purpose. The first is to use simple story problems designed in such a manner that students are most likely to develop a strategy as they solve it. These are worthwhile tasks that do not require a full period to do and discuss. Rathmell, Leutzinger, and Gabriele (2000) suggest a simple story problem and discussion in a 5- to 10-minute period to start nearly every day. Their teachers report that students develop and use a variety of effective strategies for mastering basic facts. In the discussion of these solution methods, you can focus attention on the methods that are most useful. You can have all students try the methods others have developed.

A second possible approach is a bit more direct. A lesson may revolve around a special collection of facts for which a particular type of strategy is appropriate. You can discuss how these facts might all be alike in some way, or you might suggest an approach and see if students are able to use it on similar facts.

There is a huge temptation simply to tell students about a strategy and then have them practice it. Though this can be effective for some students, many others will not personally relate to your ideas or may not be ready for them. Continue to discuss strategies invented in your class and plan lessons that encourage strategies.

Drill of Efficient Methods and Strategy Selection

It is appropriate here to make a distinction between drill and practice. Practice refers to problem-based activities in which students are encouraged to develop (invent, consider, try—but not master) flexible and useful strategies that are meaningful. The types of lessons just described can be thought of as practice lessons. Whether from story problems or from consideration of a collection of similar facts, students are wrestling with the development of strategies that they can use themselves.

Drill refers to repetitive non-problem-based activity. Drill activity is appropriate for children who have a strategy that they understand, like, and know how to use but have not yet become facile with it. Drill with an in-place strategy focuses students' attention on that strategy and helps to make it more automatic.

Drill plays a significant role in fact mastery, and the use of old-fashioned methods such as flash cards and fact games can be effective if used wisely.

Avoid Premature Drill

It is critical that you do not introduce drill too soon. Suppose that a child does not know the 9 + 5 fact and has no way to deal with it other than to count fingers or use counters. These are inefficient methods. Premature drill introduces no new information and encourages no new connections. It is both a waste of time and a frustration to the child.

As you read through this chapter, you may feel that the strategies for some facts, especially the harder multiplication facts, do not seem to be efficient at all. However, as long as the strategy is completely mental and does not rely on a model, picture, or tedious counting, repeated use of the strategy will almost certainly render it automatic. The strategy provides a mental path from fact to answer. Soon the fact and answer are "connected" as the strategy becomes almost unconscious.

The discussion in this chapter focuses on one strategy at a time. It is not at all unreasonable for students to be engaged in drill activities with one strategy before they have developed (via practice or problem-based activity) strategies for other facts.

Many of the activities suggested in the chapter are simple drills—flash cards, matching games, dice, or spinner activities—in which the objective is quick response. Do not misinterpret these activities that are clearly drills as the way to introduce or develop strategies. Drill should only be used when an efficient strategy is in place.

Practice Strategy Selection or Strategy Retrieval

Strategy selection or *strategy retrieval* is the process of deciding what strategy is appropriate for a particular fact. If you don't think to use a strategy, you probably won't. Many teachers who have tried teaching fact strategies report that the method works well while the children are focused on whatever strategy they are working on. They acknowledge that children can learn and use strategies. But, they continue, when the facts are all mixed up or the child is not in "fact practice" mode, old counting habits return.

For example, suppose that your children have been practicing the near-doubles facts for addition: Use the better-known double, 7 + 7, to derive the unknown 8 + 7. Children become quite skilled at doubling the smaller number and adding 1. All of the facts they are practicing are selected to fit this model. On other days, they have learned and practiced other strategies. Later, on a worksheet or in a mental math exercise, the children are presented with a mixture of facts. In a single exercise, a child might see

$$\begin{array}{cccc} 7 & 4 & 2 & 8 \\ +\,6 & +\,9 & +\,6 & +\,5 \end{array}$$

There is no mind-set or reminder to use different processes for each. Especially if the children have previously been habituated to counting to get answers, they will very likely revert to counting and ignore the efficient methods that were the focus of recent drills. When they were drilling the strategy, there was no need to decide what strategy might be useful. All of the facts in the near-doubles practice were near-doubles, and the strategy worked. Later, however, there is no one to suggest the strategy.

A simple activity that is useful is to prepare a list of facts selected from two or more strategies and then, one fact at a time, ask children to name a strategy that would work for that fact. They should explain why they picked the strategy and demonstrate its use. This type of activity turns the attention to the features of a fact that lend it to this or that strategy.

Overview of the Approach

For each particular strategy, from development to eventual drill when the strategy is well understood, the general approach for instruction is very similar.

FROM CONCEPTS AND STRATEGIES TO FACT MASTERY

Make Strategies Explicit in the Classroom

As has been discussed, your students will develop strategies as they solve word problems or as they investigate a category of facts you present. When a student suggests a new strategy, be certain that everyone else in the room understands how it is used. Suppose that Helen explains how she figured out 3 × 7 by starting with double 7 (14) and then adding 7 more. She knew that 6 more onto 14 is 20 and one more is 21. You can ask another student to explain what Helen just shared. This requires students to attend to ideas that come from their classmates. Now explore with the class to see what other facts would work with Helen's strategy. This discussion may go in a variety of directions. Some may notice that all of the facts with a 3 in them will work. Others may say that you can always add one more set on if you know the smaller fact. For example, for 6 × 8 you can start with 5 × 8 and add 8.

Don't expect to have a strategy introduced and understood with just one word problem or one exposure such as this. Try on several successive days problems in which the same type of strategy might be used. Children need lots of opportunities to make a strategy their own. Many children will simply not be ready to use an idea the first few days, and then all of a sudden something will click and a useful idea will be theirs.

It is a good idea to write new strategies on the board or make a poster of strategies students develop. Give the strategies names that make sense. (*Double and add one more set. Helen's idea. Use with 3s.* Include an example.)

No student should be forced to adopt someone else's strategy, but every student should be required to understand strategies that are brought to the discussion.

Drill Established Strategies

When you are comfortable that children are able to use a strategy without recourse to physical models and that they are beginning to use it mentally, it is time to drill it. You might have as many as ten different activities for each strategy or group of facts. File folder or boxed activities can be used by children individually, in pairs, or even in small groups. With a large number of activities, children can work on strategies they understand and on the facts that they need the most.

Flash cards are among the most useful approaches to fact strategy practice. For each strategy, make several sets of flash cards using all of the facts that fit that strategy. On the cards, you can label the strategy or use drawings or cues to remind the children of the strategy. Examples appear throughout the chapter.

Other activities involve the use of special dice made from wooden cubes or foam rubber, teacher-made spinners, matching activities where a helping fact or a relationship is matched with the new fact being learned, and games of all sorts. A game or drill suggested for one strategy can usually be adapted to another.

Individualize

To some extent, you want to individualize drills in such a way that students are using their preferred strategy in the drills. This is not as difficult as it may seem at first.

Different students will likely invent or adopt different strategies for the same collection of facts. For example, there are several methods or strategies that use 10 when adding 8 or 9. Therefore, a drill that includes all of the addition facts with an 8 or a 9 can accommodate any child who has a strategy for that collection. Two children can be playing a spinner drill game, each using different strategies.

It is imperative that you listen to your students. Keep track of what strategies different students are using. This will help you occasionally create groups of students that can all benefit from the same drills. This will also help you know which students have yet to develop an efficient strategy for one or more collection of facts. If you are not sure who knows what facts, gather small groups of students to take a diagnostic test, a simple fact test with facts mixed randomly. Explain that you want them to first answer only those facts that they "know" without any counting. Then they should go back and attempt the unknown facts. Listen to find out how they approach these strategies.

Practice Strategy Selection

After children have worked on two or three strategies, strategy selection drills are very important. These can be conducted quickly with the full class or a group, or independent games and activities can be prepared. Examples are described toward the end of the chapter.

Strategies for Addition Facts

The strategies for addition facts are directly related to one or more number relationships. In Chapter 2, numerous activities were suggested to develop these relationships. When the class is working on addition facts, the number relationship activities can and should be included with those described here. The teaching task is to help children connect these number relationships to the basic facts.

One-More-Than and Two-More-Than Facts

Each of the 36 facts highlighted in the chart has at least one addend of 1 or 2. These facts are a direct application of the one-more-than and two-more-than relationships.

Join or part-part-whole problems in which one of the addends is a 1 or a 2 are easy to make up. For example, *When Tommy was at the circus, he saw 8 clowns come out in a little car. Then 2 more clowns came out on bicycles. How many clowns did Tommy see in all?* Ask different students to explain how they got the answer of 10. Some will count on from 8. Some may still need to count 8 and 2 and then count all. Others will say they knew that 2 more than 8 is 10. The last response gives you an opportunity to talk about facts where you can use the two-more-than idea.

+	0	1	2	3	4	5	6	7	8	9
0		1	2							
1	1	2	3	4	5	6	7	8	9	10
2	2	3	4	5	6	7	8	9	10	11
3		4	5							
4		5	6							
5		6	7							
6		7	8							
7		8	9							
8		9	10							
9		10	11							

The different responses will provide you with a lot of information about students' number sense. As students are ready to use the two-more-than idea without counting all, they can begin to practice with activities such as the following.

One-/Two-More-Than Dice

Make a die labeled +1, +2, +1, +2, "one more," and "two more." Use with another die labeled 4, 5, 6, 7, 8, and 9. After each roll of the dice, children should say the complete fact: "Four and two is six."

One-/Two-More-Than Match

In a matching activity, children can begin with a number, match that with the one that is two more, and then connect that with the corresponding basic fact.

Lotto for +1/+2

A lotto-type board can be made on a file folder. Small fact cards can be matched to the numbers on the board. The back of each fact card can have a small answer number to use as a check.

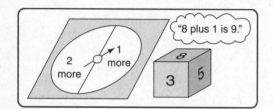

Figure 4.1 illustrates some of these activities and shows several possibilities for flash cards. Notice that activities such as the dice or spinner games and the lotto-type activity can be modified for almost all of the strategies in the chapter. These are not repeated for each strategy.

Facts with Zero

Nineteen facts have zero as one of the addends. Though such problems are generally easy, some children overgeneralize the idea that answers to addition are bigger. Word problems involving zero will be especially helpful. In the discussion, use drawings that show two parts with one part empty.

+	0	1	2	3	4	5	6	7	8	9
0	0	1	2	3	4	5	6	7	8	9
1	1									
2	2									
3	3									
4	4									
5	5									
6	6									
7	7									
8	8									
9	9									

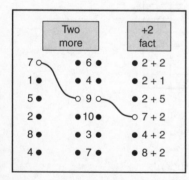

FIGURE 4.1 • • • • • • • • • • • • • • • • •

One-more and two-more facts.

What's Alike? Zero Facts

Write about ten zero facts on the board, some with the zero first and some with the zero second. Discuss how all of these facts are alike. Have children use counters and a part-part-whole mat to model the facts at their seats.

Chapter **4**   HELPING CHILDREN MASTER THE BASIC FACTS

Doubles

There are only ten doubles facts from 0 + 0 to 9 + 9, as shown here. These ten facts are relatively easy to learn and become a powerful way to learn the near-doubles (addends one apart). Some children use them as anchors for other facts as well.

+	0	1	2	3	4	5	6	7	8	9
0	0									
1		2								
2			4							
3				6						
4					8					
5						10				
6							12			
7								14		
8									16	
9										18

ACTIVITY 4.5

Double Images

Have students make picture cards for each of the doubles, and include the basic fact on the card as shown in Figure 4.2.

Word problems can focus on pairs of like addends. *Alex and Zack each found 7 seashells at the beach. How many did they find together?*

ACTIVITY 4.6

Calculator Doubles

Use the calculator and enter the "double maker" (2 ⊠ ⊟). Let one child say, for example, "Seven plus seven." The child with the calculator should press 7, try to give the double (14), and then press ⊟ to see the correct double on the display. (Note that the calculator is also a good way to practice +1 and +2 facts.)

Near-Doubles

Near-doubles are also called the "doubles-plus-one" facts and include all combinations where one addend is one more than the other. The strategy is to double the

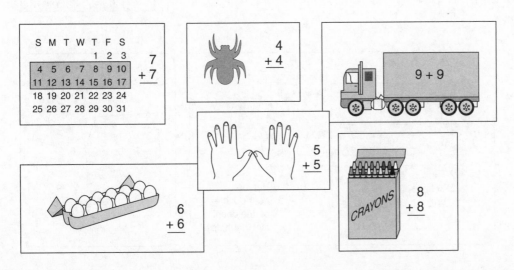

FIGURE 4.2

Doubles facts.

smaller number and add 1. Be sure students know the doubles before you focus on this strategy.

To introduce the strategy to the class, write about ten near-doubles facts on the board. Use vertical and horizontal formats, and vary which addend is the smaller.

Have students work independently to write the answers. Then discuss their ideas for "good" (that is, efficient) methods of answering these facts. Some may double the smaller number and add one and others may double the larger and subtract. If no one uses a near-double strategy, write the corresponding doubles for some of the facts and ask how these facts could help.

Before using the following activity or the two shown in Figure 4.3, be sure to try word problems involving near-doubles. The discussion will give you a good idea of who is ready to drill this strategy.

+	0	1	2	3	4	5	6	7	8	9
0		1								
1	1		3							
2		3		5						
3			5		7					
4				7		9				
5					9		11			
6						11		13		
7							13		15	
8								15		17
9									17	

ACTIVITY 4.7

Double Dice Plus One

Roll a single die with numerals or dot sets and say the complete double-plus-one fact. That is, for 7, students should say, "Seven plus eight is fifteen."

Make-Ten Facts

These facts all have at least one addend of 8 or 9. One strategy for these facts is to build onto the 8 or 9 up to 10 and then add on the rest. For 6 + 8, start with 8, then 2 more makes 10, and that leaves 4 more for 14.

+	0	1	2	3	4	5	6	7	8	9
0										
1										10
2									10	11
3									11	12
4									12	13
5									13	14
6									14	15
7									15	16
8		10	11	12	13	14	15	16	17	
9		10	11	12	13	14	15	16	17	18

FIGURE 4.3 ••••••••
Near-doubles facts.

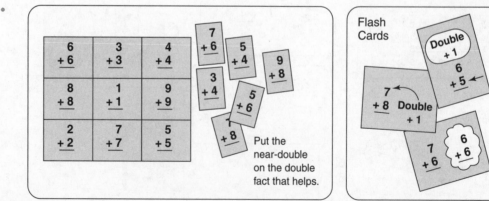

Before using this strategy, be sure that children have learned to think of the numbers 11 to 18 as 10 and some more. Many second- and third-grade children have not constructed this relationship. (Refer to "Relationships for Numbers 10 to 20" in Chapter 2.)

The next activity is a good way to introduce the make-ten strategy.

ACTIVITY 4.8

Make 10 on the Ten-Frame

Give students a mat with two ten-frames (see Figure 4.4). Flash cards are placed next to the ten-frames, or a fact can be given orally. The students should first model each number in the two ten-frames and then decide on the easiest way to show (without counting) what the total is. The obvious (but not the only) choice is to move counters into the frame showing either 8 or 9. Get students to explain what they did. Focus especially on the idea that 1 (or 2) can be taken from the other number and put with the 9 (or 8) to make 10. Then you have 10 and whatever is left.

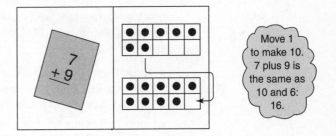

Provide a lot of time with the make-ten activity. Encourage discussion and exploration of "easy ways" to think about adding two numbers when one of them is 8 or 9. Perhaps discuss why this is not a useful idea for a fact such as 6 + 5 where neither number is near 10.

Note that children will have many other ways of using 10 to add with 8 or 9. For example, with the fact 9 + 5, some will add 10 + 5 and subtract 1. This is a perfectly good strategy, and it uses 10. You may want to give efficient strategies unique names determined by the children and discuss which ones seem especially useful.

When children seem to have the make-ten idea or a similar strategy, try the same activity without counters. Use the little ten-frame cards found in the Blackline Masters. Make a transparency set for the overhead. Show an 8 (or 9) card on the overhead. Place other cards beneath it one at a time. Suggest *mentally* "moving" two dots into the 8 ten-frame. Have students say orally what they are doing. For 8 + 4, they might say, "Take 2 from the 4 and put it with 8 to make 10. Then 10 and 2 left over is 12." The activity can be done independently with the little ten-frame cards.

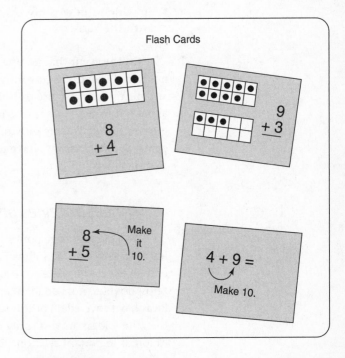

FIGURE 4.4

Make-ten facts.

> As has been noted, there is more than one way to efficiently use 10 in a strategy for facts involving 8 or 9. Imagine two or three children who have on the table a small ten-frame card for 9 so that all can see. One at a time, other cards are turned up and the students are to name the total of the two cards. How many different efficient methods involving 10 can you think of that can be accommodated by this simple activity?

A Generic Task

So far the suggested activities each focus on a particular strategy. In contrast, the next activity can be thought of as a generic task that can be posed for any fact. Use it as a possible introduction to strategies for a new collection, or use it after several strategies for a collection of facts have already been introduced. This activity gives every student the message that *their ideas are OK*. For those students who do not think of a good strategy, they will benefit from the discussion.

ACTIVITY 4.9

If You Didn't Know

Pose the following task to the class: If you did not know the answer to 8 + 5 (or any fact that you want students to think about), what are some really good ways you can use to get the answer? Explain that "really good" means that you don't have to count and you can do it in your head. Encourage students to come up with more than one way. Use a think-pair-share approach in which students discuss their ideas with a partner before they share them with the class.

In the event that no one comes up with a practical strategy you can offer one that a fictional friend shared with you—perhaps a student that you heard about in another school. You can also use this ploy to introduce a strategy that no one has thought about but which you think is possibly more efficient than those that have been suggested thus far. You are only offering ideas for consideration, not forcing them on students. You don't always have to rely on the students to come up with every strategy that they need.

Other Strategies and the Last Six Facts

To appreciate the power of strategies for fact learning, consider the following. We have discussed only five ideas or strategies (one or two more than, zeros, doubles, near-doubles, and make-ten), yet these ideas have covered 88 of the 100 addition facts! Further, these ideas are not really new but rather the application of important relationships. The 12 remaining facts are really only six facts and their respective turnarounds as shown on the chart.

+	0	1	2	3	4	5	6	7	8	9
0										
1										
2										
3						8	9	10		
4							10	11		
5				8				12		
6				9	10					
7				10	11	12				
8										
9										

Before trying to develop any particular strategies for these facts, spend several days with word problems where these facts are the addends. Listen carefully to the ideas that students use in figuring out the answers.

Doubles Plus Two, or Two-Apart Facts

Of the six remaining facts, three have addends that differ by 2: 3 + 5, 4 + 6, and 5 + 7. There are two possible relationships that might be useful here, each depending on knowledge of doubles. Some children find it easy to extend the idea of the near-doubles to double plus 2. For example, 4 + 6 is double 4 and 2 more. A different idea is to take 1 from the larger addend and give it to the smaller. Using this idea, the 5 + 3 fact is transformed into the double 4 fact—*double the number in between.*

Make-Ten Extended

Three of the six facts have 7 as one of the addends. The make-ten strategy is frequently extended to these facts as well. For 7 + 4, the idea is *7 and 3 more makes 10 and 1 left is 11*. You may decide to suggest this idea at the same time that you initially introduce the make-ten strategy. It is interesting to note that Japan, mainland China, Korea, and Taiwan all teach an addition strategy of building through 10 and do so in the first grade. Many U.S. second graders do not know what 10 plus any number is.

Counting On

Counting on is the most widely promoted strategy. It is generally taught as a strategy for all facts that have 1, 2, or 3 as one of the addends and, thus, includes the one- and two-more-than facts. For the fact 3 + 8, the child starts with 8 and counts three counts: *9, 10, 11*. There are several reasons you may want to downplay this approach. First, it is frequently applied to facts where it is not efficient, such as 8 + 5. It is difficult to explain to young children that they should count for some facts but not others. Second, it is much more procedural than conceptual. Finally, if other strategies are used, it is not necessary.

Ten-Frame Facts

If you have been keeping track, all of the remaining six facts have been covered by the discussion so far, with a few being touched by two different thought patterns. The ten-frame model is so valuable in seeing certain number relationships that these ideas cannot be passed by in thinking about facts. The ten-frame helps children learn the combinations that make 10. Ten-frames immediately model all of the facts from 5 + 1 to 5 + 5 and the respective turnarounds. Even 5 + 6, 5 + 7, and 5 + 8 are quickly seen as two fives and some more when depicted with these powerful models (see Figure 4.5).

+	0	1	2	3	4	5	6	7	8	9
0						5				
1						6				10
2						7			10	
3						8		10		
4						9	10			
5	5	6	7	8	9	10	11	12	13	14
6					10	11				
7				10		12				
8			10			13				
9		10				14				

A good idea might be to group the facts shown in the chart here and practice them using one or two ten-frames as a cue to the thought process.

The next two activities suggest the types of relationships that can be developed.

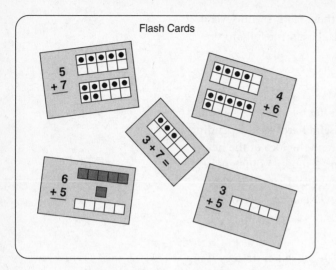

Flash Cards

6 and 4 is 10.

FIGURE 4.5

Ten-frame facts.

ACTIVITY 4.10

A Plus-Five Machine

Use the calculator to practice adding five. Enter ⊞ 5 ⊟. Next enter any number and say the sum of that number plus 5 before pressing ⊟. Continue with other numbers. (The ⊞ 5 ⊟ need not be repeated.) If a ten-frame is present, the potential for strengthening the 5 and 10 relationships is heightened.

Obviously, the calculator can be made into a machine for adding any number and is a powerful drill device..

ACTIVITY 4.11

Say the Ten Fact

Hold up a ten-frame card and have children say the "ten fact." For a card with 7 dots, the response is "seven and three is ten." Later, with a blank ten-frame drawn on the board, say a number less than 10. Children start with that number and complete the "ten fact." If you say, "four," they say, "four plus six is ten." Use the same activities in independent or small group modes.

Strategies for Subtraction Facts

Subtraction facts prove to be more difficult than addition. This is especially true when children have been taught subtraction through a "count-count-count" approach; for 13 – 5, *count* 13, *count* off 5, *count* what's left. There is little evidence that anyone who has mastered subtraction facts has found this approach helpful. Unfortunately, many sixth, seventh, and eighth graders are still counting.

Subtraction as Think-Addition

In Figure 4.6, subtraction is modeled in such a way that students are encouraged to think, "What goes with this part to make the total?" When done in this *think-addition* manner, the child uses known addition facts to produce the unknown quantity or part. (You might want to revisit the discussion of missing-part activities in Chapter 2 and part-part-whole subtraction concepts in Chapter 3.) If this important relationship between parts and wholes—between addition and subtraction—can be made, subtraction facts will be much easier. When children see 9 – 4, you want them to think spontaneously, "Four and *what* makes nine?" By contrast, observe a third-grade child who struggles with this fact. The idea of thinking addition never occurs. Instead, the child will begin to count either back from 9 or up from 4. The value of think-addition cannot be overstated.

Word problems that promote think-addition are those that sound like addition but have a missing addend: *join, initial part unknown; join, change unknown;* and *part-part-whole, part unknown* (see Chapter 3). Consider this problem: *Janice had 5 fish in her aquarium. Grandma gave her some more fish. Then she had 12 fish. How many fish did Grandma give Janice?* Notice that the action is join and, thus, suggests addition. There is a high probability that students will think *5 and how many more makes 12.* In the discussion in which you use problems such as this, your task is to connect this thought process with the subtraction fact, 12 – 5.

Subtraction Facts with Sums to 10

Think-addition is most immediately applicable to subtraction facts with sums of 10 or less. These are generally introduced with a goal of mastery in the first grade. Sixty-four of the 100 subtraction facts fall into this category.

If think-addition is to be used effectively, it is essential that addition facts be mastered first. Evidence suggests that children learn very few, if any, subtraction facts without first mastering the corresponding addition facts. In other words, mastery of 3 + 5 can be thought of as prerequisite knowledge for learning the facts 8 – 3 and 8 – 5.

Facts involving 0, 1, and 2 may be solved by different children in many different ways including think-addition. These facts are closely related to important basic number relationships. If children experience difficulties with facts such as 8 – 0 or 7 – 2, it would be a good idea to investigate their number concepts. A child who says that 7 – 0 is 6 may have overgeneralized that subtraction makes the number smaller.

Connecting Subtraction to Addition Knowledge

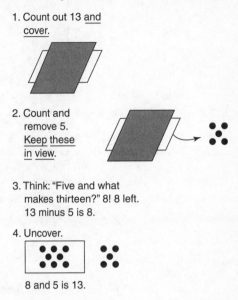

1. Count out 13 <u>and</u> <u>cover.</u>

2. Count and remove 5. <u>Keep these in view.</u>

3. Think: "Five and what makes thirteen?" 8! 8 left. 13 minus 5 is 8.

4. Uncover.

8 and 5 is 13.

FIGURE 4.6

Using a think-addition model for subtraction.

Assessment Note

Before working on mastery of subtraction facts, it is a good idea to check on students' mastery of addition facts and see if they are beginning to make connections between addition and subtraction. Prepare a drill by writing about 20 facts on a transparency that you will show to students one fact at a time. The 20 facts should be made of 10 pairs—a subtraction fact and the corresponding addition fact. For example, if you have 9 – 4 in the list, include 4 + 5 elsewhere in the list. Have students number their papers 1 to 20. On the overhead show only one fact at a time for about 5 or 6 seconds. Students write the answers as you go. They may not go back to facts they missed. Keep the pace quick so that students will not have a chance to count on their fingers.

In an activity such as this, it is essential to explain that you are simply trying to find out what they know so that you can help them. This is not a test or quiz. They should do their best to write what they think the answers are without counting.

If students know the addition facts but not the subtraction facts, more effort should be placed on developing the addition–subtraction connection. Use missing-part activities and join-type story problems in which the change amount

(continued)

is unknown. Discuss the way that both an addition sentence and a subtraction sentence can be written for these situations. Be very overt in your own modeling of think-addition. For 9 – 4 you might say, "I know that 4 and 5 make 9, so 9 minus 4 is 5." Draw a part-whole picture to go with this explanation.

This simple diagnostic exercise can be repeated at various times to see how well students are connecting addition and subtraction. This same approach can be used in a diagnostic interview format. After students have completed the problems, have them go back over those that they hesitated on, especially the subtraction facts. Ask them to think aloud about how they would get the answer. If they have answered an addition fact but not the corresponding subtraction fact, ask if they can think of any way that the addition fact could help with the subtraction fact. Remember, interview time is a time to gather information—not to teach.

The 36 "Hard" Subtraction Facts: Sums Greater Than 10

STOP Before reading further, look at the three subtraction facts shown here and try to reflect on what thought process you use to get the answers. Even if you "just know them," think about what a likely process might be.

$$\begin{array}{ccc} 14 & 12 & 15 \\ -\ 9 & -\ 6 & -\ 6 \end{array}$$

Many people will use a different strategy for each of these facts. For 14 – 9, it is easy to start with 9 and work up through 10: *9 and 1 more is 10, and 4 more makes 5.* For the 12 – 6 fact, it is quite common to hear "double 6," a think-addition approach. For the last fact, 15 – 6, 10 is used again but probably by working backward from 15—a take-away process: *Take away 5 to get 10, and 1 more leaves 9.* We could call these three approaches, respectively, build up through 10, think-addition, and back down through 10. Each of the remaining 36 facts with sums of 11 or more can be learned using one or more of these strategies. Figure 4.7 shows how these facts, in three overlapping groups, correspond to these three strategies. Keep in mind that these are not required strategies. Some children may use a think-addition method for all. Others may have a completely different strategy for some or all of these. The three approaches suggested here are based on ideas already developed: the relationship between addition and subtraction and the power of 10 as a reference point.

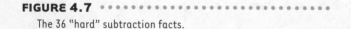

11	11	11	11	11	11	11	11
–2	–3	–4	–5	–6	–7	–8	–9

12	12	12	12	12	12	12
–3	–4	–5	–6	–7	–8	–9

13	13	13	13	13	13
–4	–5	–6	–7	–8	–9

14	14	14	14	14
–5	–6	–7	–8	–9

15	15	15	15
–6	–7	–8	–9

16	16	16
–7	–8	–9

17	17
–8	–9

18
–9

Build up through 10

Back down through 10

Think-addition (any fact)

FIGURE 4.7
The 36 "hard" subtraction facts.

Build Up Through 10
This group includes all facts where the part or subtracted number is either 8 or 9. Examples are 13 – 9 and 15 – 8.

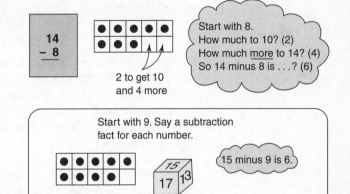

ACTIVITY 4.12

Build Up Through the Ten-Frame

On the board or overhead, draw a ten-frame with 9 dots. Discuss how you can build numbers between 11 and 18, starting with 9 in the ten-frame. Stress the idea of *one more to get to 10* and then the rest of the number. Repeat for a ten-frame showing 8. Next, with either the 8 or 9 ten-frame in view, call out numbers from 11 to 18, and have students explain how they can figure out the difference between that number and the one on the ten-frame. Later, use the same approach but show fact cards to connect this idea with the symbolic subtraction fact (see Figure 4.8).

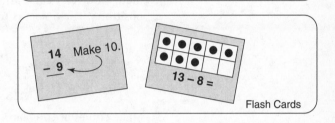

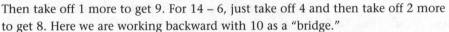

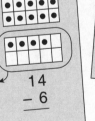

FIGURE 4.8 • • • • • • • • • • • • • • • • •

Build up through 10.

Back Down Through 10

Here is one strategy that is really take-away and not think-addition. It is useful for facts where the ones digit of the whole is close to the number being subtracted. For example, with 15 – 6, you start with the total of 15 and take off 5. That gets you down to 10. Then take off 1 more to get 9. For 14 – 6, just take off 4 and then take off 2 more to get 8. Here we are working backward with 10 as a "bridge."

EXPANDED LESSON

(pages 120–121)
A complete lesson plan based on "Build Up Through the Ten-Frame" can be found at the end of this chapter.

ACTIVITY 4.13

Back Down Through the Ten-Frame

Start with two ten-frames on the overhead, one filled completely and the other partially filled as in Figure 4.9. For 13, for example, discuss what is the easiest way to think about taking off 4 counters or 5 counters. Repeat with other numbers between 11 and 18. Have students write or say the corresponding fact.

Extend Think-Addition

Think-addition remains one of the most powerful ways to think about subtraction facts. When the think-addition concept of subtraction is well developed, many children will use that approach for all subtraction facts. (Notice that for division virtually everyone uses a think-multiplication approach. Why?)

What may be most important is to listen to children's thinking as they attempt to answer subtraction facts that they have not yet mastered. If they are not using one of the three ideas suggested here, it is a good bet that they are counting—an inefficient method.

The activities that follow are all of the think-addition variety. There is, of course, no reason why these activities could not be used for all of the subtraction facts. They need not be limited to the "hard facts."

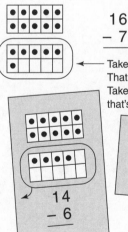

FIGURE 4.9 • • • • • • • • • • • • • • •

Back down through 10.

Missing-Number Cards

Show children, without explanation, families of numbers with the sum circled as in Figure 4.10(a). Ask why they think the numbers go together and
why one number is circled. When this number family idea is fairly well
understood, show some families with one number replaced by a question
mark, as in Figure 4.10(b), and ask what number is missing. When students
understand this activity, explain that you have made some missing-number
cards based on this idea. Each card has two of three numbers that go together
in the same way. Sometimes the circled number is missing (the sum), and
sometimes one of the other numbers is missing (a part). The cards can be
made both vertically and horizontally with the sum appearing in different
positions. The object is to name the missing number.

Missing-Number Worksheets

Make copies of the blank form found in the Blackline Masters to make a wide
variety of drill exercises. In a row of 13 "cards," put all of the combinations
from two families with different numbers missing, some parts and some
wholes. Put blanks in different positions. An example is shown in Figure 4.11.
After filling in numbers, run the sheet off, and have students fill in the missing numbers. Another idea is to group facts from one strategy or number relation or perhaps mix facts from two strategies on one page. Have students
write an addition fact and a subtraction fact to go with each missing-number
card. This is an important step because many children are able to give the
missing part in a family but do not connect this knowledge with subtraction.

FIGURE 4.10 • • • • • • • • • • • • •

Introducing missing-number cards.

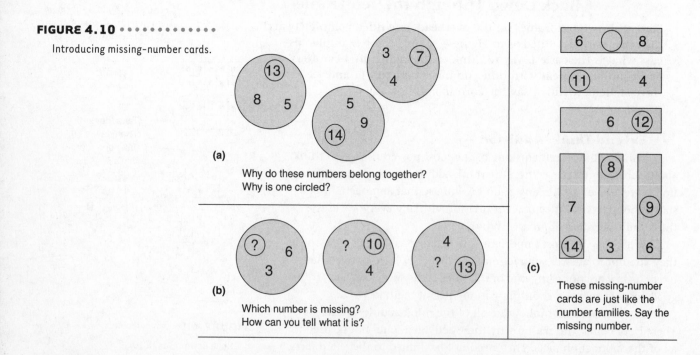

(a)

Why do these numbers belong together?
Why is one circled?

(b)

Which number is missing?
How can you tell what it is?

(c)

These missing-number
cards are just like the
number families. Say the
missing number.

FIGURE 4.11 • • • • • • •

Missing-part worksheets. The blank version can be used to fill in any sets of facts you wish to emphasize (see Blackline Masters).

Make-ten facts | Near-doubles | Two fact families (7, 8, 15) (4, 8, 12)

BLM 11

ACTIVITY 4.16

Find a Plus Fact to Help

Select a group of subtraction facts that you wish to practice. Divide a sheet of paper into small cards, about 10 or 12 to a sheet. For each subtraction fact, write the corresponding addition fact on one of the cards. Two subtraction facts can be related to each addition fact. Duplicate the sheet and have students cut the cards apart. Now write one of the subtraction facts on the board. Rather than call out answers, students find the addition fact that helps with the subtraction fact. On your signal, each student holds up the appropriate fact. For 12 – 4 or 12 – 8, the students would select 4 + 8. The same activity can be made into a matching card game.

Strategies for Multiplication Facts

Multiplication facts can also be mastered by relating new facts to existing knowledge.

It is imperative that students completely understand the commutative property (go back and review Figure 3.9, p. 85). For example, 2 × 8 is related to the addition fact double 8. But the same relationship also applies to 8 × 2 that many children think about as 2 + 2 + 2 + 2 + 2 + 2 + 2 + 2. Most of the fact strategies are more obvious with the factors in one order than in the other, but turnaround facts should always be learned together.

Of the five groups or strategies discussed next, the first four strategies are generally easier and cover 75 of the 100 multiplication facts. You are continually reminded that these strategies are suggestions, not rules, and that the most general approach with children is to have them discuss ways that *they* can use to think of facts easily.

Doubles

Facts that have 2 as a factor are equivalent to the addition doubles and should already be known by students who know their addition facts. The major problem is to realize that not only is 2 × 7 double 7, but so is 7 × 2. Try word problems where 2 is the number of sets. Later use problems where 2 is the size of the sets.

×	0	1	2	3	4	5	6	7	8	9
0			0							
1			2							
2	0	2	4	6	8	10	12	14	16	18
3			6							
4			8							
5			10							
6			12							
7			14							
8			16							
9			18							

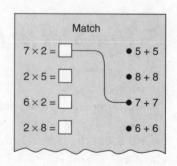

ACTIVITY 4.17

Calculator 2× Facts

Review the concept of doubles from addition. Play "Say the Double." You say a number, and the children say the double of that number. Use the calculator to practice doubles (press 2 ⊠ ═).

Make and use flash cards with the related addition fact or word *double* as a cue (see Figure 4.12).

Fives Facts

This group consists of all facts with 5 as the first or second factor, as shown here.

Practice counting by fives to at least 45. Connect counting by fives with rows of 5 dots. Point out that six rows is a model for 6 × 5, eight rows is 8 × 5, and so on.

×	0	1	2	3	4	5	6	7	8	9
0						0				
1						5				
2						10				
3						15				
4						20				
5	0	5	10	15	20	25	30	35	40	45
6						30				
7						35				
8						40				
9						45				

FIGURE 4.12 • • • • • • •

Multiplication doubles.

FIGURE 4.13 • • • • • • •

Fives facts.

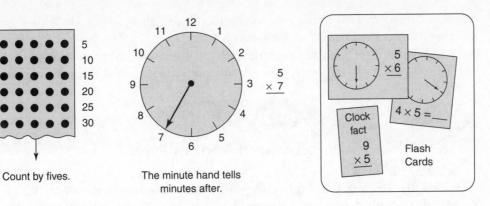

Count by fives.

The minute hand tells minutes after.

Flash Cards

ACTIVITY 4.18

Clock Facts

Focus on the minute hand of the clock. When it points to a number, how many minutes after the hour is it? Draw a large clock face, and point to numbers 1 to 9 in random order. Students respond with the minutes after. Now connect this idea to the multiplication facts with 5. Hold up a flash card, and then point to the number on the clock corresponding to the other factor. In this way, the fives facts become the "clock facts."

Include the clock idea on flash cards or to make matching activities (see Figure 4.13).

Zeros and Ones

Thirty-six facts have at least one factor that is either 0 or 1. These facts, though apparently easy, tend to get confused with "rules" that some children learned for addition. The fact $6 + 0$ stays the same, but 6×0 is always zero. The $1 + 4$ fact is a one-more idea, but 1×4 stays the same. The concepts behind these facts can be developed best through story problems. Above all else, avoid rules that sound arbitrary and without reason such as "Any number multiplied by zero is zero."

×	0	1	2	3	4	5	6	7	8	9
0	0	0	0	0	0	0	0	0	0	0
1	0	1	2	3	4	5	6	7	8	9
2	0	2								
3	0	3								
4	0	4								
5	0	5								
6	0	6								
7	0	7								
8	0	8								
9	0	9								

Nifty Nines

Facts with a factor of 9 include the largest products but can be among the easiest to learn. The table of nines facts includes some nice patterns that are fun to discover. Two of these patterns are useful for mastering the nines: (1) The tens digit of the product is always one less than the "other" factor (the one other than 9), and (2) the sum of the two digits in the product is

×	0	1	2	3	4	5	6	7	8	9
0										0
1										9
2										18
3										27
4										36
5										45
6										54
7										63
8										72
9	0	9	18	27	36	45	54	63	72	81

always 9. These two ideas can be used together to get any nine fact quickly. For 7 × 9, *1 less than 7 is 6, 6 and 3 make 9, so the answer is 63.*

Children are not likely to invent this strategy simply by solving word problems involving a factor of 9. Therefore, consider building a lesson around the following task.

ACTIVITY 4.19

Patterns in the Nines Facts

In column form, write the nines table on the board (9 × 1 = 9, 9 × 2 = 18, . . . , 9 × 9 = 81). The task is to find as many patterns as possible in the table. (Do not ask students to think of a strategy.) As you listen to the students work on this task, be sure that somewhere in the class the two patterns necessary for the strategy have been found. After discussing all the patterns, a follow-up task is to use the patterns to think of a clever way to figure out a nine fact if you didn't know it. (Note that even for students who know their nines facts, this remains a valid task.)

Once children have invented a strategy for the nines, practice activities such as those shown in Figure 4.14 are appropriate. Also consider word problems with a factor of 9 and check to see if the strategy is in use.

Warning: Although the nines strategy can be quite successful, it also can cause confusion. Because two separate rules are involved and a conceptual basis is not apparent, children may confuse the two rules or attempt to apply the idea to other facts. It is not, however, a "rule without reason." It is an idea based on a very interesting pattern that exists in the base-ten numeration system. One of the values of patterns in mathematics is that they help us do seemingly difficult things quite easily. The nifty-nine pattern illustrates clearly one of the values of pattern and regularity in mathematics.

An alternative strategy for the nines is almost as easy to use. Notice that 7 × 9 is the same as 7 × 10 less one set of 7, or 70 – 7. This can easily be modeled by displaying rows of 10 cubes, with the last one a different color, as in Figure 4.15. For students who can easily subtract 4 from 40, 5 from 50, and so on, this strategy may be preferable.

You might introduce this idea by showing a set of bars such as those in the figure with only the end cube a different color. After explaining that every bar has ten cubes, ask students if they can think of a good way to figure out how many are yellow.

Helping Facts

The chart shows the remaining 25 multiplication facts. It is worth pointing out to children that there are actually only 15 facts remaining to master because 20 of them consist of 10 pairs of turnarounds.

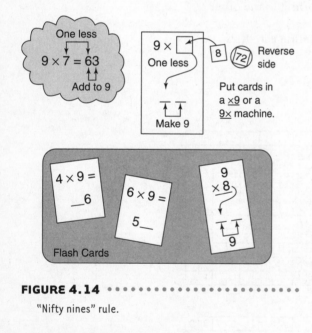

FIGURE 4.14 •

"Nifty nines" rule.

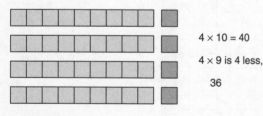

4 × 10 = 40

4 × 9 is 4 less,

36

FIGURE 4.15 • • • • • • • • • • • • • • • • • • •

Another way to think of the nines.

These 25 facts can be learned by relating each to an already known fact or *helping* fact. For example, 3 × 8 is connected to 2 × 8 (double 8 and 8 more). The 6 × 7 fact can be related to either 5 × 7 (5 sevens and 7 more) or to 3 × 7 (double 3 × 7). The helping fact must be known, and the ability to do the mental addition must also be there. For example, to go from 5 × 7 is 35 and then add 7 for 6 × 7, a student must be able to add 35 and 7. If you see finger counting at that stage, the idea of make-ten can be extended: 35 and 5 more is 40 and 2 left makes 42.

How to find a helping fact that is useful varies with different facts and sometimes depends on which factor you focus on. Figure 4.16 illustrates models for four overlapping groups of facts and the thought process associated with each.

The *double and double again* approach is applicable to all facts with 4 as one of the factors. Remind children that the idea works when 4 is the second factor as well as when it is the first. For 4 × 8, double 16 is also a difficult fact. Help children with this by noting, for example, that 15 + 15 is 30, 16 + 16 is two more, or 32. Adding 16 + 16 on paper defeats the purpose.

Double and one more set is a way to think of facts with one factor of 3. With an array or a set picture, the double part can be circled, and it is clear that there is one more set. Two facts in this group involve difficult mental additions.

If either factor is even, a *half then double* approach can be used. Select the even factor, and cut it in half. If the smaller fact is known, that product is doubled to get the new fact. For 6 × 7, half of 6 is 3. 3 times 7 is 21. Double 21 is 42. For 8 × 7, the double of 28 may be hard, but it remains an effective approach to that traditionally hard fact. (Double 25 is 50 + 2 times 3 is 56.)

Many children prefer to go to a fact that is "close" and then *add one more set* to this known fact. For example, think of 6 × 7 as 6 sevens. Five sevens is close: That's 35. Six sevens is one more seven, or 42. When using 5 × 8 to help with 6 × 8, the set language "6 eights" is very helpful in remembering to add 8 more and not 6 more. Admittedly difficult, this approach is used by many children, and it becomes the best way to think of one or two particularly difficult facts. "What is seven times eight? Oh, that's 49 and 7 more—56." The process can become almost automatic.

The relationships between easy and hard facts are fertile ground for good problem-based tasks. Rather than tell students what helping facts to use and how to use them, select a fact from one of the strategies. Use the same formulation as in Activity 4.9, "If You Didn't Know" (p. 104). For example, "If you didn't know what 6 × 8 is, how could you

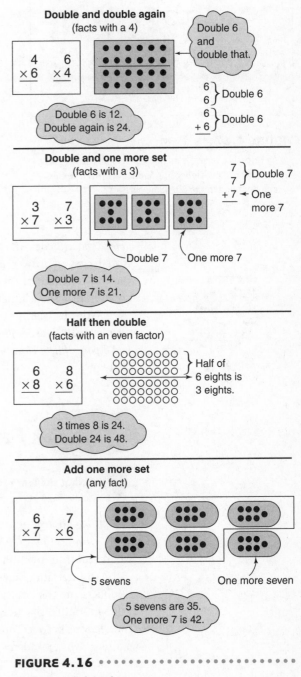

FIGURE 4.16 • • • • • • • • • • • • • • • • •
Finding a helping fact.

STRATEGIES FOR MULTIPLICATION FACTS

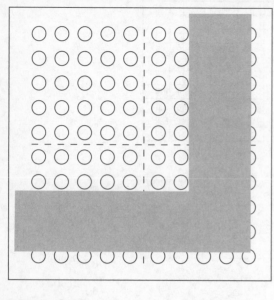

FIGURE 4.17 ●

An array is a useful model for developing strategies for the hard multiplication facts. An array like this can be found in the Blackline Masters.

BLM 12

figure it out by using something that you do know?" Students should be challenged to find as many as possible interesting and useful ways to answer a hard multiplication fact.

> **Go through each of the 20 "hard facts" and see how many of the strategies in Figure 4.16 you can use for each one. Many children will not think in terms of the arrays shown but rather will use a symbolic representation. For example, for 6 × 8 they might think of a vertical sum of six 8s or eight 6s. Try to see how this type of representation works for the ideas in Figure 4.16.**

Since arrays are a powerful thinking tool for these strategies, provide students with copies of the ten-by-ten dot array (Figure 4.17, also in Blackline Masters). A tagboard *L* is used to outline specific product arrays. The lines in the array make counting the dots easier and often suggest the use of the easier fives facts as helpers. For example, 7 × 7 is 5 × 7 plus double 7 ⟶ 35 + 14.

Don't forget to use word problems as a vehicle for developing these harder facts. Consider this problem: *Connie bundled up all of her old crayons into bags of 7 crayons each. She was able to make 8 bags with 3 crayons left over. How many crayons did she have?* As students work to get an answer, many of the strategies just discussed are possible. Plus there is the added benefit of the assessment value gained by listening to the methods different children bring to a situation that does not look like a fact drill.

Word problems can also be structured to prompt a strategy. *Carlos and Jose kept their baseball cards in albums with 6 cards on each page. Carlos had 4 pages filled, and Jose had 8 pages filled. How many cards did each boy have?* (Do you see the half-then-double strategy?)

⋮ *Division Facts and "Near Facts"*

> **STOP** What thought process do you use to recall facts such as 48 ÷ 6 or 36 ÷ 9?

If we are trying to think of 36 ÷ 9, we tend to think, "Nine times what is thirty-six?" For most, 42 ÷ 6 is not a separate fact but is closely tied to 6 × 7. (Would it not be wonderful if subtraction were so closely related to addition? It can be!)

An interesting question to ask is, "When children are working on a page of division facts, are they practicing division or multiplication?" There is undoubtedly some value in limited practice of division facts. However, mastery of multiplication facts and connections between multiplication and division are the key elements of division fact mastery. Word problems continue to be a key vehicle to create this connection.

Exercises such as 50 ÷ 6 might be called "near facts." Divisions that do not come out evenly are much more prevalent in computations and in real situations than division facts or division without remainders. To determine the answer to 50 ÷ 6, most people run through a short sequence of the multiplication facts, comparing each product to 50: "6 times 7 (low), 6 times 8 (close), 6 times 9 (high). Must be 8. That's 48 and 2 left over." This process can and should be drilled. That is, children should be able to do problems with one-digit divisors and one-digit answers plus remainders mentally and with reasonable speed.

ACTIVITY 4.20

How Close Can You Get?

To practice "near facts," try this exercise. As illustrated, the idea is to find the one-digit factor that makes the product as close as possible to the target without going over. Help children develop the process of going through the multiplication facts that was just described. This can be a drill with the full class by preparing a list for the overhead, or it can be a worksheet activity.

> Find the largest factor without going over the target number.

$4 \times \square \longrightarrow 23, \square$ left over
$7 \times \square \longrightarrow 52, \square$ left over
$6 \times \square \longrightarrow 27, \square$ left over
$9 \times \square \longrightarrow 60, \square$ left over

Effective Drill

There is little doubt that strategy development and general number sense (number relationships and operation meanings) are the best contributors to fact mastery. Drill in the absence of these factors has repeatedly been demonstrated as ineffective. However, the positive value of drill should not be completely ignored. Drill of nearly any mental activity strengthens memory and retrieval capabilities (Ashcraft & Christy, 1995).

When and How to Drill

Teachers and parents hold tenaciously to their belief in drill. Undoubtedly, far too much time is devoted to inefficient drill of basic facts, often with a negative impact on students' attitudes toward mathematics and beliefs in their abilities.

Avoid Inefficient Drill

Adopt this simple rule and stick with it: *Do not subject any student to fact drills unless the student has developed an efficient strategy for the facts included in the drill.* Drill can strengthen strategies with which students feel comfortable—ones they "own"—and will help to make these strategies increasingly automatic. Therefore, drill of strategies such as those discussed in this chapter will allow students to use them with increased efficiency, even to the point of recalling the fact without being conscious of using a strategy. Counting on fingers and making marks on paper can never result in automatic fact recall regardless of the amount of drill. Drill without an efficient strategy present offers no assistance.

Individualize Drill

It is unreasonable to expect every student in your class to develop and be comfortable with the same strategies. As you have seen, there are multiple paths to most facts. Different students will bring different number tools to the task and will develop strategies at different rates. This means that there are few drills that are likely to be efficient for a full class at any given time. That is why so many of the suggested activities are designed as flash cards, games, or simple repeatable worksheets. By creating a large number of drill activities promoting different strategies and addressing different collections of facts, it is not at all unreasonable to direct students to activities that are most useful for them.

By third grade, students can help you with this individualization process by keeping their own chart of facts mastered and facts yet to be mastered. If games and drill activities are well labeled, students can even select the activities they are ready to work on.

Drill for Strategy Retrieval

When a fact is presented without a reminder of a strategy, students need to select from their memory the mental method that works best for that fact. Drills can be devised that help students look at a fact and recall a strategy that works. The next two activities suggest how this might be done.

ACTIVITY 4.21

Circle the Strategy

On a worksheet, have students circle the facts that belong to a strategy they have been working on and answer only those facts. The same approach can be used with two or three strategies on one sheet.

ACTIVITY 4.22

Sort Them as You Do Them

Mix ordinary flash cards from two or more strategies into a single packet. Prepare simple pictures or labels for the strategies in the packet. Students first match a card with a strategy and then use the strategy to answer that fact.

Both of these activities can be tailored to match the strategies that an individual student is using and working on. Talk with the students, and have them help you put the activity together.

Technology Note

There are literally hundreds of software programs that offer drill of basic facts. Nearly all fact programs offer games or exercises at various difficulty levels. Unfortunately, there do not seem to be any programs that organize facts the way they are organized in this chapter. It should be clear that computerized fact practice should be used only after students have developed some strategies.

Many commercial programs automatically keep performance records of individual students. Almost all provide immediate feedback and many provide options for the number of problems, the size of the numbers, and whether or not to time the student.

What About Timed Tests?

Consider the following:

> Teachers who use timed tests believe that the tests help children learn basic facts. This makes no instructional sense. Children who perform well under time pressure display their skills. Children who have difficulty with skills, or who work more slowly, run the risk of reinforcing wrong learning under pressure. In addition, children can become fearful and negative toward their math learning. (Burns, 2000, p. 157)

Think about this quotation whenever you are tempted to give a timed test. Reasoning and pattern searching are never facilitated by restricting time. Some children simply cannot work well under pressure or in situations that provoke stress.

Although speed may encourage children to memorize facts, it is effective only for students who are goal oriented and who can perform in pressure situations. The pressure of speed can be debilitating and provides no positive benefits.

The value of speed drills or timed tests as a learning tool can be summed up as follows:

Timed tests

- Cannot promote reasoned approaches to fact mastery
- Will produce few long-lasting results
- Reward few
- Punish many
- Should generally be avoided

Assessment Note

If there is any defensible purpose for a timed test of basic facts it may be for diagnosis—to determine which combinations are mastered and which remain to be learned. Even for diagnostic purposes there is little reason for a timed test more than once every couple of months.

EXPANDED LESSON

Build Up Through the Ten-Frame

Based on: Activity 4.12, p. 109

GRADE LEVEL: Second grade or early third grade.

MATHEMATICS GOALS

- To continue development of ten-structured thinking: When finding the difference between a number less than 10 and one in the teens, it is useful to think of that distance in two parts—from the smaller number up to 10 and from 10 to the larger number.
- To utilize 10 in some way as a strategy for subtraction facts in which the whole is greater than 10 and the subtrahend is either 8 or 9.

THINKING ABOUT THE STUDENTS

Students should have mastered all of the addition facts for sums to 10. They should be exploring the relationship between addition and subtraction through story problems—especially join problems with change unknown. They should have discussed and been familiar with the idea that a number in the teens is 10 and some more; for example, 15 is 10 and 5.

MATERIALS AND PREPARATION

No materials other than a chalk board are required. Students will write in their journals or on plain paper.

lesson

BEFORE

Brainstorm

- On the board or overhead, draw a ten-frame with 9 dots.
- Ask: *How many dots? How many more dots do I need to draw to have 14?* (Write 14 on the board.) Have one or more students explain their reasoning. Repeat the question with 17, 12, and 15 dots.
- If students' explanations involve first filling in one dot on the ten-frame and then adding the rest to make the required number, have them come to the board to explain again by drawing the required dots.
- Change the ten-frame to 8 dots. Ask: *How many more dots do I need to have 13?* (Write 13 on the board.) Repeat with other numbers in the teens. Again, look for and focus on explanations that involve the use of 10.

The Task

- Draw two prominent ten-frames side by side on the board, one with 8 dots and one with 9 dots. Beneath write the following five facts:

$$
\begin{array}{ccccc}
13 & 17 & 11 & 15 & 13 \\
-\,9 & -\,9 & -\,8 & -\,9 & -\,8 \\
\end{array}
$$

- The task is for students to describe a good way to think about subtracting 14 − 8 that makes getting the answer easy—no counting, something they can do in their heads.
- Students should use the same idea to answer each of the five subtraction problems.

DURING

- Students may have difficulty articulating an idea. Look for students who are not writing anything and ask them what the answer to 14 – 9 is. Ask: *How do you know? What did you think about to get the answer?* Help students use what they say to write down an idea. Do *not* push students to use an add-up-through-ten strategy or even any approach that involves 10. Allow students to use their own ideas.
- Some students may be helped by simply focusing their attention on the two ten-frames and reminding them of the discussion in the first part of the lesson.
- Identify students who you will have share their ideas.

AFTER

- Ask several students to share their ideas. Include several different ideas. Be sure to find at least one or two students who worked up through 10 that you identified in the during stage.
- After a student shares how he or she worked up through 10, ask all students to try that strategy on 15 – 8. Also, have students try other strategies that are suggested when the strategy seems to be efficient (does not involve counting). Some students may work down through 10 and others may use a known fact as a helper.

ASSESSMENT NOTES

- Look for students who count on or back and do not use 10 at all. These students will need further help with their understanding of the teen numbers.
- Some students may use 10 but not efficiently. They may have to count by ones for one or both of the two parts. These students need help with the other part of 10 and also with understanding the teens as 10 and some more.
- For students having difficulty, check to see if they know the corresponding addition facts (14 – 9 and 9 + 5).

- -

next steps

- Students not effectively using 10 may benefit from building a teen number on a pair of ten-frames using counters. Present the numbers in random order. Discuss easy ways to put the counters on the two ten-frames without having to count.
- These same students may benefit from ten-frame flash cards and also from telling the total dots on two ten-frames when one of them is an 8 or 9. (See Activity 4.8, p. 103.)

- Make flash cards for facts involving –8 or –9 with a single ten-frame showing 8 or 9 dots accordingly. (See Figure 4.8 on p. 109.) Have students practice using these flash cards or plain flash cards for the same facts. Be sure that students using the flash cards have an efficient strategy and are not counting to get answers.

BASE-TEN CONCEPTS AND PLACE VALUE

A complete understanding of place value, including decimal numeration, develops over the full K–6 grade span. However, the most critical period in this development occurs in grades K to 3. In grades K
and 1 children count and are exposed to patterns in the numbers to 100. Most importantly, they begin to think about groups of
ten things as a unit. By second grade, these
initial ideas of patterns and groups of ten
are formally connected to our place-value
system of numeration. This is no small
achievement! Ample time should be given
to this development. In grade 3 the system
is extended to three or four digits.

As a significant part of this development in grades 2 and 3, students should
begin to work at putting numbers together
and taking them apart in a wide variety of
ways as they solve addition and subtraction problems with two- and three-digit
numbers. Rather than learn traditional
algorithms, children's struggles with the
invention of their own methods of computation will both enhance their understanding of place value and provide a firm
foundation for flexible methods of computation. Computation and place-value
development need not be entirely separated as they have been traditionally.

big ideas

1 Sets of ten (and tens of tens) can be perceived as single
entities. These sets can then be counted and used as
a means of describing quantities. For example, three
sets of ten and two singles is a base-ten method of
describing 32 single objects. This is the major principle of
base-ten numeration.

2 The positions of digits in numbers determine what they represent—which size
group they count. This is the major principle of *place-value* numeration.

3 There are patterns to the way that numbers are formed. For example, each
decade has a symbolic pattern reflective of the 1-to-9 sequence.

4 The groupings of ones, tens, and hundreds can be taken apart in different
ways. For example, 256 can be 1 hundred, 14 tens, and 16 ones. Taking numbers apart and recombining them in flexible ways is a significant skill for
computation.

5 "Really big" numbers are best understood in terms of familiar real-world referents. It is difficult to conceptualize quantities as large as 1000 or more.
However, the number of people that will fill the local sports arena is, for
example, a meaningful concept for those who have experienced that crowd.

Children's Pre-Base-Ten Concepts

It is tempting to think that children know a lot about numbers with two digits (10 to 99) even as early as kindergarten. After all, most kindergartners can and should learn to count to 100 and count out sets of things with as many as 20 or 30 objects. They do daily calendar activities, count children in the room, turn to specified page numbers in their books, and so on. However, their understanding is quite different from yours. It is based on a one-more-than or count-by-ones approach to quantity.

Children's Pre-Base-Ten View of Number

Ask first- or second-grade children to count out 53 tiles, and most will be able to do so or will make only careless errors. It is a tedious but not formidable task. If you watch closely, you will note that the children count out the tiles one at a time and put them into the pile with no use of any type of grouping. Have the children write the number that tells how many tiles they just counted. Most children will be able to write it. Some may write "35" instead of "53," a simple reversal.

So far, so good. Now ask the children to write the number that is 10 more than the number they just wrote. Most will begin to count, probably starting from 53. When counting on from 53, they find it necessary to keep track of the counts, probably on their fingers. Many, if not most, children in the first and early second grades will not be successful at this task, and almost none will know immediately that 10 more is 63. Asking for the number that is 10 less is even more problematic.

Finally, show a large collection of cards, each with a ten-frame drawn on it. Explain that the cards each have ten spaces and that each will hold ten tiles. Demonstrate putting tiles on the cards by filling up one of the ten-frames with tiles. Now ask, "How many cards like this do you think it will take if we want to put all of these tiles [the 53 counted out] on the cards?" A response of "53" is not unusual. Other children will say they do not know, and a few will try to put the tiles on the cards to figure it out.

Assessment Note

The questions outlined in the last three paragraphs form a very nice interview protocol that you can use with your students in grades K to 2. Additional assessment tasks are provided throughout this chapter. These simple questions will give you a fair appreciation for how difficult it is for children to think in terms of tens and ones.

Quantity Tied to Counts by Ones

The children just described know that there are 53 tiles "because I counted them." Writing the number and saying the number are usually done correctly, but their understanding of 53 derives from and is connected to the count by ones.

Children do not easily or quickly develop a meaningful use of groups of ten to represent quantities.

With minimal instruction, children can tell you that in the numeral 53, the 5 is in the tens place or that there are "3 ones." However, it is likely that this is simply a naming of the positions with little understanding. If children have been exposed to base-ten materials, they may name a rod of ten as a "ten" and a small cube as a "one." These same children, however, may not be readily able to tell how many ones are required to make a ten. It is easy to attach words to both materials and groups without realizing what the materials or symbols represent.

Children do know that 53 is "a lot" and that it's more than 47 (because you count past 47 to get to 53). They think of the "53" that they write as a single numeral. They do not know that the 5 represents five groups of ten things and the 3 three single things (Fuson et al., 1997; Ross, 1989). Fuson and her colleagues refer to children's pre-base-ten understanding of number as "unitary." That is, there are no groupings of ten, even though a two-digit number is associated with the quantity. They rely on unitary counts to understand quantities.

Goals of Place-Value Development

Place-value understanding requires an integration of new and difficult-to-construct concepts of grouping by tens (the base-ten concept) with procedural knowledge of how groups are recorded in our place-value scheme, how numbers are written, and how they are spoken.

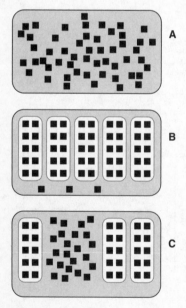

A **Unitary**
or count-by-ones
view

B **Base-ten**
or groups-of-ten
view

C **Equivalent**
or nonstandard
base-ten view

FIGURE 5.1 •

Three equivalent groupings of 53 objects. Group A is 53 because "I counted them (by ones)." Group B has 5 tens and 3 more. Group C is the same as B, but now some groups are broken into singles.

Integration of Base-Ten Groupings with Counts by Ones

Recognizing that children can count out a set of 53, we want to help them see that making groupings of tens and leftovers is a way of counting that same quantity. Each of the groups in Figure 5.1 has 53 tiles. We want children to construct the idea that all of these are the same and that the sameness is clearly evident by virtue of the groupings of tens.

There is a subtle yet profound difference between two groups of children: those who know that group B is 53 because they understand the idea that 5 groups of 10 and 3 more is the same amount as 53 counted by ones and those who simply say, "It's 53," because they have been told that when things are grouped this way, it's called 53. The latter children may not be sure how many they will get if they count the tiles in set B by ones or if the groups were "ungrouped" how many there would then be. The children who understand will see no need to count set B by ones. They understand the "fifty-threeness" of sets A and B to be the same.

Have a child make 5 bars of ten Unifix cubes. Add three more cubes and ask, "How many cubes do we have all together?" A few children will say there are 8, counting each of the bars as one. These children are not ready to see a group of cubes as simultaneously ten things and one thing.

Many children will count each of the cubes by ones, even though they've made the bars themselves. They recognize more than one in a group but are not ready to utilize the groupings to facilitate their own counting.

Other children will count by tens and respond correctly with "fifty-three." Ask these children to break all of the bars apart and make a large pile of cubes. Now repeat the question: "How many cubes are there in the pile?" Children who begin counting the cubes (this is not at all unusual) fail to see an equivalence between the single cubes and the grouped cubes. It is important not to be fooled by students who can name a quantity shown as groups of ten and singles as they are typically pictured in standard textbooks. Correct responses often hide children's rather shallow understanding.

Recognition of the equivalence of groups B and C is another step in children's conceptual development. Groupings with fewer than the maximum number of tens can be referred to as *equivalent groupings* or *equivalent representations*. Understanding the equivalence of B and C indicates that grouping by tens is not just a rule that is followed but that any grouping by tens, including all or some of the singles, can help tell how many. Many computational techniques are based on equivalent representations of numbers.

The Role of Counting in Constructing Base-Ten Ideas

Counting plays a key role in constructing base-ten ideas about quantity and connecting these concepts to symbols and oral names for numbers.

Children can count sets such as those in Figure 5.1 in three different ways. Each way helps children think about the quantities in a different way.

1. *Counting by ones.* This is the method children have to begin with. Initially, a count by ones is the only way they are able to name a quantity or "tell how many." All three of the sets in Figure 5.1 can be counted by ones. Before base-ten ideas develop, this is the only way children can be convinced that all three sets are the same.

2. *Counting by groups and singles.* In group B in Figure 5.1, counting by groups and singles would go like this: "One, two, three, four, five bunches of 10, and one, two, three singles." Consider how novel this method would be for a child who had never thought about counting a group of things as a single item. Also notice how this counting does not tell directly how many items there are. This counting must be coordinated with a count by ones before it can be a means of telling "how many."

3. *Counting by tens and ones.* This is the way adults would probably count group B and perhaps group C: "Ten, twenty, thirty, forty, fifty, fifty-one, fifty-two, fifty-three." While this count ends by saying the number that is there, it is not as explicit as the

second method in counting the number of groups. Nor will it convey a personal understanding of "how many" unless it is coordinated with the more meaningful count by ones.

Regardless of the specific activity that you may be doing with children, helping them integrate the grouping-by-tens concept with what they know about number from counting by ones should be your foremost objective. Children should frequently have the opportunity to count sets of objects in several ways. If first counted by ones, the question might be, "What will happen if we count these by groups and singles (or by tens and ones)?" If a set has been grouped into tens and singles and counted accordingly, "How can we be really certain that there are 53 things here?" or "What do you think we will get if we count by ones?" It is inadequate to *tell* children that these counts will all be the same. That is a relationship they must construct themselves through reflective thought, not because the teacher says it works that way.

Integration of Groupings with Words

The way we say a number such as "fifty-three" must also be connected with the grouping-by-tens concept. The counting methods provide a connecting mechanism. The count by tens and ones results in saying the number of groups and singles separately: "five tens and three." This is an acceptable, albeit nonstandard, way of naming this quantity. Saying the number of tens and singles separately in this fashion can be called *base-ten language* for a number. Children can associate the base-ten language with the usual language: "five tens and three—fifty-three."

Notice that there are several variations of the base-ten language for 53—5 tens and 3; 5 tens and 3 ones; 5 groups of 10 and 3 leftovers; 5 tens and 3 singles; and so on. Each may be used interchangeably with the standard name, "fifty-three."

It can easily be argued that base-ten language should be used throughout the second grade, even in preference to standard oral names.

Integration of Groupings with Place-Value Notation

In like manner, the symbolic scheme that we use for writing numbers (ones on the right, tens to the left of ones, and so on) must be coordinated with the grouping scheme. Activities can be designed so that children physically associate a tens and ones grouping with the correct recording of the individual digits, as Figure 5.2 indicates.

FIGURE 5.2 • • • • • • • • • •

Groupings by 10 are matched with numerals, placed in labeled places, and eventually written in standard form.

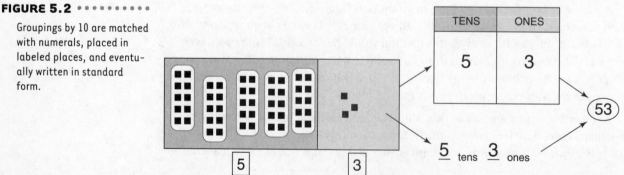

Chapter 5   BASE-TEN CONCEPTS AND PLACE VALUE

Language again plays a key role in making these connections. The explicit count by groups and singles matches the individual digits as the number is written in the usual left-to-right manner.

A similar coordination is necessary for hundreds.

Models for Place Value

Physical models for base-ten concepts can play a key role in helping children develop the idea of "a ten" as both a single entity and as a set of 10 units. Remember, though, that the models do not "show" the concept to the children. The children must construct the concept and impose it on the model.

Base-Ten Models and the Ten-Makes-One Relationship

A good base-ten model for ones, tens, and hundreds is *proportional*. That is, a ten model is physically ten times larger than the model for a one, and a hundred model is ten times larger than the ten model. Base-ten models can be categorized as *groupable* and *pregrouped*.

Groupable Models

Models that most clearly reflect the relationships of ones, tens, and hundreds are those for which the ten can actually be made or grouped from the singles. When children bundle 10 Popsicle sticks, the bundle of 10 literally *is the same as* the 10 ones from which it was made. Examples of these groupable models are shown in Figure 5.3(a). These could also be called "put-together-take-apart" models.

Of the groupable models, beans or counters in cups are the cheapest and easiest for children to use. (Plastic portion cups can be purchased from stores specializing in paper supplies.) Plastic connecting cubes are attractive and provide a good transition to pregrouped tens sticks. Plastic chain links in ten-link chains are another popular model. Bundles of Popsicle sticks or coffee stirrers are well-known models, but small hands have trouble with rubber bands and actually making the bundles. With most groupable materials, hundreds are possible but are generally not practical for most activities in the classroom.

(a) Groupable Base-Ten Models

Counters and cups. Ten single counters are placed in a cup. Hundreds: ten cups in a margarine tub.

Interlocking cubes. Ten single cubes form a bar of 10. Hundreds: not very convenient.

Bundles of sticks (wooden craft sticks, coffee stirrers). (If bundles are left intact, these are a pregrouped model.) Hundreds: ten bundles in a big bundle.

(b) Pregrouped Base-Ten Models

Strips and squares: Teacher-made from mount board and poster board. See Blackline Masters. Plastic versions are available through catalogs.

Base-ten blocks: wooden or plastic units, longs, flats, and blocks. Expensive, durable, easily handled, the only model with 1000.

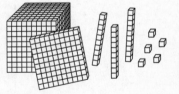

Bean sticks. Beans glued to craft sticks. Ten sticks can be bundled for 100.

FIGURE 5.3 •
Groupable and pregrouped base-ten models.

As children become more and more familiar with these models, collections of tens can be made up in advance by the children and kept as ready-made tens. Lids can be purchased for the plastic portion cups, and the connecting cubes or the links can be left prebundled. This is a good transition into the pregrouped models described next.

Pregrouped or Trading Models

Models that are pregrouped are commonly shown in textbooks and have become very popular. (See Figure 5.3b.) However, children cannot actually take them apart or put them together. When 10 single pieces are accumulated, they must be exchanged or *traded* for a ten, and likewise, tens must be traded for hundreds.

The chief advantage of these models is their ease of use and the efficient way they model large numbers. A significant disadvantage is the potential for children to use them without reflecting on the ten-to-one relationships or without really understanding what they are doing. For example, if children are told to trade 10 ones for a ten, it is quite possible for them to make this exchange without attending to the "tenness" of the piece they call a ten. Similarly, children can learn to "make the number 42" by simply selecting 4 tens and 2 ones pieces without understanding that if the pieces all came apart there would be 42 ones pieces that could be counted by ones.

No model, including a groupable model, will guarantee that children are reflecting on the ten-to-one relationships in the materials. With pregrouped models we need to make an extra effort to see that children understand that a ten piece really is the same as 10 ones.

BLMs 13–14

See the Blackline Masters for making base-ten strips and squares and the bean sticks.

Technology Note

Computer versions of base-ten blocks are becoming more common. In 2004, the Scott Foresman textbook company introduced a *Number Blocks* tool as part of an array of virtual manipulatives. Students can quickly stamp as many ones, tens, hundreds, or thousands onto the screen as they wish. A hammer cursor is used to break larger pieces into ten smaller ones. Using a glue-bottle cursor, students identify 10 ones, 10 tens, or 10 hundreds, which will then group together into the next larger piece. The National Library of Virtual Manipulatives at Utah State had a similar tool at the time this book was being written (http://matti.usu.edu/nlvm/nav/vlibrary.html). Other software of a similar nature will surely be developed or already exists.

Compared to physical models, virtual models are cheap and in endless supply. A good model will have the option of a symbolic "counter" to match the pieces on the screen. The Scott Foresman model allows for two separate groupings, each with its own counter and the counter can be shown in three different modes: 386, 3 hundreds + 8 tens + 6 ones, or 300 + 80 + 6. Computer models allow students to print out the work that they have done with the materials. With physical models, students' work is generally lost when the blocks are put away.

On the other hand, the computer model is no more conceptual than a physical model and, like the physical model, is only a representation for the students who understand what is being shown.

Nonproportional Materials

In this book, colored counters, abacuses, and money are not considered to model base-ten ideas because the materials play no part in developing those relationships. With an abacus, ten beads in one column are exchanged for one bead in the next column to the left. There is nothing in the representation that illustrates the relationship between ten beads and the single bead to its left. The exchange is simply an arbitrary rule. Nonproportional materials can keep track of numbers within a position but they do not illuminate an understanding of the relationship between positions.

Once understood, money can be a useful aid in developing flexible approaches to computation. For example, if the sum of 76 and 28 is thought of in terms of quarters and pennies, the task is quite simple. However, money does not help in the early development of place value.

Developing Place-Value Concepts and Procedures

Now that you have a sense of the task of helping children develop place-value concepts, we can begin to focus on activities that can help with this task. This section focuses separately on three main components of place value: base-ten concepts or grouping by tens, standard oral names for numbers, and written forms of numbers. The central idea of counting groups of ten to describe quantities is clearly the most important component to be developed. However, you should understand that the separation of the three goals in this section is to help you understand the objectives. In the classroom, these three goals can and should be developed together. Although kindergarten children are unlikely to understand base-ten concepts, it is still very important to expose them to counting beyond ten and to the patterns found on the hundreds chart.

Grouping Activities

Because children come to their development of base-ten concepts with a count-by-ones idea of number, you must begin there. You cannot arbitrarily impose grouping by 10 on children. We want children to experiment with showing amounts in groups of like size and perhaps to come to an agreement that 10 is a very useful size to use. The following activity could be done in late first grade or second grade and is designed as an example of a first effort at developing grouping concepts.

ACTIVITY 5.1

Counting in Groups

Find a collection of things that children might be interested in counting— perhaps the number of eyes in the classroom or the number of shoes, a mystery jar of buttons or cubes, a long chain of plastic links, or the number of crayons in the crayon box. The quantity should be countable, some- where between 25 and 100. Pose the question, "How could we count our

(continued)

shoes in some way that would be easier than counting by ones?" Whatever suggestions you get, try to implement them. After trying several methods, you can have a discussion of what worked well and what did not. If no one suggests counting by tens, you might casually suggest that as possibly another idea.

One teacher had her second-grade students find a good way to count all the connecting cubes being held by the children after each had been given a cube for each of their pockets. The first suggestion was to count by sevens. That was tried but did not work very well because none of the second graders could count by sevens. In search of a faster way, the next suggestion was to count by twos. This did not seem to be much better than counting by ones. Finally, they settled on counting by tens and realized that this was a pretty good method, although counting by fives worked pretty well also.

This and similar activities provide you with the opportunity to suggest that materials actually be arranged into groups of tens before the "fast" way of counting is begun. Remember that children may count "ten, twenty, thirty, thirty-one, thirty-two" but not fully realize the "thirty-two-ness" of the quantity. To connect the count-by-tens method with their understood method of counting by ones, the children need to count both ways and discuss why they get the same result.

The idea in the next activity is for children to make groupings of 10 and record or say the amounts. Number words are used so that children will not mechanically match tens and ones with individual digits. It is important that children confront the actual quantity in a manner meaningful to them.

ACTIVITY 5.2

Groups of 10

Prepare bags of counters of different types. Bags may have toothpicks, buttons, beans, plastic chips, connecting cubes, craft sticks, or other items. Children have a record sheet similar to the top example in Figure 5.4. The bags can be placed at stations around the room, or each pair of children can be given one. Children dump out and count the contents. The amount is recorded as a number word. Then the counters are grouped in as many tens as possible. The groupings are recorded on the form. Bags are traded, or children move to another station after returning all counters to the bag.

If children have difficulty writing the number words, a chart can be displayed for students to copy from (see Figure 5.5).

Variations of the "Groups of 10" activity are suggested by the other record sheets in Figure 5.4. In "Get This Many," the children count the dots and then count out the corresponding number of counters. Small cups in which to put the groups of 10 should be provided. Notice that the activity requires students to address quantities in a way they understand, record the amount in words, and then make the groupings.

The "Groups of 10" activity and the variations in Figure 5.4 start where the students are and develop the idea of groups. "Fill the Tens" and "Loop This Many" begin with a verbal name (number word), and students must count the indicated amount and then make groups.

FIGURE 5.4 • • • • • • • • • • • • • • •

Number words and making groups of 10.

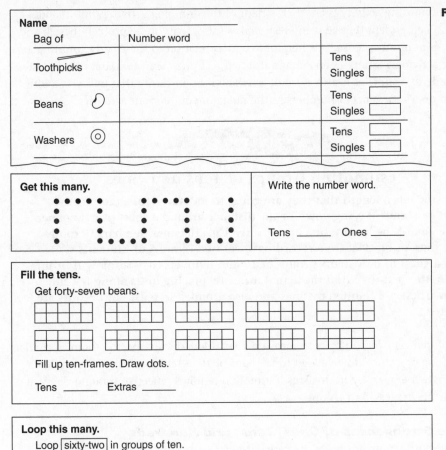

Name _____

Bag of	Number word		
Toothpicks		Tens	☐
		Singles	☐
Beans		Tens	☐
		Singles	☐
Washers		Tens	☐
		Singles	☐

Get this many.

Write the number word.

_____

Tens _____ Ones _____

Fill the tens.

Get forty-seven beans.

Fill up ten-frames. Draw dots.

Tens _____ Extras _____

Loop this many.

Loop sixty-two in groups of ten.

Tens _____ Ones _____

Assessment Note

As you watch children doing these activities, you will be able to learn a lot about their base-ten concept development. For example, how do children count out the objects? Do they make groupings of 10 as they go? Do they count to 10 and then start again at 1? Children who do that are already using the base-ten structure. But what you will more likely see early on is children counting a full set without any stopping at tens and without any effort to group the materials in piles. A second-grade teacher had her students count a jar of small beans. After they had recorded the number, they were to ask for plastic cups in which to make cups of 10. Several children, when asked how many cups they thought they might need, had no idea or made random guesses.

Number Words

eleven	ten	one
twelve	twenty	two
thirteen	thirty	three
fourteen	forty	four
fifteen	fifty	five
sixteen	sixty	six
seventeen	seventy	seven
eighteen	eighty	eight
nineteen	ninety	nine

FIGURE 5.5 •

A chart to help children write number words.

The following activity is another variant of the grouping activities but includes an estimation component that adds interest, makes the activity more problem based, and contributes to number sense. It is helpful to add estimation to these early counting and grouping activities. Estimates encourage children to think about total quantities. Listening to students' estimates is also a useful assessment opportunity that tells you a lot about children's concepts of numbers in the range of your current activities.

EXPANDED LESSON

(pages 155–156)

A complete lesson plan based on "Estimating Groups of Tens and Ones" can be found at the end of this chapter.

ACTIVITY 5.3

Estimating Groups of Tens and Ones

Show students a length that they are going to measure—for example, the length of a student lying down or the distance around a sheet of newspaper. At one end of the length, line up 10 units (e.g., 10 cubes in a bar, 10 toothpicks, rods, or blocks). On a recording sheet (see Figure 5.6), students write down a guess of how many groups of 10 and leftovers they think will fit into the length. Next they find the actual measure, placing units along the full length. These are counted by ones and also grouped in tens. Both results are recorded.

Children can work in pairs to measure several lengths around the room. A similar estimation approach could be added to "Groups of 10" (Activity 5.2), where students first estimate the quantity in the bags. Estimation requires reflective thought concerning quantities expressed in groups.

The Strangeness of Ones, Tens, and Hundreds

Reflect for a moment on how strange it must sound to say "seven ones." Certainly children have never said they were "seven ones" years old. The use of the word *ten* as a singular group name is even more mysterious. Consider the phrase "Ten ones makes one ten." The first *ten* carries the usual meaning of 10 things, the amount that is 1 more than 9 things. But the other *ten* is a singular noun, a thing. How can something the child has known for years as the name for a lot of things suddenly become one thing? Bunches, bundles, cups, and groups of 10 make more sense in the beginning than "a ten."

As students begin to make groupings of 10, the language of these groupings must also be introduced. At the start, language such as "groups of 10 and leftovers" or

FIGURE 5.6 • • • • • • • • •

Record sheet for estimating groups of tens and ones.

NAME ___Jessica_____

OBJECT	ESTIMATE	ACTUAL
_desk_____	_5_ TENS _6_ SINGLES	_3_ TENS _2_ SINGLES
		ThirTy-TWO_____
		Number Word
_____	___ TENS ___ SINGLES	___ TENS ___ SINGLES
		_____
		Number Word

"bunches of tens and singles" is most meaningful. For tens, use whatever terminology fits: bars of 10, cups of 10, bundles of 10. Eventually you can abbreviate this simply to "ten." There is no hurry to use the word "ones" for the leftovers. Language such as "four tens and seven" works very well.

The word *hundred* is equally strange and yet usually gets less attention. It must be understood in three ways: as 100 single objects, as 10 tens, and as a singular thing. These word names are not as simple as they seem!

Equivalent Representations

An important variation of the grouping activities is aimed at the equivalent representations of numbers. For example, with children who have just completed the "Groups of 10" activity for a bag of counters, ask, "What is another way you can show your 42 besides 4 groups and 2 singles? Let's see how many ways you can find." Interestingly, most children will go next to 42 singles. The following activities are also directed to the idea of equivalent representations.

ACTIVITY 5.4

Odd Groupings

Show a collection of materials that are only partly grouped in sets of 10. For example, you may have 5 chains of 10 links and 17 additional links. Be sure the children understand that the groups each have 10 items. Count the number of groups, and also count the singles. Ask, "How many in all?" Record all responses and discuss before you count. Let the children use whatever way they wish to count. Next change the groupings (make a ten from the singles or break apart one of the tens) and repeat the questions and discussion. Do not change the total number from one time to the next. Once students begin to understand that the total does not change, ask in what other ways the items could be grouped if you use tens and singles.

The next activity is similar but is done using pregrouped materials and is appropriate for third grade.

ACTIVITY 5.5

Three Other Ways

Students work in groups or pairs. First they show "four hundred sixty-three" on their desks with strips and squares in the standard representation. Next they find and record at least three other ways of showing this number.

After children have had sufficient experiences with pregrouped materials, a "dot, stick, and square" notation can be used for recording ones, tens, and hundreds. By third grade, children can use small squares for hundreds, as shown in Figure 5.7. Use the drawings as a means of telling the children what pieces to get out of their own place-value kits and as a way for children to record results.

The next activity begins to incorporate oral language with equivalent representation ideas.

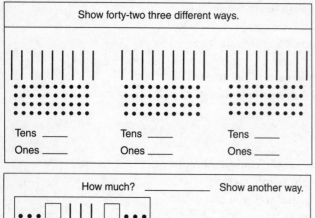

Show forty-two three different ways.

Tens _____   Tens _____   Tens _____
Ones _____   Ones _____   Ones _____

How much? _____ Show another way.

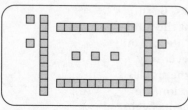

FIGURE 5.7 •

Equivalent representation exercises using square-stick-dot pictures.

"Four tens and seven ones—forty-seven"

FIGURE 5.8 •

Mixed model of 47.

Base-ten riddles can be presented orally or in written form. In either case, children should use base-ten materials to help solve them. The examples here illustrate a variety of possibilities with different levels of difficulty.

I have 23 ones and 4 tens. Who am I?
I have 4 hundreds, 12 tens, and 6 ones. Who am I?
I have 30 ones and 3 hundreds. Who am I?
I am 45. I have 25 ones. How many tens do I have?
I am 341. I have 22 tens. How many hundreds do I have?
I have 13 tens, 2 hundreds, and 21 ones. Who am I?
If you put 3 more tens with me, I would be 115. Who am I?
I have 17 ones. I am between 40 and 50. Who am I?
I have 17 ones. I am between 40 and 50. How many tens do I have?

Oral Names for Numbers

The standard name of the collection in Figure 5.8 is "forty-seven." A more explicit terminology in *base-ten language* is "four tens and seven ones." Base-ten language is rarely misunderstood by children working with base-ten materials and encourages thinking in terms of groups instead of a large pile of singles.

Two-Digit Number Names

In first and second grades, children need to connect the base-ten concepts with the oral number names they have used many times. They know the words but have not thought of them in terms of tens and ones.

Almost always use base-ten models while teaching oral names. Use base-ten language paired with standard language. Emphasize the teens as exceptions. Acknowledge that they are formed "backward" and do not fit the patterns.

Use a 10 × 10 array of dots on the overhead projector. Cover up all but two rows, as shown in Figure 5.9(a). "How many tens? (2.) Two tens is called *twenty*." Have the class repeat. "Sounds a little like *twin*." Show another row. "Three tens is called *thirty*. Four tens is *forty*. Five tens should have been

fivety rather than *fifty*." The names *sixty, seventy, eighty,* and *ninety* all fit the pattern. Slide the cover up and down the array, asking how many tens and the name for that many.

Use the same 10 × 10 array to work on names for tens and ones. Show, for example, four full lines, "forty." Next expose one dot in the fifth row. "Four tens and one. Forty-one." Add more dots one at a time. "Four tens and two. Forty-two." "Four tens and three. Forty-three." This is shown in Figure 5.9(b). When that pattern is established, repeat with other decades from twenty through ninety.

Repeat this basic approach with other base-ten models. The next activity shows how this might be done.

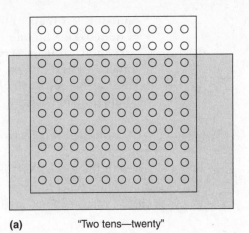

(a)   "Two tens—twenty"

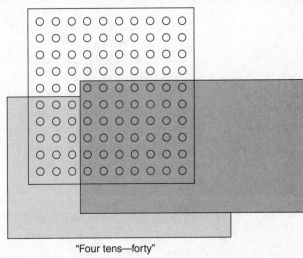

"Four tens—forty"
(b)   "Four tens and three—forty-three"

FIGURE 5.9 ●

10 × 10 dot arrays are used to model sets of 10 and singles.

ACTIVITY 5.8

Counting with Base-Ten Models

Show some tens pieces on the overhead. Ask how many tens. Ask for the usual name. Add a ten or remove a ten and repeat the questions. Next add some ones. Always have children give the base-ten name and the standard name. Continue to make changes in the materials displayed by adding or removing 1 or 2 tens and by adding and removing ones. For this activity, show the tens and ones pieces in different arrangements rather than the standard left-to-right order for tens and ones. The idea is to connect the names to the materials, not the order they are in.

Reverse the activity by having children use base-ten pieces at their desks. For example, you say, "Make 63." The children make the number with the models and then give the base-ten name.

Note that Activities 5.7 and 5.8 will be much enhanced by discussion. Have children explain their thinking. If you don't require children to reflect on these responses, they soon learn how to give the response you want, matching number words to models, without actually thinking about the total quantities.

ACTIVITY 5.9

Tens, Ones, and Fingers

Ask your class, "How can you show 37 fingers?" (It is fun to precede this question by asking for different ways to show 6 fingers, 8 fingers, and other

(continued)

DEVELOPING PLACE-VALUE CONCEPTS AND PROCEDURES

amounts less than 10.) Soon children will figure out that four children are required. Line up four children, and have three hold up 10 fingers and the last child 7 fingers. Have the class count the fingers by tens and ones. Ask for other children to show different numbers. Emphasize the number of sets of 10 fingers and the single fingers (base-ten language) and pair this with the standard language.

In the last three activities, it is important occasionally to count an entire representation by ones. Remember that the count by ones is the young child's principal linkage with the concept of quantity. For example, suppose you have just had children use connecting cubes to make 42. Try asking, "Do you think there really are 42 blocks there?" Many children are not convinced, and the count by ones is very significant.

Three-Digit Number Names

The approach to three-digit number names is essentially the same as for two-digit names. Show mixed arrangements of base-ten materials. Have children give the base-ten name and the standard name. Vary the arrangement from one example to the next by changing only one type of piece. That is, add or remove only ones or only tens or only hundreds.

Similarly, have children at their desks model numbers that you give to them orally using the standard names. By the time that children are ready for three-digit numbers, the two-digit number names, including the difficulties with the teens, have usually been mastered. The major difficulty is with numbers involving no tens, such as 702. As noted earlier, the use of base-ten language is quite helpful here. The zero-tens difficulty is more pronounced when writing numerals. Children frequently write 7002 for "seven hundred two." The emphasis on the meaning in the oral base-ten language form will be a significant help.

Written Symbols

The discussion so far has stressed the ideas of groups of 10 and the connection of these base-ten concepts to oral number names. No one would expect that written numbers are completely absent during this development. At the same time, it is correct to focus on the ideas of base-ten concepts before emphasizing the written numbers.

Place-Value Mats

Place-value mats are simple mats divided into two or three sections to hold ones and tens or ones, tens, and hundreds pieces as shown in Figure 5.10. You can suggest to your students that the mats are a good way to organize their materials when working with base-ten pieces. Explain that the standard way to use a place-value mat is with the space for the ones on the right and tens and hundreds places to the left.

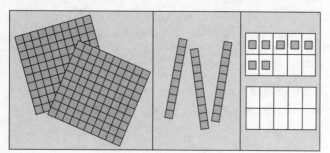

Strips and squares show
237 on three-place mat.

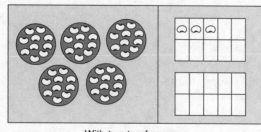

With two ten-frames,
cups and beans show 53.

FIGURE 5.10 ••••••••••••••••••••••••••••••••••

Place-value mats with two ten-frames in the ones place to organize the counters and promote the concept of groups of 10.

Though there is no requirement to have anything printed on the mats, it is strongly recommended that two ten-frames be drawn in the ones place as shown. (See Blackline Masters.) That way, the amount of ones on the ten-frames is always clearly evident, eliminating the need for frequent and tedious counting. The ten-frame also makes it very clear how many additional counters would be needed to make the next set of 10. If children are modeling two numbers at the same time, one ten-frame can be used for each number. Most illustrations of place-value mats in this book will show two ten-frames, even though that feature is not commonly seen in standard texts.

BLM 15

As children use their place-value mats, they can be shown how the left-to-right order of the pieces is also the way that numbers are written. The place-value mat becomes a link between the base-ten models and the written form of the numbers. Once again, be aware of how easy it would be for a child to show a number on a mat using tens and ones pieces and learn to write the number without any understanding of what the number represents. First- and second-grade textbooks often show a model and have children record numbers in this manner:

<u> 7 </u> tens and <u> 3 </u> ones is <u> 73 </u> in all.

It is all too easy to copy down the number of sticks and single blocks and rewrite these digits in a single number 73 and not confront what these symbols stand for.

Assessment Note

Most of the activities suggested so far serve as opportunities to find out what children know and understand about place value. They are performance tasks. A lot of the assessment information you will need can come from watching and listening as children do these tasks.

- How do children count or estimate quantities? Do they spontaneously use sets of tens?
- When materials are already arranged in groups of 10 (counters in cups, dots in ten-frames) or in groups of 100, do the children use these structures to tell how many?
- How flexible are children with their thinking about numbers? Can they take them apart and combine them in ways that reflect an understanding of ones, tens, and hundreds?

The Hundreds Chart

The hundreds chart (Figure 5.11) is such an important tool in the development of place-value concepts that it deserves special attention. K–2 classrooms should have a hundreds chart displayed prominently. Activities in which even kindergarten and first-grade children explore patterns on the hundreds chart were described in Chapter 2. (See pp. 56–58.) As children explore number patterns on the hundreds chart and become more and more adept at filling in missing numbers on the chart, they are learning about the structure of the written numbers in our place-value system. (See Activity 2.29, p. 57.)

FIGURE 5.11 • • • • • • • • •

A hundreds chart.

1	2	3	4	5	6	7	8	9	10
11	12	13	14	15	16	17	18	19	20
21	22	23	24	25	26	27	28	29	30
31	32	33	34	35	36	37	38	39	40
41	42	43	44	45	46	47	48	49	50
51	52	53	54	55	56	57	58	59	60
61	62	63	64	65	66	67	68	69	70
71	72	73	74	75	76	77	78	79	80
81	82	83	84	85	86	87	88	89	90
91	92	93	94	95	96	97	98	99	100

BLMs 9, 10, and 16

As mentioned in Chapter 2, a pocket chart version of a hundreds chart is very useful. You can remove numerals from the chart and have students return them to the appropriate places. An overhead transparency of a blank 10 × 10 grid serves as another form for a blank chart on which numbers can be written. A master for a blank grid, a matching hundreds chart, and a set of four smaller hundreds charts that can be duplicated for students can all be found in the Blackline Masters.

In addition to the patterns described in Chapter 2, other patterns you might have students explore include numbers that have a 7 in them, numbers where the digits add up to four, and various skip-count patterns.

ACTIVITY 5.10

Skip-Count Patterns

As a full class activity, have students skip count by twos, threes, fours, and so on. After skip counting as a class, have students record a specific skip-count pattern on their own copy of the hundreds chart by coloring in each number they count. Every skip count produces an interesting pattern on the chart. You should also discuss the patterns in the numbers. For example, when you skip count by fours, you only land on numbers that you get when you count by twos. Which counts make column patterns, and which counts make diagonal patterns?

In the beginning, skip counting may be quite difficult for children. As they become more comfortable with skip counts, you can challenge students to skip count without the aid of the hundreds chart. Skip-counting skills show a readiness for multiplication combinations and also help children begin to look for interesting and useful patterns in numbers.

More and Less on the Hundreds Chart

Begin with a blank or nearly blank chart. Circle a particular missing number. Students are to fill in the designated number and its "neighbors," the numbers to the left, right, above, and below. This can be done with the full class on the overhead projector, or worksheets can be prepared using a blank hundreds chart or 10 × 10 grid. After students become 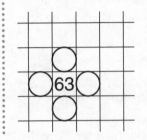 comfortable naming the neighbors of a number, ask what they notice about the neighbor numbers. The numbers to the left and right are one more and one less than the given number. Those above and below are ten less and ten more, respectively. By discussing these relationships on the chart, students begin to see how the sequence of numbers is related to the numeric relationships in the numbers.

Notice that children will first use the hundreds chart to learn about the patterns in the sequence of numbers. Many students, especially at the K or 1 level, will not understand the corresponding numeric relationships such as those discussed in the last activity. In the following activity, number relationships on the chart are made more explicit by including the use of base-ten models.

Models with the Hundreds Chart

This activity has several variations that can be conducted with the full class or can be made into an activity in which two students work together to explore an idea and write about what they have discovered. Use any physical model for two-digit numbers with which the students are familiar.

- Give children one or more numbers to first make with the models and then find on the chart. Use groups of two or three numbers either in the same row or the same column.
- Have students make all of the numbers in a row or in a column. How are the numbers in the row (or column) alike? How are they different? What happens at the end of the row?
- Indicate a number on the chart. What would you have to change to make each of its neighbors (the numbers to the left, right, above, and below)?

It is becoming more and more popular to have a chart that extends to 200, even in the first grade. Perhaps a more powerful idea is to extend the hundreds chart to 1000.

The Thousands Chart

Provide students with several sheets of the blank hundreds charts from the Blackline Masters. Assign groups of three or four students the task of creating a 1-to-1000 chart. The chart is to be made by taping ten charts together in a long strip. Students should decide how they are going to divide up the task with different students taking different parts of the chart.

The thousands chart should be discussed as a class to examine how numbers change as you count from one hundred to the next, what the patterns are, and so on. In fact, the earlier hundreds chart activities can all be extended to a thousands chart. You may want to make a blank thousands chart (clearly indicating each 100-square). Use the students' charts for other discussions.

More Connections with Numbers

The next three activities are designed to help children make connections among all three representations: models, oral language, and written forms. They can be done with two- or three-digit numbers in grades 1–4.

ACTIVITY 5.14

Say It/Press It

Display some ones and tens (and hundreds) so that the class can see. (Use the overhead projector or simply draw on the board using the square-stick-dot method.) Arrange the materials in a mixed design, not in the standard left-to-right format. Students say the amount shown in base-ten language ("four hundreds, one ten, and five") and then in standard language ("four hundred fifteen"), and finally they enter it on their calculators. Have someone share his or her display and defend it. Make a change in the materials and repeat.

"Say It/Press It" is especially good for helping with teens (note the example in the activity description) and for three-digit numbers with zero tens. If you show 7 hundreds and 4 ones, the class says "seven hundreds, zero tens, and four—seven hundred (*slight pause*) four." The pause and the base-ten language suggest the correct three-digit number to press or write. Many students have trouble with this example and write "7004," writing exactly what they hear in the standard name. Similarly, first- and second-grade children often write "504" for fifty-four. This activity will help. The next activity simply changes the representation that is presented first to the students.

ACTIVITY 5.15

Show It/Press It

Say the standard name for a number (with either two or three digits). At their desks, students use their own base-ten models to show that number and press it on their calculators (or write it). Again, pay special attention to the teens and the case of zero tens.

The following activity has been popular for decades and remains a useful challenge for students in the early stages of place-value development.

ACTIVITY 5.16

Digit Change

Have students enter a specific two- or three-digit number on the calculator. The task is to then change one of the digits in the number without simply entering the new number. For example, change 48 to 78. Change 315 to 305 or to 295. Changes can be made by adding or subtracting an appropriate amount. Students should write or discuss explanations for their solutions.

Assessment Note

Children are often able to disguise their lack of understanding of place value by following directions, using the tens and ones pieces in prescribed ways, and using the language of place value.

The diagnostic tasks presented here are designed to help you look more closely at children's understanding of place value. They are not suggested as definitive tests but as means of obtaining information for the thoughtful teacher. These tasks have been used by several researchers and are adapted primarily from Labinowicz (1985) and Ross (1986). The tasks are designed for one-on-one settings. They should not be used as instructional activities nor should they be done all at once.

Counting Skills

A variety of oral counting tasks provides insight into the counting sequence.

- Count forward for me, starting at 77.
- Count backward, starting at 55.
- Count by tens.
- Count by tens, starting at 34.
- Count backward by tens, starting at 130.

In the tasks that follow, the manner in which the child responds is as important as the answers.

One More and Ten More, One Less and Ten Less

Write the number 342. Have the child read the number. Then have the child write the number that is 1 more than the number. Next ask for the number that is 10 more than the number. You may wish to explore further with models. One less and 10 less can be checked the same way. Of course, this can also be done with a two-digit number.

Digit Correspondence

Dump out 36 blocks. Ask the child to count the blocks, and then have the child write the number that tells how many there are. Circle the 6 in 36 and ask, "Does this part of your 36 have anything to do with how many blocks there are?" Then circle the 3 and repeat the question exactly. Do not give clues. Based on responses to the task, Ross (1989) has identified five distinct levels of understanding of place value:

1. *Single numeral.* The child writes 36 but views it as a single numeral. The individual digits 3 and 6 have no meaning by themselves.
2. *Position names.* The child identifies correctly the tens and ones positions but still makes no connections between the individual digits and the blocks.
3. *Face value.* The child matches 6 blocks with the 6 and 3 blocks with the 3.

(continued)

4. *Transition to place value.* The 6 is matched with 6 blocks and the 3 with the remaining 30 blocks but not as 3 groups of 10.

5. *Full understanding.* The 3 is correlated with 3 groups of 10 blocks and the 6 with 6 single blocks.

Using Tens

Dump out 47 counters, and have the child count them. Next show the child at least ten cards, each with a ten-frame drawn on it. Ask, "If we wanted to put these counters in the spaces on these cards, how many cards could we fill up?" (If the ten-frame has been used in class to model sets of 10, use a different frame such as a 10-pin arrangement of circles. Be sure the child knows there are 10 spaces on each card.)

Using Groups of 10

Prepare cards with beans or other counters glued to the cards in an obvious arrangement of 10. Supply at least ten cards and a large supply of the beans. After you are sure that the child has counted several cards of beans and knows there are 10 on each, say, "Show me 34 beans." (Does the child count individual beans or use the cards of 10?) The activity can also be done with hundreds.

Number Sense Development

The discussion so far has addressed the three main components of place-value understanding: the integration of base-ten groupings, oral names, and written names. But students need to expand these ideas beyond basic numeration concepts and reading and writing numerals in order to develop number sense. These activities should be an ongoing feature of your instruction.

Relative Magnitude

Relative magnitude refers to the size relationship one number has with another—is it much larger, much smaller, close, or about the same? There are several quick activities that can be done with a number line sketched on the board. The number line can help children see how one number is related to another.

ACTIVITY 5.17

Who Am I?

Sketch a line labeled 0 and 100 at opposite ends. Mark a point with a ? that corresponds to your secret number. (Estimate the position the best you can.) Students try to guess your secret number. For each guess, place and label a mark on the line.

Continue marking each guess until your secret number is discovered. As a variation, the endpoints can be other than 0 and 100. For example, try 0 and 1000, 200 and 300, or 500 and 800.

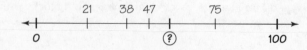

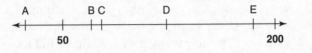
Who Could They Be?

Label two points on a number line (not necessarily the ends).

Ask students what numbers they think different points labeled with letters might be and why they think that. In the example shown here, B and C are less than 100 but probably more than 60. E could be about 180. You can also ask where 75 might be or where 400 is. About how far apart are A and D? Why do you think D is more than 100?

```
    A         B C        D              E
  ←─┼─────────┼─┼────────┼──────────────┼──→
    50                                 200
```

In the next activity, some of the same ideas are discussed without benefit of a number line.

ACTIVITY 5.19

Close, Far, and in Between

Put any three numbers on the board. For first and second grade, use two-digit numbers and modify the questions accordingly.

With these three numbers as referents, ask questions such as the following, and encourage discussion of all responses:

Which two are closest? Why?
Which is closest to 300? To 250?
Name a number between 457 and 364.
Name a multiple of 25 between 219 and 364.
Name a number that is more than all of these.
About how far apart are 219 and 500? 219 and 5000?
If these are "big numbers," what are some small numbers? Numbers about the same? Numbers that make these seem small?

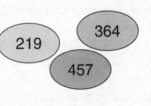

Connections to Real-World Ideas

We should not permit children to study place-value concepts without encouraging them to see number in the world about them. You do not need a prescribed activity to bring real numbers into the classroom.

Children in the second grade should be thinking about numbers under 100 first and, soon after, numbers up to 1000. Quantities larger than that are difficult to think about. Where are numbers like this? Around your school: the number of children in each class, the numbers on the school buses, the number of minutes devoted to mathematics each day and then each week, the number of cartons of chocolate and plain milk served in the cafeteria each day, the numbers on the calendar (days in a week, month, year), the number of days since school has started. And then there are measurements, numbers at home, numbers on a field trip, and so on.

What do you do with these numbers? Turn them into interesting graphs, write stories using them, make up problems, devise contests.

The particular way you bring number and the real world together in your class is up to you. But do not underestimate the value of connecting the real world to the classroom.

Assessment Note

Listen to your children throughout the day when they are using numbers in connection with real quantities. Do they use numbers that are appropriate for their age in meaningful ways? When they count things, make measurements, or talk about quantities in their reading or social studies lessons, do they exhibit an understanding of the relative size of these numbers? For example, when estimating how many people might attend a movie or go to a Little League baseball game, are the numbers they choose reasonable for the situation? Everyday usage of numbers by your students can give you insight into their understanding of quantities connected to the real world.

Approximate Numbers and Rounding

In our number system, some numbers are "nice." They are easy to think about and work with. What makes a nice number is sort of fuzzy. However, numbers such as 100, 500, and 750 are easier to use than 94, 517, and 762. Multiples of 100 are very nice, and multiples of 10 are not bad either. Multiples of 25 (50, 75, 425, 675, etc.) are nice because they combine into 100s and 50s rather easily, and we can mentally place those between multiples of 100s. Multiples of 5 are a little easier to work with than other numbers.

Flexible thought with numbers and many estimation skills are related to the ability to substitute a nice number for one that is not so nice. The substitution may be to make a mental computation easier, to compare it to a familiar reference, or simply to store the number in memory more easily.

In the past, students were taught rules for rounding numbers to the nearest 10 or nearest 100. Unfortunately, the emphasis was placed on applying the rule correctly. (If the next digit is 5 or more, round up; otherwise, leave the number alone.) A context to suggest why they may want to round numbers was usually a lesser consideration.

The activities here are designed to help students recognize what nice numbers are and to identify a nice-number substitute. (*Authors' note:* The term *nice number* is not found in standard textbooks. There is no commonly accepted definition.)

ACTIVITY 5.20

Nice-Number Skip Counts

Count by 5s, 10s, 25s, and 50s with your students. The 5s and 10s are fairly easy, but the skill is certainly worth practicing. Counts by 25s or 50s may be hesitant at first. Students can use a calculator to assist with their counting and connect the counts with numerals (press ⊞ 25 ⊟ ⊟ ⊟ . . .). At first, start all counts at zero. Later, start at some multiple of your skip amount. For example, begin at 275 and count by 25s. Counts by 10s should also begin at numbers ending in 5 as well as multiples of 10. Also count backward by these same amounts (press 650 ⊟ 50 ⊟ ⊟ ⊟ . . .).

To round a number simply means to substitute a nice number that is close so that some computation can be done more easily. The close number can be any nice number and need not be a multiple of 10 or 100, as has been traditional. It should be whatever makes the computation or estimation easier or simplifies numbers sufficiently in a story, chart, or conversation. You might say, "Last night it took me 57 minutes to do my homework" or "Last night it took me about one hour to do my homework." The first expression is more precise; the second substitutes a rounded number for better communication.

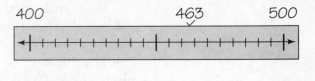

FIGURE 5.12

A blank number can be labeled in different ways to help students with near and nice numbers.

A number line with nice numbers highlighted can be useful in helping children select near nice numbers. An unlabeled number line like the one shown in Figure 5.12 can be made using three strips of poster board taped end to end. Labels are written above the line on the chalkboard. The ends can be labeled 0 and 100, 100 and 200, . . . , 900 and 1000. The other markings then show multiples of 25, 10, and 5. Indicate a number above the line that you want to round. Discuss the marks (nice numbers) that are close.

Activities for Flexible Thinking

The separation of place-value development from computation has long been the norm. Most likely this is because traditional computation has been almost completely directed at one specified algorithm for each operation. Students have not typically been asked to develop their own methods for computation. As pointed out in the NCTM *Standards* document, "It is not necessary to wait for students to fully develop place-value understandings before giving them opportunities to solve problems with two- and three-digit numbers" (NCTM, 2000, p. 82). The interdependence of place-value understanding with the personal development of strategies for computation—especially addition and subtraction—suggests that students will develop or refine place-value concepts while working on computational methods.

The next chapter focuses completely on computational development. However, in order to highlight the value of interaction between place-value concepts and computation, the following computational activities are suggested here. In addition to the activities that follow, second- and third-grade teachers should consider challenging their students to solve story problems with multidigit computation—either mentally or using their own invented strategies. (See Chapter 6 for suggestions.)

Working with Tens and Hundreds

We are so accustomed to thinking about addition and subtraction computation as involving "regrouping"—the trading of 10 ones for a ten or vice versa—that we tend to believe that regrouping is an integral part of computation. In fact, virtually all invented strategies for computation as well as mental strategies involve no regrouping at all. Rather, what happens in most cases might be called "bridging a ten" or "using a system of tens." The row structure of the hundreds chart is especially useful in developing this understanding of bridging across ten.

For example, in the sum of 38 and 24, one might first add 38 and 20 to get 58 and then add 4 more to 58. This last sum can be done with the same reasoning as adding 8 + 4; add 2 to get to 10 and then 2 more is 12. So, for 58 and 4, add 2 onto 58 to get to 60 and then 2 more is 62. Alternatively, a student might add 38 + 24 by adding 30 + 20, then 8 + 4, and combine the results: 50 and 12 is 62. In neither case are 10 ones traded for a ten. There is no carrying. Subtraction works in a similar manner. Rarely, if ever, will a student using his or her own invented strategies regroup a ten into 10 ones.

> **STOP** As you consider the activities in this section and the next, you will find that although you are adding and subtracting multidigit numbers, you will not be borrowing or carrying. If you find yourself using a traditional technique, do the activity again. Focus on bridging tens rather than regrouping. Avoid using the traditional algorithms to solve these problems.

Many of the skills of invented strategies appear in the next activity, which combines symbolism with base-ten representations. In all of these activities, class discussion should have children explain how they did the exercises or tell how they thought about them.

ACTIVITY 5.21

Numbers, Squares, Sticks, and Dots

As illustrated in Figure 5.13, prepare a worksheet or overhead transparency on which a numeral and some base-ten pieces are shown. Use small squares, sticks, and dots for base-ten pieces to keep drawing simple. Students write the totals that they compute mentally.

Figure 5.14 is a take-away version of the same activity. As shown, the amount removed can be either the numeral or the squares and sticks. Try it both ways.

Thinking About Parts of Numbers

Another important focus involves thinking about a number in terms of two parts, especially thinking about a missing part, which is the agenda of the next several activities.

Often in computations it is useful to recognize that a number can be made up of a "nice" number and some more. The nice part (maybe a multiple of 50 or 100) is dealt with first and then the smaller leftover piece can be considered.

ACTIVITY 5.22

50 and Some More

Say a number between 50 and 100. Students respond with "50 and ____." For 63, the response is "50 and 13." Use other numbers that end in 50 such as "450 and some more."

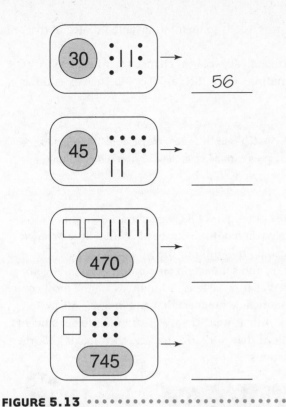

56

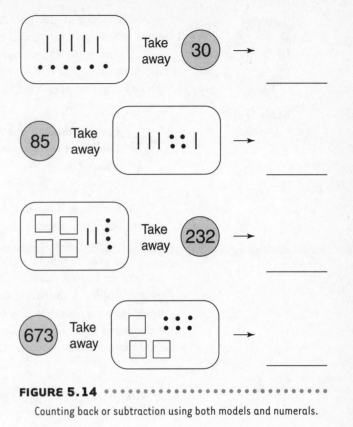

FIGURE 5.13 • • • • • • • • • • • • • • • • • • •

Flexible counting on or addition using both models and numerals.

FIGURE 5.14 • • • • • • • • • • • • • • • • • •

Counting back or subtraction using both models and numerals.

Nice numbers also are often broken apart in computations. The next two activities are extremely useful for developing the thinking required for counting-up approaches to subtraction. Introduce these activities to the full class using the overhead projector. Have students share their thinking strategies.

ACTIVITY 5.23

The Other Part of 100

Two students work together with a set of little ten-frame cards. One student makes a two-digit number. Then both students work mentally to determine what goes with the ten-frame amount to make 100. They write their solutions on paper and then check by making the other part with the cards to see if the total is 100. Students take turns making the original number. Figure 5.15 shows three different thought processes that students might use.

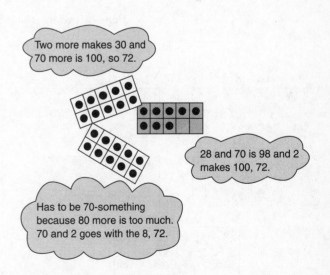

FIGURE 5.15 • • • • • • • • • • • • • • • • • • •

Using little ten-frames to help think about the "other part of 100."

147

Being able to give the other part of 100 is so useful in invented strategies that students should get quite good at it.

If your students are adept at parts of 100, you can change the whole from 100 to another number. At first try other multiples of 10 such as 70 or 80. Then extend the whole to any number less than 100.

 STOP Suppose that the whole is 83. Sketch four little ten-frame cards showing 36. Looking at your "cards," what goes with 36 to make 83? How did you think about it?

What you just did in finding the other part of 83 was subtract 36 from 83. You did not borrow or regroup. Most likely you did it in your head. With a little practice students as early as the third grade can do this without the aid of the cards.

Compatible numbers for addition and subtraction are numbers that go together easily to make nice numbers. Numbers that make tens or hundreds are the most common examples. Compatible sums also include numbers that end in 5, 25, 50, or 75, since these numbers are easy to work with as well. The teaching task is to get students accustomed to looking for combinations that work together and then looking for these combinations in computational situations.

ACTIVITY 5.24

Compatible Pairs

Searching for compatible pairs can be done as a worksheet activity or with the full class using the overhead projector. Prepare a transparency or duplicate a page with a search task. Five possibilities of different difficulty levels are shown in Figure 5.16. Students call out or connect the compatible pairs as they see them.

Here are two more activities that combine some of the ideas we have been exploring.

ACTIVITY 5.25

Calculator Challenge Counting

Students press any number on the calculator (e.g., 17), then [+] 8. They say the sum before they press [=]. Then they continue to add 8 mentally, challenging themselves to say the number before they press [=]. They should see how far they can go before making a mistake.

The constant addend in "Challenge Counting" can be any number, even a two- or three-digit number. Try 20 or 25. Try 40 and then 48. As an added challenge, after a student has progressed eight or ten counts, have the student reverse the process by pressing [−] followed by the same number and then, [=], [=], ... Discuss patterns that appear.

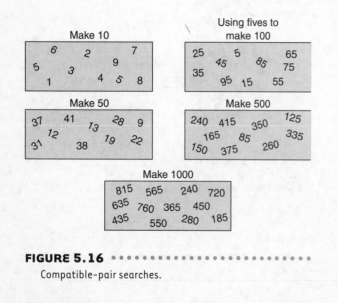

FIGURE 5.16 •
Compatible-pair searches.

Little Ten-Frame
Addition and Subtraction

Provide a set of little ten-frame cards for each of two students. Each student makes a number with his or her cards. When both have their number ready, they place it out so both can see. Then they try to be the first to tell the total. For the subtraction version, one student makes a number greater than 50 and the other writes a number on paper that is less than 50. The written number is to be subtracted from the modeled number. Students should be encouraged to share strategies to see how fast they can get.

Although activities like those in this section can be done independently or in pairs, it is good to occasionally do them with the full class so that strategies can be discussed.

Assessment Note

Students who exhibit difficulty with any of these activities will also have difficulty with almost any type of invented computation. For example, how do students go about the exercises in Activity 5.21, "Numbers, Squares, Sticks, and Dots"? This activity demands that children have sufficient understanding of base-ten concepts that they can use them in meaningful counts. If students are counting by ones, perhaps on their fingers, then more practice with these activities may be misplaced. Consider additional counting and grouping activities where students have the opportunity to see the value of groups of ten.

The following activity is frequently used in interviews with individual students but could easily be a task posed to the whole class or a small group for discussion. As you listen to how children solve these problems, you will realize that there is a lot more information to be found out about their thinking beyond simply getting the answer correct.

ACTIVITY 5.27

Mystery Mats

First, show a mat or board with some base-ten pieces covered and some showing. Tell the child how many pieces are hidden under the cover and ask him or her to figure out how much is on the board altogether, as in Figure 5.17(a).

After that, show a board partially covered as before. Tell the child how many pieces are on the board altogether and ask how many are hidden, as in Figure 5.17(b).

Activity 5.27 could also involve hundreds. The amounts that you tell the child could be given in written form instead of orally.

FIGURE 5.17 •••••••

Two useful assessment
activities.

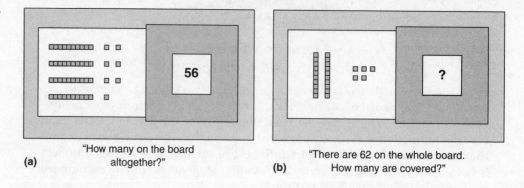

"How many on the board
altogether?"

(a)

"There are 62 on the whole board.
How many are covered?"

(b)

Helping Children Work with Money

Money skills such as counting and making change are perennial problems for the primary teacher. Most first- and second-grade books have one or more chapters devoted exclusively to money, and teachers find the subject to be difficult for their students. Although there are no easy answers, it is useful to consider what skills and concepts are required for working with money. Here is a list of the money ideas and skills typically required in the primary grades:

- Coin recognition
- Values of coins
- Using the values of coins
  - Counting sets of coins (including comparing two sets)
  - Equivalent collections of coins (same amounts, different coins)
  - Selecting coins for a given amount
  - Making change

Coin Recognition and Values

The recognition of coins is not a mathematical skill at all. The names of our coins are conventions of our social system. Students learn these names the same way that they learn the names of any physical objects in their daily environment—through exposure and repetition.

The value of each coin—a nickel is worth 5¢, a dime is worth 10¢, and so on—is also a convention that students must simply be told. However, a student can say, "A dime is worth 10 cents" and not really understand what that means. For these values to make sense, students must have an understanding of 5, 10, and 25. More than that, they need to be able to think of these quantities without seeing countable objects. Nowhere else do we say, "this is five," while pointing to a single item. A child whose number concepts remain tied to counts of objects is not going to be able to understand the values of coins. The social concept of having an *equivalent worth* or *value* is nontrivial for the young child. If your students seem to have good concepts of small numbers but still have difficulties with the values of single coins, then your lessons should focus on purchase power—a dime can *buy the same thing* that 10 pennies can buy.

Using Coin Values

The remaining items in the list are all a form of mental computation and/or compound skip counting. To name the total value of the coins shown is the same as mentally computing the following sum: 25 + 10 + 5 + 5 + 5 + 1 + 1. The coin task has the added difficulty that the values must also be called to mind with no numerals visible. Unfortunately, the task with coins comes well before students would be required to do the symbolic sum mentally.

There is nothing wrong with asking second-grade students to do the mental math required in counting a collection of coins. Even though it is actually mental computation, the numbers are fortunately restricted to multiples of 5 and 10 with some ones added at the end. The task can be seen either as skip counting or as addition. The skip-counting approach can help students develop their understanding of the patterns in our number system. To this end, the next activity extends "Nice-Number Skip Counts" (Activity 5.20) as a preparation for counting money.

ACTIVITY 5.28

Money Counts

Explain to the students that they will start counting by one number and at your signal they will shift to a count by a different number. Begin with only two different amounts, say, 25 and 10. Write these numbers on the board. Point to the larger number (25), and have students begin to count. After three or more counts, raise your hand to indicate a pause in the counting. Then lower your hand and point to the smaller number (10). Children continue the count from where they left off but now count by 10s. Use any two of these numbers: 100, 50, 25, 10, 5, 1. Always start with the larger. Later, try three numbers, still in descending order.

Note that the counts in "Money Counts" are the same as are used when counting coins or money. These skills can also be applied to bills and coins.

Assessment Note

When a collection of coins is not arranged in descending order of values, students must first impose this order on the collection. This is a skill based only on the ability to compare numbers and recognize the value of the coins. Check to see if students can put a string of numbers such as this in order from greatest to least: 5, 1, 5, 25, 10, 1, 25, 10. For a student experiencing difficulty with this task, try a collection with no duplicates. If there is still difficulty,

(continued)

it is clear that the student needs more experiences with counting, with the hundreds chart, and with other basic place-value concept-development activities.

If the student can put the numeral string in order but cannot order a set of coins, the problem is most likely a failure to have learned the values of the coins.

Remember that working with coins requires not only adding up the values but also first mentally giving each coin a value and then ordering the coins. A good readiness activity is the following one in which students add a mixed collection of numbers, each of which is the value of a coin.

ACTIVITY 5.29

Coin-Number Addition

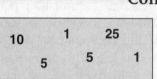

On the board or overhead, write a small collection of numbers in haphazard form. All numbers are the same as coin values.

How many numbers or whether you use 25s and 50s will vary with the experiences of your students. Begin with only 10s and 1s. Then add some 5s and eventually 25s (and 50s, if these are in your curriculum). The students' task is to add the numbers mentally. Do not suggest how they add the numbers or in what order because there is almost always more than one good way to do this. For example, rather than add from the largest values to the smallest—the typical way coins are taught in books—it is also reasonable to use the 5s to make tens or other methods. For this collection, note that it is easy to add 5 and 25, then 10, then 7 (the last 5 and two 1s). Discuss with students how they added the collection.

When discussing solutions to this last activity, be sure to value any approach that works. However, pay special attention to those students who begin with the larger values and those who put nice combinations together utilizing thinking with tens. There is no reason to require students to add in any particular order, not with this activity or with coins.

After students have gathered experiences with coin-numbers, try the same activity with coins. Simply spill some plastic coins on the overhead or draw "coins" on the board. (Draw circles with P, N, D, or Q inside, not numbers.) Equivalent exercises are found in most standard textbooks.

Making Change

Last in the list of money skills is making change. This is very similar to subtracting by adding on, an extremely valuable way to subtract mentally or with the aid of writing intermediate steps on paper.

 Before reading further, solve this problem mentally. How far is it from 46 to 83? Do this now.

There are several methods that you may have used. If you tried in some manner to take 46 away from 83, try another method. This time do something that involves finding what you have to add to 46 to make 83.

Among the methods you may have tried, your first steps may have been one of these:

- Add 4 to get to 50.

- Add 40 to get to 86 (or count by tens to 86).

- Add 30 to get to 76 (or count by tens to 76).

From these starts you would continue to add on or subtract (from 86) to find out that you need 37. (This process is discussed further in Chapter 6.) However, notice that you had to keep track of the intermediate values. If, for example, you began by adding 4, you have to "store" the 4 in your head. Then you might add 30 onto the 50, storing 30 more for a new total of 34. Now you add 3 more onto the stored 34 to get the answer. The stored numbers could have been written on paper, perhaps crossing out old ones as you went along.

Writing the stored numbers is certainly an aid for students who are just learning this process. Notice that it is not necessary to accumulate the stored numbers as you go if you are writing them down. In the example we just did, you might have written "4, 30, 3." A simple glance at these would tell you the answer. Before cash registers told them what change to give, store clerks used this exact same method to make change. The stored numbers were the coins they took out of the drawer as they added on: first pennies to get to a ten, then larger coins to get to the amount tendered. It was not necessary to actually add up the amount of the change but just count it out to the customer.

Why is this process so difficult for students? Most important, in traditional curricula, this is the only place where students are asked to add on to find a difference, so it is a very foreign type of task. Second, they are generally asked to create the difference or change in a prescribed manner. Finally, they must do it with coins instead of numerals.

Because adding on to find a difference is such a valuable skill—significantly easier than the traditional subtraction algorithm and lending itself to mental work—it makes sense to give students a lot of experience with adding on to find differences before asking them to make change. As students become more skillful at adding on, they can see the process of making change as an extension of a skill already acquired.

A good place to begin is with the activity "The Other Part of 100" (Activity 5.23) in the previous section. The use of the little ten-frame cards encourages students to first add up to the next ten, although, as noted, that is not the only method.

Follow "The Other Part of 100" with the next activity, which is similar.

ACTIVITY 5.30

How Much More?

Write a target number on the board. This number should be the same as an amount that might be given to a store clerk in a purchase, most likely 25, 50, 75, or 100. To the left of this target, write a smaller starting number and an arrow. Here are some examples:

$$13 \rightarrow 25$$
$$56 \rightarrow 75$$
$$29 \rightarrow 50$$

(continued)

Think in terms of purchases. If the target is 75, that means you gave the clerk 75¢. You would only do this for items costing more than 50¢. Similarly, for a target of 50, use numbers greater than 25. For a target of 100, any smaller number would be fine since you may have given the clerk a dollar bill. The students are to tell how much more is needed to add on to the starting number to get to the target. Students may write down intermediate results in any way they wish. A list of four of these is a reasonably short task. Discuss the methods of solution used by different students. To demonstrate how to write intermediate results, when a student is explaining his or her method, write the numbers on the board as described in the earlier discussion.

Do not explain this last activity as a money activity, only as a mental math exercise. Students will almost certainly use only ones and tens in their solutions. That is, they will not add on 25 or even 5 at a time. However, they are using the same methods they will use with coins. You are actually preparing these students for subtraction in general. The activity is especially useful for students who have learned the subtraction algorithm and resist adding on to subtract.

Next, modify "How Much More?" to the following activity.

ACTIVITY 5.31

How Much More with Coin Numbers?

At the top of the board, write the values of the coins: 25, 10, 5, 1. Include 50 if half-dollars are in your curriculum. Write four start and target numbers as in "How Much More?" In this task, however, students must use only numbers in the list to create the difference. They should write down each number they use as they use it. Furthermore, they should try to use as many of the larger numbers as possible, or, in other words, as few "coins" as possible. For example, if the target is 75 with a start of 58, they would write 1, 1, 10, 5. When students share their solutions, do not criticize those who do not use a minimal number of "coins." Rather, always ask if anyone can do it with fewer "coins." Ask this even when the solution is the desired one.

"How Much More with Coin Numbers?" is exactly the same as the task of making change except that students do not have to think about coins, only numbers. Furthermore, they are allowed to do it any way they wish. Obviously, the task can be extended to values greater than a dollar (greater than targets of 100).

This sequence of suggested activities is not a surefire solution to the difficulties students experience with money. It is designed to build on prerequisite number and place-value skills and concepts without or before using coins. The last two activities are also excellent readiness for subtraction as an "adding up" procedure.

These money activities are part of a good blend between computation and place-value development.

EXPANDED LESSON

Estimating Groups of Tens and Ones

Based on: Activity 5.3, p. 132

GRADE LEVEL: Late first or second grade.

MATHEMATICS GOALS
- To connect a count-by-ones understanding to a count based on the number of groups of 10 and leftovers for quantities to 100.
- To provide opportunities to measure lengths using non-standard measures.

THINKING ABOUT THE STUDENTS
Students have not yet developed a full understanding of two-digit numbers in terms of tens and ones. They are able to count a collection of objects to 100. They have talked about numbers in terms of bunches of tens and have discussed number patterns on the hundreds chart.

MATERIALS AND PREPARATION
- Decide on about 8 lengths for the students to measure. All lengths must be such that students can place measuring units end-to-end along the full length. Vertical distances can be measured with Unifix cubes or other snap cubes that can easily be made into a long bar.
- For each length, make a corresponding measurement "kit." Each kit should have more than enough individual units to measure the length it is paired with. Also, for each kit prepare 10 connected units, for example, a bar of 10 Unifix cubes, a chain of 10 paper clips, or 10 toothpicks sandwiched between two pieces of transparent tape.

FOR UNIT	USE LENGTHS
Unifix	2 to 5½ feet (60 cm to 180 cm)
Small paper clips	2 to 9 feet (60 cm to 270 cm)
Large paper clips	3 to 12 feet (90 cm to 4 m)
Toothpicks	5 to 12 feet (1.8 m to 4 m)

- A transparency of the recording sheet and a copy for each student. (See the Blackline Master L-3.)
- A kit of units that can be used in the BEFORE portion of the lesson.

lesson

BLM L-3

BEFORE

Begin with a Simpler Version of the Task
- Decide on a unit of length, such as Unifix cubes. Show students a length that is somewhere between 25 and 45 units long. For example, you might use the edge of a teacher's desk, a length of ribbon or rope, or a poster set on the chalk tray.
- Explain that you want to make an estimate of how long it is in terms of Unifix cubes. Accept some estimates. Expect students' guesses to be quite varied. Then suggest that it might be helpful to estimate in terms of groups of 10 units and leftovers. Show students a bar of 10 Unifix (or 10 of whatever unit you are using).
- Hold the 10 units at one end of the length to be measured and accept students' new estimates. Write the first child's estimate in the blank on the transparency. Explain that an *estimate* is what you think it might be by looking at the 10 units. It is not just a wild guess.
- Pass out the recording sheets and have students record their own estimate in the first box. Ask several students what their estimates are.
- Have two students use individual units to measure the length. It is important that they line units along the entire length so that when they have finished they will have as many actual units as required for the measure. Have two students put the units into groups of 10. Count the groups of 10 and count any leftovers separately. Record this in blanks labeled "Actual" on the recording sheet transparency and have students do likewise on their papers.
- Finally, ask students how many units there are. Have the class count the entire group by ones as you set them aside or point to each. Write the number word and the number (e.g., *thirty-four 34*) on the transparency. Have students record on their papers.

The Task

- For each length and corresponding unit, students are to see how good an estimate of the length they can make in terms of groups of 10 and leftovers.
- They then check their estimates by actually measuring, making, and counting groups of 10 and leftovers and, finally, counting all of the units.

Establish Expectations

- Explain that there are measuring kits and a length for each kit. For each length, students are to:
  - Hold the 10 units at one end of the length and estimate the measure of the length in terms of 10 and leftovers. Each student should record his or her estimate on the recording sheet. They may want to do this step independently to see who is the better estimator.
  - They are then to measure the lengths by using units—laying them end to end.
  - When they have placed units along the full length, they should make sets of 10. They count and record the number of groups of 10 and leftovers.
  - Finally, they should count all of the units and record this as a number word and as a number. Refer to your example.
- Students are only to measure three different lengths. As long as they use the kit that goes with the length, it does not make any difference which lengths they measure.

DURING

- Be sure that students are making and recording estimates by comparing the length to the provided strip of 10. They are not to change their estimates.
- Pay attention to how students count the total number of units. Some may already know that 4 tens and 6 leftovers is 46. However, most should probably be counting the total by ones. Challenge students who just count groups: *Are you sure you will get 46 if you count them all by ones?*

AFTER

When all students have completed at least three estimates and measures, discuss what it means to estimate—it is not the same as a guess. Ask: *How did using a group of ten units help you make an estimate? How does counting the groups of tens and leftovers help tell you how many units you had?* This last question is the key to this lesson. Avoid telling students how to relate the groups and leftovers to the actual number.

ASSESSMENT NOTES

- Look for students who do not make connections between the groups and leftovers, and the actual counts. These students have not yet developed base-ten concepts.
- Students who confidently state the total when they have the number of groups and leftovers have indicated at least a beginning understanding of base-ten concepts.

- -

next steps

- Students who need more base-ten experiences can benefit by counting groups by ones first and then putting them into groups of ten (see Activity 5.2, p. 130). Putting numbers in the correct place on a blank hundreds chart is also a good activity for these students.
- Students should also be working on the oral names for numbers and beginning to see how numbers can be made with other groupings of tens and ones (e.g., 47 is 3 tens and 17 ones). See Activities 5.4, 5.5, and 5.6.
- Before becoming too confident about students who seem to understand this activity, try some of the assessments in the Assessment Note on pp. 141–142.

STRATEGIES FOR WHOLE-NUMBER COMPUTATION

Much of the public sees computational skill as the hallmark of what it means to know mathematics at the elementary school level. Although this is far from the truth, the issue of computational skills with whole numbers is, in fact, a very important part of the elementary curriculum, especially in grades 2 to 6.

Rather than constant reliance on a single method of subtracting (or any operation), methods can and should change flexibly as the numbers and the context change. In the spirit of the *Standards,* the issue is no longer a matter of "knows how to subtract three-digit numbers"; rather it is the development over time of an assortment of flexible skills that will best serve students in the real world.

Toward Computational Fluency

With today's technology the need for doing tedious computations by hand has essentially disappeared. At the same time, we now know that there are numerous methods of computing that can be handled either mentally or with pencil-and-paper support. In most everyday instances, these alternative strategies for computing

big ideas

1 Flexible methods of computation involve taking apart and combining numbers in a wide variety of ways. Most of the partitions of numbers are based on place value or "compatible" numbers—number pairs that work easily together, such as 25 and 75.

2 Invented strategies are flexible methods of computing that vary with the numbers and the situation. Successful use of the strategies requires that they be understood by the one who is using them—hence, the term *invented*. Strategies may be invented by a peer or the class as a whole; they may even be suggested by the teacher. However, they must be constructed by the student.

3 Flexible methods for computation require a good understanding of the operations and properties of the operations, especially the turnaround property and the distributive property for multiplication. How the operations are related—addition to subtraction, addition to multiplication, and multiplication to division—is also an important ingredient.

4 The traditional algorithms are clever strategies for computing that have been developed over time. Each is based on performing the operation on one place value at a time with transitions to an adjacent position (trades, regrouping, "borrows," or "carries"). These algorithms work for all numbers but are often far from the most efficient or useful methods of computing.

are easier and faster, can often be done mentally, and contribute to our overall number sense. The traditional algorithms (procedures for computing) do not have these benefits. Consider the following problem.

Mary has 114 spaces in her photo album. So far she has 89 photos in the album. How many more photos can she put in before the album is full?

 Try solving the photo album problem using some method other than the one you were taught in school. If you want to begin with the 9 and the 4, try a different approach. Can you do it mentally? Can you do it in more than one way? Work on this before reading further.

Here are just four of many methods that have been used by students in the primary grades to solve the computation in the photo album problem:

89 + 11 is 100. 11 + 14 is 25.

90 + 10 is 100 and 14 more is 24 plus 1 (for 89, not 90) is 25.

Take away 14 and then take away 11 more or 25 in all.

89, 99, 109 (that's 20). 110, 111, 112, 113, 114 (keeping track on fingers) is 25.

Strategies such as these can be done mentally, are generally faster than the traditional algorithms, and make sense to the person using them. Every day, students and adults resort to error-prone, traditional strategies when other, more meaningful methods would be faster and less susceptible to error. Flexibility with a variety of computational strategies is an important tool for successful daily living. It is time to broaden our perspective of what it means to compute.

Figure 6.1 lists three general types of computing. The initial, inefficient direct modeling methods can, with guidance, develop into an assortment of invented strategies that are flexible and useful. As noted in the diagram, many of these methods can be handled mentally, although no special methods are designed specifically for mental computation. The traditional pencil-and-paper algorithms remain in the mainstream curricula. However, the attention given to them should, at the very least, be debated.

Direct Modeling

The developmental step that usually precedes invented strategies is called *direct modeling:* the use of manipulatives or drawings along with counting to represent directly the meaning of an operation or story problem. Figure 6.2 provides an example using base-ten materials, but often students use simple counters and count by ones.

Students who consistently count by ones most likely have not developed base-ten grouping concepts. That does not mean that they should not continue to solve problems involving two-digit numbers. As you work with

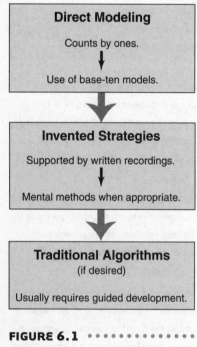

FIGURE 6.1

Three types of computational strategies.

these children, suggest (don't force) that they group counters by tens as they count. Perhaps instead of making large piles, they might make bars of ten from connecting cubes or organize counters in cups of ten. Some students will use the ten-stick as a counting device to keep track of counts of ten, even though they are counting each segment of the stick by ones.

When children have plenty of experience with base-ten concepts and models, they begin to use these ideas in the direct modeling of the problems. Even when students use base-ten materials, they will find many different ways to solve problems.

Invented Strategies

We will refer to any strategy other than the traditional algorithm and that does not involve the use of physical materials or counting by ones as an *invented strategy*. These invented strategies might also be called *personal and flexible strategies*. At times, invented strategies are done mentally. For example, 75 + 19 can be done mentally (75 + 20 is 95, less 1 is 94). For 847 + 256, some students may write down intermediate steps to aid in memory as they work through the problem. (Try that one yourself.) In the classroom, some written support is often encouraged as strategies develop. Written records of thinking are more easily shared and help students focus on the ideas. The distinction between written, partially written, and mental is not important, especially in the development period.

Over the past two decades, a number of research projects have focused attention on how children handle computational situations when they have not been taught a specific algorithm or strategy. Three elementary curricula each base the development of computational methods on student-invented strategies. These are often referred to as "reform curricula" (*Investigations in Number, Data, and Space, Trailblazers,* and *Everyday Mathematics*)."There is mounting evidence that children both in and out of school can construct methods for adding and subtracting multidigit numbers without explicit instruction" (Carpenter et al., 1998, p. 4).

Not all students invent their own strategies. Strategies invented by class members are shared, explored, and tried out by others. However, no student should be permitted to use any strategy without understanding it.

Contrasts with Traditional Algorithms

There are significant differences between invented strategies and the traditional algorithms.

1. *Invented strategies are number oriented rather than digit oriented.* For example, an invented strategy for 618 – 254 might begin with 600 – 200 is 400. Another approach might begin with 254. Adding 46 is 300 and then 300 more to 600. In either case, the computation begins with complete three-digit numbers rather than the individual digits 8 – 4 as in the traditional algorithm. Using the traditional algorithm for 45 + 32, children never think of 40 and 30 but rather 4 + 3. Kamii, long a crusader against standard algorithms, claims that they "unteach" place value (Kamii & Dominick, 1998).

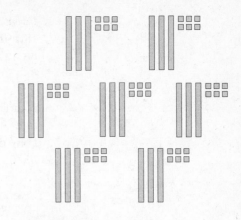

FIGURE 6.2 • • • • • • • • • • • • • • • •

A possible direct modeling of 36 × 7 using base-ten models.

2. *Invented strategies are left-handed rather than right-handed.* Invented strategies begin with the largest parts of numbers, those represented by the leftmost digits. For 86 – 17, an invented strategy might begin with 80 – 10, 80 – 20, or perhaps 86 – 10. These and similar left-handed beginnings provide a quick sense of the size of the answer. With the traditional approach, after borrowing from the 8 and computing 16 – 7, all we know is that the answer ends in 9. By beginning on the right with a digit orientation, traditional methods hide the result until the end. Long division is an exception.

3. *Invented strategies are flexible rather than rigid.* As in 1 and 2 above, several different strategies can be used to begin an addition or subtraction computation. Invented strategies also tend to change or adapt to the numbers involved. Try each of these mentally: 465 + 230 and 526 + 98. Did you use the same method? The traditional algorithm suggests using the same tool on all problems. The traditional algorithm for 7000 – 25 typically leads to student errors, yet a mental strategy is relatively simple.

Benefits of Invented Strategies

The development of invented strategies delivers more than computational facility. Both the development of these strategies and their regular use have positive benefits that are difficult to ignore.

- *Base-ten concepts are enhanced.* There is a definite interaction between the development of base-ten concepts and the process of inventing computational strategies (Carpenter et al., 1998). "Invented strategies demonstrate a hallmark characteristic of understanding" (p. 16). The development of invented strategies should be integrated with the development of base-ten concepts, even as early as first grade.

- *Students make fewer errors.* Research has found that when students use their own strategies for computation they tend to make fewer errors because they understand their own methods (e.g., see Kamii and Dominick, 1997). Decades of trying to teach the traditional algorithms, no matter how conceptually, have continually demonstrated that students make numerous, often systematic errors that they use again and again. Systematic errors are not typical with invented strategies.

- *Less reteaching is required.* Students rarely use an invented strategy they do not understand. The supporting ideas are firmly networked with a sense of number, thus making the strategies more permanent. In contrast, students are frequently seen using traditional algorithms without being able to explain why they work (Carroll & Porter, 1997).

- *Invented strategies provide the basis for mental computation and estimation.* Since traditional algorithms are poorly suited to mental computation and estimation strategies, students are forced to temporarily abandon the very strategies that were taught and learn new, number-oriented, left-handed methods. It makes much more sense to teach these methods from the beginning. As students become more and more proficient with these flexible methods using pencil-and-paper support, they soon are able to use them mentally or adapt them to estimation methods. Again we find that time is saved in the curriculum.

- *Flexible, invented strategies are often faster than the traditional algorithms.* It is sad to see a student (or even adults) tediously regrouping for computations such as 300 − 98 or 4 × 75. Much of the computation that adults do daily when technology is not available is of the type that lends itself to methods than can often be done very quickly with a nontraditional approach.

- *Invented strategies serve students at least as well on standard tests.* Evidence suggests that students not taught traditional algorithms fare about as well in computation on standardized tests as students in traditional programs (Campbell, 1996; Carroll, 1996, 1997; Chambers, 1996). As an added bonus, students tend to do quite well with word problems, since they are the principal vehicle for developing invented strategies. The pressures of external testing do not dictate a focus on the traditional algorithms.

Mental Computation

A mental computation strategy is simply any invented strategy that is done mentally. What may be a mental strategy for one student may require written support by another. Initially, students should not be asked to do computations mentally, as this may threaten those who have not yet developed a reasonable invented strategy or who are still at the direct modeling stage. At the same time, you may be quite amazed at the ability of students (and at your own ability) to do computations mentally.

Try your own hand with this example:

$$342 + 153 + 481$$

STOP For the addition task just shown, try this method: Begin by adding the hundreds, saying the totals as you go—*3 hundred, 4 hundred, 8 hundred.* Then add on to this the tens in successive manner and finally the ones. Do it now.

As your students become more adept, they can and should be challenged from time to time to do appropriate computations mentally. Do not expect the same skills of all students.

Traditional Algorithms

Teachers often ask, "How long should I wait until I show them the 'regular' way?" The question is based on a fear that without learning the same methods that all of us grew up with, students will somehow be disadvantaged. For addition and subtraction this is simply not the case. The primary goal for all computation should be students' ability to compute in some efficient manner—not what algorithms are used. That is, the *method* of computing is not the objective; the ability to compute is the goal. For multiplication and division, many teachers will see a greater need for traditional approaches, especially with three or more digits involved. However, even with those operations, the traditional algorithms are not necessary.

Abandon or Delay Traditional Algorithms

Flexible left-handed methods done mentally with written support are absolutely all that are necessary for addition and subtraction. Developed with adequate practice in the primary grades, these flexible approaches will become mental and very efficient for most students by fifth grade and will serve them more than adequately throughout life. You may find this difficult to accept for two reasons: first, because the traditional algorithms have been a significant part of your mathematical experiences, and second, because *you* may not have learned these skills. These are not reasons to teach the traditional algorithms for addition and subtraction.

For multiplication and division, the argument may not be quite as strong as the number of digits involved increases. However, through the third grade where students need only multiply or divide by a single digit, invented strategies are not only adequate but will provide the benefits of understanding and flexibility mentioned earlier. It is worth noting again that there is evidence that students do quite well on the computation portions of standardized tests even if they are never taught the traditional methods.

If, for whatever reason you feel you must teach the traditional algorithms, consider the following:

- Students will not invent the traditional methods because right-handed methods are simply not natural. This means that you will have to introduce and explain each algorithm.

- No matter how carefully you suggest that these right-handed borrow-and-carry methods are simply another alternative, students will sense that these are the "right ways" or the "real ways" to compute. *This is how Mom and Dad do it. This is what the teacher taught us.* As a result, most students will abandon any flexible left-handed methods they may have been developing.

It is not that the traditional algorithms cannot be taught with a strong conceptual basis. Textbooks have been doing an excellent job of explaining these methods for years. The problem is that the traditional algorithms, especially for addition and subtraction, are not natural methods for students. As a result, the explanations generally fall on deaf ears. Far too many students learn them as meaningless procedures, develop error patterns, and require an excessive amount of reteaching or remediation. If you are going to teach the traditional algorithms, you are well advised to spend a significant amount of time—months, not weeks—with invented methods. Delay! The understanding that children gain from working with invented strategies will make it much easier for you to teach the traditional methods.

Traditional Algorithms Will Happen

You probably cannot keep the traditional algorithms out of your classroom. Children pick them up from older siblings, last year's teacher, or well-meaning parents. Traditional algorithms are in no way evil, and so to forbid their use is somewhat arbitrary. However, students who latch on to a traditional method often resist the invention of more flexible strategies. What do you do then?

First and foremost, apply the same rule to traditional algorithms as to all strategies: *If you use it, you must understand why it works and be able to explain it.* In an atmosphere that says, "Let's figure out why this works," students can profit from making sense of these algorithms just like any other. But the responsibility should be theirs, not yours.

Accept a traditional algorithm (once it is understood) as one more strategy to put in the class "tool box" of methods. But reinforce the idea that like the other strategies, it may be more useful in some instances than in others. Pose problems where a mental strategy is much more useful, such as 504 – 498 or 25 + 62. Discuss which method seemed best. Point out that for a problem such as 4568 + 12,813, the traditional algorithm has some advantages. But in the real world, most people do those computations on a calculator.

Development of Invented Strategies: A General Approach

Students do not spontaneously invent wonderful computational methods while the teacher sits back and watches. Among different reform or progressive programs, students tended to develop or gravitate toward different strategies suggesting that teachers and the programs do have an effect on what methods students develop. This section discusses general pedagogical methods for helping children develop invented strategies.

Use Story Problems Frequently

When computational tasks are embedded in simple contexts, students seem to be more engaged than they are with bare computations. Furthermore, the choice of story problems influences the strategies students use to solve them. Consider these problems:

> **Max had already saved 68 cents when Mom gave him some money for running an errand. Now Max has 93 cents. How much did Max earn for his errand?**

> **George took 93 cents to the store. He spent 68 cents. How much does he have left?**

The computation 93 – 68 solves both problems, but the first is more likely than the second to be solved by an add-on method. In a similar manner, fair-share division problems are more likely to encourage a share strategy than a measurement or repeated subtraction problem.

Not every task need be a story problem. Especially when students are engaged in figuring out a new strategy, bare arithmetic problems are quite adequate.

Use the Three-Part Lesson Format

The three-part lesson format described in Chapter 1 is a good structure for an invented-strategy lesson. The task can be one or two story problems or even a bare computation but always with the expectation that the method of solution will be discussed.

Allow plenty of time to solve a problem. Listen to the different strategies students are using, but do not interject your own. Challenge able students to find a second method, solve a problem without models, or improve on a written explanation. Allow children who are not ready for thinking with tens to use simple counting methods. Students who finish quickly may share their methods with others before sharing with the class.

The most important portion of the lesson comes when students explain their solution methods. Help students write their explanations on the board or overhead. Encourage students to ask questions of their classmates. Occasionally have the class try a particular method with different numbers to see how it works.

Remember, not every student will invent strategies. However, students can and will try strategies that they have seen and that make sense to them.

Select Numbers with Care

With the traditional algorithms you are used to distinguishing between problems that require regrouping and those that do not. When encouraging students to develop their own methods, there are more factors to consider. For addition, 35 + 42 is generally easier than 35 + 47. However, 30 + 20 is easier than both and can help students begin to think in terms of tens. Paired with this might be 46 + 10 or 20 + 63. At grade 1, 10 + 11 can provide challenge, a variety of methods, and the start of thinking with tens. Two-digit plus one-digit sums can also serve as a useful stepping-stone. For addition, *Will the sum go over 100?* is a thought to consider.

Think about how multiples of ten might help. For subtraction, learning to add up to a multiple of 10 and especially to 100 is particularly useful. Therefore, tasks such as 30 – 12 and 100 – 35 can provide important readiness for later problems. Tasks such as 417 – 103 or 417 – 98 may each encourage students to subtract 100 and then adjust.

There is no best sequence of problem types. Listen to the strategies students use and select numbers that can build on those ideas or help others in the class to see a new way of thinking. Similar care can and should be given to the selection of multiplication and division tasks.

Integrate Computation with Place-Value Development

In Chapter 5 we made the point that students can begin to develop computational strategies as they are learning about tens and ones. It is not necessary to wait until students have learned place value before they begin computing. Notice how the examples in the preceding section on number selection can help reinforce the way that our number system is built on a structure of groups of tens. In Chapter 5 there is a section entitled "Activities for Flexible Thinking" (p. 145). The activities in that section are appropriate for grades 2 and 3 and complement the development of invented strategies, especially for addition and subtraction.

Progression from Direct Modeling

Direct modeling involving tens and ones can and will lead eventually to invented strategies. However, students may need to be encouraged to move away from the direct modeling process. Here are some ideas:

- Record students' verbal explanations on the board in ways that they and others can model. Have the class follow the recorded method using different numbers.

- Ask children to make a written numeric record of what they did when they solved the problem with models. Explain that they are then going to try to use the same method on a new problem.

- Ask students who have just solved a problem with models to see if they can do it in their heads.

- Pose a problem to the class, and ask students to solve it mentally if they are able.

Invented Strategies for Addition and Subtraction

Research has demonstrated that children will invent a lot of different strategies for addition and subtraction. Your goal might be that each of your children has at least one or two methods that are reasonably efficient, mathematically correct, and useful with lots of different numbers. Expect different children to settle on different strategies.

It is not at all unreasonable for students to be able to add and subtract two-digit numbers mentally by third grade. However, daily recording of strategies on the board not only helps communicate ideas but also helps children who need the short-term memory assistance of recording intermediate steps.

Adding and Subtracting Single Digits

Children can easily extend addition and subtraction facts to higher decades.

> Tommy was on page 47 of his book. Then he read 8 more pages. How many pages did Tommy read in all?

If students are simply counting on by ones, the following activity may be useful. It is an extension of the make-ten strategy for addition facts.

ACTIVITY 6.1

Ten-Frame Adding and Subtracting

Quickly review the make-ten idea from addition facts using two ten-frames. (Add on to get up to ten and then add the rest.) Challenge children to use the same idea to add on to a two-digit number as shown in Figure 6.3. Two students can work together. First, they make a specified two-digit number with the little ten-frame cards. They then stack up all of the less-than-ten cards and turn them over one at a time. Together they talk about how to get the total quickly.

The same approach is used for subtraction. For instance, for 53 – 7, take off 3 to get to 50, then 4 more is 46.

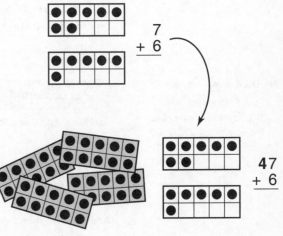

FIGURE 6.3

Little ten-frame cards can help children extend the make-ten idea to larger numbers.

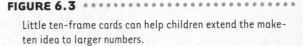

Notice how building up through ten (as in 47 + 6) or down through ten (as in 53 – 7) is different from carrying and borrowing. No ones are exchanged for a ten or tens for ones. The ten-frame cards encourage students to work with multiples of ten without regrouping.

Another important model to use in the second and third grades is the hundreds chart. The hundreds chart has the same tens structure as the little ten-frame cards. For 47 + 6 you count 3 to get out to 50 at the end of the row and then 3 more in the next row.

Adding and Subtracting Tens and Hundreds

Sums and differences involving multiples of 10 or 100 are easily computed mentally. Write a problem such as the following on the board:

$$300 + 500 + 20$$

Challenge children to solve it mentally. Ask students to share how they did it. Look for use of place-value words: "3 *hundred* and 5 *hundred* is 8 *hundred,* and 20 is 820."

Adding Two-Digit Numbers

For each of the examples that follow, a possible recording method is offered. These are intended to be suggestions, not prescriptions. Children have difficulty inventing recording techniques. If you record their ideas on the board as they explain their ideas, you are helping them develop written techniques. You may even discuss recording methods with individuals or with the class to decide on a form that seems to work well. Horizontal formats encourage students to think in terms of numbers instead of digits. A horizontal format is also less likely to encourage use of the traditional algorithms.

Students will often use a counting-by-tens-and-ones technique for some of these methods. That is, instead of "46 + 30 is 76," they may count "46 ⟶ 56, 66, 76." These counts can be written down as they are said to help students keep track.

Figure 6.4 illustrates four different strategies for addition of two two-digit numbers. The following story problem is a suggestion.

FIGURE 6.4 • • • • • • • •

Four different invented strategies for adding two two-digit numbers.

Invented Strategies for Addition with Two-Digit Numbers	
Add Tens, Add Ones, Then Combine 46 + 38 40 and 30 is 70. 6 and 8 is 14. 70 and 14 is 84. $\begin{array}{r} 46 \\ +38 \\ \hline 70 \\ 14 \\ \hline 84 \end{array}$	**Move Some to Make Tens** 46 + 38 Take 2 from the 46 and put it with the 38 to make 40. Now you have 44 and 40 more is 84. $\overset{2}{4\!\!6} + \overset{\longrightarrow}{38}$ 44 + 40 84
Add On Tens, Then Add Ones 46 + 38 46 and 30 more is 76. Then I added on the other 8. 76 and 4 is 80 and 4 is 84. $46 + 38 \rightarrow$ $76 + 8 \rightarrow 80, 84$	**Use a Nice Number and Compensate** 46 + 38 46 and 40 is 86. That's 2 extra, so it's 84. $46 + 38 \rightarrow$ $46 + 40 \rightarrow$ $86 - 2 \rightarrow 84$

The two Scout troops went on a field trip. There were 46 Girl Scouts and 38 Boy Scouts. How many Scouts went on the trip?

The *move to make ten* and *compensation* strategies are useful when one of the numbers ends in 8 or 9. To promote that strategy, present problems with addends like 39 or 58. Note that it is only necessary to adjust one of the two numbers.

> **STOP** Try adding 367 + 155 in as many different ways as you can. How many of your ways are like those in Figure 6.4?

Subtracting by Counting Up

This is an amazingly powerful way to subtract. Students working on the *think-addition* strategy for their basic facts can also be solving problems with larger numbers. The concept is the same. It is important to use *join with change unknown* problems or *missing-part* problems to encourage the counting-up strategy. Here is an example of each.

Sam had 46 baseball cards. He went to a card show and got some more cards for his collection. Now he has 73 cards. How many cards did Sam buy at the card show?

Juanita counted all of her crayons. Some were broken and some not. She had 73 crayons in all. 46 crayons were not broken. How many were broken?

The numbers in these problems are used in the strategies illustrated in Figure 6.5.

Invented Strategies for Subtraction by Counting Up	
Add Tens to Get Close, Then Ones	**Add Ones to Make a Ten, Then Tens and Ones**
73 – 46 $\quad$ 46 ⟩ 20	73 – 46 $\quad$ 73 – 46
46 and 20 is 66. $\quad$ 66 ⟩ 4	46 and 4 is 50. $\quad$ 46 + 4 → 50
(30 more is too much.) $\quad$ 70 ⟩ 3	50 and 20 is 70 and 3 $\quad\quad$ + 20 → 70
Then 4 more is 70 and 3 is 73. $\quad$ 73 $\quad$ ___	more is 73. The 4 and 3 $\quad\quad$ + 3 → 73
That's 20 and 7 or 27. $\quad\quad$ 27	is 7 and 20 is 27. $\quad\quad$ ___ 27
Add Tens to Overshoot, Then Come Back	
73 – 46 $\quad$ 73 – 46	Similarly, $\quad$ 46 + 4 → 50
46 and 30 is 76. $\quad$ 46 + 30 → 76 – 3 → 73	46 and 4 is 50. $\quad$ 50 + 23 → 73
That's 3 too $\quad$ 30 – 3 = 27	50 and 23 is 73. $\quad$ 23 + 4 = 27
much, so it's 27.	23 and 4 is 27.

FIGURE 6.5

Subtraction by counting up is a powerful method.

Emphasize the value of using tens by posing problems involving multiples of 10. In 50 – 17, the use of ten can happen by adding up from 17 to 20, or by adding 30 to 17. Some students may reason that it must be 30-something because 30 and 17 is less than 50 and 40, and 17 is more than 50. Because it takes 3 to go with 7 to make 10, the answer must be 33. Work on naming the missing part of 50 or 100 is also valuable. (See Activity 5.23, "The Other Part of 100," p. 147.)

Take-Away Subtraction

Using take-away is considerably more difficult to do mentally. However, take-away strategies are common, probably because traditional textbooks emphasize take-away as the meaning of subtraction and take-away is the basis of the traditional algorithm. Four different strategies are shown in Figure 6.6.

....

There were 73 children on the playground. The 46 second-grade students came in first. How many children were still outside?

....

The two methods that begin by taking tens from tens are reflective of what most students do with base-ten pieces. The other two methods leave one of the numbers intact and subtract from it. Try 83 – 29 in your head by first taking away 30 and adding 1 back. This is a good mental method when subtracting a number that is close to a multiple of ten.

EXPANDED LESSON

(pages 184–185)

The Expanded Lesson for this chapter has students explore subtraction of two-digit numbers.

 Try computing 82 – 57. Use both take-away and counting-up methods. Can you use all of the strategies in Figures 6.5 and 6.6 without looking?

FIGURE 6.6 ••••••••

Take-away strategies work reasonably well for two-digit problems. They are a bit more difficult with three digits.

Invented Strategies for Take-Away Subtraction	
Take Tens from the Tens, Then Subtract Ones 73 – 46 70 minus 40 is 30. Take away 6 more is 24. Now add in the 3 ones ⟶ 27. $73 - 46$ $70 - 40 \to 30 - 6 \to$ $24 + 3 \to 27$ Or 70 minus 40 is 30. I can take those 3 away, but I need 3 more from the 30 to make 27. $\begin{array}{r} 7\cancel{3} \\ -\ 46 \\ \hline 30 \\ -\ 3 \\ \hline 27 \end{array}$	**Take Away Tens, Then Ones** 73 – 46 73 minus 40 is 33. Then take away 6: 3 makes 30 and 3 more is 27. $73 - 40 \to 33 - 3$ $30 - 3 \to 27$ **Take Extra Tens, Then Add Back** 73 – 46 73 take away 50 is 23. That's 4 too many. 23 and 4 is 27. $73 - 50 \to 23 + 4$ 27 **Add to the Whole If Necessary** 73 – 46 Give 3 to 73 to make 76. 76 take away 46 is 30. Now give 3 back ⟶ 27. $\overset{+3}{73 - 46}$ $76 - 46 \to 30$ $-3 \to 27$

Extensions and Challenges

Each of the examples in the preceding sections involved sums less than 100 and all involved *bridging a ten;* that is, if done with a traditional algorithm, they require carrying or borrowing. Bridging, the size of the numbers, and the potential for doing problems mentally are all issues to consider.

Bridging

For most of the strategies, it is easier to add or subtract when bridging is not required. Try each strategy with 34 + 52 or 68 – 24 to see how it works. Easier problems instill confidence. They also permit you to challenge your students with a "harder one." There is also the issue of bridging 100 or 1000. Try 58 + 67 with different strategies. Bridging across 100 is also an issue for subtraction. Problems such as 128 – 50 or 128 – 45 are more difficult than ones that do not bridge 100.

Larger Numbers

Most curricula will expect third graders to add and subtract three-digit numbers. Your state standards may even require work with four-digit numbers. Try seeing how *you* would do these without using the traditional algorithms: 487 + 235 and 623 – 247. For subtraction, a counting-up strategy is usually the easiest. Occasionally, other strategies appear with larger numbers. For example, "chunking off" multiples of 50 or 25 is often a useful method. For 462 + 257, pull out 450 and 250 to make 700. That leaves 12 and 7 more $\longrightarrow$ 719.

Traditional Algorithms for Addition and Subtraction

The traditional computational methods for addition and subtraction are significantly different from nearly every invented method. In addition to starting with the rightmost digits and being digit oriented (as already noted), the traditional approaches involve the concept generally referred to as *regrouping* (a very strange term), exchanging 10 in one place-value position for 1 in the position to the left ("carrying")—or the reverse, exchanging 1 for 10 in the position to the right ("borrowing"). The terms *borrowing* and *carrying* are obsolete and conceptually misleading. The word *regroup* also offers no conceptual help to young children. A preferable term is *trade*. Ten ones are *traded* for a ten. A hundred is *traded* for 10 tens.

Terminology aside, the trading process is quite different from the bridging process used in all invented and mental strategies. Consider the task of adding 28 + 65. Using the traditional method, we first add 8 and 5. The resulting 13 ones must be separated into 3 ones and 1 ten. The newly formed ten must then be combined with the other tens. This process of "carrying a ten" is conceptually difficult and is different from the bridging process that occurs in invented strategies. In fact, nearly all major textbooks now teach this process of regrouping prior to and separate from direct instruction with the addition and subtraction algorithm, an indication of the difficulties involved. The process is even more difficult for subtraction, especially across a zero in the tens place where two successive trades are required.

Compounding all of this is the issue of recording each step. The traditional algorithms do not lend themselves to mental computation and so students must learn to record. The literature of the past 50 years is replete with the errors that students make with these recording methods.

It is also a serious error to focus on nonregrouping problems before tackling regrouping. Teaching nonregrouping problems first causes bad habits that children must later unlearn. The most common result is for students to completely ignore the numbers involved and focus only on adding in each column. When regrouping is eventually introduced, there is a strong tendency to not regroup at all, recording 615 as the sum of 28 and 47. When carrying is finally emphasized, many students compensate by carrying all of the time, even when not needed. Similar difficulties arise in subtraction.

All of these observations are offered to encourage you to abandon the traditional algorithms for addition and subtraction and, failing that, to alert you to the difficulties that your students will likely experience. Having said that, we offer some guidance for you if you must teach the standard procedures. Since it will never occur to students to add or subtract beginning in the ones place, you will have to use a more direct approach to instruction rather than a strictly problem-oriented approach.

The Addition Algorithm

Explain to the students that they are going to learn a method of adding that most "big people" learned when they were in school. It is not the only way or even the best way; it is just a method you want them to learn.

Begin with Models Only

BLM 15

In the beginning, avoid any written work except for the possible recording of an answer. Provide children with place-value mats and base-ten models. A mat with two ten-frames in the ones place (Blackline Masters) is suggested.

Have students make one number at the top of the mat and a second beneath it as shown in Figure 6.7. A groupable model such as counters in cups is most helpful.

You will need to explain two rules. First: *Begin in the ones column.* Second: *Do not keep more than 9 pieces in any column. Make a trade if possible.* You can let students solve problems on their own using base-ten models and following these rules. You will likely still need to work on the idea of trading. Do not begin written records until students are comfortable and fluent with this process.

Develop the Written Record

The general idea at this stage is to have students record each step *as they do it* with manipulatives. A useful suggestion is to have students turn their lined paper a quarter turn and use the lines to keep the columns separate. For the first few times, guide each step carefully. Most textbooks do quite a good job of illustrating the process.

Another suggestion is to have children work in pairs. One child is responsible for the models and the other for recording the steps. Children reverse roles with each problem.

Figure 6.8 shows a variation of the traditional recording scheme that is quite reasonable, at least for up to three digits. It avoids the little "carried ones" and focuses attention on the value of the digits. If students were permitted to start adding on the left as they are inclined to do, this

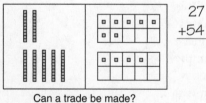

$$\begin{array}{r} 27 \\ +54 \\ \hline \end{array}$$

Can a trade be made?
How can you tell?

FIGURE 6.7 • • • • • • • • • • • • • •

Setting up the addition algorithm.

recording procedure is the same as that shown for the invented strategy "Add tens, add ones, then combine" (Figure 6.4, p. 166).

The Subtraction Algorithm

The general approach to developing the subtraction algorithm is the same as for addition. When the procedure is completely understood with models, a do-and-write approach connects it with a written form.

Begin with Models Only

Start by having children model only the top number in a subtraction problem on the top half of their place-value mats. For the amount to be subtracted, have children write each digit on a small piece of paper and place these pieces near the bottom of their mats in the respective columns, as in Figure 6.9. Explain to children that they are to begin working with the ones column first, as they did with addition. To avoid inadvertent errors, suggest making trades before removing any pieces. That way, the full amount on the paper slip can be taken off at once.

Anticipate Difficulties with Zeros

Exercises in which zeros are involved anywhere in the problem tend to cause special difficulties. Give extra attention to these cases while still using models.

The very common error of "borrowing across zero" is best addressed at the modeling stage. For example, in 403 – 138, children must make a double trade, exchanging a hundreds piece for 10 tens and then one of the tens for 10 ones.

Develop the Written Record

The process of recording each step as it is done is the same as was suggested for addition.

When children can explain symbolism, that is a signal for moving children on to a completely symbolic level. Again, be attentive to problems with zeros.

If students are permitted to follow their natural instincts and begin with the big pieces (from the left instead of the right), recording schemes similar to that shown in Figure 6.10 are possible. The trades are made from the pieces remaining *after* the subtraction in the column to the left has been done. A "borrow across zero" difficulty will still occur, but in problems like this: 462 – 168. Try it.

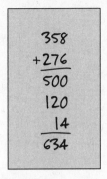

FIGURE 6.8

An alternative recording scheme for addition. Notice that this can be used from left to right as well as from right to left.

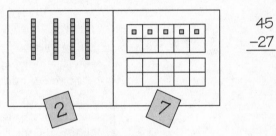

Not enough ones to take off 7.
Trade a ten for 10 ones.

FIGURE 6.9

Setting up the subtraction algorithm.

Assessment Note

It is not unusual for some children in the second grade to use inefficient count-by-ones methods for a long time, showing little or no interest in trying strategies that involve the use of tens. When children do not progress to the more efficient methods that have been illustrated here it can be very disturbing, especially with the pressures of external testing to worry about.

FIGURE 6.10

A left-hand recording scheme for subtraction. Other methods can also be devised.

(continued)

TRADITIONAL ALGORITHMS FOR ADDITION AND SUBTRACTION

A first response should be patience. Many children simply need more time to develop methods that utilize tens. Having said that, it is not sufficient to wait indefinitely with the hope that sooner or later these children will adapt more efficient strategies. There are at least two possible reasons for students' continued use of inefficient methods.

- *Comfort!* Some students are simply not willing to be risk takers. If you have been very accepting of inefficient methods (as you should be), some students develop security with an approach that works for them however tedious it may be and ignore more efficient strategies used by their peers. Perhaps you simply need to challenge these students to find a method that does not require all of that counting or to try a particular tens strategy that was just suggested by one of their classmates.

- *Inadequate base-ten concepts.* In an environment that allows students to build on their own ideas, a student with weak base-ten understanding will not likely use base-ten strategies for computation. This is a more fundamental issue. It suggests that you consider some diagnostic strategies to help decide on next steps.

For some children you may need to find out more about their underlying conceptual understanding of base-ten concepts. It can be useful to stop and listen more carefully to a single child by conducting a short (5- to 10-minute) interview. Often you can do this while others are working on a problem you have given to the class.

Pose a word problem or computation and ask the student to "think out loud" while she works. Explain that you want to find out how she is thinking. Avoid any teaching at this time and make no evaluative comments. Show interest in the student's thinking. Ask questions to clarify thinking that may not be clear. However, if the child is only using count-by-ones methods, you will not be learning what she knows about base-ten ideas. Ask if she can show you how to do the task with base-ten models or the little ten-frame cards. If you feel that there is a real weakness with base-ten ideas, try the more direct diagnoses of base-ten concepts found in Chapter 5 on p. 141.

If you find that your students need more development time with base-ten concepts, consider some of these ideas:

- Present challenges or activities with the hundreds chart. (See Activities 5.11 and 5.12.) Also ask students to solve computation problems using the hundreds chart and focus on those solutions that utilize the rows of ten.

- Do some grouping activities that encourage students to make groups of ten to count. (See Activities 5.7, 5.8, and 5.9.)

- Try activities found in the Chapter 5, "Activities for Flexible Thinking" (p. 145). Look especially at "Numbers, Squares, Sticks, and Dots" (Activity 5.21).

- Have students use the little ten-frame cards to solve the addition computation problems you give them.

Invented Strategies for Multiplication

Computation strategies for multiplication are considerably more complex than for addition and subtraction. Often, but by no means always, the strategies that students invent are very similar to the traditional algorithm. The big difference is that students think about numbers, not digits. They always begin with the large or left-hand numbers.

For multiplication, the ability to break numbers apart in flexible ways is even more important than in addition or subtraction. The distributive property is another concept that is important in multiplication computation. For example, to multiply 43 × 5, one might think about breaking 43 into 40 and 3, multiplying each by 5, and then adding the results. Children require ample opportunities to develop these concepts by making sense of their own ideas and those of their classmates.

Useful Representations

The problem 34 × 6 may be represented in a number of ways, as illustrated in Figure 6.11. Often the choice of a model is influenced by a story problem. To determine how many Easter eggs 34 children need if each colors 6 eggs, children may model 6 sets of 34 (or possibly 34 sets of 6). If the problem is about the area of a rectangle that is 34 cm by 6 cm, then some form of an array is likely. But each representation is appropriate for thinking about 34 × 6 regardless of the context, and students should get to a point where they select ways to think about multiplication that are meaningful to them.

How children represent a product interacts with their methods for determining answers. The groups of 34 might suggest repeated additions—perhaps taking the sets two at a time. Double 34 is 68 and there are three of those, so 68 + 68 + 68. From there a variety of methods are possible.

The six sets of base-ten pieces might suggest breaking the numbers into tens and ones: 6 times 3 tens or 6 × 30 and 6 × 4. Some children use the tens individually: 6 tens make 60. So that's 60 and 60 and 60 (180). Then add on the 24 to make 204.

It is not uncommon to arrange the base-ten pieces in a nice array, even if the story problem does not suggest it. The area model is very much like an arrangement of the base-ten pieces.

All of these ideas should be part of students' repertoire of models for multidigit multiplication. Introduce different representations (one at a time) as ways to explore multiplication until you are comfortable that the class has a collection of useful ideas. At

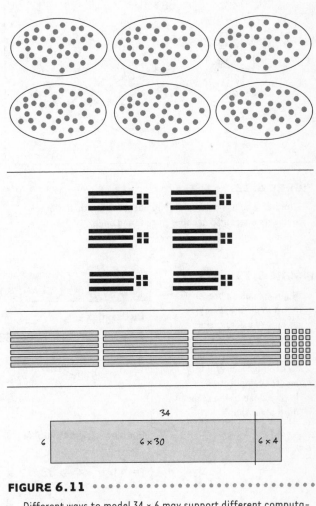

FIGURE 6.11 ●

Different ways to model 34 × 6 may support different computational strategies.

the same time, do not force students who reason very well without drawings to use models when they are not needed.

Multiplication by a Single-Digit Multiplier

As with addition and subtraction, it is helpful to place multiplication tasks in contextual story problems. Let students model the problems in ways that make sense to them. Do not be concerned about mixing of factors (6 sets of 34 or 34 sets of 6). Nor should you be timid about the numbers you use. The problem 3 × 24 may be easier than 7 × 65, but the latter provides challenge. The types of strategies that students use for multiplication are much more varied than for addition and subtraction. However, the following three categories can be identified from the research to date.

Complete-Number Strategies

Children who are not yet comfortable breaking numbers into parts using tens and ones will approach the numbers in the sets as single groups. For students who think this way, Figure 6.12 illustrates two methods they may use. These children will benefit from listening to children who use base-ten models. They may also need more work with base-ten grouping activities where they take numbers apart in different ways.

Partitioning Strategies

Children break numbers up in a variety of ways that reflect an understanding of base-ten concepts, at least four of which are illustrated in Figure 6.13. The "By Decades" approach is the same as the standard algorithm except that students always begin with the large values. It extends easily to three digits and is very powerful as a mental math strategy. Another valuable strat-

---

Complete-Number Strategies for Multiplication

$$63$$
$$\underline{+\ 63}$$
$$126$$
$$\underline{+\ 63}$$
$$189$$
$$\underline{+\ 63}$$
$$252$$
$$\underline{+\ 63}$$
$$315$$

63×5

$$\begin{array}{c} 63 \\ 63 \end{array} \Big\rangle 126$$
$$\begin{array}{c} 63 \\ 63 \end{array} \Big\rangle 126 \Big\rangle 315$$
$$\begin{array}{c} 63 \\ 63 \end{array} \Big\rangle 189$$
$$63$$

FIGURE 6.12 •

Children who use a complete-number strategy do not break numbers apart into decades or tens and ones.

FIGURE 6.13 • • • • • • •

Numbers can be broken apart in different ways to make easier partial products, which are then combined. Partitioning by decades is useful for mental computation and is very close to the standard algorithm.

Partitioning Strategies for Multiplication

By Decades

27×4

$$\begin{array}{l} 4 \times 20 = 80 \\ 4 \times 7 = 28 \end{array} \Big\rangle 108$$

268×7

$$\begin{array}{l} 7 \times 200 = 1400 \\ 7 \times 60 = 420 \end{array} \Big\rangle 1820$$
$$7 \times 8 = 56 \diagdown$$
$$1876$$

By Tens and Ones

27×4

$$\begin{array}{l} 10 \times 4 = 40 \\ 10 \times 4 = 40 \end{array} \Big\rangle 80$$
$$7 \times 4 = 28 \diagup \Big\rangle 108$$

Partitioning the Multiplier

46×3

Double $\quad 46 \rightarrow 92$
$$\diagdown$$
$$138$$

Other Partitions

27×8

So $25 \times 4 \rightarrow 100$
$$25 \times 8 \rightarrow 200$$
$$2 \times 8 = 16 \Big\rangle 216$$

---

egy for mental methods is found in the "Other Partitions" example. It is easy to compute mentally with multiples of 25 and 50 and then add or subtract a small adjustment. All partition strategies rely on the distributive property.

Compensation Strategies

Children look for ways to manipulate numbers so that the calculations are easy. In Figure 6.14, the problem 27 × 4 is changed to an easier one, and then an adjustment or compensation is made. In the second example, one factor is cut in half and the other doubled. This is often used when a 5 or a 50 is involved. Because these strategies are so dependent on the numbers involved, they can't be used for all computations. However, they are powerful strategies, especially for mental math and estimation.

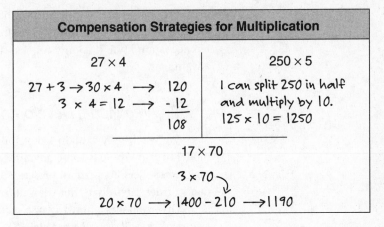

FIGURE 6.14 •

Compensation methods use a product related to the original. A compensation is made in the answer, or one factor is changed to compensate for a change in the other factor.

Using Multiples of 10 and 100

There is a value in exposing students early to products involving multiples of 10 and 100.

• •

The Scout troop wanted to package up 400 fire starter kits as a fundraising project. If each pack will have 12 fire starters, how many fire starters are the Scouts going to need?

• •

Children will use 4 × 12 = 48 to figure out that 400 × 12 is 4800. There will be discussion around how to say and write "forty-eight hundred." Be aware of students who simply tack on zeros without understanding why. Try problems such as 3 × 60 or 210 × 4 at grade 3.

The Traditional Algorithm for Multiplication

The traditional multiplication algorithm is probably the most difficult of the four algorithms if students have not had plenty of opportunities to explore their own strategies. Time spent allowing your students to develop a range of invented strategies will pay off in their understanding of the traditional algorithm. While your children are working on multiplication using their invented strategies, be sure to emphasize partitioning techniques, especially those that are similar to the "By Decades" approach shown in Figure 6.13. These strategies tend to be the most efficient and are very close to the traditional algorithm. In fact, students who are using one or more partitioning strategies with a one-digit multiplier have no real need to learn any other approach.

The traditional algorithm can, like the "By Decades" approach, be developed with either a repeated addition model or an area model. For single-digit multipliers, the difference is minimal. It is only for two-digit multipliers that the area model has some advantages.

An Area Model Development

We will briefly explain a development of the traditional algorithm using an area model because there is some advantage to this approach when students move to two-digit multipliers. As with all prescribed algorithms, you will have to direct your students rather carefully rather than utilize a full problem-oriented approach.

Give students a drawing of a rectangle 47 cm by 6 cm. *How many small square centimeter pieces will fit in the rectangle?* (What is the area of the rectangle in square centimeters?) Let students solve the problem in groups before discussing it as a class.

As shown in Figure 6.15, the rectangle can be "sliced" or separated into two parts so that one part will be 6 ones by 7 ones, or 42 ones, and the other will be 6 ones by 4 tens, or 24 tens. Notice that the base-ten language "6 ones times 4 tens is 24 tens" tells how many *pieces* (sticks of ten) are in the big section. To say "6 times 40 is 240" is also correct and tells how many units or square centimeters are in the section. Each section is referred to as a *partial product*. By adding the two partial products, you get the total product or area of the rectangle.

To avoid the tedium of drawing large rectangles and arranging base-ten pieces, use the base-ten grid paper found in the Blackline Masters. On the grid paper, students can easily draw accurate rectangles showing all of the pieces. Check to be sure students understand that for a product such as 74 × 8, there are two partial products, 70 × 8 = 560 and 4 × 8 = 32, and the sum of these is the product. Do not force any recording technique on students until they understand how to use the two dimensions of a rectangle to get a product.

BLM 19

Develop the Written Record

When the two partial products are written separately as in Figure 6.16(a), there is little new to learn. Students simply record the products and add them together. As illustrated, it is possible to teach students how to write the first product with a carried digit so that the combined product is written on one line. This traditional recording scheme is known to be problematic. The little carried digit is often the source of difficulty—it gets added in before the second multiplication or is forgotten.

FIGURE 6.15 • • • • • • • • •

A rectangle filled with base-ten pieces is a useful model for two-digit-by-one-digit multiplication.

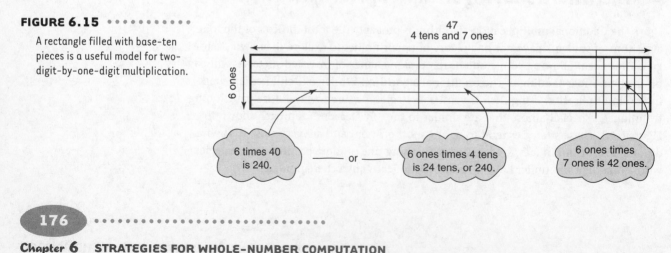

There is absolutely no practical reason why students can't be allowed to record both partial products and avoid the errors related to the carried digit. When you accept that, it makes no difference in which order the products are written. Why not simply permit students to do written multiplication as shown in Figure 6.16 without carrying? Furthermore, that is precisely how this is done mentally.

Most standard curricula progress from two digits to three digits with a single-digit multiplier. Students can make this progression easily. They still should be permitted to write all three partial products separately and not have to bother with carrying.

Two-Digit Multipliers

With the area model, the progression to a two-digit multiplier is relatively straightforward. Rectangles can be drawn on base-ten grid paper, or full-sized rectangles can be filled in with base-ten pieces. There will be four partial products, corresponding to four different sections of the rectangle. Figure 6.17 shows a rectangle partitioned into the usual partial products.

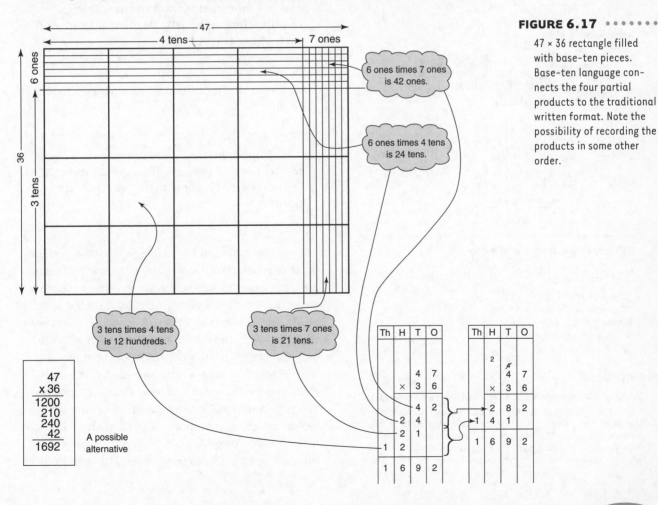

FIGURE 6.16 ● ● ● ● ● ● ● ● ● ● ● ● ● ● ● ●

(a) In the standard form, the product of ones is recorded first. The tens digit of this first product can be written as a "carried" digit above the tens column. (b) It is quite reasonable to abandon the carried digit and permit the partial products to be recorded in any order.

FIGURE 6.17 ● ● ● ● ● ● ●

(a) In the standard form, the product of ones is recorded first. The tens digit of this first product can be written as a "carried" digit above the tens column. (b) It is quite reasonable to abandon the carried digit and permit the partial products to be recorded in any order.

47 × 36 rectangle filled with base-ten pieces. Base-ten language connects the four partial products to the traditional written format. Note the possibility of recording the products in some other order.

6 ones times 7 ones is 42 ones.

6 ones times 4 tens is 24 tens.

3 tens times 4 tens is 12 hundreds.

3 tens times 7 ones is 21 tens.

```
  47
x 36
1200
 210
 240
  42
1692
```
A possible alternative

● ●

THE TRADITIONAL ALGORITHM FOR MULTIPLICATION

Invented Strategies for Division

In our discussion of division facts (Chapter 4), we included something we called "near facts." In a near fact, the divisor and quotient are both less than ten but there is a remainder, as in 44 ÷ 8. Third-grade students should have ample experiences with near facts. When these problems are expanded to those in which the quotients are more than 9 (e.g., 73 ÷ 6), the process evolves into invented strategies for division. Third grade is not too soon for students to begin exploring division strategies, but there is little need to teach the standard algorithm.

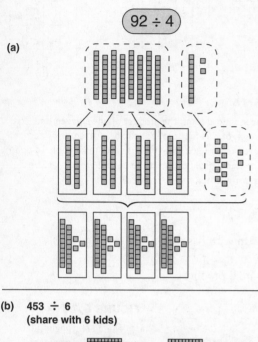

(a) 92 ÷ 4

(b) 453 ÷ 6
(share with 6 kids)

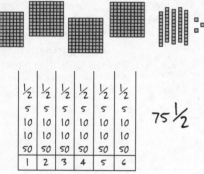

75 ½

(c) 143 jelly beans shared with 8 kids

Try 14 × 8 → 112
12 groups of 8 is 96.
12 groups in 100 leaves 4.
5 groups of 8 is 40.
And 3 more left over.
12 + 5 is 17 with 7 left.

FIGURE 6.18

Students use both models and symbols to solve division tasks.

Source: Adapted from *Developing Mathematical Ideas: Numbers and Operations, Part I: Building a System of Tens Casebook,* by D. Schifter, V. Bastable, & S. J. Russell. Copyright © 1999 by Education Development Center, Inc. Published by Dale Seymour Publications, an imprint of Pearson Learning. Used by permission.

Sharing and Measurement Problems

Recall that there are two concepts of division. First is the partition or fair-sharing idea, illustrated by this story problem:

> **The bag has 783 jelly beans, and Laura and her four friends want to share them equally. How many jelly beans will Laura and each of her friends get?**

Then there is the measurement or repeated subtraction concept:

> **Jumbo the elephant loves peanuts. His trainer has 625 peanuts. If he gives Jumbo 20 peanuts each day, how many days will the peanuts last?**

Students should be challenged to solve both types of problems. However, the fair-share problems are often easier to solve with base-ten pieces. Furthermore, the traditional algorithm is built on this idea. Eventually, students will develop strategies that they will apply to both types of problems, even when the process does not match the action of the story.

Figure 6.18 shows some strategies that fourth-grade children have used to solve division problems. The first example illustrates 92 ÷ 4 using base-ten pieces and a sharing process. A ten is traded when no more tens can be passed out. Then the 12 ones are distributed, resulting in 23 in each set. This direct modeling approach with base-ten pieces is quite easy even for third-grade students to understand and use.

In the second example, the student sets out the base-ten pieces and draws a "bar graph" with six columns. After noting that there are not enough hundreds for each kid, he mentally splits the 3 hundreds in half, putting 50 in each column. That leaves him with 1 hundred, 5 tens, and 3 ones. After trading the hundred for tens (now 15 tens), he gives 20 to each, recording 2 tens in each bar. Now he is left with 3 tens and 3 ones, or 33. He knows that 5×6 is 30, so he gives each kid 5, leaving him with 3. These he splits in half and writes $\frac{1}{2}$ in each column.

The child in the third example is solving a sharing problem but tries to do it as a measurement process. She wants to find out how many 8s are in 143. Initially she guesses. By multiplying 8 first by 10, then by 20, and then by 14, she knows the answer is more than 14 and less than 20. After some more work (not shown), she rethinks the problem as how many 8s in 100 and how many in 40.

Missing Factor Strategies

You can see in Figure 6.18 how the use of base-ten pieces tends to lead to a digit-by-digit strategy—share the hundreds first, then the tens, then the ones. Although this is precisely the conceptual background behind the traditional algorithm, it is digit oriented as opposed to an approach that helps students think of the whole value of the dividend. In Figure 6.18(c), the student is using a multiplicative approach. She is trying to find out, "What number times 8 will be close to 143 with less than 8 left over?" This is a good method to suggest to students in grade 3 or 4. It will build on their multiplication skills, it is a method that lends itself to mental estimation, and it can work quite well for most purposes.

> **STOP** Before reading further, consider the task of determining the quotient of $318 \div 7$ by trying to figure out *what number times 7 (or 7 times what number)* is close to 318 without going over. Do not use the standard algorithm.

There are several places to begin solving this problem. For instance, since 10×7 is 70 and 100×7 is 700, it has to be between 10 and 100, probably closer to 10. You might start adding up 70s:

70

+ 70 is 140

+ 70 is 210

+ 70 is 280

+ 70 is 350

So four 70s is not enough and five is too much. It has to be forty-something. At this point you could guess at numbers between 40 and 50. Or you might add on 7s. Or you could notice that forty 7s (280) leaves you with 20 plus 18 or 38. Oh—five 7s will be 35 of the 38 with 3 left over. In all, that's $40 + 5$ or 45 with a remainder of 3.

INVENTED STRATEGIES FOR DIVISION

This missing-factor approach is likely to be invented by some students if they are solving measurement problems such as the following:

> Grace can put 6 pictures on one page of her photo album. If she has 82 pictures, how many pages will she need?

Alternatively, you can simply pose a task such a 82 ÷ 6 and ask students, "What number times 6 would be close to 82?" and continue from there.

The Traditional Algorithm for Division

Long division is the one traditional algorithm that starts with the left-hand or big pieces. The conceptual basis for the algorithm most often taught in textbooks is the partition or fair-share method.

Typically, the division algorithm with one-digit divisors is introduced in the third grade. If done well, it should not have to be retaught.

Begin with Models

Return again to the first example in Figure 6.18. The student is using base-ten models to solve 92 ÷ 4. Notice that the first step is to share the tens. *There are 9 tens. How many tens can be put in each of the 4 groups?* The tens are distributed, 2 per group, and then there is only one left. This last ten is exchanged for 10 ones, making a total of 12 ones. Since 4 × 3 is 12, 3 ones can be put in each group with none left over.

If students use a pregrouped base-ten model such as those shown in Figure 6.18, they will need to understand the concept of trading a ten for 10 ones (and later a hundred for 10 tens). This is not difficult but may require some extra work.

 Try the distributing or sharing process yourself using base-ten pieces (or draw squares, sticks, and dots). Use the problem 524 ÷ 3. Try to talk through the process without using "goes into." Think sharing.

Develop the Written Record

The recording scheme for the long-division algorithm is not completely intuitive. You will need to be quite directive in helping children learn to record the fair sharing with models. There are essentially four steps:

1. *Share* and record the number of pieces put in each group.
2. *Record* the number of pieces shared in all. Multiply to find this number.
3. *Record* the number of pieces remaining. Subtract to find this number.
4. *Trade* (if necessary) for smaller pieces and combine with any that are there already. Record the new total number in the next column.

When students model problems with a one-digit divisor, steps 2 and 3 seem unnecessary. Explain that these steps really help when you don't have the pieces there to count.

Figure 6.19 details each step of the recording process just described. On the left, you see the traditional algorithm. To the right is a suggestion that matches the actual action with the models by explicitly recording the trades. Instead of the somewhat mysterious "bring-down" procedure, the traded pieces are crossed out, as is the number

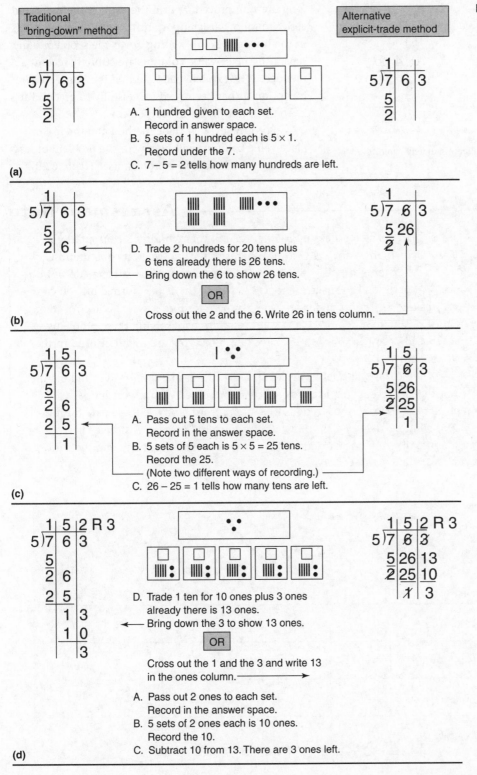

Traditional "bring-down" method

Alternative explicit-trade method

(a)
A. 1 hundred given to each set.
   Record in answer space.
B. 5 sets of 1 hundred each is 5 × 1.
   Record under the 7.
C. 7 − 5 = 2 tells how many hundreds are left.

(b)
D. Trade 2 hundreds for 20 tens plus 6 tens already there is 26 tens.
   Bring down the 6 to show 26 tens.

   OR

   Cross out the 2 and the 6. Write 26 in tens column.

(c)
A. Pass out 5 tens to each set.
   Record in the answer space.
B. 5 sets of 5 each is 5 × 5 = 25 tens.
   Record the 25.
   (Note two different ways of recording.)
C. 26 − 25 = 1 tells how many tens are left.

(d)
D. Trade 1 ten for 10 ones plus 3 ones already there is 13 ones.
   Bring down the 3 to show 13 ones.

   OR

   Cross out the 1 and the 3 and write 13 in the ones column.

A. Pass out 2 ones to each set.
   Record in the answer space.
B. 5 sets of 2 ones each is 10 ones.
   Record the 10.
C. Subtract 10 from 13. There are 3 ones left.

FIGURE 6.19 • • • • • • • • • • • •

The traditional and explicit-trade methods are connected to each step of the division process. Every step can and should make sense.

of existing pieces in the next column. The combined number of pieces is written in this column using a two-digit number. In the example, 2 hundreds are traded for 20 tens, combined with the 6 that were there for a total of 26 tens. The 26 is therefore written in the tens column.

Students who are required to make sense of the long-division procedure find the explicit-trade method easier to follow. It is important to spread out the digits in the dividend when writing down the problem. Lines separating place-value columns are strongly recommended. (The explicit-trade method is a Van de Walle invention. It has been used successfully in grades 3 to 8. You will not find it in textbooks.)

Both the explicit-trade method and the use of place-value columns will help with the problem of leaving out a middle zero in a problem (see Figure 6.20).

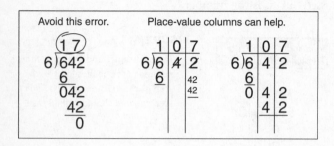

FIGURE 6.20 •••••••••••••••••••••••••••••••••••

Using lines to mark place-value columns can help avoid forgetting to record zeros.

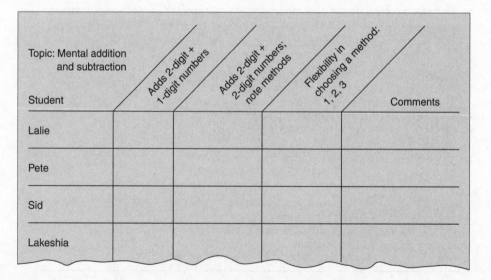

Assessment Note

Parents are perhaps more interested in their children's computational skills than in any other area. When students do well on computation tests, parents are pleased. But what do you know when students do not do well? At best you can make inferences based on the papers turned in. You can look for basic-fact errors and carelessness or perhaps find a systematic error in an algorithm. What you do not know is how children are solving these problems and what ideas and strategies they have developed that are useful or need further development.

When computational strategies and algorithms are developed in the manner suggested in this chapter, every day you are presented with a wealth of assessment data. The important thing is to gather, record, and use these data for individual children the same as you would for tests and quizzes. A simple chart something like the one in Figure 6.21 may be all you need. Note that the third

FIGURE 6.21 •••••••

A checklist with space for comments or notes lets you record daily observations of students' direct modeling and invented strategies.

Topic: Mental addition and subtraction Student	Adds 2-digit + 1-digit numbers	Adds 2-digit + 2-digit numbers; note methods	Flexibility in choosing a method: 1, 2, 3	Comments
Lalie				
Pete				
Sid				
Lakeshia				

column includes a minirubric or a three-point scale. Students' names can be arranged in groups, by how they sit in the room, or alphabetically—any way that makes them easy to find.

   As you walk around in the during portion of your lessons, and also in the after portion when children explain their computation strategies and reasoning, you can make notes on the chart. Make a new chart each week but keep the old ones to provide evidence of growth over time. These charts can be useful for grading and for parent conferences. There is no harm in giving an occasional quiz or test of computational skills. But avoid giving more value to tests simply because they are objective.

THE TRADITIONAL ALGORITHM FOR DIVISION

EXPANDED LESSON

Exploring Subtraction Strategies

GRADE LEVEL: Second or third grade.

MATHEMATICS GOALS
- To develop flexible strategies for subtracting two-digit numbers with an emphasis on adding-up methods.
- To promote the use of tens in computational strategies.

THINKING ABOUT THE STUDENTS
The students have been working on a variety of invented strategies for adding two-digit numbers. It is not necessary that this skill be mastered before beginning subtraction. This lesson may or may not be the first subtraction lesson. The assumption is that students have not been taught the traditional algorithms for addition or subtraction.

MATERIALS AND PREPARATION
Prepare two story problems either on a transparency or duplicate on a sheet of paper. If duplicated, leave half of the page for each problem.

lesson

BEFORE

The Task
- Provide students with two story problems either on paper or on the overhead. Here are two possibilities:

    David's book has 72 pages. He has already read 35 pages. How many more pages does David have to read to finish his book?

    Tara keeps her books on two bookshelves. She has 24 books in all. On the top shelf she has 16 books. How many books does Tara have on the bottom shelf?

  Students are to solve each problem using any method that they want.

Brainstorm
- Read the first problem together with the students. Have them think how they would go about solving the problem. What would they do first?
- Give students some time to think of a way to solve the problem and then call on several students to share their ideas. Try to elicit some details. For example, if a student says, "I would start with 35 and add up to 72," ask what she would add on first. You want to give students who do not know where to begin some good ideas. Ask other students if they would begin differently. It is not sufficient to say, "I would subtract." If students use a take-away strategy or even a counting-by-ones approach, that is okay. Do not force any method.

Establish Expectations
- Students are to show how they solved each problem. They should provide enough information so that if someone picked up their paper they would be able to tell how they got the answers. Remind students that they will be sharing their ideas with the class.

DURING

- Monitor students' work. For students who are stuck, ask them to tell you what ideas they have thought about. Try to make a suggestion that builds on the student's ideas. For example, if the student says, "I want to take 35 from 72," you might suggest that the student try taking away 10 at a time. After making a suggestion, walk away. Do not be overly guiding.
- Watch for students who solve the problem but have not written enough to explain their solution. Ask them about their method and then require them to write some more to explain what they have just told you. You may have to help some students with ways to record their ideas.

- Do not correct students who have made errors.
- Watch for students to share their methods. If usually reluctant students have a solution, advise them that you may call on them to share their ideas.
- Challenge early finishers with a three-digit problem: 314 – 197.

AFTER

- When all students have completed their work, ask for answers to the first problem. Record these on the board. Pick one of the answers and ask, *Who got this answer?* Select a student to share his or her method.
- As the students explain their thinking, try to record their process on the board. Avoid aligning the two numbers vertically as in the traditional algorithm. One good strategy is to use a blank number line. As students explain what they did, you can indicate each portion on the number line, recording each jump as they explain. For example, suppose that a student starts with 35 and adds 10 and 10 and 10 (to get to 65), then adds 5 (to get to 70), and then 2 more. Your record on the board may look like this:

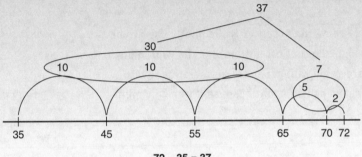

72 – 35 = 37

- For each jump on the number line, indicate the size of the jump. For adding-up strategies, the answer will usually be the sum of the jumps. For take-away strategies, the answer will be where the jumps end.
- When more than one answer has been offered, be sure to have a method shared for each answer. By asking the class if they agree with, understand, or have questions for the student who is sharing, the responsibility for deciding what is correct falls to the class, not you. In any case, try to get several solution methods for the problem.
- Have students share their solution strategies for the second problem in a similar manner.

ASSESSMENT NOTES

- Watch for students who are solving these problems by counting by ones. Some may even count both numbers by ones rather than count on. Others may make tallies or use counters for the larger number and then mark off or remove the subtrahend.
- Try to keep track of students who are using a take-away method and those who use an adding-on approach. For some problems, take-away strategies are often more difficult.

- Students who are not using tens at all (counting by ones) will benefit by solving similar problems using the little ten-frame cards. (See Activity 5.26, p. 149.) Also consider other activities from the "Activities for Flexible Thinking" section of Chapter 5.
- If few or none of your students used an adding-on strategy, try Activity 5.23, "The Other Part of 100" and Activity 5.24, "Compatible Pairs."

- Even if students are successful with these problems, it is appropriate to provide a lot of additional practice conducted in a similar manner to this lesson. It is not necessary to always use story problems, nor is it necessary to restrict the tasks to two-digit numbers. As students become more proficient, challenge those who are able to solve problems such as these mentally.

next steps

EXPANDED LESSON

GEOMETRIC THINKING AND GEOMETRIC CONCEPTS

Geometry in K–8 is finally being taken seriously. Geometry used to be the chapter that was skipped or put off until late in the year. Many teachers were not comfortable with geometry, associating it with high school and proofs. Nor was geometry seen as important because it was only minimally tested on standardized tests. Now geometry is a strand of the curriculum in nearly every state and district.

This change is due in large part to the influence of the NCTM standards movement beginning in 1989. A second significant influence is an attention to a theoretical perspective that has helped us understand how students reason about spatial concepts.

Geometry Goals for Your Students

It is useful to think about your geometry objectives in terms of two quite different yet related frameworks: spatial reasoning, or spatial sense, and the specific content such as that most likely found in your state or district objectives. The first of these frameworks has to do with the way students think and reason about shape and space. There is a well-researched theoretical basis for organizing the development of geometric thought that guides this framework. The second framework is content in the more traditional sense—knowing about symmetry, triangles, parallel lines, and so forth. The NCTM *Principles and Standards for*

big ideas

1 What makes shapes alike and different can be determined by an array of geometric properties. For example, shapes have sides that are parallel, perpendicular, or neither; they have line symmetry, rotational symmetry, or neither; they are similar, congruent, or neither.

2 Shapes can be moved in a plane or in space. These changes can be described in terms of translations (slides), reflections (flips), and rotations (turns).

3 Shapes can be described in terms of their location in a plane or in space. Coordinate systems can be used to describe these locations precisely. In turn, the coordinate view of shape offers another way to understand certain properties of shapes, changes in position (transformations), and how they appear or change size (visualization).

4 Shapes can be seen from different perspectives. The ability to perceive shapes from different viewpoints helps us understand relationships between two- and three-dimensional figures and mentally change the position and size of shapes.

School Mathematics authors have helped describe content goals across the grades. We need to understand both of these aspects of geometry—thought and content—so that we can best help students grow.

Spatial Sense

Spatial sense can be defined as an intuition about shapes and the relationships among shapes. Individuals with spatial sense have a feel for the geometric aspects of their surroundings and the shapes formed by objects in the environment.

Spatial sense includes the ability to visualize objects and spatial relationships—to turn things around in your mind. It includes a comfort with geometric descriptions of objects and position. People with spatial sense appreciate geometric form in art, nature, and architecture. They are able to use geometric ideas to describe and analyze their world.

Many people say they aren't very good with shape or that they have poor spatial sense. The typical belief is that you are either born with spatial sense or not. This simply is not true! We now know that rich experiences with shape and spatial relationships, when provided consistently over time, can and do develop spatial sense. Without geometric experiences, most people do not grow in their spatial sense or spatial reasoning. Between 1990 and 1996, NAEP data indicated a steady, continuing improvement in students' geometric reasoning at all three grades tested—grades 4, 8, and 12 (Martin & Strutchens, 2000). Students did not just get smarter. More likely there has been an increasing emphasis on geometry at all grades. Still, much more needs to be done if U.S. children are to rise to the same level as their European and Asian counterparts.

Geometric Content

For too long, the geometry curriculum in the United States has been somewhat of an eclectic mix of activities and lists of "bold print words"—too much emphasis has been placed on learning terminology. At the same time, the growing emphasis placed on geometry has spawned a huge assortment of wonderful tasks for students. Fortunately, the authors of *Principles and Standards for School Mathematics* have provided a content framework for the pre-K–12 curriculum. As with each of the content standards, the geometry standard has a number of goals that apply to all grade levels. The four goals for geometry can be loosely summarized with these headings: *Shapes and Properties, Transformation, Location,* and *Visualization.* A very brief description of these headings is offered next.

- *Shapes and Properties* includes a study of the properties of shapes in both two and three dimensions, as well as a study of the relationships built on properties.

- *Transformation* includes a study of translations, reflections, and rotations (slides, flips, and turns) and the study of symmetries.

- *Location* refers primarily to coordinate geometry or other ways of specifying how objects are located in the plane or in space.

- *Visualization* includes the recognition of shapes in the environment, developing relationships between two- and three-dimensional objects, and the ability to draw and recognize objects from different perspectives.

GEOMETRY GOALS FOR YOUR STUDENTS

The value of these content goals is that a content framework finally exists that cuts across grades so that both teachers and curriculum planners can examine growth from year to year.

You are strongly encouraged to read the geometry goals for grades pre-K–2 and 3–5 in *Principles and Standards* (NCTM, 2000).

Geometric Thought: Reasoning About Shapes and Relationships

Not all people think about geometric ideas in the same manner. Certainly, we are not all alike, but we are all capable of growing and developing in our ability to think and reason in geometric contexts. The research of two Dutch educators, Pierre van Hiele and Dina van Hiele-Geldof, has provided insight into the differences in geometric thinking and how the differences come to be.

The van Hieles' work began in 1959 and immediately attracted a lot of attention in the Soviet Union but for nearly two decades received little notice in this country (Hoffer, 1983; Hoffer & Hoffer, 1992). But today, the van Hiele theory has become the most influential factor in the American geometry curriculum.

The van Hiele Levels of Geometric Thought

The most prominent feature of the model is a five-level hierarchy of ways of understanding spatial ideas. Each of the five levels describes the thinking processes used in geometric contexts. The levels describe how we think and what types of geometric ideas we think about, rather than how much knowledge we have. A significant difference from one level to the next is the objects of thought—what we are able to think about geometrically.

Level 0: Visualization

The objects of thought at level 0 are shapes and what they "look like."

Students recognize and name figures based on the global, visual characteristics of the figure—a gestalt-like approach to shape. Students operating at this level are able to make measurements and even talk about properties of shapes, but these properties are not abstracted from the shapes at hand. It is the appearance of the shape that defines it for the student. A square is a square "because it looks like a square." Because appearance is dominant at this level, appearances can overpower properties of a shape. For example, a square that has been rotated so that all sides are at a 45-degree angle to the vertical may now be a diamond and no longer a square. Students at this level will sort and classify shapes based on their appearances—"I put these together because they are all pointy" (or "fat," or "look like a house," or are "dented in sort of," and so on). With a focus on the appearances of shapes, students are able to see how shapes are alike and different. As a result, students at this level can create and begin to understand classifications of shapes.

The products of thought at level 0 are classes or groupings of shapes that seem to be "alike."

Level 1: Analysis

The objects of thought at level 1 are classes of shapes rather than individual shapes.

Students at the analysis level are able to consider all shapes within a class rather than a single shape. Instead of talking about *this* rectangle, it is possible to talk about *all* rectangles. By focusing on a class of shapes, students are able to think about what makes a rectangle a rectangle (four sides, opposite sides parallel, opposite sides of the same length, four right angles, congruent diagonals, etc.). The irrelevant features (e.g., size or orientation) fade into the background. At this level, students begin to appreciate that a collection of shapes goes together because of properties. Ideas about an individual shape can now be generalized to all shapes that fit that class. If a shape belongs to a particular class such as cubes, it has the corresponding properties of that class. "All cubes have six congruent faces, and each of those faces is a square." These properties were only implicit at level 0. Students operating at level 1 may be able to list all the properties of squares, rectangles, and parallelograms but not see that these are subclasses of one another, that all squares are rectangles and all rectangles are parallelograms. In defining a shape, level 1 thinkers are likely to list as many properties of a shape as they know.

The products of thought at level 1 are the properties of shapes.

Level 2: Informal Deduction

The objects of thought at level 2 are the properties of shapes.

As students begin to be able to think about properties of geometric objects without the constraints of a particular object, they are able to develop relationships between and among these properties. "If all four angles are right angles, the shape must be a rectangle. If it is a square, all angles are right angles. If it is a square, it must be a rectangle." With greater ability to engage in "if–then" reasoning, shapes can be classified using only minimum characteristics. For example, four congruent sides and at least one right angle can be sufficient to define a square. Rectangles are parallelograms with a right angle. Observations go beyond properties themselves and begin to focus on logical arguments *about* the properties. Students at level 2 will be able to follow and appreciate an informal deductive argument about shapes and their properties. "Proofs" may be more intuitive than rigorously deductive. However, there is an appreciation that a logical argument is compelling. An appreciation of the axiomatic structure of a formal deductive system, however, remains under the surface.

The products of thought at level 2 are relationships among properties of geometric objects.

Level 3: Deduction

The objects of thought at level 3 are relationships among properties of geometric objects.

At level 3, students begin to appreciate the need for a system of logic that rests on a minimum set of assumptions and from which other truths can be derived. This is the level of the traditional high school geometry course.

The products of thought at level 3 are deductive axiomatic systems for geometry.

Level 4: Rigor

The objects of thought at level 4 are deductive axiomatic systems for geometry.

At the highest level of the van Hiele hierarchy, the objects of attention are axiomatic systems themselves, not just the deductions within a system. This is generally the level of a college mathematics major who is studying geometry as a branch of mathematical science.

The products of thought at level 4 are comparisons and contrasts among different axiomatic systems of geometry.

We have given brief descriptions of all five levels to illustrate the scope of the van Hiele theory. At the K–3 level you will be interested primarily in levels 0 and 1.

Characteristics of the van Hiele Levels

You no doubt noticed that the products of thought at each level are the same as the objects of thought at the next. This object–product relationship between levels of the van Hiele theory is illustrated in Figure 7.1. The objects (ideas) must be created at one level so that relationships among these objects can become the focus of the next level. In addition to this key concept of the theory, four related characteristics of the levels of thought merit special attention.

1. The levels are sequential. To arrive at any level above level 0, students must move through all prior levels. To move through a level means that students have experienced geometric thinking appropriate for that level and have created in their own minds the types of objects or relationships that are the focus of thought at the next level.
2. The levels are not age dependent in the sense of the developmental stages of Piaget. A third grader or a high school student could be at level 0. Indeed, some students and adults remain forever at level 0, and a significant number of adults never reach level 2. But age is certainly related to the amount and types of geometric experiences that we have. Therefore, it is reasonable to assume that most children in the K–2 range as well as many children in grades 3 and 4 are at level 0.
3. Geometric experience is the greatest single factor influencing advancement through the levels. Activities that permit students to explore, talk about, and interact with content at the next level, while increasing their experiences at their current level, have the best chance of advancing the level of thought for those students. Some researchers believe that it is possible to be at one level with respect to a familiar area of content and at a lower level with less familiar ideas (Clements & Battista, 1992).
4. When instruction or language is at a level higher than that of the students, there will be a lack of communication. Students required to wrestle with objects of thought that have not been constructed at the earlier level may be forced into rote learning and achieve only temporary and superficial success. Students can, for example, memorize that all squares are rectangles without having constructed that relationship. Students may memorize a geometric proof but fail to create the steps or understand the rationale involved (Fuys, Geddes, & Tischler, 1988; Geddes & Fortunato, 1993).

The van Hiele Theory of Geometric Thought

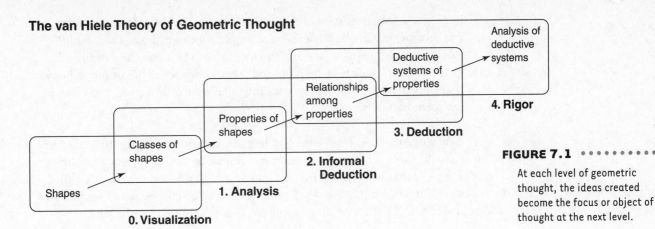

FIGURE 7.1 • • • • • • • • • • • •

At each level of geometric thought, the ideas created become the focus or object of thought at the next level.

Implications for Instruction

If the van Hiele theory is correct—and there is much evidence to support it—then a major goal of the K–8 curriculum must be to advance students' level of geometric thought. If students are to be adequately prepared for the deductive geometry curriculum of high school, then it is important for their thinking to have grown to level 2 by the end of the eighth grade.

Not every child will be ready to move to the next level. However, all teachers should be aware that the experiences they provide are the single most important factor in moving children up this developmental ladder. Every teacher should be able to see some growth in geometric thinking over the course of the year.

The van Hiele theory and the developmental perspective of this book highlight the necessity of teaching at the child's level of thought. However, almost any activity can be modified to span two levels of thinking, even within the same classroom. For many activities, how we interact with individual children will adapt the activity to their levels and encourage them or challenge them to operate at the next higher level.

Explorations help develop relationships. The more students play around with the ideas in activities, the more relationships they will discover. However, students need to learn how to explore ideas in geometry and play around with the relationships in order for ideas to develop and become meaningful.

The following sections contain descriptions of the types of activity and questioning that are appropriate for the first two levels. Apply these descriptors to the tasks that you pose to students, and use them to guide your interaction with students. The use of physical materials, drawings, and computer models is a must at every level.

Instruction at Level 0

Instructional activities in geometry appropriate for level 0 should:

- Involve lots of sorting and classifying. Seeing how shapes are alike and different is the primary focus of level 0. As students learn more content, the types of things that they notice will become more sophisticated. At an early stage they may talk about very nongeometric-sounding attributes of shape such as "fat" or even the color of the pieces. When properties such as symmetry and numbers of sides and corners are introduced, students should be challenged to use these features to classify shapes.

GEOMETRIC THOUGHT: REASONING ABOUT SHAPES AND RELATIONSHIPS

- Include a sufficient variety of examples of shapes so that irrelevant features do not become important. Students need ample opportunities to draw, build, make, put together, and take apart shapes in both two and three dimensions. These activities should be built around specific characteristics or properties so that students develop an understanding of geometric properties and begin to use them naturally.

To help students move from level 0 to level 1, students should be challenged to test ideas about shapes for a variety of examples from a particular category. Say to them, "Let's see if that is true for other rectangles," or "Can you draw a triangle that does *not* have a right angle?" In general, students should be challenged to see if observations made about a particular shape apply to other shapes of a similar kind.

Instruction at Level 1

Instructional activities in geometry appropriate for level 1 should:

- Focus more on the properties of figures rather than on simple identification. As new geometric concepts are learned, the number of properties that figures have can be expanded.

- Apply ideas to entire classes of figures (e.g., *all* rectangles, *all* prisms) rather than on individual models. Analyze classes of figures to determine new properties. For example, find ways to sort all possible triangles into groups. From these groups, define types of triangles.

Assessment Note

Nearly all of your students in grades K to 3 will be at level 0. However, by at least grade 3 teachers certainly want to begin to challenge students who seem able.

No simple test exists to pigeonhole students at a certain level. However, examine the descriptors for the first two levels. As you conduct an activity, listen to the types of observations that students make. Can they talk about shapes as classes? Do they refer, for example, to "rectangles" rather than basing discussion around a particular rectangle? Do they generalize that certain properties are attributable to a type of shape or simply the shape at hand? Do they understand that shapes do not change when the orientation changes? With simple observations such as these, you will soon be able to distinguish between levels 0 and 1.

Content and the Levels of Thinking

This chapter offers a sample of activities organized around the four content areas: shapes and properties, transformations, location, and visualization. A section of the chapter is devoted to each of these areas. The van Hiele theory applies to all geometric activity, regardless of content. However, it is within the content area of shapes and properties that the theory is most clearly seen. For that reason the activities in that section are subdivided into those appropriate for level 0 and level 1 thinkers. You will find this subdivision helpful for matching activities to your students and encouraging student development of thinking to higher levels. The three remaining sections focus on activities for developing spatial sense through location, transformation, and visualization. Each of these sections is organized in a progression of difficulty and sophistication.

Understand that all of these subdivisions are quite fluid; that is, the content areas overlap and build on each other. Activities in one section may help develop geometric thinking in another area. For example, developing spatial sense through an investigation of symmetry can help students move from level 0 to level 1. A more sophisticated analysis of symmetry can continue to help students move to level 2. In most instances, an activity described for one level of thinking can easily be adapted to an adjacent level simply by the way it is presented to students.

Shapes and Properties Activities

Children need experiences with a rich variety of both two- and three-dimensional shapes. It is useful for students to be able to identify common shapes, notice likenesses and differences among shapes, become aware of the properties that different shapes have, and eventually use these properties to further define and understand their geometric world. As students find out more about shapes over time, they can begin to appreciate how definitions of special shapes come to be.

This gradual development of student understanding of shapes and their properties clearly reflects the van Hiele theory of geometric thought. Within this category of geometric content, an awareness and application of the theory to your instruction is most important.

Activities for Level 0 Thinkers

The emphasis at level 0 is on the shapes that students can observe, feel, build, take apart, and perceive in many ways. The general goal is to explore how shapes are alike and different and use these ideas to create classes of shapes (both physically and mentally). Some of these classes of shapes have names—rectangles, triangles, prisms, cylinders, and so on. Properties of shapes, such as parallel sides, symmetry, right angles, and so on, are included at this level but only in an informal, observational manner. Triangles should be more than just equilateral. Shapes should have curved sides, straight sides, and combinations of these. Along the way, the names of shapes and their properties can be introduced casually.

Sorting and Classifying

As young students work at classification of shapes, be prepared for them to notice features that you do not consider to be "real" geometric attributes, such as "curvy" or "looks like a rocket." Children at this level will also attribute to shapes ideas that are not part of the shape, such as "points up" or "has a side that is the same as the edge of the geoboard."

For variety in two-dimensional shapes, create your own materials. A good set found in the Blackline Masters is called 2-D Shapes. Make multiple copies so that groups of children can all work with the same shapes. The shapes in Figure 7.2 are similar to those in the Blackline Masters, but you will want many more. Once you have your sets constructed, the following activities provide several ideas.

FIGURE 7.2 • • • • • • • • •

An assortment of shapes for sorting.

BLMs 20–26

EXPANDED LESSON

(pages 221–222)

A complete lesson plan based on "Shape Sorts" can be found at the end of this chapter.

Shapes with curved edges

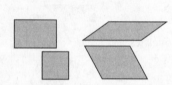

Opposite sides "go the same way"—parallelograms

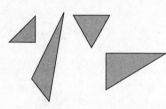

Three sides—triangles

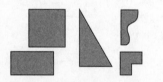

Shapes with a "square corner"—right angle

These all "dent in"—concave

FIGURE 7.3 •

By sorting shapes, students begin to recognize properties.

ACTIVITY 7.1

Shape Sorts

Have students work in groups of four with a set of 2-D Shapes similar to those in Figure 7.2. Here are several related activities that might be done in order:

- Each child randomly selects a shape. In turn, the students tell one or two things they find interesting about their shape. There are no right or wrong responses.
- Children each randomly select two shapes. The task is to find something that is alike about their two shapes and something that is different. (Have them select their shapes before they know the task.)
- The group selects one shape at random and places it in the center of the workspace. Their task is to find all other shapes that are like the target shape, but all according to the same rule. For example, if they say "This one is like our shape because it has a curved side and a straight side," then all other shapes that they put in the collection must have these properties. Challenge them to do a second sort with the same target shape but using a different property.
- Have students share their sorting rules with the class and show examples. All students then draw a new shape that will also fit in the group according to the same rule. They should write about their new shape and why it fits the rule.
- Do a "secret sort." You or one of the students creates a small collection of about five shapes that fit a secret rule. Leave others that belong in your group in the pile. The other students try to find additional pieces that belong to the set and/or guess the secret rule.

🛑 **STOP** *Why do you think that the teacher should not say things such as, "Find all the pieces with straight sides," or "Find the triangles," and instead have students choose how to sort?*

In any sorting activity, the students should decide how to sort, not the teacher. This allows the students to do the activity using ideas *they* own and understand. By listening to the kinds of attributes that they use in their sorting, you will be able to tell what properties they know and use and how they think about shapes. Figure 7.3 illustrates a few of the many possible ways a set might be sorted.

The secret sorting activity is one option for introducing a new property. For example, sort the shapes so that all have at least one right angle or "square corner." When students discover your rule, you have an opportunity to talk more about that property.

The following activity is also done with the 2-D Shapes.

What's My Shape?

From the Blackline Masters for Assorted Shapes, make a set of 2-D Shapes on paper. Cut out about a third of the shapes and paste each inside a folded half-sheet of construction paper to make "secret shape" folders.

   In a group, one student is designated the leader and given a secret-shape folder. The other students are to find the shape that matches the shape in the folder. To this end, they ask questions to which the leader can answer only "yes" or "no." The group can sort the shapes as they ask questions to help narrow down the possibilities. They are not allowed to point to a piece and ask, "Is it this one?" Rather, they must continue to ask questions that reduce the choices to one shape. The final piece is tested against the one in the leader's folder.

   The difficulty of Activity 7.2 is largely dependent on the shape in the folder. The more shapes in the collection that resemble the secret shape, the more difficult the task.

   Most of the activities in "Shape Sorts" can and should be done with three-dimensional shapes as well. The difficulty is finding or making a collection that has sufficient variability. Geoblocks are a large set of wooden blocks available through various distributors. The variety is good, but no blocks have curved surfaces. Check catalogs for other collections. Consider combining several different sets to get variation. Another option is to collect real objects such as cans, boxes, balls, and Styrofoam shapes. Figure 7.4 illustrates some classifications of solids.

Assessment Note

The ways in which children describe shapes in "Shape Sorts" and similar activities with three-dimensional shapes is a good clue to their level of thinking. The classifications made by level 0 thinkers will generally be restricted to the shapes that they can actually put into a group. As they

(continued)

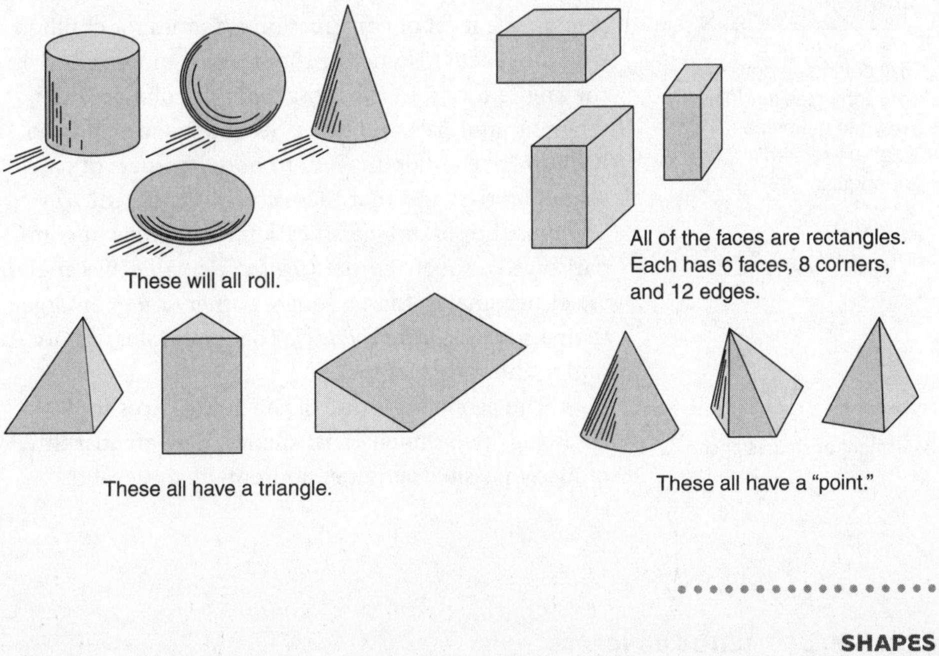

FIGURE 7.4

Early classifications of three-dimensional shapes.

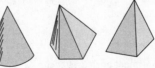

These will all roll.

All of the faces are rectangles. Each has 6 faces, 8 corners, and 12 edges.

These all have a triangle.

These all have a "point."

195

SHAPES AND PROPERTIES ACTIVITIES

begin to think in terms of the properties of shapes, they will create categories based on properties and their language will indicate that there are many more shapes in the group than those that are physically present. Students may say things like, "These shapes have square corners sort of like rectangles," or "These look like boxes. All the boxes have square [rectangular] sides."

Constructing and Dissecting Shapes

Children need to freely explore how shapes fit together to form larger shapes and how larger shapes can be made of smaller shapes. Among two-dimensional shapes for these activities, pattern blocks and tangrams are the best known. In a 1999 article, Pierre van Hiele describes an interesting set of tiles he calls the mosaic puzzle (see Figure 7.5). Another excellent tile set for building is a set of triangles cut from squares (isosceles right triangles). Patterns for the mosaic puzzle and tangrams can be found in the Blackline Masters.

BLM 27

Figure 7.6 shows four different types of tangram puzzles in increasing order of difficulty. Numerous resource books are available devoted entirely to tangrams and NCTM's *e-Standards* includes a tangram applet (Example 4.4). One form of the applet includes eight figures that can be made using all seven of the pieces. The e-version of tangrams has the advantage of motivation and the fact that you must be much more deliberate in arranging the shapes.

Like the tangram pieces, van Hiele's mosaic puzzle pieces fit together in many interesting ways. (See Figure 7.7 on p. 198.) The mosaic puzzle is a bit more challenging because only two of the pieces are congruent (exactly alike), and there are many more different lengths on the various sides than in the tangram puzzle. In a similar manner, the puzzle is more varied than pattern blocks. As a result, the mosaic puzzle provides a good alternative at the second and third grades to step up the level of construction activities for children who are ready. Also notice that there is more variety in the angles found in the mosaic puzzle compared to tangrams and pattern blocks. Second grade is not too early to have children begin to notice corners of shapes (*angles*) and that these come in different sizes. The most important classification of angles is in comparison to a square corner (*right angle*). All other angles are either smaller than a square corner (*acute*) or larger than a square corner (*obtuse*). The terminology is not important at this level.

The geoboard is one of the best devices for "drawing" two-dimensional shapes. Here are just three of many possible activities appropriate for level 0.

Pattern blocks

The 7-piece mosaic puzzle is built on an isometric grid (van Hiele, 1999).

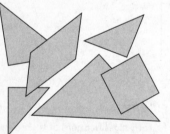

Tangrams

Try cutting up squares or rectangles in other ways to get pieces that are related (Lindquist, 1987b).

Triangles cut from squares

FIGURE 7.5 •

Activities with tiles can involve an assortment of shapes or can be designed with just one shape.

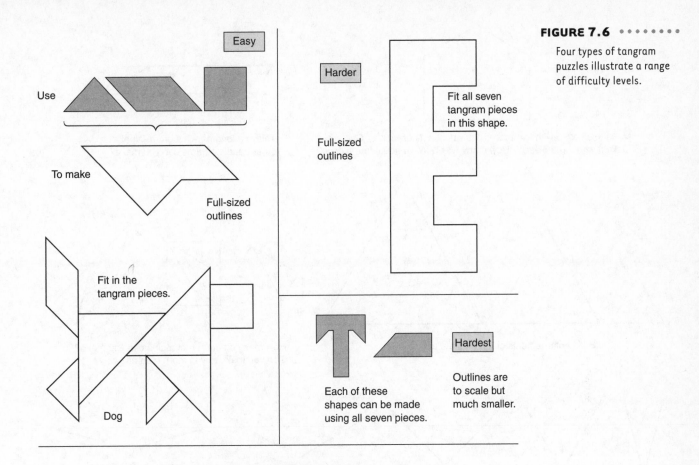

FIGURE 7.6 • • • • • • • •

Four types of tangram puzzles illustrate a range of difficulty levels.

Easy

Use

To make

Full-sized outlines

Fit in the tangram pieces.

Dog

Harder

Full-sized outlines

Fit all seven tangram pieces in this shape.

Hardest

Each of these shapes can be made using all seven pieces.

Outlines are to scale but much smaller.

ACTIVITY 7.3

Geoboard Copy

Copy shapes, designs, and patterns from prepared cards as in Figure 7.8. Begin with designs shown with dots as on a geoboard and later have students copy designs drawn without dots.

ACTIVITY 7.4

Parts That Are Alike

Copy a shape from a card, and have students subdivide or cut it into smaller shapes on their geoboards. Specify the number of smaller shapes. Also specify whether they are all to be congruent or simply of the same type as shown in Figure 7.9 on p. 199. Depending on the shapes involved, this activity can be made to be quite easy or relatively challenging.

Have lots of geoboards available in the classroom. It is better for two or three children to have 10 or 12 boards at a station than for each to have only one. That way, a variety of shapes can be made and compared before they are changed.

Teach students from the very beginning to copy their geoboard designs. Paper copies permit students to create complete sets of drawings that fulfill a particular task.

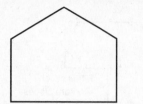

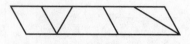

Make this house with two pieces. Now do it a different way. Can you make it with three pieces? How many ways? What about four pieces?

This is a long parallelogram. What other parallelograms can you make?

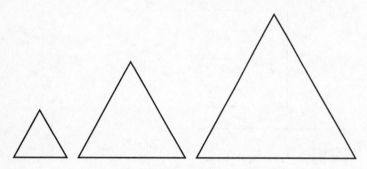

Build enlargements of the equilateral triangle.

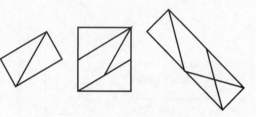

How many different rectangles can you make? Can you make any in more than one way?

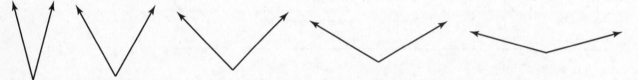

How many different-sized angles can you find in the set of pieces? Put them in order from smallest to largest.

FIGURE 7.7 •

A sample of activities with the mosaic puzzle.

Reprinted with permission from van Hiele, P. M., Developing geometric thinking through activities that begin with play. *Teaching Children Mathematics*, 5, 310–316. Copyright © 1999 by the National Council of Teachers of Mathematics. All rights reserved.

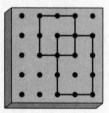

Have children copy shapes from pattern cards onto a geoboard.

Besides pattern cards with and without dots, have children copy <u>real</u> shapes—tables, houses, letters of the alphabet, etc.

FIGURE 7.8 •

Shapes on geoboards.

Chapter 7 **GEOMETRIC THINKING AND GEOMETRIC CONCEPTS**

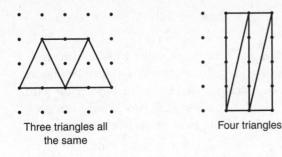

Three triangles all
the same

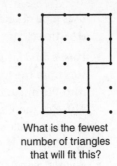

Four triangles

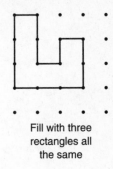

What is the fewest
number of triangles
that will fit this?

Fill with three
rectangles all
the same

Start with a shape and cut it into smaller shapes.
Add special conditions to make the activity challenging.

FIGURE 7.9 • • • • • • • •

Subdividing shapes.

Drawings can be placed on the bulletin board for classification and discussion, made into booklets illustrating a new idea that is being discussed, and sent home to show parents what is happening in geometry.

Younger students can use paper with a single large geoboard on each sheet. Later, a paper board about 10 cm square is adequate. Both are found in the Blackline Masters.

To help children in the very early grades copy geoboard designs, suggest that they first mark the dots for the corners of their shape. Encourage students to say a name for each peg, such as, "second row, end peg" as they point to it on their geoboard. Then they can use the name to find and mark the corresponding dot on their paper. With the corners identified, it is much easier for them to draw lines to make the shape.

BLMs 28–29

Technology Note

The *e-Standards* provides a very good electronic geoboard. Although found in the K–2 section and entitled "Investigating the Concept of a Triangle," this is actually a great geoboard applet for any grade. It allows you to select and delete bands, and select and delete vertices. The *Geoboard* applet from the National Library of Virtual Manipulatives (http://matti.usu.edu/nlvm/nav/vlibrary.html) is essentially the same but with some additional features.

Assorted dot and grid papers provide an alternative to geoboards. Virtually all of the activities suggested for tiles and geoboards can also be done on dot or grid paper. Changing the type of paper changes the activity and provides new opportunity for insight and discovery. The Blackline Masters have a variety of dot and grid paper.

Building three-dimensional shapes is a little more difficult compared with two-dimensional shapes. A variety of commercial materials permit fairly creative construction of geometric solids (e.g., 3D Geoshapes, and Polydron). The 3D Geoshapes and Polydron are examples of materials consisting of plastic polygons that snap together to make three-dimensional models. The following are three highly recommended home-made approaches to skeletal models.

BLMs 30–36

- *Plastic coffee stirrers with modeling clay or pipe cleaners.* Plastic stirrers can be easily cut to different lengths. One method of connecting corers is to use small chunks of clay (about 1 to 2 cm in diameter). This is a good model as long as the structures are not too elaborate. An alternative connection method uses pipe cleaners cut in 2-inch lengths. These are inserted into the ends of the stirrers.

- *Plastic drinking straws with flexible joints.* Cut the straws lengthwise with scissors from the top down to the flexible joint. These slit ends can then be inserted into the uncut bottom ends of other straws, making a strong but flexible joint. Three or more straws are joined in this fashion to form two-dimensional polygons. To make skeletal solids, use tape or wire twist ties to join polygons side to side.

- *Rolled newspaper rods.* Fantastic superlarge skeletons can be built using newspaper and masking tape. Roll three large sheets of newspaper on the diagonal to form a rod. The more tightly the paper is rolled, the less likely the rod is to bend. Secure the roll at the center with a bit of masking tape. The rods are thin and flexible for about 6 inches in from each end where there is less paper. Connect rods by bunching this thin part together and fastening with tape. Use masking tape freely, wrapping it several times around each joint. Additional rods can be joined after two or three are already taped (see Figure 7.10).

With these homemade models, students should compare the rigidity of a triangle with the lack of rigidity of polygons with more than three sides. Point out that triangles are used in many bridges, in the long booms of construction cranes, in gates, and in the structural parts of buildings. Discuss why this may be so. As children build large skeleton structures, they will find that they need to add diagonal members to form triangles. The more triangles, the less likely their structure will collapse.

The newspaper rod method is exciting because the structures quickly become large. Let students work in groups of three or four. They will soon discover what makes a structure rigid and ideas of balance and form. Although your students will generally create free-form structures, it is exciting to see how tall and how sturdy they can be made.

Tessellations

A *tessellation* is a tiling of the plane using one or more shapes in a repeated pattern with no holes or gaps. Making tessellations is an artistic way for level 0 students from first grade forward to explore patterns in shapes and to see how shapes combine to form other shapes. Many exciting tessellations can be made using just one shape,

FIGURE 7.10

Large skeletal structures and special shapes can be built with tightly rolled newspaper. Young children can build free-form sculptures. Older children can be challenged to build shapes with specific properties. Overlap the ends about 6 inches to ensure strength.

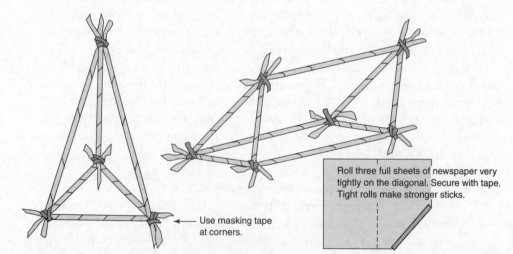

← Use masking tape at corners.

Roll three full sheets of newspaper very tightly on the diagonal. Secure with tape. Tight rolls make stronger sticks.

Chapter 7   **GEOMETRIC THINKING AND GEOMETRIC CONCEPTS**

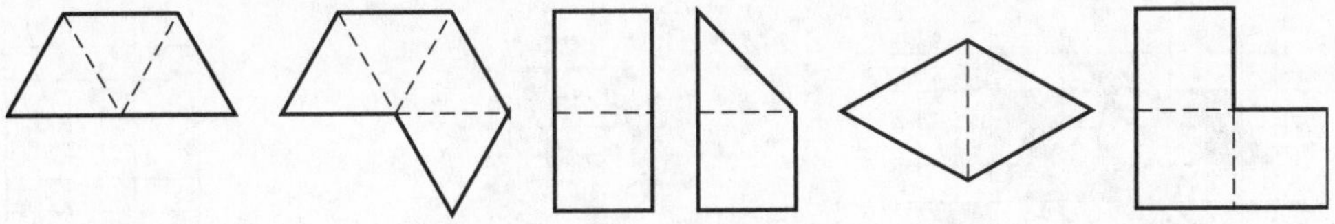

FIGURE 7.11 • • • • • • •

These simple shapes are good tiles to use for tessellations in the early grades. The dotted gray lines show how the shapes are made from squares or equilateral triangles. They are not included on the students' tiles.

which is appropriate for most students in the K–3 range. Adding a second or third shape to a tessellation significantly increases the difficulty of the task.

Even single-shape tessellations are more easily made with some shapes than others. For example, squares or equilateral triangles tessellate quite easily, although these provide very minimal geometric challenge. Several shapes that make good early tessellation tiles are shown in Figure 7.11.

There are two tasks in making an artistic tessellation. First, the shapes must be assembled in a pattern that can continue indefinitely. That means that the pattern, if it were extended, would be the same all over the plane. The second task is to apply a color scheme to the tessellation so that the colors also are in a repeating pattern. A checkerboard is an example of a simple coloring of a simple tessellation. In contrast, children commonly use pattern blocks to make radiating patterns. Although these are fun to construct and quite pretty, they are not tessellations. As the blocks radiate out from the center, the manner in which they are arranged changes.

For children in the K–3 range, it is useful to separate the geometric pattern task from that of creating a color pattern. First, have them experiment with constructing a tessellation using just one shape in a single color. A good idea is to precut the tiles from construction paper or even corrugated cardboard using a paper cutter. Children select a supply of a single tile and work on a large sheet of paper as a mat. Help them "talk" their pattern to see how it repeats. ("Two up, then two sideways, two up. . . .") Avoid the tendency to make the patterns line up with the edge of the mat or to put a border on the pattern. The tiles can spill over the edge. For many tiles, such as 5 cm by 10 cm rectangles, there are numerous different tiling patterns, and children should explore making different patterns before any tiles are glued to the paper.

Once students have found a tessellation pattern they like, they can use two colors of the tile and make the same geometric pattern but now add a color pattern. Even with one geometric pattern, numerous color patterns can be imposed on the design. Once the paper tiles are all arranged in a pattern, they can be glued to the paper to create a wonderful artwork.

Figure 7.12 provides some examples of tessellations using a single tile and two colors as well as several additional shapes that can be used. Creating a tessellation involves geometric problem solving in terms of finding out how different shapes fit together. The next activity suggests some additional challenges.

ACTIVITY 7.5

Tessellation Challenges

In the process of making a tessellation, students can be challenged to:

- Find different tessellation patterns using the same shape.
- Outline the smallest portion of the tessellation that repeats completely. This may be an arrangement of several tiles that essentially forms a larger tile.

(continued)

FIGURE 7.12 • • • • • •

Tessellations.

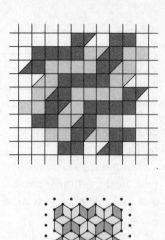
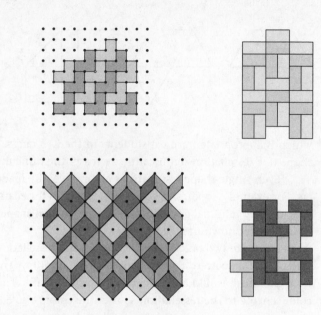

Tessellations can be drawn on grids or made of construction paper tiles. They are challenging and provide an opportunity for both artistic creativity and spatial reasoning.

Once a tessellation is made, students can be challenged to:

- Find shapes within the pattern. (What two or more shapes make a new shape that you can find?)
- Look for examples of symmetry, both line symmetry and rotational symmetry, within the tessellation. (Symmetries are discussed later in this chapter.)
- Find efficient methods of counting the number of tiles in the pattern.
- Using the shortest edge of a tile as a unit, find the shortest distance from one point on the tessellation to another, assuming that the path must be along the edges of the tiles.
- Use the tessellation for area and perimeter explorations. Find two subsets of tiles with the same number of tiles (same area) but with different perimeters. Find two subsets with different numbers of tiles with the same perimeters.

Activities for Level 1 Thinkers

A significant difference between level 1 and level 0 is the object of students' thought. Although students will continue to use models and drawings of shapes, they begin to see these as representatives of classes of shapes. Their understanding of the properties of shapes—such as symmetry, perpendicular and parallel lines, and so on—continues to be refined.

For the sake of clarity, the important definitions of two- and three-dimensional shapes are provided here. You will notice that shape definitions include relationships between and among shapes.

Special Categories of Two-Dimensional Shapes

Table 7.1 lists some important categories of two-dimensional shapes. Examples of these shapes can be found in Figure 7.13 on p. 204.

TABLE 7.1 •
Categories of Two-Dimensional Shapes

Shape	Description
Simple Closed Curves	
Concave, convex	An intuitive definition of *concave* might be "having a dent in it." If a simple closed curve is not concave, it is *convex*. A more precise definition of *concave* may be interesting to explore with older students.
Symmetrical, nonsymmetrical	Shapes may have one or more lines of symmetry and may or may not have rotational symmetry. These concepts will require more detailed investigation.
Polygons Concave, convex Symmetrical, nonsymmetrical	Simple closed curves with all straight sides.
Regular	All sides and all angles are congruent.
Triangles	
Triangles	Polygons with exactly three sides.
Classified by sides Equilateral Isosceles Scalene	All sides are congruent. At least two sides are congruent. No two sides are congruent.
Classified by angles Right Acute Obtuse	Has a right angle. All angles are smaller than a right angle. One angle is larger than a right angle.
Convex Quadrilaterals	
Convex quadrilaterals	Convex polygons with exactly four sides.
Kite	Two opposing pairs of congruent adjacent sides.
Trapezoid Isosceles trapezoid	At least one pair of parallel sides. A pair of opposite sides is congruent.
Parallelogram Rectangle Rhombus Square	Two pairs of parallel sides. Parallelogram with a right angle. Parallelogram with all sides congruent. Parallelogram with a right angle and all sides congruent.

In the classification of quadrilaterals and parallelograms, the subsets are not all disjoint. For example, a square is a rectangle and a rhombus. All parallelograms are trapezoids, but not all trapezoids are parallelograms.* Children at level 1 have difficulty seeing this type of subrelationship. They may quite correctly list all the properties of a square, a rhombus, and a rectangle and still identify a square as a "nonrhombus" or a "nonrectangle." Is it wrong for students to refer to subgroups as disjoint sets? By fourth or fifth grade, it is only wrong to encourage such thinking. Burger (1985) points out that upper elementary students correctly use such classification schemes in other

---

*Some definitions of trapezoid specify *only one* pair of parallel sides, in which case parallelograms would not be trapezoids. The University of Chicago School Mathematics Project (UCSMP) uses the "at least one pair" definition, meaning that parallelograms and rectangles are trapezoids.

FIGURE 7.13 ● ● ● ● ● ● ●

Classification of two-
dimensional shapes.

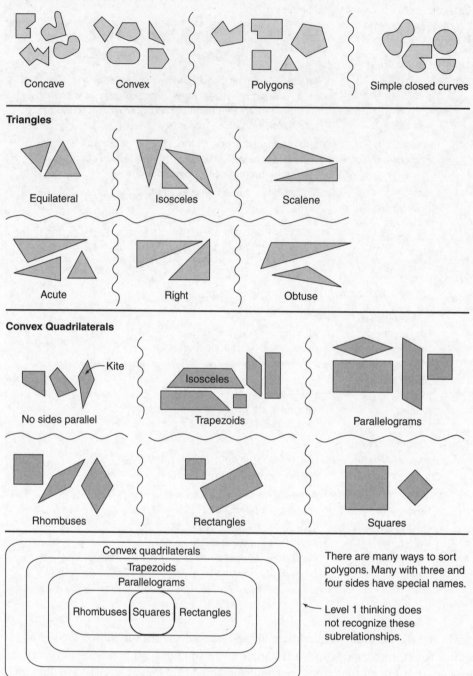

There are many ways to sort
polygons. Many with three and
four sides have special names.

Level 1 thinking does
not recognize these
subrelationships.

contexts. For example, individual students in a class can belong to more than one club.
A square is an example of a quadrilateral that belongs to two other clubs.

Special Categories of Three-Dimensional Shapes

Important and interesting shapes and relationships also exist in three dimensions. Table 7.2 describes classifications of solids. Figure 7.14 on p. 206 shows exam-

TABLE 7.2 ●●●
Categories of Three-Dimensional Shapes

Shape	Description
Sorted by Edges and Vertices	
Sphere and "egglike" shapes	Shapes with no edges and no vertices (corners). Shapes with edges but no vertices (e.g., a flying saucer). Shapes with vertices but no edges (e.g., a football).
Sorted by Faces and Surfaces	
Polyhedron	Shapes made of all faces (a face is a flat surface of a solid). If all surfaces are faces, all the edges will be straight lines. Some combination of faces and rounded surfaces (cylinders are examples, but this is not a definition of a cylinder). Shapes with curved surfaces. Shapes with and without edges and with and without vertices. Faces can be parallel. Parallel faces lie in places that never intersect.
Cylinders	
Cylinder	Two congruent, parallel faces called *bases.* Lines joining corresponding points on the two bases are always parallel. These parallel lines are called *elements* of the cylinder.
Right cylinder	A cylinder with elements perpendicular to the bases. A cylinder that is not a right cylinder is an *oblique cylinder.*
Prism	A cylinder with polygons for bases. All prisms are special cases of cylinders.
Rectangular prism	A cylinder with rectangles for bases.
Cube	A square prism with square sides.
Cones	
Cone	A solid with exactly one face and a vertex that is not on the face. Straight lines (elements) can be drawn from any point on the edge of the base to the vertex. The base may be any shape at all. The vertex need not be directly over the base.
Circular cone	Cone with a circular base.
Pyramid	Cone with a polygon for a base. All faces joining the vertex are triangles. Pyramids are named by the shape of the base: *triangular* pyramid, *square* pyramid, *octagonal* pyramid, and so on. All pyramids are special cases of cones.

ples of cylinders and prisms. Note that prisms are defined here as a special category of cylinder—a cylinder with a polygon for a base. Figure 7.15 shows a similar grouping of cones and pyramids.

 Explain the following: Prisms are to cylinders as pyramids are to cones. How is this relationship helpful in learning volume formulas?

FIGURE 7.14 • • • • • • •

Cylinders and prisms.

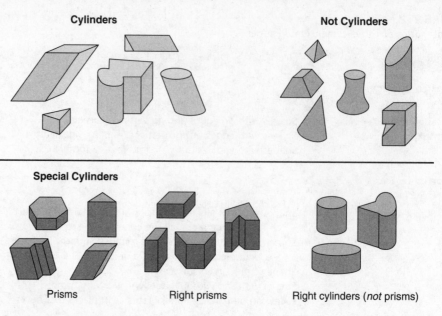

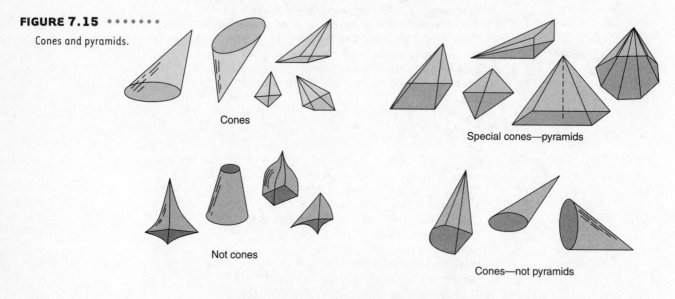

Cylinders have two parallel faces, and parallel lines join corresponding points on these faces. If the parallel faces are polygons, the cylinder can be called a prism.

FIGURE 7.15 • • • • • • •

Cones and pyramids.

Cones and cones with a polygon base (pyramids) all have straight-line elements joining every point of the base with the vertex. (Yes, a pyramid is just a special type of cone.)

Many textbooks define cylinders strictly as circular cylinders. These books do not have special names for other cylinders. Under that definition, the prism is not a special case of a cylinder. This points to the fact that definitions are conventions, and not all conventions are universally agreed upon.

Sorting and Classifying Activities

The next activity provides a good method when you want to introduce a category of shapes.

ACTIVITY 7.6

Mystery Definition

Use the overhead or chalkboard to conduct activities such as the example in Figure 7.16. For your first collection be certain that you have allowed for all possible variables. In Figure 7.16, for example, a square is included in the set of rhombi. Similarly, choose nonexamples to be as close to the positive examples as is necessary to help with an accurate definition. The third or mixed set should also include those nonexamples with which students are most likely to be confused.

Rather than confirm the choice of shapes in the third set, students should write an explanation for their choice.

The value of the "Mystery Definition" approach is that students develop ideas and definitions based on their own concept development. After their definitions have been discussed and compared, you can offer the usual "book" definition for the sake of clarity.

For defining types or categories of triangles, the next activity is especially good and uses a different approach.

Sorting of shapes at level 1 focuses on the properties of shapes rather than what they look like. For example, students can sort a collection of shapes consisting of only triangles. With some prodding from you, students in the third grade might be helped to discover that triangles can be sorted according to the relationships in their sides or by their angles. (See Figure 7.13.)

The following activity focuses only on quadrilaterals or polygons with four sides. When completed as intended, the activity is generally beyond the third-grade level. However, students who have explored a lot of properties, such as right angles, parallel lines, symmetries, and congruence, could certainly profit from this exploration. It is offered here primarily as a clear example of the difference between levels 0 and 1.

ACTIVITY 7.7

Property Lists for Quadrilaterals

Prepare worksheets for parallelograms, rhombi, rectangles, and squares. On each sheet are three or four examples of that category of shape. Examples are illustrated in Figure 7.17. Assign students working in groups of three or four to one type of quadrilateral. Their task is to list as many properties as

(continued)

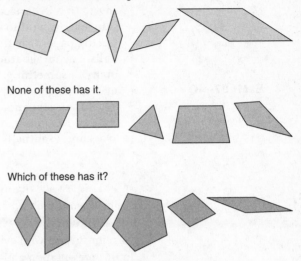

All of these have something in common.

None of these has it.

Which of these has it?

The name of a property is not necessary for it to be understood. It requires more careful observation of properties to discover what shapes have in common.

FIGURE 7.16 •

All of these, none of these: a mystery definition.

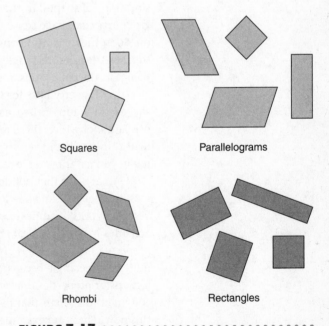

Squares

Parallelograms

Rhombi

Rectangles

FIGURE 7.17 •

Shapes for "Property Lists for Quadrilaterals" worksheets can be found in the Blackline Masters.

SHAPES AND PROPERTIES ACTIVITIES

they can. Each property listed must be applicable to all of the shapes on their sheet. They will need a simple index card to check right angles, to compare side lengths, and to draw straight lines. Mirrors (to check line symmetry) and tracing paper (for angle congruence and rotational symmetry) are also useful tools. Encourage students to use the words "at least" when describing how many of something: for example, "rectangles have at least two lines of symmetry," since squares—included in the rectangles—have four.

Have students prepare their property lists under these headings: Sides, Angles, Diagonals, and Symmetries. Groups then share their lists with the class and eventually a class list for each shape will be developed.

This last activity may take two or three days. Share lists beginning with parallelograms, then rhombi, then rectangles, and finally squares. Have one group present its list. Then others who worked on the same shape should add to or subtract from it. The class must agree with everything that is put on the list. As new relationships come up in this presentation-and-discussion period, you can introduce proper terminology. For example, if two diagonals intersect in a square corner, then they are *perpendicular*. Other terms such as *parallel, congruent, bisect, midpoint,* and so on can be clarified as you help students write their descriptions.

Progression from Level 0 to Level 1 to Level 2

Compare the last activity, "Property Lists for Quadrilaterals," with Activity 7.1, "Shape Sorts" (p. 194). In "Shape Sorts," the objects of children's thought are the very shapes that are in front of them. What comes out of that activity are collections or classifications of shapes. In the very early years, these classifications will be nonstandard groupings that make sense to the students—fat, tall, pointy, looks like houses, and so on. Soon they will also construct standard groupings that have standard names— squares, triangles, rectangles, prisms, and so on. You will supply the appropriate names as the collections are developed.

In "Property Lists for Quadrilaterals," the students only see a small collection of shapes at the top of their paper. However, the object of their thinking is the entire class of shapes for which these few are representative. In "Property Lists" the object of student thinking is the very type of thing (a class of shapes) that was the product of thinking in "Shape Sorts" at level 0.

An activity that builds on "Property Lists" illustrates how the thinking again progresses at level 2. Imagine a class of fifth- or sixth-grade students who have completed "Property Lists" and have agreed on lists for each shape. They can now use the lists in activities in which logical arguments are made based on the lists. For example, every property of a rectangle is also a property of squares. Therefore, if a shape is a square, it must be a rectangle because it has those properties. Students can look for short subcollections of properties that will guarantee the shape. For instance, a quadrilateral with congruent diagonals that bisect each other will necessarily be a rectangle. Try sketching this now. These are examples of level 2 reasoning. The objects of thought are properties of shapes—also the product of thought at level 1.

At the beginning of this chapter we talked about two kinds of goals for your students: goals of spatial sense and geometric thinking and goals of geometric content. This section on shapes and properties has been organized to help you gain some perspective on these two agendas. By planning your assessment of geometric thinking as well as and separately from content, you can avoid the trap of teaching to content objectives in a superficial way. Activities that do not appear to directly match a content objective should at least have a growth objective.

In the early grades, when you can expect your students to be level 0 thinkers, you want to be sure that their thinking is increasing in its sophistication and is moving toward level 1. Here are suggestions for things to look for:

- Child attends to a variety of characteristics of shapes in sorting and building activities.
- Child uses language that is descriptive of geometric shapes.
- Child shows evidence of geometric reasoning in solving puzzles, exploring shapes, creating designs, and analyzing shapes.
- Child recognizes shapes in the environment.
- Child solves spatial problems.

Each of these statements can be assessed as indicative of either a level 0 thinker or a level 1 thinker. For example, at level 0, the types of characteristics that students are likely to pay attention to are not properties of general classes of shapes ("pointy," "fat," "has five sides," "goes up," etc.). Properties such as "parallel" or "symmetrical" may be used by level 0 thinkers as well as those at level 1. The distinction is found in what the properties are attributed to. At level 0, students are restricted in thought to the shapes they are currently working with, while at level 1, students attribute properties to classes of shapes (*all* rectangles or *all* cylinders). Language, reasoning, shape recognition, and spatial problem solving can all be assessed as being appropriate for level 0 or level 1. By thinking in this manner, teachers can begin to get a sense of the geometric growth of their students beyond the specific content knowledge that may have been developed.

Transformation Activities

Transformations are also called "rigid motions"—movements that do not change the size or shape of the object moved. Usually, three transformations are discussed: *translations* or slides, *reflections* or flips, and *rotations* or turns. Interestingly, the study of symmetry is also included under the study of transformations. Do you know why?

Slides, Flips, and Turns

At the primary level, the terms *slide, flip,* and *turn* are adequate. The goal is to help students recognize and apply these transformations. You can use a nonsymmetric shape on the overhead to introduce these terms (see Figure 7.18). Most likely your

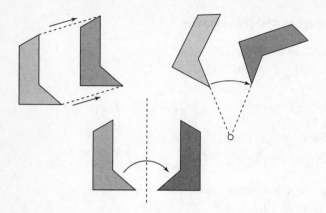

FIGURE 7.18 ••••••••••••••••••••••

Translation (slide), reflection (flip), rotation (turn).

textbook will use only the center of a shape as the point of rotation and restrict reflections to vertical and horizontal lines through the center. These restrictions are not necessary and may even be misleading.

The Motion Man described in the next activity can also be given to students to introduce the *slide, flip,* and *turn* terms. In the activity, rotations are restricted to $\frac{1}{4}$, $\frac{1}{2}$, and $\frac{3}{4}$ turns in a clockwise direction. The center of the turn will be the center of the figure. Reflections will be flips over vertical or horizontal lines. These restrictions are for simplicity. In the general case, the center of rotation can be anywhere on or off the figure. Lines of reflection can also be anywhere.

ACTIVITY 7.8

Motion Man

Using the Motion Man Blackline Masters, make copies of the first Motion Man and then copy the mirror image on the backs of these copies. Experiment first. You want the back image to match the front image when held to the light. Cut off the excess paper to leave a square. Give all students a two-sided Motion Man.

BLMs 41–42

Demonstrate each of the possible motions. A slide is simply that. The figure does not rotate or turn over. Demonstrate $\frac{1}{4}$, $\frac{1}{2}$, and $\frac{3}{4}$ turns. Emphasize that only clockwise turns will be used for this activity. Similarly, demonstrate a horizontal flip (top goes to bottom) and a vertical flip (left goes to right). Practice by having everyone start with his or her Motion Man in the same orientation. As you announce one of the moves, students slide, flip, or turn Motion Man accordingly.

Then display two Motion Men side by side in any orientation. The task is to decide what motion or combination of motions will get the man on the left to match the man on the right. Students use their own man to work out a solution. Test the solutions that students offer. If both men are in the same position, call that a slide.

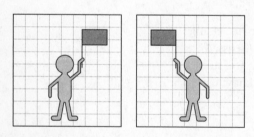

FIGURE 7.19 •••••••••••••••••••

The Motion Man is printed back to back. Use to show slides, flips, and turns. (See Blackline Masters.)

Begin with the Motion Man in the left position shown in Figure 7.19. Now place a second Motion Man next to the first. Will it take one move or more than one move (transformation) to get from the first to the second Motion Man? Can you describe all of the positions that require more than one move? Are there any positions that require more than two moves?

At first, students will be confused when they can't get their Motion Man into the new position with one move. This causes an excellent problem. Don't be too quick to suggest that it may take two moves. If you allow for flips across each of the two diagonals as well as vertical and horizontal flips, Motion Man can assume any new position in exactly one move. This provides a challenge for students. Two students begin with their Motion Man figures in the same position. One student then changes his or her Motion Man and challenges the other student to say what motion is required to make the two Motion Men match. The solution is then tested and the roles reversed.

Line and Rotational Symmetry

If a shape can be folded on a line so that the two halves match, then it is said to have *line symmetry* (or mirror symmetry). Notice that the fold line is actually a line of reflection—the portion of the shape on one side of the line is reflected onto the other side. That is the connection between line symmetry and transformations.

One way to introduce line symmetry to children is to show examples and nonexamples using an all-of-these/none-of-these approach as in Figure 7.16 on p. 207. Another approach is to have students fold a sheet of paper in half and cut out a shape of their choosing. When they open the paper, the fold line will be a line of symmetry. A third way is to use mirrors. When you place a mirror on a picture or design so that the mirror is perpendicular to the table, you see a shape with symmetry when you look in the mirror. Here is an activity with line symmetry.

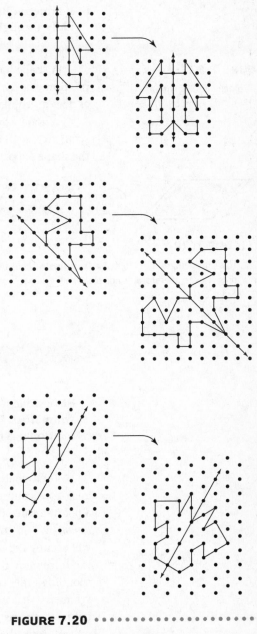

ACTIVITY 7.9

Pattern Block Mirror Symmetry

Students need a plain sheet of paper with a straight line through the middle. Using about six to eight pattern blocks, students make a design completely on one side of the line that touches the line in some way. The task is to make the mirror image of their design on the other side of the line. When finished, they use a mirror to check their work. They place the mirror on the line and look into it from the side of the original design. With the mirror in place they should see exactly the same image as they see when they lift the mirror. You can also challenge them to make designs with more than one line of symmetry.

Building symmetrical designs with pattern blocks tends to be easier if the line is "pointing" at the student, that is, with a left and a right side. With the line oriented horizontally or diagonally, the task is harder.

The same task can be done with a geoboard. First, stretch a band down the center or from corner to corner. Make a design on one side of the line and its mirror image on the other. Check with a mirror. This can also be done on either isometric or rectangular dot grids as shown in Figure 7.20.

FIGURE 7.20

Exploring symmetry on dot grids.

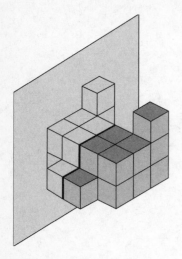

A plane of symmetry in three dimensions is analogous to a line of symmetry in two dimensions. Figure 7.21 illustrates a shape built with cubes that has a plane of symmetry.

FIGURE 7.21 • • • • • • • • •

A block building with one plane of symmetry.

A shape has *rotational symmetry* if it can be rotated about a point and land in a position exactly matching the one in which it began. A square has rotational symmetry as does an equilateral triangle.

A good way to understand rotational symmetry is to take a shape with rotational symmetry, such as a square, and trace around it on a piece of paper. Call this tracing the shape's "box." The order of rotational symmetry will be the number of ways that the shape can fit into its box without flipping it over. A square has rotational symmetry of *order* 4, whereas an equilateral triangle has rotational symmetry of *order* 3. The parallelogram in Figure 7.22 has rotational symmetry of order 2. Some books would call order 2 symmetry "180-degree symmetry." The number of degrees refers to the smallest angle of rotation required before the shape matches itself or fits into its box. A square has 90-degree rotational symmetry.

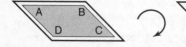

FIGURE 7.22 • • • • • • • • • • • • • • • • •

This parallelogram fits in its box two ways without flipping it over. Therefore, it has rotational symmetry of order 2.

Rotational symmetry in the plane (also referred to as *point symmetry*) also has an analogous counterpart in three dimensions. Whereas a figure in a plane is rotated about a point, a three-dimensional figure is rotated about a line. This line is called an *axis of symmetry*. As a solid with rotational symmetry revolves around an axis of symmetry, it will occupy the same position in space (its "box") but in different orientations. A solid can have more than one axis of rotation. For each axis of symmetry, there is a corresponding order of rotational symmetry. A regular square pyramid has only one axis of symmetry that runs through the tip of the pyramid and the center of the square. A cube, by contrast, has a total of 13 axes of symmetry: three (through opposite faces) of order 4, four (through diagonally opposite vertices) of order 3, and six (through midpoints of diagonally opposite edges) of order 2.

Location Activities

In kindergarten children learn about everyday positional descriptions—*over, under, near, far, between, left,* and *right.* These are the beginnings of the *Standards'* goal of specifying locations. These informal indicators of location are useful for everyday interactions. However, spatial understandings are enhanced by helping students refine the way they answer questions of direction, distance, and location. Geometry, measurement, and algebra are all supported by the use of a grid system with numbers or coordinates attached that can specify the location on a grid. As students become more sophisticated, their use of coordinates progresses along with them. However, there is no reason that students at the primary level cannot begin to think in terms of a grid system to identify location. If this preparation for more sophisticated coordinate geometry is made in the early years, students will not find coordinates at all mysterious in later years.

The next activity can serve as a readiness task for coordinates and help students see the value of a way to specify location without pointing.

ACTIVITY 7.12

Hidden Positions

For the game boards, draw an 8-inch square on tagboard. Subdivide the squares into a 3 × 3 grid. Two students sit with a "screen" separating their desktop space so that neither student can see the other's grid (see Figure 7.23). Each student has four different pattern blocks. The first player places a block on four different sections of the grid. He then tells the other player where to put blocks on her grid to match his own. When all four pieces are positioned, the two grids are checked to see if they are alike. Then the players switch roles. Model the game once by taking the part of the first student. Use words such as *top row, middle, left,* and *right.* Students can play in pairs as a station activity.

The "Hidden Positions" game can easily be extended to a 4 × 4 or even 5 × 5 grid. As the grid size increases, the need for a system of labeling positions increases.

Students can begin to use a simple coordinate system as early as the first grade. Draw a coordinate grid on the board or on the overhead projector such as the one shown in Figure 7.24. Explain how to use two numbers to designate an intersection point on the grid. The first number tells how far to move to the right. The second number tells how far to move up. For younger children use the words along with the numbers: 3 right and 0 up. Be sure to include 0 in your introduction. Select a point on the grid and have students decide what two numbers name that point. If your point is at (2,4) and students incorrectly say "four, two," then simply indicate where the point is that they named. Emphasize that when they say or write the two numbers, the first number is the number of steps to the right and the second is the number of steps up.

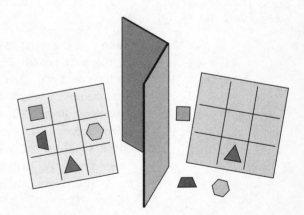

FIGURE 7.23

The "Hidden Positions" game. Players must communicate verbally the positions of their blocks on the grid.

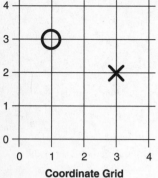

FIGURE 7.24 • • • • • • • • •

A simple coordinate grid. The X is at (3,2) and the 0 is at (1,3). Use the grid to play Three in a Row (like Tic-Tac-Toe). Put marks on intersections, not spaces.

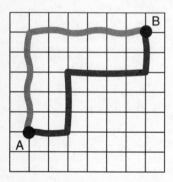

FIGURE 7.25 • • • • • • • • •

Coloring in different paths on a grid. What is the fewest number of turns needed to get from A to B? The most?

The next activity explores the notion of different paths on a grid.

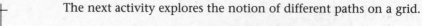

ACTIVITY 7.13

Paths

On a sheet of 2-cm grid paper, mark two different points A and B as shown in Figure 7.25. Using the overhead or the chalkboard, demonstrate how to describe a path from A to B. For the points in the figure, one path is "up 5 and right 6." Another path might be "right 2, up 2, right 2, up 3, right 2." Count the length of each path. As long as you always move toward the target point (in this case either right or up), the path lengths will always be the same. Here they are 11 units long. Students draw three paths on their papers from A to B using different colored crayons. For each path they write directions that describe their paths. They should check the lengths of each path. Ask, "What is the greatest number of turns that you can make in your path?" "What is the smallest number?" "Where would A and B have to be in order to get there with no turns?"

If you add a coordinate system on the grid in "Paths," students can describe their paths with coordinates: For example, the path in Figure 7.25 is described as follows:

$$(1,2) \rightarrow (3,2) \rightarrow (3,5) \rightarrow (7,5) \rightarrow (7,7).$$

Technology Note

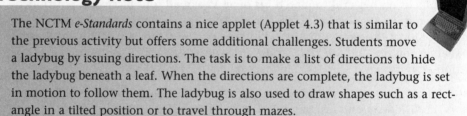

The NCTM *e-Standards* contains a nice applet (Applet 4.3) that is similar to the previous activity but offers some additional challenges. Students move a ladybug by issuing directions. The task is to make a list of directions to hide the ladybug beneath a leaf. When the directions are complete, the ladybug is set in motion to follow them. The ladybug is also used to draw shapes such as a rectangle in a tilted position or to travel through mazes.

Once a coordinate system has been introduced, students may want to use it in a simple game similar to the commercial game called "Battleship." Each player has a grid similar to the one in Figure 7.24. Players secretly put their initials on five intersections of their own grid. Then, with the grids kept separate as in "Hidden Positions," the players take turns trying to "hit" the other player's targets by naming a point on the grid using coordinates. The other player indicates if the "shot" was a hit or a miss. When a player scores a hit, he or she gets another turn. Each player keeps track of where he or she has taken shots, recording an "X" for a hit and an "0" for a miss. The game ends when one player has hit all of the other player's targets.

At this level, students are simply using coordinates to describe positions. Although important, this is not very challenging or exciting. By grade 3, students can begin to use coordinates to describe changes on a coordinate grid. In this spirit, consider the following activity if you feel your students are ready. In it, students use coordinates to cause a shape to change location in the plane—to slide or translate it.

Coordinate Slides

Students will need a sheet of centimeter grid paper on which to draw two coordinate axes near the left and bottom edges. Have them plot and connect about five or six points on the grid to form a small shape. (See Figure 7.26.) If you direct them to use only coordinates between 5 and 12, the figure will be reasonably small and near the center of the paper. Select one point of their shape and have students add 6 to the first coordinate (typically called the *x*-coordinate) leaving the second coordinate the same. Students plot this new point. For example, for the point (5, 10) a new point (11, 10) is plotted. Have students repeat this process for each vertex of their figure, adding 6 to each first coordinate. When new points for each point in the figure have been plotted, these are connected as before. Students will notice that the new shape is identical to the original and in the same orientation. The new shape is a translation of the original, or a slide six units to the right. Students then create a second figure by adding 9 to each second coordinate. This will create a slide 9 units up. As a challenge, ask students to predict how they would change the coordinates to create a new figure that is a slide down 5 units and to the right 4 units. (Subtract 5 from the second coordinates and add 4 to the first coordinates.)

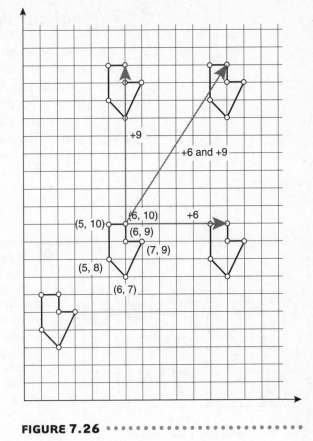

FIGURE 7.26 •

Coordinate slides.

In the last activity the figure did not twist or turn, flip over, or change size or shape. It slid along a path. Lines can be drawn between corresponding points of the original figure to the new figure. These lines will all be parallel to each other and exactly the same length. The lines show the direction and distance of the slide. Therefore, the change was one of the three rigid motions—a translation or slide.

> **STOP** What do you think would happen if, instead of adding or subtracting, you multiplied each of the coordinates by 2 or by 3? What if you multiplied each coordinate by $\frac{1}{2}$? Try this on a sheet of grid paper before you read on.

When the coordinates of a shape are multiplied, each by the same factor, the shape either gets larger or smaller. The size is changed but not the shape. The new shape is similar to the old shape. This is called a *dilation*. Your students may enjoy exploring this phenomenon.

Reflections and rotations can also be explored and described with coordinates, but the process is too difficult for students in the early grades. Students might be interested to know that changing coordinates of a shape is essentially the way that computers create computer animations, mathematically changing a shape from one position to another.

Visualization Activities

Visualization activities involve seeing and understanding shapes from different perspectives. As with other aspects of geometry, students' ability to visualize shapes in different orientations and with different representations (e.g., drawings of three-dimensional objects) will improve with appropriate experiences.

Finding out how many different shapes can be made with a given number of simple tiles demands that students mentally flip and turn shapes in their minds and find ways to decide if they have found them all. That is the focus of the next activity.

ACTIVITY 7.15

Pentominoes

A pentomino is a shape formed by joining five squares as if cut from a square grid. Each square must have at least one side in common with another. Provide students with five square tiles and a sheet of square grid paper for recording. Challenge them to see how many different pentomino shapes they can find. Shapes that are flips or turns of other shapes are not considered different. Do not tell students how many pentomino shapes there are. Good discussions will come from deciding if some shapes are really different and if all shapes have been found.

Once students have decided that there are just 12 pentominoes (see Figure 7.27), the 12 pieces can then be used in a variety of activities. Paste the grids with the children's pentominoes onto tagboard and let them cut out the 12 shapes. These can be used in the next two activities. It is also fun to explore the number of shapes that can be made from six equilateral triangles or from four 45-degree right triangles (halves of squares). With the right triangles, sides that touch must be the same length. How many of each of these "ominoes" do you think there are?

Lots of activities can be done with pentominoes. For example, try to fit all 12 pieces into a 6 × 10 or 5 × 12 rectangle. (This is very difficult.) Also, each of the 12 shapes can be used as a tessellation tile. Another task is to examine each of the 12 pentominoes and decide which will fold up to make an open box. For those that are "box makers," which square is the bottom? The following activity also uses the 12 pentomino pieces and is an excellent visualization task for young children.

There are 12 pentominoes.

Finding all possible shapes made with five squares—or six squares (called "hexominoes") or six equilateral triangles and so on—is a good exercise in spatial problem solving.

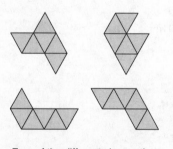

Four of the different shapes that six equilateral triangles will make.

Four of the different shapes that four "half-square" triangles will make.

FIGURE 7.27

Pentominoes and related shape challenges.

ACTIVITY 7.16

Pentomino Squeeze

This game for two students requires one set of the 12 pentominoes cut out and an 8 × 8 grid of squares the same size as those from which the pentominoes were cut. One-inch squares work well. In turn, each player selects a pentomino and places it on the grid. The squares of the pentomino must match up with the squares on the grid. The pentominoes may be turned over or rotated in any manner. However, pentominoes may not overlap any previously played pieces! Once on the board they may not be moved. The winner is the last person to be able to play.

Another aspect of visualization for young children is to be able to think about solid shapes in terms of their faces or sides. For these activities you will need to make "face cards" by tracing around the different faces of a shape, making either all faces on one card or a set of separate cards with one face per card (see Figure 7.28).

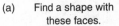

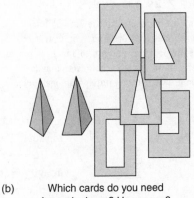

(a)　Find a shape with these faces.

(b)　Which cards do you need for each shape? How many?

FIGURE 7.28 • • • • • • • • • • • • • •

Matching face cards with solid shapes.

ACTIVITY 7.17

Face Matching

There are two versions of the task: Given a face card, find the corresponding solid, or given a solid, find the face card. With a collection of single-face cards, students can select the cards that go with a particular block. For another variation, stack all of the single-face cards for one block face down. Turn them up one at a time as clues to finding the block.

The ability to discern shapes in the environment is part of the visualization agenda. A search for shapes can be modified to accommodate both level 0 and level 1 students at the same time by altering the object of the search.

ACTIVITY 7.18

Shape Hunts

Have students search (inside and outside or as a homework assignment) not just for triangles, circles, squares, and rectangles but also for properties of shapes. A shape hunt will be much more successful if you let students look for either one thing or for a specific list. Different groups can hunt for different things. For example:

- Parallel lines (lines "going in the same direction")
- Right angles ("square corners")
- Curved surfaces or curved lines
- Two or more shapes that make another shape
- Circles inside each other (concentric)
- Shapes with "dents" (concave) or without "dents" (convex)
- Solids that are like a box, a cylinder, a pyramid, a cone
- Five shapes that are alike in some way
- Shapes that have line or rotational symmetry

The following activity has been adapted from NCTM's *Principles and Standards* book and is found in the pre-K–2 section on geometry (NCTM, 2000, p. 101).

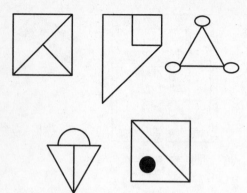

FIGURE 7.29 • • • • • • • • • • • • • • • • • •

Examples of designs to use in the "Quick Images" activity. Draw each on acetate so that the design is about 4 to 5 inches across. Briefly show students the design and have them draw it on their paper from memory.

Quick Images

Draw some simple sketches on transparencies so that they can be shown to students one sketch at a time. They should be drawings that students can easily reproduce. Some examples are shown in Figure 7.29. On the overhead projector display one of the sketches for about 5 seconds. Then have students attempt to reproduce the sketch on their own paper. Show the same sketch again for a few seconds and allow students to modify their drawings. Repeat with additional sketches.

In your discussions with students, ask them to tell how they thought about the sketch or to describe it in words that helped them remember what they saw. As students learn to verbally describe what they see, their visual memory will improve.

In the last activity, visual memory as well as the ability to create a sketch played a big role. Thinking about position of lines and features of the sketch is also important. In the next activity students must mentally move shapes and predict the results. The activity combines ideas about line symmetry (reflections) as well as visualization and spatial reasoning.

Notches and Holes

Use a half sheet of paper that will easily fit on the overhead. Fold it in half and then half again, making the second fold in the opposite direction from the first. Students make a sketch of the paper when it is opened, showing a line for each fold. With the paper folded, cut notches in one or two sides and/or cut off one or two corners. You can also use a paper punch to make a hole or two. While still folded, place the paper on the overhead showing the notches and holes. The folded edges should be to the left and at the bottom (see Figure 7.30). The task is for students to draw the notches and holes that they think will appear when you open the paper.

To introduce this activity, begin with only one fold and only two cuts. Stay with one fold until students are ready for a more difficult challenge.

In "Notches and Holes" students will eventually learn which cuts create holes and how many and which cuts make notches in the edges or on the corners. Notice how line symmetry or reflection plays a major role in the activity. Symmetry determines the position, the shape, and the number of holes created by each cut.

 Stop now and try the "Notches and Holes" activity yourself. Try cuts in various places on the folded paper and see what is involved in this well-known activity.

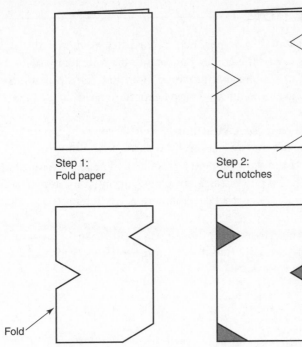

Step 1:
Fold paper

Step 2:
Cut notches

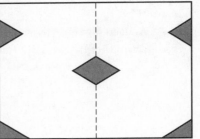

Fold

Step 3:
Show on overhead projector

Step 4:
Students draw their predictions

FIGURE 7.30 • • • • • • •

An example showing how the "Notches and Holes" activity is done. Students make either one or two folds and cut notches and/or punch holes in the folded paper. (Only one fold is shown here.) Before unfolding, they draw a sketch predicting the result when the paper is unfolded.

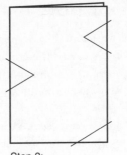

Technology Note

Geometry is one area of the curriculum for which a variety of fascinating computer programs exist. Many programs allow students to "stamp" geometric shapes such as tangrams or pattern blocks onto the screen and then manipulate them. We have already discussed e-geoboards, and e-tangrams. Here are some more examples.

Shape Up (Sunburst, 1995) and *Shapes* (Clements & Sarama, 1995) are two good examples of computer versions of physical tiles. Both programs include a pattern block and tangram format in which students can stamp pieces onto a blank screen. Pieces are easily moved around, rotated, or flipped through either a vertical or horizontal line. In *Shapes,* two or more pieces can be "glued together" to create new shapes. The pattern blocks include a quarter circle that adds to the variability. Both programs allow shapes to be enlarged or reduced in size. Some puzzles are included with the packages, and new puzzles are easily created. *Shape Up* has a third mode in which six regular shapes can be manipulated and each can be cut into many smaller shapes and rearranged in endless ways.

It is not clear that any greater geometric benefit is gained with the virtual versions of these blocks. However, the environment and the variability are sufficiently different to warrant the use of this type of program along with physical models. Students who have difficulty with fine motor control are often unable to produce drawings or cut-and-paste recordings of their geometry activities. Because the computer permits students to print colorful copies of their work and include written journal entries, these students take real pride in the products they produce.

Assessment Note

Principles and Standards is extremely helpful for articulating growth in geometric content across the grades. For each of the four goals articulated by the standards (shape and properties, location, transformations, and visualization) examine the grade-level expectations at the K–2 and 3–5 grade bands.

Try to include a sense of growth over time in your assessment of content. If you limit your assessment to a mastery of skills or definitions, the spirit of exploration that you want in your geometry program will be lost. We most often teach in a manner that reflects our assessment plans. Although mastery of some ideas is perhaps important, conceptual development is rarely reflected in memorizing definitions.

In deciding what to assess and how, it is best to take a long-term view of geometry rather than a more traditional mastery-oriented approach.

EXPANDED LESSON

Shape Sorts
Based on: Activity 7.1, p. 194

GRADE LEVEL: Kindergarten through second grade or early third grade.

MATHEMATICS GOALS
- To develop an awareness of the wide variety of ways that two-dimensional shapes can be alike.
- To establish classifications of shapes by various properties, both traditional categorizations and informal, student-generated categories.
- To introduce the names of common shapes or important properties (when and if the opportunity arises within the activity).

THINKING ABOUT THE STUDENTS
Students need no prerequisite knowledge for this lesson. The activity will naturally adjust itself to the ideas held by the students. The level of vocabulary and the types of observations that students make will depend on the geometric experiences of the students and their verbal skills.

MATERIALS AND PREPARATION
- Each group of three to five students will need a collection of 2-D Shapes. Blackline Masters 20 to 26 provide a collection of 49 shapes. Duplicate each set on a different color of card stock and cut out the shapes. You may want to laminate the card stock before you cut out the shapes.
- Students will need a large surface (floor or table) on which to spread out the shapes.

lesson

BEFORE

Begin with a Simpler Version of the Task:
- Gather students in a circle where all can see and have access to one set of shapes.
- Have each student select a shape. Ask students to think of things that they can say about their shape. Go around the group and ask students to hold up their shape and tell one or two of their ideas.
- Return all shapes to the pile and you select one shape. Place this "target" shape for all to see. Each student is to find a shape that is like the target shape in some way. Again, have students share their ideas. You may want to repeat this with another shape.

The Task
- Each group of students is to select a shape from the collection to be the target shape just as you did. Then they are to find as many other shapes that are like the target shape as they can. However, all the shapes they find must be like the target shape *in the same way*. For example, if they use "has straight sides" as a rule, they cannot also use "has a square corner." That would be two different ways or two rules.

Establish Expectations
- Explain that when you visit each group, you want to see a collection of shapes that go together according to the same rule. You will see if you can guess their rule by looking at the shapes they have put together.
- When you have checked their first rule, you will select a new target shape for them. They should make a new collection of shapes using a different rule. When they have finished, each student should draw a new shape on paper that would fit the rule. All of the drawings should then be alike in the same way. (For kindergarten and first-grade students, you will probably explain this part as you visit their group.)

DURING
- Listen carefully for the types of ideas that students are using. Are they using "nongeometric" language such as "pointy," "looks like a house," "has a straight bottom," or are they beginning to talk about more geometric ideas such as "square corners,"

"sides that go the same way" (parallel), or "dented in" (concave)? If they are using shape names, are they using them correctly?

- Gently correct incorrect language or, when appropriate, introduce correct terms. However, do not make terminology and definitions a focus of the activity. Allow students to use their own ideas.
- You may want to challenge students by quickly creating a small group of shapes that go together according to a secret rule. See if they can figure out what the rule is and find other shapes that go with your collection.

AFTER

- Collect students' drawings, keeping the groups intact. Gather students together so that all will be able to see the drawings. (This could be done the day after the DURING portion of the lesson.)
- Display the drawings from one group. Have students from other groups see if they can guess the rule for the drawings. If the drawings are not adequate to see the rule, have those who made the drawings find a few shapes from the collection of shapes that fit the rule.
- To expand students' ideas or interject new ideas, you may want to create a set using a secret rule as described previously. Base your rule on an attribute of the shapes that the students have not yet thought of.

ASSESSMENT NOTES

- Do not think of this activity as something that students should master. This lesson can profitably be repeated two or three times over the course of the year. As students have more and more experiences with shapes, they will be able to create different, more sophisticated sorting rules.
- Watch for students who talk about shapes in terms of relative attributes such as "bottom," "pointing up," or "has a side near the windows." These same students will not recognize a square as such if it has been turned to look like a "diamond." When this happens, pick up the shape, turn it slowly, and ask the student if it is still pointing up (or whatever). Point out that the shape doesn't change, only the way it is positioned.
- If you have introduced vocabulary that is important, you can informally assess students' knowledge of that vocabulary during this activity. Every type of shape that a primary-grade student needs to know is included in the set. There are examples of right angles, parallel lines, concave and convex shapes, shapes with line symmetry, and shapes with rotational symmetry.

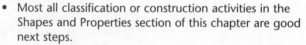

- It is always fun to do secret sorts. These can be done quickly by simply showing a small collection of the shapes that go together by a secret rule that you have devised. This is a good way to introduce a new shape or property to the students. A secret sort can be a 10-minute activity at any time.

next steps

- Activity 7.2, "What's My Shape," is a good follow-up to this lesson.
- Most all classification or construction activities in the Shapes and Properties section of this chapter are good next steps.

DEVELOPING MEASUREMENT CONCEPTS

Measurement is a complex area of the curriculum. Unfortunately, the measurement curriculum in most states asks that students learn something about nearly every type of measurement almost every year, even in the primary grades. Traditional textbooks, in an attempt to respond to state mandates, pack all of this information into what often becomes a superficial "covering of the material."

A goal for the primary teacher is to help students understand what it means to measure length, volume, weight, and area, and to help students understand the most important measuring instrument for young children—the ruler. Familiarity with a few standard units is another goal, although most curricula are too ambitious in this regard.

big ideas

1 Measurement involves a comparison of an attribute of an item or situation with a unit that has the same attribute. Lengths are compared to units of length, areas to units of area, time to units of time, and so on. Before anything can be measured meaningfully, it is necessary to understand the attribute to be measured.

2 Meaningful measurement and estimation of measurements depend on a personal familiarity with the unit of measure being used.

3 Estimation of measures and the development of personal benchmarks for frequently used units of measure help students increase their familiarity with units, prevent errors in measurements, and aid in the meaningful use of measurement.

4 Measurement instruments are devices that replace the need for actual measurement units. It is important to understand how measurement instruments work so that they can be used correctly and meaningfully.

The Meaning and Process of Measuring

Suppose that you asked your students to measure an empty bucket. The first thing they would need to know is *what* about the bucket is to be measured. They might measure the height or depth, diameter (distance across), or circumference (distance around). All of these are length measures. The surface area of the side could be determined. A bucket also has capacity and weight. Each of these *aspects that can be measured* is an *attribute* of the bucket.

Once they determine the attribute to be measured, they need to choose a unit of measure. The unit must have the attribute that is being measured. Length is measured with units that have length, volume with units that have volume, and so on.

Technically, a *measurement* is a number that indicates a comparison between the attribute of the object (or situation or event) being measured and the same attribute of a given unit of measure. We commonly use small units of measure to determine in some way a numeric relationship (the measurement) between what is measured and the unit. For example, to measure a length, the comparison can be done by lining up copies of the unit directly against the length being measured. To measure weight, which is a pull of gravity or a force, the weight of the object might first be applied to a spring. Then the comparison is made by finding out how many units of weight produce the same effect on the spring. In either case, the number of units is the measure of the object.

For most of the attributes that are measured in schools, we can say that *to measure* means that the attribute being measured is "filled" or "covered" or "matched" with a unit of measure with the same attribute (as illustrated in Figure 8.1). This concept of filling or covering is a good way to talk with children about measurement. It is appropriate with this understanding, then, to say that the measure of an attribute is a count of how many units are needed to fill, cover, or match the attribute of the object being measured.

In summary, to measure something, one must perform three steps:

1. Decide on the attribute to be measured.
2. Select a unit that has that attribute.
3. Compare the units, by filling, covering, matching, or some other method, with the attribute of the object being measured.

Measuring instruments such as rulers, scales, protractors, and clocks are devices that make the filling, covering, or matching process easier. A ruler lines up the units of length and numbers them. A clock lines up units of time and marks them off.

FIGURE 8.1 ●

Measuring different attributes of a bucket.

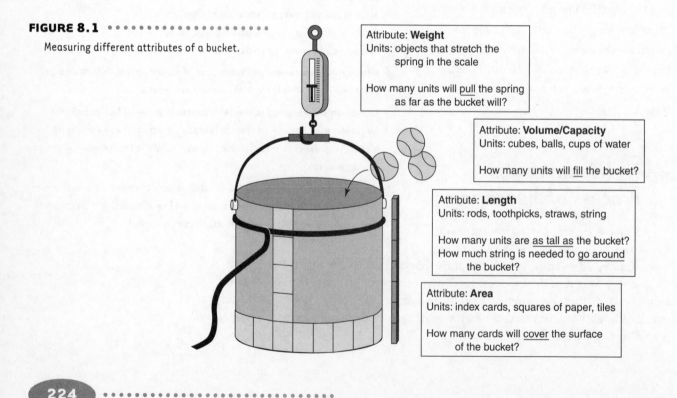

Attribute: **Weight**
Units: objects that stretch the
    spring in the scale

How many units will <u>pull</u> the spring
    as far as the bucket will?

Attribute: **Volume/Capacity**
Units: cubes, balls, cups of water

How many units will <u>fill</u> the bucket?

Attribute: **Length**
Units: rods, toothpicks, straws, string

How many units are <u>as tall as</u> the bucket?
How much string is needed to <u>go around</u>
    the bucket?

Attribute: **Area**
Units: index cards, squares of paper, tiles

How many cards will <u>cover</u> the surface
    of the bucket?

Developing Measurement Concepts and Skills

A typical group of first graders measures the length of their classroom by laying strips 1 meter long end to end. But the strips sometimes overlap, and the line weaves in a snakelike fashion around the desks. Do they understand the concept of length as an attribute of the classroom? Do they understand that each strip of 1 meter has this attribute of length? Do they understand that their task is to fill smaller units of length into the longer one? More than likely these students are attempting to follow the teacher's directions to make a line of strips stretching from wall to wall (and from their vantage point, they are doing quite well). They are performing a procedure instrumentally without a conceptual basis.

A General Plan of Instruction

A basic understanding of measurement suggests three steps to help children develop a conceptual knowledge of measuring. These are summarized in Table 8.1.
Let's briefly discuss each of these three instructional components.

Making Comparisons

The first and most critical goal is for students to understand the attribute they are going to measure. When students compare objects on the basis of some measurable

TABLE 8.1 •
Plan for Measurement Instruction

Step One

Goal: Students will understand the attribute to be measured.

Type of Activity: Make comparisons based on the attribute. For example, longer/shorter, heavier/lighter. Use direct comparisons whenever possible.

Notes: When it is clear that the attribute is understood, there is no further need for comparison activities.

Step Two

Goal: Students will understand how filling, covering, matching, or making other comparisons of an attribute with measuring units produces a number called a measure.

Type of Activity: Use physical models of measuring units to fill, cover, match, or make the desired comparison of the attribute with the unit.

Notes: In most instances it is appropriate to begin with informal units. Progress to the direct use of standard units when appropriate and certainly before using formulas or measuring tools.

Step Three

Goal: Students will use common measuring tools with understanding and flexibility.

Type of Activity: Make measuring instruments and use them in comparison with the actual unit models to see how the measurement tool is performing the same function as the individual units. Be certain to make direct comparisons between the student-made tools and the standard tools.

Notes: Student-made tools are usually best made with informal units. Without a careful comparison with the standard tools, much of the value in making the tools can be lost.

attribute, that attribute becomes the focus of the activity. For example, is the capacity of one box more than, less than, or about the same as the capacity of another? No measurement is required, but some manner of comparing one volume to the other must be devised. The attribute of "capacity" (how much a container can hold) is inescapable.

Many attributes can be compared directly, such as placing one length directly in line with another. In the case of volume or capacity, some indirect method is probably required, such as filling one box with beans and then pouring the beans into the other box. Using a string to compare the height of a wastebasket to the distance around is another example of an indirect comparison. The string is the intermediary. It is impossible to compare these two lengths directly.

Using Models of Units

The second goal is for students to understand what a unit of measure is and how it is used to produce a measurement. For most attributes that are measured in elementary schools, it is possible to have physical models of the units of measure. Time and temperature are exceptions. Unit models can be found for both informal units and standard units. For length, for example, drinking straws (informal) or tagboard strips 1 foot long (standard) might be used as units.

The most easily understood use of unit models is actually to use as many copies of the unit as are needed to fill or match the attribute measured. The length of the room could be measured with giant footprints by placing tagboard copies of the footprint end to end, completely "covering" the length of the room. It is somewhat more difficult to use a single copy of a unit in an iteration process. For the footprint example, one footprint could be placed down and then moved to take the space of the second footprint, and so on. However, not only is this more difficult for younger children, but also it obscures the meaning of the measurement—to see how many units will fill the length.

It is useful to measure the same object with different-sized units. Results should be predicted in advance and discussed afterward. This will help students understand that the unit used is as important as the attribute being measured. The fact that smaller units produce larger numeric measures, and vice versa, is hard for young children to understand. This inverse relationship can only be constructed by reflecting on measurements with varying-sized units. Predictions and discussions of results add to the reflective nature of the activities.

Making and Using Measuring Instruments

An understanding of the devices we use to measure is the third goal. In the sixth National Assessment of Educational Progress (Kenney & Kouba, 1997), only 24 percent of fourth-grade students and 62 percent of eighth-grade students could give the correct measure of an object not aligned with the end of a ruler, as in Figure 8.2. These results point to the difference between using a measuring device and understanding how it works.

If students actually make simple measuring instruments using unit models with which they are familiar, it is more likely that they will understand how an instrument measures. A ruler is the most important measurement tool that primary students need to learn about. If students line up physical units, such as paper clips, along a strip of tagboard and mark them off, they can see that it is the *spaces* on rulers and not the marks or numbers that are important.

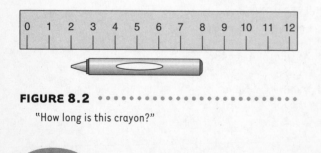

FIGURE 8.2

"How long is this crayon?"

It is essential that the measurement with actual unit models be compared with the measurement using an instrument. A chain of paper clips can be used as a ruler to make this transition more apparent. Without this comparison, students may not understand that these two methods are really two means to the same end.

A discussion of student-made measuring instruments for each attribute is provided in the text that follows. Of course, children should also use standard, ready-made instruments such as rulers and scales and should compare the use of these devices with the use of the corresponding unit models.

Informal Units and Standard Units: Reasons for Using Each

It is common in primary grades to use nonstandard or informal units to measure length and sometimes area. The use of informal units for beginning measurement activities is beneficial at all grade levels. It is useful to understand the reasons that we use informal units so that we can do so wisely.

- Informal units make it easier to focus directly on the attribute being measured. For example, in a discussion of how to measure the area of an irregular shape, units such as lima beans, square tiles, or circular counters may be suggested. Each unit covers area and each will give a different result. The discussion focuses on what it means to measure area.
- By selecting units carefully, the size of the numbers in early measurements can be kept reasonable. The measures of length for first-grade students can be kept less than 20 even when measuring long distances simply by using longer units.
- Informal units provide a good rationale for standard units. A discussion of the need for a standard unit can have more meaning after groups in your class have measured the same objects with their own units and arrived at different answers.
- Using informal units can be fun.

The use of standard units is also important in your measurement program at any grade level.

- Knowledge of standard units is a valid objective of a measurement program and must be addressed. Students must not only develop a familiarity with standard units but must also learn appropriate relationships between them.
- Once a measuring concept is fairly well developed, it is frequently just as easy to use standard units. If there is no good instructional reason for using informal units, why not use standard units and provide the exposure?

At the K–3 level, it is certainly reasonable to begin the measurement of any attribute with informal units. The move to standard units should be guided by how well you believe your students are developing an understanding of measurement of that attribute and the requirements of your curriculum to be familiar with standard units. Especially for K–1 students, a discussion of inches, feet, centimeters, and meters can obscure what it means to measure. By third grade, students probably have used informal units to measure length and can develop unit familiarity by measuring with standard units. When informal units have served their purpose, move on.

The Role of Estimation in Learning Measurement

It is very important to have students estimate a measurement before they make it. This is true with both informal and standard units. There are at least three good reasons for including estimation in measurement activities:

- Estimation helps students focus on the attribute being measured and the measuring process. Think how you would estimate the area of the front of this book with standard playing cards as the unit. To do so, you have to think about what area is and how the units might be fitted into the book cover.

- Estimation provides intrinsic motivation to measurement activities. It is fun to see how close you can come in your estimate or if your team can make a better estimate than the other teams in the room.

- When standard units are used, estimation helps develop familiarity with the unit. If you estimate the height of the door in meters before measuring, you have to devise some way to think about the size of a meter.

The Approximate Nature of Measurement

In all measuring activities, emphasize the use of approximate language. The desk is *about* 15 orange rods long. The chair is *a little less than* 4 straws high. The use of approximate language is very useful for younger children because many measurements do not come out even. In fact, all measurements include some error. The use of smaller units or fractional units does produce a greater degree of *precision*. For example, a length measure can never be more than one-half unit in error. And yet, since there is mathematically no "smallest unit," there is always some error involved.

Measuring Length

Length is usually the first attribute students learn to measure. Be aware, however, that length measurement is not immediately understood by young children.

Comparison Activities

At the kindergarten level, children should begin with direct comparisons of two or more lengths.

ACTIVITY 8.1

Longer, Shorter, Same

Make a sorting-by-length station at which students sort objects as longer, shorter, or about the same as a specified object. It is easy to have several such stations in your room. The reference object can be changed occasionally to produce different sorts. A similar task is to put objects in order from shortest to longest.

Length (or Unit) Hunt

Give pairs of students a strip of tagboard, a stick, a length of rope, or some other object with an obvious length dimension. The task on one day might be to find five things in the room that are shorter than, longer than, or about the same length as their object. They can draw pictures or write the names of the things they find.

By making the target length a standard unit (e.g., a meter stick or a 1-meter length of rope), the activity can be repeated to provide familiarity with important standard units.

It is important to compare lengths that are not in straight lines. One way to do this is with string or rope. Students can wrap string around objects in a search for things that are, for example, as long around as the distance from the floor to their belly button or as long as the distance around one's head or waist. Body measures are always fun.

Indirect comparisons are used in the next activity.

Crooked Paths

Make some crooked or curvy paths on the floor with masking tape. As a comparison task, students are to decide which of two paths is longer. Provide students with string or rope that is longer than either path but do not require that they use it. Do not show them a method of deciding. Be sure that students explain their methods of comparison.

EXPANDED LESSON

(pages 249–250)
A complete lesson plan based on "Crooked Paths" can be found at the end of this chapter.

In "Crooked Paths" some students may argue that the path that "looks longer" is the longer path although a crooked and more compact path may be longer. Respond simply that this is not a very convincing argument. Students who use the rope to create an equivalent length to one path must have a transitive understanding of measurement. If A is equal in length to B (the rope) and B is equal in length to (or shorter/longer than) C, then A must be equal in length to (or shorter/longer than) C. Although transitivity is crucial to understanding measurement, not all grade K or 1 students will be able to follow this argument.

Other good questions to ask in connection with this or other comparison tasks are: "How much longer is this path than that one?" "Try to make a straight line that is just as long as this path. How can you tell that your line is just as long?"

Using Units of Length

Students can use a variety of informal units to begin measuring length, for example:

- *Giant footprints:* Make about 20 copies of a large footprint about $1\frac{1}{2}$ to 2 feet long cut out of poster board.

- *Measuring ropes:* Cut cotton clothesline into lengths of 1 m. These are useful for measuring curved lines and the circumference of large objects such as the teacher's desk.

- *Plastic straws:* Drinking straws are inexpensive and provide large quantities of a useful unit. Straws are easily cut into smaller units. You can link straw units together with a long string. The string of straws is an excellent bridge to a ruler or measuring tape.

- *Short units:* Toothpicks, connecting cubes, wooden cubes, and paper clips are all useful units for measuring shorter lengths. Cuisenaire rods are one of the nicest sets of units because they come in ten different lengths, are easily placed end to end, and can be related to each other. Paper clips can readily be made into chains as can plastic chain links, available from suppliers of manipulatives.

The temptation is to carefully explain to students how to use these units to measure and then send them off to practice measuring. This approach will shift students' attention to the procedure (following your instruction) and away from developing an understanding of measurement using units. In the following activity students are provided with a measuring task but are required to develop their own approach. Correct ideas about measurement can be developed out of a discussion of the results.

ACTIVITY 8.4

How Long Is the Teacher?

Explain that you have just received an important request from the principal. She needs to know exactly how tall each teacher is. The students are to decide how to measure the teachers and write a note to the principal explaining how tall their teacher is and how they decided. Next, explain that it may be easier if you lay down and students measure how long you are instead of how tall. Do this at several stations around the room. Have students make marks at your feet and head and draw a straight line between your "head" and "foot."

Explain that the principal says you can use any ONE of these things to measure with. (Provide several choices. For each choice of unit, supply enough units to more than cover your length. Be aware of the numbers that will result so be sure to use units that are at least 6 inches long.) Put students in pairs and allow them to select one unit with which to measure.

The value of the last activity will come from the discussion. Good questions include "How did different children measure?" "Did students who measured with the same unit get the same answers? Why not?" "How could the principal make a line that was just as long as the teacher?" In your discussion, focus on the value of lining units up carefully, end to end. Discuss what happens if you overlap units or don't stay in a straight line.

Repeat the basic task of "How Long Is the Teacher?" with other measuring tasks, each time providing a choice of units and the requirement that students explain their measures. It is always helpful if the same lengths (heights, distances around) are measured by several pairs of students so that possible errors can be discussed and the measuring process refined. The following similar activity adds an estimation component.

Guess and Measure

Make lists of things in the room to measure (see Figure 8.3). For younger children, run a piece of masking tape along the dimension of each object to be measured. On the list, designate the units to be used. Do not forget to include curves or other distances that are not straight lines. Include estimates before the measures. Young children will not be very good at estimating distances at first.

For students in the second or third grade, the "Guess and Measure" activity can easily be done with standard units. For students beginning to learn about two-digit numbers, add the following task to the activity: Have students make a row or chain of exactly ten units to use in helping them with their estimates. They first lay ten units against the object and then make their guess.

Rather than try to explain to young students that larger units will create a smaller measure and vice versa (an idea that is often confusing to them), create an activity where this issue is a focus.

Changing Units

Have students measure a length with one unit; then provide them with a different unit and see if they can predict the measure of the same length with the new unit. Students should write down their predictions and explanations of how they were made. Then have them make the actual measurement. In the class discussions that follow, the predictions and explanations will be the most educational part of the activity.

Name _____

Around your outline

Unit: ⟨_____⟩
                    straw

Guess _____ straws

Measured _____ straws

The teacher's desk
Unit: orange rod

Teacher's desk

Guess _____ rods

Measured _____ rods

Around math book
Unit: paper clip

Math Book

Guess _____ clips

Measured _____ clips

FIGURE 8.3 • • • • • • • • • • • • • • • • • • •

Record sheet for measuring with informal length units.

When first doing the "Changing Units" activity, show the second unit and discuss only if the measurement will be smaller or larger using this unit. Be sure to do the activity with a switch from smaller to larger units as well as larger to smaller units. You will find that many students will think that the larger units will give the larger measure. By second grade, you can explore the activity a bit more by having students make numeric predictions of the second measure based on a comparison of the units. For example, if a measurement made with yellow Cuisenaire rods was 12 rods, what will the measurement be if the orange rod is used instead? (The orange rod is twice as long as the yellow, so the measurement should be half as big, or 6 rods.) Do not explain the solution to the students. Instead allow students to struggle with their reasoning and test their conjectures by actually measuring.

Assessment Note

You will probably be able to tell a lot about how well your students understand length measurement by observing them in activities such as those just described. Here are a few tasks that you might use as assessments, perhaps in an interview format:

- Provide a box with assorted units of different sizes. Cuisenaire rods would be suitable. Have the student use the materials in the box to measure a given length. Observe if the student understands that all units must be of like size. If different lengths of units are used, ask how the student would describe his or her measurement.
- Ask students to draw a line or mark off a distance of a prescribed number of units (informal or formal, depending on what has been used). Observe whether the students know to align the units in a straight line without overlaps or gaps.
- Have students measure two different objects. Then ask how much longer is the longer object. Observe if the student can use the measurements to answer or if a third measurement must be made of the difference. (The student must be capable of determining the difference numerically for this task to be valuable.)
- Provide a length of string. Tell students that the string is 6 units long. How could they use the string to make a length of 3 units? How could they make a length of 9 units? In this task, you are looking to see if students can mentally subdivide the given length (string) based on an understanding of its measure. That is, can students visualize that 6 units are matched to the string length and half of these would be 3 units?

The jump from using units to using rulers to measure is not trivial. One of the best methods of helping students understand rulers is to have them make their own rulers out of actual units. One approach is to precut narrow strips of construction paper into lengths of 5 cm each. Use two different colors of paper. Discuss how the strips could be used to measure by laying them end to end. Provide long strips of tagboard about 5 cm wide. Students paste the strips end to end along the edge of the tagboard, alternating colors, as shown in Figure 8.4.

Pasting down copies of the units on a ruler maximizes the connection between the spaces on a ruler and the actual units. Older children can make rulers by using a real unit to make marks along a tagboard strip and then coloring in the spaces. Children should not be encouraged to use the end of a ruler as a starting point; many real rulers are not made that way. If the first unit on a ruler does not coincide with the end of the ruler, the student is forced to attend to aligning the units on the ruler with the object measured.

Students should eventually put numbers on their homemade rulers, as shown in Figure 8.5. For young children, numbers can be written in the center of each unit to make it clear that the numbers are a way of precounting the units. When numbers are written in the standard way, at the ends of the units, the ruler becomes a number line. This format is more sophisticated and should be carefully discussed with children.

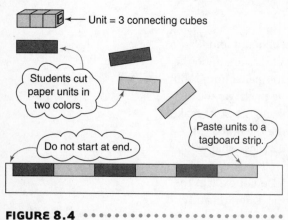

FIGURE 8.4

Making a simple ruler.

Using Rulers and Tape Measures

It is important to use the rulers students have made. In addition to the estimate-and-measure activities mentioned earlier, have teams measure items once with a ruler and a second time with actual unit models. Although the results should be the same, inaccuracies or incorrect use of the ruler may produce differences that are important to discuss. Also use the ruler to measure lengths that are longer than the ruler.

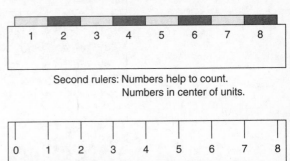

First rulers: Students count units.

Second rulers: Numbers help to count.
Numbers in center of units.

Standard rulers: Numbers are at ends of units. Notice where 0 is.

FIGURE 8.5 •

Give meaning to numbers on rulers.

ACTIVITY 8.7

More Than One Way

Challenge students to find different ways to measure the same length with one ruler. (Start from either end; start at a point not at the end; measure different parts of the object and add the results.)

Much of the value of student-made rulers can be lost if you do not transfer this knowledge to standard rulers. Give children a standard ruler and discuss how it is like and how it differs from the ones they have made. What are the units? Could you make a ruler with paper units the same as this? Could you make some cardboard units and measure the same way as with the ruler? What do the numbers mean? What are the other marks for? Where do the units begin?

Assessment Note

Research indicates that when students see standard rulers with the numbers on the hash marks, they often believe that the numbers are counting the marks rather than indicating the units or spaces between the marks. Not only is this an incorrect understanding of rulers, but also it can lead to wrong answers when using rulers. As an assessment provide students with a ruler, as shown in Figure 8.6, with hash marks but no numbers. Have students use the ruler to measure an item that is shorter than the ruler. A correct understanding of rulers is indicated if students count spaces between the hash marks.

Another good assessment of ruler understanding is to have students measure with a "broken" ruler, one with the first two units broken off. Some students will say that it is impossible to measure with such a ruler because there is no starting point. Those who understand rulers will be able to match and count the units

(continued)

FIGURE 8.6 • • • • • • • • • • • • • • •

Use an unmarked ruler and ask students to measure an object. Does the student count spaces or hash marks? In the example shown, the correct length is 8 units. A student counting hash marks would respond with 9 units.

meaningfully in their measures. (See Barrett, Jones, Thornton, & Dickson, 2003, for a complete discussion of student development of length measurement including the use of rulers.)

Observing how children use a ruler to measure an object that is longer than the ruler is also informative. Children who are simply reading the last mark on the ruler may not be able to do this task because they do not understand how a ruler is a representation of a row of units.

Measuring Area

Area is a measure of the space inside a region or how much it takes to cover a region. As with other attributes, students must first understand the attribute of area before measuring.

Comparison Activities

One of the purposes of early comparison activities with areas is to help students distinguish between size (or area) and shape, length, and other dimensions. A long, skinny rectangle may have less area than a triangle with shorter sides. This is an especially difficult concept for young children to understand. Piagetian experiments indicate that many 8- or 9-year-olds do not understand that rearranging areas into different shapes does not affect the amount of area.

Direct comparison of two areas is nearly always impossible except when the shapes involved have some common dimension or property. For example, two rectangles with the same width can be compared directly, as can any two circles. Comparison of these special shapes, however, fails to deal with the attribute of area. Instead, activities in which one area is rearranged are suggested. Cutting a shape into two parts and reassembling it in a different shape can show that the before and after shapes have the same area, even though they are different shapes. This idea is not at all obvious to children in the K–2 grade range.

ACTIVITY 8.8

Two-Piece Shapes

Cut a large number of rectangles of the same size, about 3 inches by 5 inches. Each pair of students needs six rectangles. Have students fold and cut the rectangles on the diagonal, making two identical triangles. Next, have them rearrange the triangles into different shapes, including the original rectangle. The rule is that only sides of the same length can be matched up and must be matched exactly. Have each group find all the shapes that can be made this way, pasting the triangles on paper as a record of each shape (see Figure 8.7). Discuss the size and shape of the different results. Is one shape bigger than the rest? How is it bigger? Did one take more paper to make, or do they all have the same amount of paper? Help children conclude that although each figure is a different shape, all the figures have the same *area*. (*Size* in this context is a useful substitute for *area* with very young children, although it does not mean exactly the same thing.)

In the preceding task, students are making shapes of like areas by rearranging parts of like rectangles. A slightly different task follows.

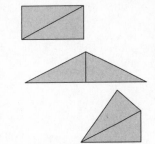

FIGURE 8.7 • • • • • • • • •

Different shapes, same size.

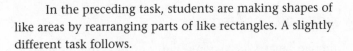

ACTIVITY 8.9

Rectangle Comparison—No Units

Provide students with pairs of rectangles as follows.

Pair A: 2 × 9 and 3 × 6
Pair B: 1 × 10 and 3 × 5
Pair C: 3 × 8 and 4 × 5

The rectangles should be blank except for the labels. The students' task is to decide in each pair which rectangle has the greater area or if the two are the same size. They are allowed to cut or fold the rectangles in any way they wish, but they must include an explanation for their decision in each pair. Pair C will cause the most difficulty and you may wish to reserve it as a challenge.

 Consider how you would compare each pair of rectangles in the preceding activity without relying on a formula or drawing squares.

In the first two pairs, the skinny rectangle can be folded and cut to either match (pair A) or be easily compared (pair B) to the second rectangle. For pair C, one rectangle can be placed on the other and then the extended pieces compared.

Tangrams can be used for the same purpose. The standard set of seven tangram pieces is cut from a square, as shown in Figure 8.8. The two small triangles can be used to make the parallelogram, the square, and the medium triangle. Four small triangles will make the large triangle. This permits a similar discussion about the pieces having the same size (area) but different shapes. (Tangram pieces can be found in the Blackline Masters.) The following activity suggests a method for comparing areas without measuring.

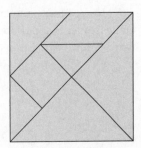

7 tangram shapes

These two make

The two small triangles make each of the medium shapes.

ACTIVITY 8.10

Tangram Areas

Draw the outline of several shapes made with tangram pieces, as in Figure 8.9. Let students use tangrams to decide which shapes are the same size, which are larger, and which are smaller. Let students explain how they came to their conclusions.

(continued)

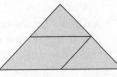

Two small triangles with any of the medium pieces will make the large triangle.

FIGURE 8.8 •

Tangrams provide a nice opportunity to investigate size and shape concepts.

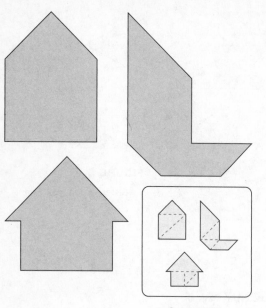

FIGURE 8.9

Compare shapes made of tangram pieces.

One solution

There are several different approaches to this task, and it is best if students determine their own solutions rather than blindly follow your directions.

Using Units of Area

Although squares are very nice units of area (and the most commonly used), any tile that conveniently fills up a plane region can be used. Even filling a region with uniform circles or lima beans provides a useful idea of what it means to measure areas. Here are some suggestions for area units that are easy to gather or make in the large quantities you will need.

- Round plastic chips, pennies, or lima beans can be used. It is not necessary at a beginning stage that the area units fit with no gaps.
- Color Tiles (1-inch squares) are an excellent small unit.
- Cut squares from cardboard. Large squares (about 20 cm on a side) work well for large areas. Smaller units should be about 5 to 10 cm on a side.
- Sheets of newspaper make good units for very large areas.
- Index cards or old business cards make good medium-sized units.
- Pattern blocks provide six different units. The hexagon, trapezoid, blue rhombus, and triangle can be related to each other in a manner similar to the tangrams.

Children can use units to measure surfaces in the room such as desktops, bulletin boards, or books. Large regions can be outlined with masking tape on the floor. Small regions can be duplicated on paper so that students can work at their desks. Odd shapes and curved surfaces provide more challenge and interest.

In area measurements, there may be lots of units that only partially fit. By third grade, students should begin to wrestle with partial units and mentally put together two or more partial units to count as one (see Figure 8.10).

The following activity is a good starting point to see what ideas your students bring to their understanding of area measurement.

ACTIVITY 8.11

Fill and Compare

Draw two rectangles and a blob shape on a sheet of paper. Make it so that the three areas are not the same but with no area that is clearly largest or smallest. The students' task is to first make a guess about which is the smallest and the largest of the three shapes. After recording their guess, they should use a filler of their choice to decide. Provide small units such as circular disks, Color Tiles, or lima beans. Students should explain in writing what they found out.

Your objective in the beginning is to develop the idea that area is a *measure of covering*. Do not introduce formulas. Simply have the students fill the shapes and count

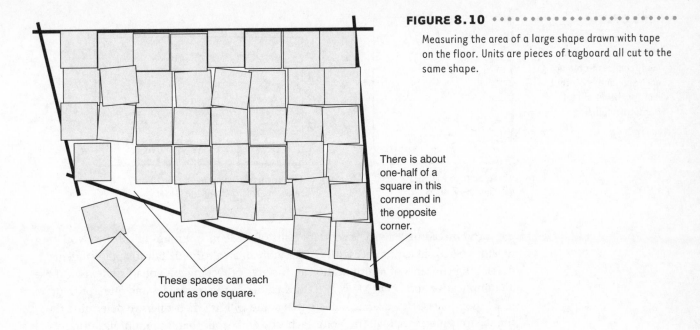

FIGURE 8.10 •

Measuring the area of a large shape drawn with tape on the floor. Units are pieces of tagboard all cut to the same shape.

There is about one-half of a square in this corner and in the opposite corner.

These spaces can each count as one square.

the units. Be sure to include estimation before measuring (this is significantly more difficult than for length), use approximate language, and relate precision to the size of the units in the same manner as with length. Groups are very likely to come up with different measures for the same region. Discuss these differences with the children, and point to the difficulties involved in making estimates around the edges. Avoid the idea that there is a "right" answer.

It is important to understand that filling regions with units and counting does little to help students develop multiplicative formulas. Even when rectangles are filled with a grid of squares, students are more likely to count the squares than to relate the number of squares to the dimensions of the rectangles.

In Activity 8.9, "Rectangle Comparison—No Units," students were encouraged to fold and cut the rectangles in order to make a direct comparison. However, third grade is not too early to begin having students relate the concept of multiplication using arrays to the area of rectangles. The following activity is a good first step in that direction.

ACTIVITY 8.12

Rectangle Compare—Square Units

Students are given a pair of rectangles that are either the same or very close in area. They are also given a model or drawing of a single square unit and an appropriate ruler. (The units can be either centimeters or inches, and the ruler should clearly measure the appropriate unit. Students must be familiar with rulers.) The students are not permitted to cut out the rectangles or even draw on them. The task is to use their rulers to determine, in any way that they can, which rectangle is larger or whether they are the same. They should use words, drawings, and numbers to explain their conclusions. Some suggested pairs are as follows:

4 × 10 and 5 × 8
5 × 10 and 7 × 7
4 × 6 and 5 × 5

FIGURE 8.11 • • • • • • •

Some students will be able to figure out how many squares fit along each side and know that multiplication will tell the total number.

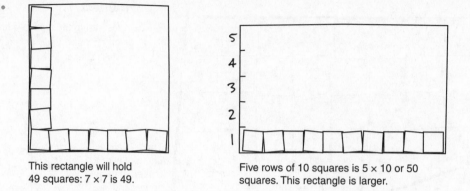

This rectangle will hold 49 squares: 7 × 7 is 49.

Five rows of 10 squares is 5 × 10 or 50 squares. This rectangle is larger.

The preceding activity is good for pairs of students or groups of three to work on together. The goal is not necessarily to develop an area formula but to apply students' developing concepts of multiplication to the area of rectangles. Not all students will use a multiplicative approach. Many will draw copies of the rectangles and attempt to draw in all the squares. However, it is likely that some will use their rulers to determine the number of squares that will fit along each side and, from that, use multiplication to determine the total area. (See Figure 8.11.) By having students share their strategies, more students can be exposed to the use of multiplication.

Measuring Volume and Capacity

Volume and *capacity* are both terms for measures of the "size" of three-dimensional regions. Volume typically refers to the amount of space that an object takes up. Volume is measured with units such as cubic inches or cubic centimeters—units that are based on linear measures. The term *capacity* is generally used to refer to the amount that a container will hold. Standard units of capacity include quarts and gallons, liters and milliliters—units used for liquids as well as the containers that hold them. Having made these distinctions, they are not ones to worry with. The term *volume* can also be used to refer to the capacity of a container.

Comparing the volumes of solid objects is very difficult. For primary grade children, it is appropriate to focus on capacity. A simple method of comparing capacity is to fill one container with something and then pour this amount into the comparison container.

Young children should have lots of experiences directly comparing the capacities of different containers. Collect a large assortment of cans, small boxes, and plastic containers. Gather as many different shapes as possible. Also gather some plastic scoops. Cut a plastic 2-liter bottle in half, and use the top portion as a funnel. Rice or dried beans are good fillers to use. Sand and water are both considerably messier.

ACTIVITY 8.13

Capacity Sort

Provide a collection of labeled containers, with one marked as the "target." The task is to sort the collection into those that hold more than, less than, or about the same amount as the target container. Provide a recording sheet on which each container is listed and a place to circle "holds more," "holds less," and "holds about the same." List the choices twice for each container. The first choice is to record a guess made by observation. The second is to record "what was found." Provide a filler (such as beans or rice), scoops, and funnels. Avoid explicit directions but later discuss students' ideas for solving the task.

ACTIVITY 8.14

Capacity Lineup

Given a series of five or six labeled containers of different sizes and shapes, the task is to order them from least capacity to most. This can be quite challenging. Do not provide answers. Let students work in groups to come up with a solution and also explain how they arrived at it.

Remember that your only goal is that students develop an understanding of the concept of capacity. Children often confuse "holds more" with "taller" or "fatter," even though these may be misleading attributes. This is why a variety of container shapes not only adds interest but also can contribute to student understanding.

The concept of volume of a solid object is similar to capacity but much more difficult for children to "see." Here, not only are the shapes of objects sometimes misleading, but a method of comparison is also difficult. To compare volumes of solids such as a ball and an apple, some method of displacement must be used. Provide students with two or three containers that will each hold the objects to be compared and a filler such as rice or beans. With this equipment some students may be able to devise their own comparison method. One approach is to first fill a container completely and then pour it into an empty holding container. Next place an object in the first container and fill it again to the top, using filler from the holding container. The volume of filler remaining is equal to the volume of the object. Mark the level of the leftover filler in the holding container before repeating the experiment with other objects. By comparing the level of the leftover filler for two or more objects, the volumes of the objects can be compared.

Using Units of Volume and Capacity

Two types of units can be used to measure volume and capacity: solid units and containers. Solid units are things like wooden cubes or old tennis balls that can be used to fill the container being measured. The other type of unit model is a small container that is filled and poured repeatedly into the container being measured. The following are a few examples of units that you might want to collect.

- Plastic caps and liquid medicine cups are all good for very small units.
- Plastic jars and containers of almost any size can serve as a unit.
- Wooden cubic blocks or blocks of any shape can be units as long as you have a lot of the same size.
- Styrofoam packing peanuts can be used. Even though they do not pack perfectly, they still produce conceptual measures of volume.

Measuring activities for capacity are similar to those for length and area. Estimation of a capacity is a lot more fun because it is much more difficult than length or area.

Volumes of rectangular boxes such as a shoe box can be determined by filling with any of the units mentioned earlier. However, here is an opportunity to prepare students for volume formulas in a manner similar to what was discussed for the area of rectangles. If students are given a box and sufficient cubes to fill it, they will most likely count the cubes rather than use any multiplicative structure. The following activity is similar to "Comparing Rectangles—Square Units."

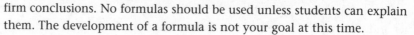

ACTIVITY 8.15

Compare Boxes—Cubic Units

Provide students with a pair of small boxes that you have folded up from poster board. (See Figure 8.12.) Use unit dimensions that match the blocks that you have. Students are given two boxes, exactly one block, and an appropriate ruler. (If you use 2-cm cubes, make a ruler with the unit equal to 2 centimeters.) The students' task is to decide which box has the greater volume or if they have the same volume.

Here are some suggested box dimensions ($L \times W \times H$):

$$6 \times 3 \times 4 \qquad 5 \times 4 \times 4 \qquad 3 \times 9 \times 3 \qquad 6 \times 6 \times 2 \qquad 5 \times 5 \times 5$$

Students should use words, drawings, and numbers to explain their conclusions.

A useful hint in the last activity is to first figure out how many cubes will fit on the bottom of the box. Some, although certainly not all, third-grade students will discover a multiplicative rule for the volume. The boxes can be filled with cubes to confirm conclusions. No formulas should be used unless students can explain them. The development of a formula is not your goal at this time.

Making and Using Measuring Cups

Instruments for measuring capacity are generally used for small amounts of liquids or pourable materials such as rice or water. These tools are commonly found in kitchens and laboratories. As with other instruments, if children make their own, they are likely to develop a better understanding of the units and the approach to the measuring process.

A measuring cup can be made by using a small container as a unit. Select a large, transparent container for the cup and a small container for a unit. Fill the unit with beans or rice, empty it into the large container, and make a mark indicating the level. Repeat until the cup is nearly full. If the unit is small, marks may only be necessary after every 5 units. Numbers need not be written on the container for every marking. Students frequently have difficulty reading scales in which not every mark is labeled or where each mark represents more than one unit. This is an opportunity to help them understand how to interpret lines on a real measuring cup.

Students should use their measuring cups and compare the measures with those made by directly filling the container from the unit. The cup is likely to produce errors due to inaccurate markings. This is an opportunity to

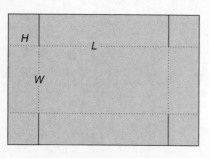

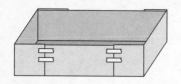

FIGURE 8.12 • • • • • • • • • • • • •

Make small boxes by starting with a rectangle and drawing a square on each corner as shown. Cut on the solid lines and fold the box up, wrapping the corner squares to the outside and tape or glue them to the sides as shown.

point out that measuring instruments themselves can be a source of error in measurement. The more accurately made the instrument, and the finer the calibration, the less the error from that source.

Measuring Weight and Mass

Weight is a measure of the pull or force of gravity on an object. *Mass* is the amount of matter in an object and a measure of the force needed to accelerate it. On the moon, where gravity is much less than on Earth, an object has a smaller weight but the identical mass as on Earth. For practical purposes, on Earth, the measures of mass and weight will be about the same. In this discussion, the terms *weight* and *mass* will be used interchangeably.

Making Comparisons

The most conceptual way for students to compare the weights of two objects is to hold one in each hand, extend their arms, and experience the relative downward pull on each—effectively communicating to a young child what "heavier" or "weighs more" means. This personal experience can then be transferred to one of two basic types of scales—balances and spring scales. Figure 8.13 shows a homemade version of each. Simple scales of each type are available through school-supply catalogs.

Children should first use their hands to estimate which of two objects is heavier. When they then place the objects in the two pans of a balance, the pan that goes down can be understood to hold the heavier object. Even a relatively simple balance will detect small differences. If two objects are placed one at a time in a spring scale, the heavier object pulls the pan down farther. Both balances and spring scales have real value in the classroom. (Technically, spring scales measure weight and balance scales measure mass. Why?)

With either scale, sorting and ordering tasks are possible with very young children. For students in grades 2 and 3, comparisons of weight are probably not necessary.

Using Units of Weight or Mass

Any collection of uniform objects with the same mass can serve as weight units. For very light objects, wooden or plastic cubes work well. Large metal washers found in hardware stores are effective for weighing slightly heavier objects. You will need to rely on standard weights to weigh things as heavy as a kilogram or more.

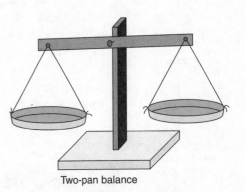

Two-pan balance

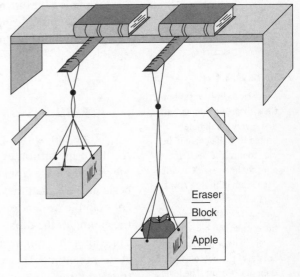

Eraser
Block
Apple

Rubber-band (spring) scales
Marks show where different objects
pulled the scale.

FIGURE 8.13

Two simple scales.

In a balance scale, place an object in one pan and weights in the other until the two pans balance. In a spring scale, first place the object in and mark the position of the pan on a piece of paper taped behind the pan. Remove the object and place just enough weights in the pan to pull it down to the same level. Discuss how equal weights will pull the spring or rubber band with the same force.

While the concept of heavier and lighter is learned rather early, the notion of units of weight or mass is a bit more mysterious. At any grade level, even a brief experience with informal unit weights is good preparation for standard units and scales.

Making and Using a Scale

Most scales that we use in our daily lives produce a number when an object is placed on or in it. There are no visible unit weights. How does the scale produce the right number? By making a scale that gives a numeric result without recourse to units, children can see how scales work in principle.

By third grade students can use informal weight units and calibrate a simple rubber band scale like the one in Figure 8.13. Mount the scale with a piece of paper behind it and place weights in the pan. After ever five weights, make a mark on the paper. The resulting marks correspond to the markings around the dial of a standard scale. The pan serves as the pointer. In the dial scale, the downward movement of the pan mechanically causes the dial to turn. The value of this activity is seeing how scales are made. Even digital readout scales are based on the same principle.

FIGURE 8.14 • • • • • • •

A plastic 1-liter water bottle with the bottom cut off and a very small hole drilled into the cap can be placed into the neck of another bottle with a wider neck. Show children how to hold a finger over the hole until before starting the timer and then place the bottle in neck of the larger bottle. If the bottom bottle is empty to start, the level of water at the end of the time period can be marked and compared with another duration. (See Kamii & Long, 2003.)

Measuring Time

Time is a bit different from the other attributes that are commonly measured in school because it cannot be seen and because it is more difficult for students to comprehend units of time or how they are matched against a given time period or duration.

Comparison of Durations

Time can be thought of as the duration of an event from its beginning to its end. As with other attributes, for students to adequately understand the attribute of time, they should make comparisons of events that have different durations. If two events begin at the same time, the shorter duration will end first and the other last longer. For example, which top spins longer? However, this form of comparison focuses on the ending of the duration rather than the duration itself. In order to think of time as something that can be measured, it is helpful to compare two events that do not start at the same time. This requires that some form of measurement of time be used from the beginning.

An informal unit of time might be the duration of a pendulum swing, the slow but steady drip of a water faucet, or water dripping from one bottle to another. In the latter case, the level of the water can indicate the beginning and the end of the time period. (See Figure 8.14.)

Which Takes Longer?

Students work in pairs. Two activities are specified and the students predict which of the two activities will take longer. One student times the other doing each of two activities and then the roles are reversed. A few tasks that might be compared are:

- Stacking 10 blocks one at a time and then removing them one at a time.
- Printing your name.
- Walking slowly around a designated path.
- Making a bar of 15 Unifix cubes.
- Copying a simple drawing such as a house.

The water timer shown in Figure 8.14 has the advantage of being continuous—there are no units to count. A tennis ball suspended on a long string from the ceiling makes a slowly swinging pendulum that will keep the counts manageable. If a 10-second sand timer is available, a unit can consist of emptying the timer and then turning it over for the next unit.

Be sure students understand how to do each of the two tasks they are comparing. Because only one student does each task, there is no competition or racing.

Clock Reading

The common instrument for measuring time is the clock. However, learning to tell time has little to do with time measurement and more to do with the skills of learning to read a dial-type instrument. Clock reading is a difficult skill to teach.

Some Difficulties

Young children's problems with clock reading may be due to the curriculum. Children are usually taught first to read clocks to the hour, then the half and quarter hours, and finally to 5- and 1-minute intervals. In the early stages of this sequence, children are shown clocks set exactly to the hour or half hour. Many children who can read a clock at 7:00 or 2:30 have no idea what time it is at 6:58 or 2:33.

Digital clocks permit students to read times easily but do not relate times very well. To know that a digital reading of 7:58 is nearly 8 o'clock, the child must know that there are 60 minutes in an hour, that 58 is close to 60, and that 2 minutes is not a very long time. These concepts have not been developed by most first-grade and many second-grade children. The analog clock (with hands) shows "close to" times without the need for understanding big numbers or even how many minutes in an hour.

Furthermore, the standard approach to clock reading ignores the distinctly different actions and functions of the two hands. The little hand indicates broad, approximate time (nearest hour), and the big hand indicates time (minutes) before or after an hour. When we look at the hour hand, we focus on where it is pointing. With the minute hand, the focus is on the distance that it has gone around the clock or the distance yet to go for the hand to get back to the top.

"About 7 o'clock"

"A little bit
past 9 o'clock"

"Halfway between
2 o'clock and 3 o'clock"

FIGURE 8.15 ·······

Approximate time with
one-handed clocks.

A Suggested Approach

The following suggestions can help students understand and read analog clocks.

1. Begin with a one-handed clock. A clock with only an hour hand can be read with reasonable accuracy. Use lots of approximate language: "It's about 7 o'clock." "It's a little past 9 o'clock." "It's halfway between 2 o'clock and 3 o'clock" (see Figure 8.15).

2. Discuss what happens to the big hand as the little hand goes from one hour to the next. When the big hand is at 12, the hour hand is pointing exactly to a number. If the hour hand is about halfway between numbers, about where would the minute hand be? If the hour hand is a little past or before an hour (10 to 15 minutes), about where would the minute hand be?

3. Use two real clocks, one with only an hour hand and one with two hands. (Break off the minute hand from an old clock.) Cover the two-handed clock. Periodically during the day, direct attention to the one-handed clock. Discuss the time in approximate language. Have students predict where the minute hand should be. Uncover the other clock and check.

4. Teach time after the hour in 5-minute intervals. After step 3 has begun, count by fives going around the clock. Instead of predicting that the minute hand is pointing at the 4, encourage students to say it is about 20 minutes after the hour. As skills develop, suggest that students always look first at the little or hour hand to learn approximately what time it is and then focus on the minute hand for precision.

5. Predict the reading on a digital clock when shown an analog clock, and vice versa; set an analog clock when shown a digital clock. This can be done with both one-handed and two-handed clocks. Cover both clocks. At various times throughout the day, uncover one clock and have students predict what is showing on the other.

Related Concepts

Students also need to learn about seconds, minutes, and hours and to develop some concept of how long these standard units of time are. You can help by making a conscious effort to note the duration of short and long events during the day. Timing small events of $\frac{1}{2}$ minute to 2 minutes is fun and useful. TV shows and commercials are a good standard. Have students time familiar events in their daily lives: brushing teeth, eating dinner, riding to school, spending time in the reading group.

As students learn more about two-digit numbers, the time after the hours can also be related to the time left before the hour. This is helpful not only for telling time but for number sense as well. Note that in the sequence suggested, time after the hour is stressed almost exclusively. Time before or till the hour can come later.

Assessment Note

Gathering useful assessment data in the area of measurement requires open-ended activities that permit students to show how they understand measurement concepts. Traditional textbook tests tend to focus on pre-scriptive, procedural skills such as conversion of units from feet to inches or the use of a formula. Examine these test items and ask yourself if they really tell you what you want to know about your students and measurement.

As you progress through your measurement unit, think about what students really need to know to develop an understanding of measurement of any given attribute.

How well do students understand the attribute being measured? Observing how students do comparison activities ("Which of these regions is the largest? How can you tell?") will tell you what you need to know. Be wary of overly directing students; make sure that the ideas you observe are theirs, not yours. Rather than directing students to measure something the way you prescribe, have students select their own methods and explain what they did and why they made the choices they made.

Introducing Standard Units

As pointed out earlier, there are a number of reasons for teaching measurement using nonstandard units. However, measurement sense demands that children be familiar with the common measurement units and that they be able to make estimates in terms of these units and meaningfully interpret measures depicted with standard units.

Perhaps the biggest error in measurement instruction is the failure to recognize and separate two types of objectives: first, understanding the meaning and technique of measuring a particular attribute and, second, learning about the standard units commonly used to measure that attribute. These two objectives can be developed separately; when both objectives are attempted together, confusion is likely.

 How many of the four reasons why you might use informal units can you recall? Which of these seem most important to you and why?

Reread the list of reasons for using informal units on p. 227. Not all reasons apply to every situation you may face. To avoid wasting time in your measurement program it is important to know why you are or are not using informal or nonstandard units. It is only when students are comfortable with measurement of an attribute that they can focus on things like cups and quarts or the number of inches in a foot or feet in a yard or have a feel for grams and kilograms.

Instructional Goals

Three broad goals relative to standard units of measure can be identified:

1. *Familiarity with the unit.* Familiarity means that students should have a basic idea of the size of commonly used units and what they measure. Without this familiarity, measurement sense is impossible. It is more important to know about how much 1 liter of water is or to be able to estimate a shelf as 5 feet long than to have the ability to measure either of these accurately.
2. *Ability to select an appropriate unit.* Related to unit familiarity is knowing what is a reasonable unit of measure in a given situation. The choice of an appropriate unit is also a matter of required precision. (Would you measure your lawn to purchase grass seed with the same precision as you would use in measuring a window to buy a pane of glass?) Students need practice in using common sense in the selection of appropriate standard units.

3. *Knowledge of a few important relationships between units.* The emphasis should be kept to those relationships that are commonly used, such as inches, feet, and yards or milliliters and liters. Tedious conversion exercises do little to enhance measurement sense. The goal of unit relationships is the least important of all measurement objectives.

Developing Unit Familiarity

Two types of activities can help develop familiarity with standard units: (1) comparisons that focus on a single unit and (2) activities that develop personal referents or benchmarks for single units or easy multiples of units.

ACTIVITY 8.17

About One Unit

Give students a model of a standard unit, and have them search for things that measure about the same as that one unit. For example, to develop familiarity with the meter, give students a piece of rope 1 meter long. Have them make lists of things that are about 1 meter. Keep separate lists for things that are a little less (or more) or twice as long (or half as long). Encourage students to find familiar items in their daily lives. In the case of lengths, be sure to include circular lengths. Later, students can try to predict if a given object is more than, less than, or close to 1 meter.

The same activity can be done with other unit lengths. Parents can be enlisted to help students find familiar distances that are about 1 mile or about 1 kilometer. Suggest in a letter that they check the distances around the neighborhood, to the school or shopping center, or along other frequently traveled paths.

For capacity units such as cup, quart, and liter, students need a container that holds or has a marking for a single unit. They should then find other containers at home and at school that hold about as much, more, and less. Remember that the shapes of containers can be very deceptive when estimating their capacity.

For the standard weights of gram, kilogram, ounce, and pound, students can compare objects on a two-pan balance with single copies of these units. It may be more effective to work with 10 grams or 5 ounces. Students can be encouraged to bring in familiar objects from home to compare on the classroom scale.

The second approach to unit familiarity is to begin with very familiar items and use their measures as references or benchmarks. A doorway is a bit more than 2 meters. A bag of flour is a good reference for 5 pounds. A bedroom may be about 10 feet long. A paper clip weighs about a gram and is about 1 centimeter wide. A gallon of milk weighs a little less than 4 kilograms.

ACTIVITY 8.18

Familiar References

For each unit of measure you wish to focus on, have students make a list of at least five familiar things and measure those things using that unit. For lengths, encourage them to include long and short things; for weight, to find both light and heavy things; and so on. The measures should be rounded off to nice whole numbers. Discuss lists in class so that different ideas are shared.

It is common practice to have students find length benchmarks on their bodies. This may be a questionable practice for primary-aged students because their rapid growth will cause their references to change. If you couple the discussion of personal benchmarks with a discussion of growth, value in this approach remains. Students can have references that they can use now. If they compare their references with their parents, they can begin to think about growth as well as develop a better sense of units.

ACTIVITY 8.19

Personal Benchmarks

Have students find personal references on their bodies for the following lengths:

> Metric: 1 cm, 10 cm, 1 meter
> Customary: 1 inch, 1 foot, 1 yard

Have them consider their feet and hands, including lengths and widths of fingers, hands, and hand spans. Heights to waist, belly button, shoulder, or head can be considered as well as lengths of arms and arm spans. Students should also have a good idea of how tall they are, their arm span, and how far they normally walk in five or ten strides.

After developing lists of benchmarks, have students use only their bodies to "measure" or estimate measures of various lengths and heights. After recording these estimates, they should measure each length with a ruler and check their accuracy.

Choosing Appropriate Units

Should the room be measured in feet or inches? Should the concrete blocks be weighed in grams or kilograms? The answers to questions such as these involve more than simply knowing how big the units are, although that is certainly required. Another consideration involves the need for precision. If you were measuring your wall in order to cut a piece of molding or woodwork to fit, you would need to measure it very precisely. The smallest unit would be an inch or a centimeter, and you would also use small fractional parts. But if you were determining how many 8-foot molding strips to buy, the nearest foot would probably be sufficient.

ACTIVITY 8.20

Guess the Unit

Find examples of measurements of all types in newspapers, on signs, or in other everyday situations. Present the context and measures but without units. The task is to predict what units of measure were used. Have students discuss their choices.

Important Standard Units and Relationships

Both the customary and metric systems include many units that are rarely if ever used in everyday life. Table 8.2 lists the units that are most common in each system. Your state or local curriculum is the best guide to help you decide which units your students should be learning. Remember that textbooks are written to satisfy the needs

TABLE 8.2 •••••••••••••••••••••••••••••••

Commonly Encountered Units of Measure

	Metric System	Customary System
Length	millimeter	inch
	centimeter	foot
	meter	yard
	kilometer	mile
Area	square centimeter	square inch
	square meter	square foot
		square yard
Volume	cubic centimeter	cubic inch
	cubic meter	cubic foot
		cubic yard
Capacity	millimeter	ounce*
	liter	teaspoon
		tablespoon
		cup
		quart
		gallon
Weight	gram	ounce*
	kilogram	pound
	metric ton	ton

*In the U.S. customary system, the term *ounce* refers to a weight or *avoirdupois* unit, 16 of which make a pound, and also a volume or capacity unit, 8 of which make a cup. Though the two units have the same name, they are not related.

of many states and so they may touch on units not in your curriculum. Too much tedious information can be boring. Unit familiarity with the most popularly used units should be the principal focus of almost all instruction with standard units. (See Activities 8.17, 8.18, and 8.19.)

The relationships between units within either the metric or customary systems are conventions. As such, students must simply be told what the relationships are and exercises must be devised to reinforce them. At the primary level, it can be safely argued that familiarity with the basic units that are commonly used is much more important than knowing how many cups in a quart or inches in a yard. Again, your curriculum should be your guide.

In the customary system there are very few patterns or rules to guide students in converting units. Liquid or capacity units involve mostly multiples of 2, 4, and 8 but there is no real pattern. The relationships between inches, feet, and yards are quite common and can be the source of good word problems involving multiplication and division.

The metric system was designed systematically around powers of ten. However, before students have an appreciation of decimal numeration, this system will be of minimal assistance.

Assessment Note ————————

In assessing students' understanding and familiarity with standard units, there is a danger of focusing on the traditional conversion tasks. Consider these two tasks:

1. 4 feet = _____ inches
2. Estimate the length of this rope in feet and then in inches. How did you decide on your estimate?

Both tasks relate feet and inches. However, the second task requires students to have a familiarity with the units as well. With the estimation task we can observe whether the student uses the first estimate to make the second (understanding and *using* the feet/inches relationship) or rather makes two separate estimates. This task also allows us to see how an estimate is made. This information is unavailable in the narrower traditional task.

The point is to ask questions that get at more than recall and ask students to *use* the information that you helped them to develop.

EXPANDED LESSON

Crooked Paths

Based on: Activity 8.3, p. 229

GRADE LEVEL: Late kindergarten or early first grade.

MATHEMATICS GOALS
- To help students understand that length is an attribute that need not be in a straight line. For example, a distance around an object or a nonstraight path has length just as does a straight object.
- To provide the opportunity to use an intermediary object as a basis of comparison.

THINKING ABOUT THE STUDENTS
Students have made comparisons of straight objects or paths and have learned the meaning of *longer* and *shorter* in that context. Students have not used units or rulers to measure lengths.

MATERIALS AND PREPARATION
- This will be a station activity. Set up three identical stations around the room. Each station consists of two

crooked paths made of masking tape. Try to make them about the same in each station. Path A is a zigzag of four straight line segments that total about 9 feet in all. Path B is more S-shaped and is about 7 feet long. Make path B "look" longer by spreading it out more.

- Make one recording sheet for every two students. (See Blackline Master L-4.)
- Use rope, string, or yarn that is at least 10 feet long for each station.

- -

lesson

BEFORE

Begin with a Simpler Version of the Task
- Show the class pairs of straight objects such as a meter stick and teacher, pencil and crayon, or two lines drawn on the board. For each pair, ask: *Which is longer? Which is shorter? How can we tell?*
- On the board draw a half circle and beneath it a line segment about as long as the diameter. Ask: *How can we tell which of these is longer?* Solicit ideas. Be sure students hear the idea that the curve is longer than the segment and that some students provide good reasons. For example, say: *If you had to walk on these, it would take longer to walk the curved path.*

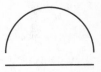

The Task
- Gather students around one station. Say, *One path might be longer or they might be the same. Your task is to decide.*

BLM L-4

Establish Expectations
- Show students the worksheets and explain how to use them. Explain that they are to circle the path that is longer or circle both paths if they think they are the same. Then they draw a picture to show how they decided. Have children work in pairs.
- Ask students which path they think is longer or whether they think they are the same. Say: *Before you begin work, put an X on the picture of the path that you think is longer. This is your guess.* Have a few students share their guesses and their reasoning.
- Show students that there is string for comparing lengths, but they can use their bodies, or blocks, or whatever materials they want to help them decide.

DURING

- Monitor station activity but do not interfere. Be sure students are completing worksheets to the best of their abilities.
- If a pair seems unable to make a decision, ask: *If a toy car was going to go along these paths, which path would it travel longer on?* Or: *Could you use some blocks from over in the block corner to help?*
- Challenge task for capable students: Make a long row of blocks in a straight line that is just as long as the curvy path.

AFTER (WHEN ALL STUDENTS HAVE COMPLETED THE STATION)

- Remind students of the task of comparing the two paths. Return their worksheets so that they can use them to talk about what they did.
- Ask: *How many thought the zigzag path was longer?* (Count and record on the board next to a zigzag.) *How many thought the curvy path was longer?* (Count and record.) *How many thought they were about the same?* (Count and record.) Ask students if the guesses they made were the same as the result that they figured out. Were they surprised? Why?
- Select pairs to explain what they did. Begin with timid students who are correct. Then ask students with different results. Get as many different ideas and methods as possible.
- If students disagree about which path is longer, have them explain their reasoning in a way that might convince those who disagree. Give students the opportunity to change their minds but ask, *What made you change your minds?*

ASSESSMENT NOTES

- Look for students who understand how length can exist on a curved path (correctly compare or make appropriate attempt). This can be a checklist item based on the discussion or observations.
- If students used the string, did they exhibit correct understanding of intermediate units? (This is not a requirement of the activity.)
- For students who used units, did they use like-sized units or make appropriate use of materials?

- -

next steps

- Students who are confused by this activity can be given an activity in which they start with two ropes or plastic chains of different lengths. Have them decide which is longer or shorter. Then have them make each into a crooked path. Repeat the longer/shorter discussion.
- The activity could be repeated as a worksheet with paths drawn on paper and students using paper clip chains to compare. An activity with paper clip chains or other chains can serve as a bridge to learning to use units to measure.
- Move on to units of measurement. See Activity 8.4, "How Long Is the Teacher?"

EARLY FRACTION CONCEPTS

For students in the upper elementary grades and even middle school, fractions present a considerable challenge. It is in the area of fractions that students often give up trying to understand and resort instead to rules. However, if approached in a developmental manner, students in the primary grades can be helped to construct a firm foundation for fraction concepts, preparing them for the skills that are later built on these ideas.

Traditional programs in grades K–2 typically offer very limited exposure to fractions. At grade 3, many state curricula demand a full development of fraction understanding. Some even include operations with fractions at grade 3. However, few if any programs provide students with adequate time or experiences to help them with this complex area of the curriculum. This chapter will explore a complete conceptual development of fraction concepts that can begin at grade 1 or 2, with most of the work appropriate for grade 3. A leap to fraction computation before the fourth grade is probably a mistake. In fact, no algorithms of any sort are required in this development.

big ideas

1 Fractional parts are equal shares or equal-sized portions of a whole or unit. A unit can be an object or a collection of things. More abstractly, the unit is counted as 1. On the number line, the distance from 0 to 1 is the unit.

2 Fractional parts have special names that tell how many parts of that size are needed to make the whole. For example, *thirds* require three parts to make a whole.

3 The more fractional parts used to make a whole, the smaller the parts. For example, eighths are smaller than fifths.

4 The denominator of a fraction indicates by what number the whole has been divided in order to produce the type of part under consideration. Thus, the denominator is a divisor. In practical terms, the denominator names the kind of fractional part that is under consideration. The numerator of a fraction counts or tells how many of the fractional parts (of the type indicated by the denominator) are under consideration. Therefore, the numerator is a multiplier—it indicates a multiple of the given fractional part.

5 Two equivalent fractions are two ways of describing the same amount by using different-sized fractional parts. For example, in the fraction $\frac{6}{8}$, if the eighths are taken in twos, then each pair of eighths is a fourth. The six-eighths then can be seen to be three-fourths.

Sharing and the Concept of Fractional Parts

The first goal in the development of fractions should be to help children construct the idea of *fractional parts of the whole*—the parts that result when the whole or unit has been partitioned into *equal-sized portions* or *fair shares*.

Children seem to understand the idea of separating a quantity into two or more parts to be shared fairly among friends. They eventually make connections between the idea of fair shares and fractional parts. Sharing tasks are, therefore, good places to begin the development of fractions.

Sharing Tasks

Considerable research has been done with children from first through eighth grades to determine how they go about the process of forming fair shares and how the tasks posed to students influence their responses (e.g., Empson, 2002; Lamon, 1996; Mack, 2001; Pothier & Sawada, 1983).

Sharing tasks are generally posed in the form of a simple story problem. *Suppose there are four square brownies to be shared among three children so that each child gets the same amount. How much (or show how much) will each child get?* Task difficulty changes with the numbers involved, the types of things to be shared (regions such as brownies, discrete objects such as pieces of chewing gum), and the presence or use of a model.

Students initially perform sharing tasks (division) by distributing items one at a time. When this process leaves leftover pieces, it is much easier to think of sharing them fairly if the items can be subdivided. Typical "regions" to share are brownies (rectangles), sandwiches, pizzas, crackers, cake, candy bars, and so on. The problems and variations that follow are adapted from Empson (2002).

· ·

Four children are sharing 10 brownies so that each one will get the same amount. How much can each child have?

· ·

Problem difficulty is determined by the relationship between the number of things to be shared and the number of sharers. Because children's initial strategies for sharing involve halving, a good place to begin is with two, four, or even eight sharers. For ten brownies and four sharers, many children will deal out two to each child and then halve each of the remaining brownies. (See Figure 9.1.)

Consider these variations in numbers:

5 brownies shared with 2 children

2 brownies shared with 4 children

5 brownies shared with 4 children

4 brownies shared with 8 children

3 brownies shared with 4 children

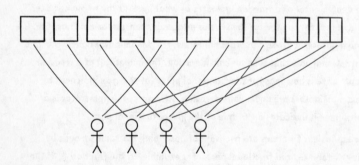

FIGURE 9.1 ·

Ten brownies shared with four children.

> **STOP** Try drawing pictures for each of the preceding sharing tasks. Which do you think is most difficult? Which of these represents essentially the same degree of difficulty? What other tasks involving two, four, or eight sharers would you consider as similar, easier, or more difficult than these?

When the numbers allow for some items to be distributed whole (five shared with two), some students will first share whole items and then cut up the leftovers. Others will slice every piece in half and then distribute the halves. When there are more sharers than items, some partitioning must happen at the beginning of the solution process.

When students who are still using a halving strategy try to share five things among four children, they will eventually get down to two halves to give to four children. For some, the solution is to cut each half in half; that is, "each child gets a whole (or two halves) and a half of a half."

It is a progression to move to three or six sharers because this will force children to confront their halving strategies.

> **STOP** Try solving the following variations using drawings. Can you do them in different ways?

4 pizzas shared with 6 children

7 pizzas shared with 6 children

5 pizzas shared with 3 children

To subdivide a region into a number of parts other than a power of two (four, eight, etc.) requires an odd subdivision at some point. This is difficult for young children.

Several types of sharing solutions might be observed. Figure 9.2 shows some different approaches.

Use a variety of representations for these problems. The items to be shared can be drawn on worksheets as rectangles or circles along with a statement of the problem. Another possibility is to cut out construction paper circles or squares. Some students may need to cut and physically distribute the pieces. Students can use connecting cubes to make bars that they can separate into pieces. Or they can use more traditional fraction models such as circular "pie" pieces.

Sharing Tasks and Fraction Language

During the discussions of students' solutions (and discussions are essential!) is a good time to introduce the vocabulary of fractional parts. This can be quite casual and, at least for younger children, should not involve any fraction symbolism. When a brownie or

(a) Four candy bars shared with six children:

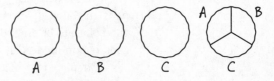

Cut all the bars in half.
Cut the last two halves into three parts.
Each child gets a half and sixth.

(b) Four pizzas shared with three children:

Pass out whole pizzas.
Cut the last pizza in three parts.
Each child gets 1 whole and one-third.

(c) Five sandwiches shared with three children:

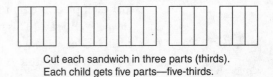

Cut each sandwich in three parts (thirds).
Each child gets five parts—five-thirds.

FIGURE 9.2 •

Three different sharing processes.

other region has been broken into equal shares, simply say, "We call these *fourths*. The whole is cut into four parts. All of the parts are the same size—fourths."

Children need to be aware of two aspects or components of fractional parts: (1) the number of parts and (2) the equality of the parts (in size, not necessarily in shape). Emphasize that the number of equal parts or fair shares that make up a whole determines the name of the fractional parts or shares. They will be familiar with halves but should quickly learn to describe thirds, fourths, fifths, and so on.

It is a mistake to think that fractional parts such as sixths or eighths are conceptually more difficult than halves and thirds. Note that in the discussion of sharing, halves, fourths, and eighths were explored prior to thirds, sixths, and fifths. This was done because successive halving of parts is a natural process for young children. The number of parts does not correlate with conceptual difficulty. Most state curricula would lead you to believe differently. In fact, if we want children to generalize the concept of fractional parts and connect to this generalization the numeric names of thirds, fourths, fifths, and so on, they must be exposed to more than just halves and thirds in the earliest stages of exploring fractions.

Models for Fractions

In the primary grades the use of models to explore fractions is essential. Students can represent fraction concepts with physical materials and drawings in many different ways. Not only should students use these models, but also they should explore fractional concepts with a wide variety of models so that fractions don't simply become "pie pieces." Some fraction models may challenge students to be more reflective about the fraction concepts than others. Be aware of the values and difficulties of different models so that you will be able to suggest appropriate materials for your students.

Region or Area Models

All of the sharing tasks involved sharing something that could be cut into smaller parts. In these situations the fractions are based on parts of an area or region. This is a good place to begin and is almost essential when doing sharing tasks. There are many good region models, as shown in Figure 9.3.

Circular "pie" piece models are by far the most commonly used area model. The main advantage of the circular region is that it emphasizes the amount that is remaining to make up a whole. The strong emphasis on the circle as a whole also has disadvantages. To use the semicircle or any other piece other than the circle to represent the whole would be very confusing. So there is no challenge for students to construct a whole given one of the pieces as a fractional part. Another disadvantage lies in the fact that each piece is a unit fraction. That is, it is not possible to pick up or point to a single piece and say, "This represents two-thirds." Finally, too great an emphasis on the circle model will encourage students to draw circular fractions in order to make an argument for a result as in deciding if $\frac{2}{3}$ is more or less than $\frac{3}{4}$. Even adults have difficulty partitioning a circle in a reasonably accurate manner. Drawings of circle models can mislead and be overused. The other models in Figure 9.3 are more flexible and allow for different-sized units or wholes. Paper grids on which students can draw fractional amounts are quite flexible. Several grid papers can be found in the Blackline Masters.

BLMs 31–36

FIGURE 9.3 • • • • • • • •

Area or region models for fractions.

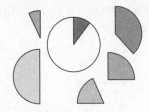

Circular "pie" pieces

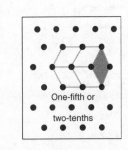

Rectangular regions

Any piece can be selected as the whole.

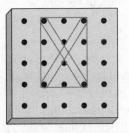

Fourths on a geoboard

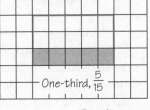

One-third, $\frac{5}{15}$

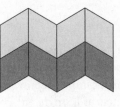

One-fifth or two-tenths

Drawings on grids or dot paper

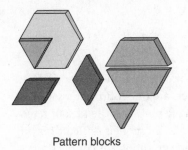

Pattern blocks

Paper folding

Length or Measurement Models

With measurement models, lengths are compared instead of areas. Either lines are drawn and subdivided, or physical materials are compared on the basis of length, as shown in Figure 9.4. Manipulative versions, especially Cuisenaire rods, provide more opportunity for trial and error and for exploration.

Fraction strips are a teacher-made version of Cuisenaire rods. Both the strips and the rods have pieces that are in lengths of 1 to 10 measured in terms of the smallest strip or rod. Each length is a different color for ease of identification. Strips of construction paper or adding-machine tape can be folded to produce equal-sized subparts.

The rod or strip model provides the most flexibility while still having separate pieces for comparisons. To make fraction strips, cut 11 different colors of poster board into strips 2 cm wide. Cut the smallest strips into 2-cm squares. Other strips are then 4, 6, 8, . . . , 20 cm, producing lengths 1 to 10 in terms of the smallest strip. Cut the last color into strips 24 cm long to produce a 12 strip. If you are using Cuisenaire rods, tape a red 2 rod to an orange 10 rod to make a 12 rod. In this chapter's

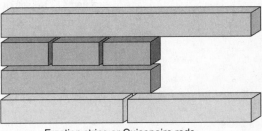

Fraction strips or Cuisenaire rods

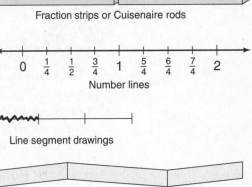

$$0 \quad \frac{1}{4} \quad \frac{1}{2} \quad \frac{3}{4} \quad 1 \quad \frac{5}{4} \quad \frac{6}{4} \quad \frac{7}{4} \quad 2$$

Number lines

Line segment drawings

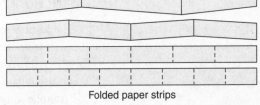

Folded paper strips

FIGURE 9.4 •

Length or measurement models for fractions.

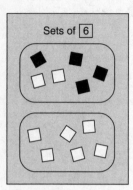

Two-color counters in arrays.
Rows and columns help show
parts. Each array makes a
whole. Here $\frac{3}{5} = \frac{9}{15}$.

XXX   XX
XX   XXX
  OO
  OOO

Drawings using
Xs and Os.
Shows $\frac{2}{3} = \frac{10}{15}$.

Sets of 6

Two-color counters in
loops drawn on paper.
Shows $1\frac{2}{6}$.

FIGURE 9.5 ● ● ● ● ● ● ● ● ● ● ● ● ● ● ● ● ● ● ●

Set models for fractions.

illustrations, the colors of the strips will be the same as the corresponding lengths of the Cuisenaire rods:

1	White	7	Black
2	Red	8	Brown
3	Light green	9	Blue
4	Purple	10	Orange
5	Yellow	12	Pink or red-orange
6	Dark green		

The number line is a significantly more sophisticated measurement model. From a child's vantage point, there is a real difference between putting a number on a number line and comparing one length to another. Each number on a line denotes the distance of the labeled point from zero, not the point itself. This distinction is often difficult for children.

Set Models

In set models, the whole is understood to be a set of objects, and subsets of the whole make up fractional parts. For example, three objects are one-fourth of a set of 12 objects. The set of 12, in this example, represents the whole or 1. It is the idea of referring to a collection of counters as a single entity that makes set models difficult for primary school children. However, the set model helps establish important connections with many real-world uses of fractions. See Figure 9.5.

Counters in two colors on opposite sides are frequently used. They can easily be flipped to change their color to model various fractional parts of a whole set.

From Fractional Parts to Fraction Symbols

As already discussed, one of the best ways to introduce the concept of fractional parts is through sharing tasks. However, the idea of fractional parts is so fundamental to a strong development of fraction concepts that it should be explored further with additional tasks.

Fractional Parts and Words

In addition to helping children use the words *halves*, *thirds*, *fourths*, *fifths*, and so on, be sure to make regular comparison of fractional parts to the whole. Make it a point to use the terms *whole*, or *one whole*, or simply *one* so that students have a language that they can use regardless of the model involved.

The following activity is a simple extension of the sharing tasks. It is important that students can tell when a region has been separated into a particular type of fractional part.

● ●

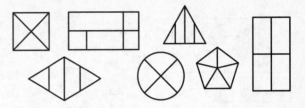

Correct Shares

As in Figure 9.6, show examples and nonexamples of specified fractional parts. Have students identify the wholes that are correctly divided into requested fractional parts and those that are not. For each response, have students explain their reasoning. The activity should be done with a variety of models, including length and set models.

In the "Correct Shares" activity, the most important part is the discussion of the nonexamples. The wholes are already partitioned either correctly or incorrectly, and the children were not involved in the partitioning. It is also useful for children to create designated equal shares given a whole, as they are asked to do in the next activity.

Finding Fair Shares

Give students models, and have them find fifths or eighths or other fractional parts using the models. (The models should never have fractions written on them.) The activity is especially interesting when different wholes can be designated in the same model. That way, a given fractional part does not get identified with a special shape or color but with the relationship of the part to the designated whole. Some ideas are suggested in Figure 9.7.

Notice when partitioning sets that children frequently confuse the number of counters in a share with the name of the share. In the example in Figure 9.7, the 12 counters are partitioned into four sets—*fourths*. Each share or part has three counters, but it is the number of shares that makes the partition show *fourths*.

Understanding Fraction Symbols

Fraction symbolism represents a fairly complex convention that is often misleading to children. It is well worth your time to help students develop a strong understanding of what the top and bottom numbers of a fraction tell us.

Fractional-Parts Counting

Counting fractional parts to see how multiple parts compare to the whole creates a foundation for the two parts

FIGURE 9.6 •

Children learning about fractional parts should be able to tell which of these figures is correctly partitioned in fourths. They should also be able to explain why the other figures are not showing fourths.

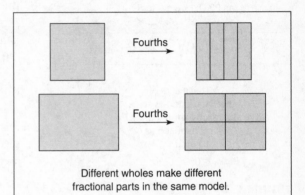

Different wholes make different fractional parts in the same model.

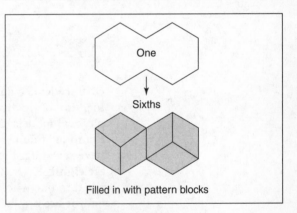

One

↓

Sixths

Filled in with pattern blocks

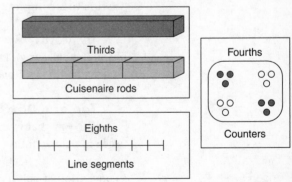

Thirds

Cuisenaire rods

Eighths

Line segments

Fourths

Counters

FIGURE 9.7 • • • • • • • • • • • • • • • • • • •

Given a whole, find fractional parts.

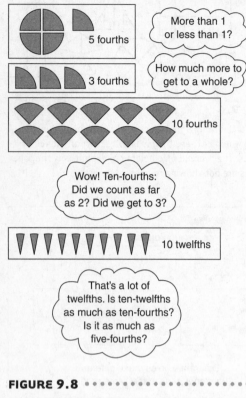

FIGURE 9.8 •

Counting fractional parts.

of a fraction. Students should come to think of counting fractional parts in much the same way as they might count apples or any other objects. If you know the kind of part you are counting, you can tell when you get to one, when you get to two, and so on. Students who understand factional parts should not need to arrange pie pieces into a circle to know that four fourths make a whole.

Display some pie-piece fraction parts in groups as shown in Figure 9.8. For each collection, tell students what type of piece is being shown and simply count them together: "*one*-fourth, *two*-fourths, *three*-fourths, *four*-fourths, *five*-fourths." Ask, "If we have five-fourths, is that more than one whole, less than one whole, or the same as one whole?"

As students count each collection of parts, discuss the relationship to one whole. Make informal comparisons between different collections. "Why did we get almost two wholes with seven-fourths, and yet we don't even have one whole with ten-twelfths?"

Also take this opportunity to lay verbal groundwork for mixed fractions. "What is another way that we could say seven-thirds?" (Two wholes and one more third or one whole and four-thirds.)

With this introduction, students are ready for the following task.

ACTIVITY 9.3

More, Less, or Equal to One Whole

Give students a collection of fractional parts (all the same type) and indicate the kind of fractional part they have. Parts can be drawn on a worksheet or physical models can be placed in plastic baggies with an identifying card. For example, if done with Cuisenaire rods or fraction strips, the collection might have seven light green rods/strips with a caption or note indicating "these are eighths." The task is to decide if the collection is less than one whole, equal to one whole, or more than one whole. Students must draw pictures and/or use numbers to explain their answer. They can also tell how close the set is to a complete whole. Several collections constitute a reasonable task.

Try Activity 9.3 with several different fraction models (although pie pieces are too much of a giveaway). Pattern blocks make a good manipulative format and are also easily drawn with a template. The same is true of Cuisenaire rods.

Top and Bottom Numbers

The way that we write fractions with a top and a bottom number and a bar between is a convention—an arbitrary agreement for how to represent fractions. (By the way, always write fractions with a horizontal bar, not a slanted one. Write $\frac{3}{4}$, not 3/4.) As a convention, it falls in the category of things that you simply tell students. However, a good idea is to make the convention so clear by way of demonstration that students will tell *you* what the top and bottom numbers stand for. The following procedure is recommended even if your students have been "using" symbolic fractions for several years.

Display several collections of fractional parts in a manner similar to those in Figure 9.8. Have students count the parts together. After each count, write the correct fraction, indicating that this is how it is written as a symbol. Include sets that are more than one, but write them as simple or "improper" fractions and not as mixed numbers. Include at least two pairs of sets with the same top numbers such as $\frac{4}{8}$ and $\frac{4}{3}$. Likewise, include sets with the same bottom numbers. After the class has counted and you have written the fraction for at least six sets of fractional parts, pose the following questions:

What does the bottom number in a fraction tell us?

What does the top number in a fraction tell us?

> **STOP** **Before reading further, answer these two questions in your own words. Don't rely on formulations you've heard before. Think in terms of what we have been talking about—namely, fractional parts and counting fractional parts. Imagine counting a set of 5 eighths and a set of 5 fourths and writing the fractions for these sets. Use children's language in your formulations and try to come up with a way to explain these meanings that has nothing to do with the type of model involved.**

Here are some reasonable explanations for the top and bottom numbers.

- *Top number:* This is the counting number. It tells how many shares or parts we have. It tells how many have been counted. It tells how many parts we are talking about. It counts the parts or shares.

- *Bottom number:* This tells what is being counted. It tells what fractional part is being counted. If it is a 4, it means we are counting *fourths;* if it is a 6, we are counting *sixths;* and so on.

This formulation of the meanings of the top and bottom numbers may seem unusual to you. It is often said that the top number tells "how many" and the bottom tells "how many parts it takes to make a whole." This may be correct but can be misleading. For example, a $\frac{1}{6}$ piece is often cut from a cake without making any slices in the remaining $\frac{5}{6}$ of the cake. That the cake is only in two pieces does not change the fact that the piece taken is $\frac{1}{6}$. Or if a pizza is cut in 12 pieces, two pieces still make $\frac{1}{6}$ of the pizza. In neither of these instances does the bottom number tell how many pieces make a whole.

There is evidence that an iterative notion of fractions, one that views a fraction such as $\frac{3}{4}$ as a count of three things called *fourths,* is an important idea for children to develop (Post, Wachsmuth, Lesh, & Behr, 1985; Tzur, 1999). The iterative concept is most clear when focusing on these two ideas about fraction symbols:

- The top number *counts.*
- The bottom number tells *what is being counted.*

The *what* of fractions are the fractional parts. They can be counted. Fraction symbols are just a shorthand for saying *how many* and *what.*

Smith (2002) points out a slightly more "mathematical" definition of the top and bottom numbers that is completely in accord with the one we've just discussed.

FROM FRACTIONAL PARTS TO FRACTION SYMBOLS

For Smith, it is important to see the bottom number as the divisor and the top as the multiplier. That is, $\frac{3}{4}$ is three *times* what you get when you *divide* a whole into four parts. This multiplier and divisor idea is especially useful when students are asked later to think of fractions as an indicated division; that is, $\frac{3}{4}$ also means $3 \div 4$.

Mixed Numbers and Improper Fractions

If you have counted fractional parts beyond a whole, your students already know how to write $\frac{13}{16}$ or $\frac{11}{3}$. Ask, "What is another way that you could say 13 *sixths*?" Students may suggest "two wholes and one-sixth more," or "two plus one-sixth." Explain that these are correct and that $2 + \frac{1}{6}$ is usually written as $2\frac{1}{6}$ and is called a *mixed number*. Note that this is a symbolism convention and must be explained to children. What is not at all necessary is to teach a rule for converting mixed numbers to common fractions and the reverse. Rather, consider the following task.

ACTIVITY 9.4

Mixed-Number Names

Give students a mixed number such as $3\frac{2}{5}$. Their task is to find a single fraction that names the same amount. They may use any familiar materials or make drawings, but they must be able to give an explanation for their result. Similarly, have students start with a fraction greater than 1, such as $\frac{17}{4}$, and have them determine the mixed number and provide a justification for their result.

Repeat the "Mixed-Number Names" task several times with different fractions. After a while, challenge students to figure out the new fraction name without the use of models. A good explanation for $3\frac{1}{4}$ might be that there are 4 fourths in one whole, so there are 8 fourths in two wholes and 12 fourths in three wholes. The extra fourth makes 13 fourths in all, or $\frac{13}{4}$. (Note the iteration concept playing a role.)

There is absolutely no reason ever to provide a rule about multiplying the whole number by the bottom number and adding the top number. Nor should students need a rule about dividing the bottom number into the top to convert fractions to mixed numbers. These rules will readily be developed by the students but in their own words and with complete understanding.

Parts-and-Whole Tasks

The three types of tasks presented here can help children develop their understanding of fractional parts as well as the meanings of the top and bottom numbers in a fraction. Models are used to represent wholes and parts of wholes. Written or oral fraction names represent the relationship between the parts and wholes. Given any two of these—whole, part, and fraction—the students can use their models to determine the third.

Any type of model can be used as long as different sizes can represent the whole. Traditional pie pieces do not work because the whole is always the circle, and all the pieces are *unit fractions*. (A *unit fraction* is a single fractional part. The fractions $\frac{1}{3}$ and $\frac{1}{8}$ are unit fractions.)

Examples of each type of exercise are provided in Figure 9.9, Figure 9.10, and Figure 9.11. Each figure includes examples with a region model (freely drawn rectangles), a length model (Cuisenaire rods or fraction strips), and set models.

These three types of problems vary in difficulty as well as in what they can help children learn. The first type, in which students find the part given the whole and fraction (Figure 9.9), is commonly encountered in textbooks. What may make it different is that the given whole is not partitioned at all. Students must know that the denominator will tell them how to partition the whole—it is the divisor. The numerator counts. Therefore, once partitioned, they count the necessary number of fractional parts. Notice that you can ask for students to show a fraction that is more than a whole even though only one whole is provided. Usually students will create a second whole and partition that as well.

In the second type of task, students are asked to find or create the whole given a part of the whole. Students will find this task a bit more difficult than the first. The struggle and discussion among students will be worth the effort. This exercise emphasizes that a fraction is not an absolute quantity; rather, it is a relationship between the part and the whole. If a white strip (1 unit long) is given as $\frac{1}{4}$, then the purple strip (4 units long) is the whole. However, if the red strip (2 units) is given as $\frac{1}{4}$, then the brown strip (8 units) is the whole. When the given part is not a unit fraction, the task is considerably more difficult. For the second example in Figure 9.10, students must first realize that the given rectangle is three of something—three-*fourths*. Therefore, if that given piece is subdivided into three parts, then one of those parts will be a fourth. From the unit fraction, counting produces the whole—four of the one-fourth pieces make a whole. Notice again how the task forces students to think of counting unit fractional parts.

The third type of exercise will likely involve some estimation, especially if drawings are used. Different estimates can prompt excellent discussion. With Cuisenaire rods or sets, there is always a single correct answer.

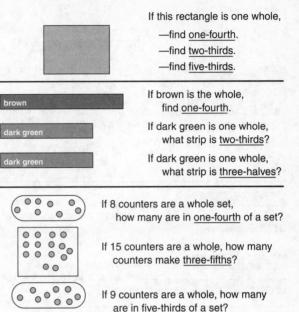

If this rectangle is one whole,
—find one-fourth.
—find two-thirds.
—find five-thirds.

brown — If brown is the whole, find one-fourth.

dark green — If dark green is one whole, what strip is two-thirds?

dark green — If dark green is one whole, what strip is three-halves?

If 8 counters are a whole set, how many are in one-fourth of a set?

If 15 counters are a whole, how many counters make three-fifths?

If 9 counters are a whole, how many are in five-thirds of a set?

FIGURE 9.9

Given the whole and the fraction, find the part.

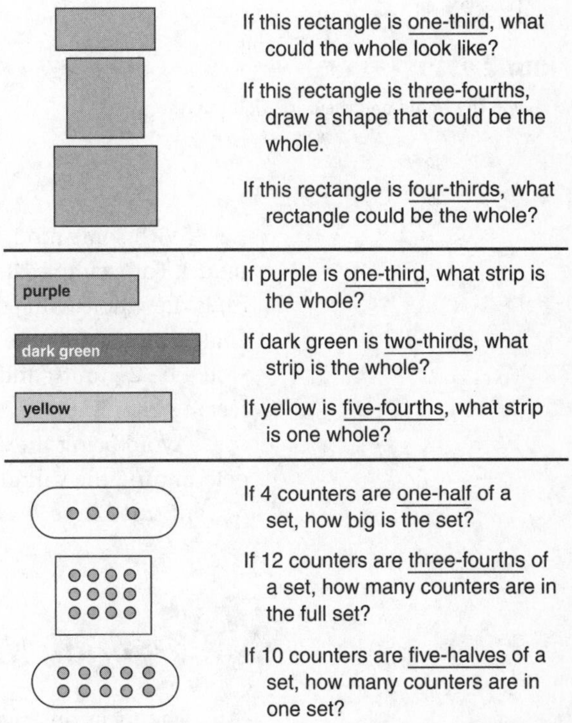

If this rectangle is one-third, what could the whole look like?

If this rectangle is three-fourths, draw a shape that could be the whole.

If this rectangle is four-thirds, what rectangle could be the whole?

purple — If purple is one-third, what strip is the whole?

dark green — If dark green is two-thirds, what strip is the whole?

yellow — If yellow is five-fourths, what strip is one whole?

If 4 counters are one-half of a set, how big is the set?

If 12 counters are three-fourths of a set, how many counters are in the full set?

If 10 counters are five-halves of a set, how many counters are in one set?

FIGURE 9.10

Given the part and the fraction, find the whole.

FROM FRACTIONAL PARTS TO FRACTION SYMBOLS

Whole — What fraction of the big square does the small square represent?

What fraction is the large rectangle if the smaller one is one whole?

Whole

dark green / yellow — If dark green is the whole, what fraction is the yellow strip?

dark green / blue — If the dark green strip is one whole, what fraction is the blue strip?

What fraction of this set is black? (Don't answer in ninths.)

If 10 counters are the whole set, what fraction of the set is 6 counters?

These 16 counters are what fraction of a whole set of 12 counters?

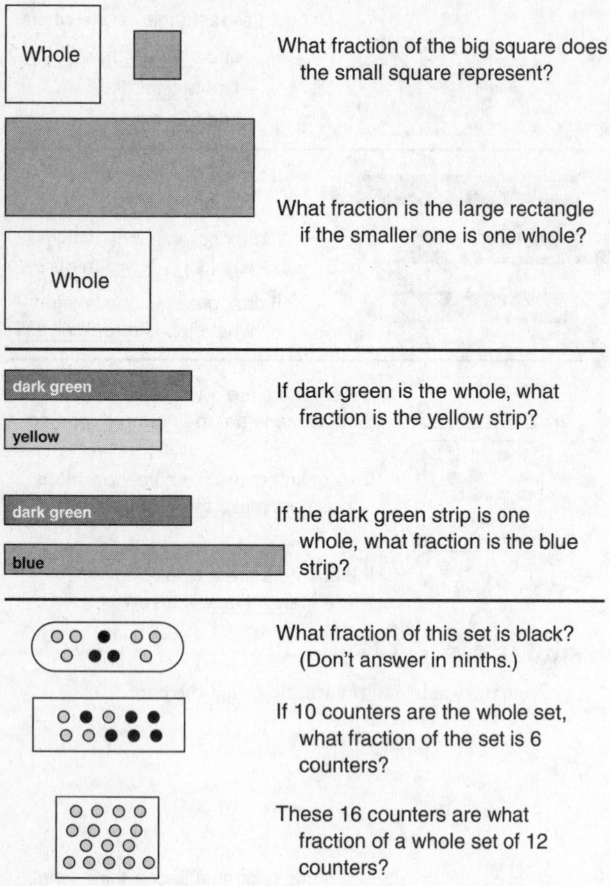

FIGURE 9.11 •

Given the whole and the part, find the fraction.

Two or three challenging parts-and-whole questions can make an excellent lesson. The tasks should be presented to the class in just the same form as in the figures. Physical models are often the best way to present the tasks so that students can use a trial-and-error approach to determine their results. As with all tasks, it should be clear that an explanation is required to justify each answer. For each task, let several students supply answers and explanations.

Sometimes it is a good idea to create simple story problems that ask the same questions.

• •

Mr. Samuels has finished $\frac{3}{4}$ of his patio. It looks like this:

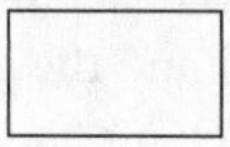

Draw a picture that might be the shape of the finished patio.

• •

The problems can also involve numbers instead of models:

• •

If the swim team sold 48 raffle tickets, it would have enough money to pay for new team shirts. So far the swimmers have $\frac{5}{8}$ of the necessary raffle tickets sold. How many more tickets do they need to sell?

• •

With some models, it is necessary to be certain that the answer exists within the model. For example, if you were using fraction strips, you could ask, "If the blue strip (9) is the whole, what strip is two-thirds?" The answer is the 6 strip, or dark green. You could not ask students to find "three-fourths of the blue strip" because each fourth of 9 would be $2\frac{1}{4}$ units, and no strip has that length. Similar caution must be taken with rectangular pieces.

Avoid being the answer book for your students. Make students responsible for determining the validity of their own answers. In these exercises, the results can always be confirmed in terms of what is given.

Fraction Number Sense

The focus on fractional parts is an important beginning. But number sense with fractions demands more—it requires that students have some intuitive feel for fractions. They should know "about" how big a particular fraction is and be able to tell easily which of two fractions is larger.

Benchmarks of Zero, One-Half, and One

The most important reference points or benchmarks for fractions are 0, $\frac{1}{2}$, and 1. For fractions less than 1, simply comparing them to these three numbers gives quite a lot of information. For example, $\frac{3}{20}$ is small, close to 0, whereas $\frac{3}{4}$ is between $\frac{1}{2}$ and 1. The fraction $\frac{9}{10}$ is quite close to 1. Since any fraction greater than 1 is a whole number plus an amount less than 1, the same reference points are just as helpful: $3\frac{3}{7}$ is almost $3\frac{1}{2}$.

ACTIVITY 9.5

Zero, One-Half, or One

On the board or overhead, write a collection of 8 to 10 fractions. A few should be greater than 1 ($\frac{9}{8}$ or $\frac{11}{10}$), with the others ranging from 0 to 1. Let students sort the fractions into three groups: those close to 0, close to $\frac{1}{2}$, and close to 1. For those close to $\frac{1}{2}$, have them decide if the fraction is more or less than $\frac{1}{2}$. The difficulty of this task largely depends on the fractions. The first time you try this, use fractions such as $\frac{1}{20}$, $\frac{53}{100}$, or $\frac{9}{10}$ that are very close to the three benchmarks. On subsequent days, use fractions with most of the denominators less than 20. You might include one or two fractions such as $\frac{2}{8}$ or $\frac{3}{4}$ that are exactly in between the benchmarks. As usual, require explanations for each fraction.

The next activity is also aimed at developing the same three reference points for fractions. In "Close Fractions," however, the students must come up with the fractions rather than sort them.

ACTIVITY 9.6

Close Fractions

Have students name a fraction that is close to 1 but not more than 1. Next have them name another fraction that is even closer to 1 than that. For the second response, they have to explain why they believe the fraction is closer to 1 than the previous fraction. Continue for several fractions in the same manner, each one being closer to 1 than the previous fraction. Similarly, try close to 0 or close to $\frac{1}{2}$ (either under or over). The first several times you try this activity, let the students use models to help with their thinking. Later, see how well their explanations work when they cannot use models or drawings. Focus discussions on the relative size of fractional parts.

Understanding why a fraction is close to 0, $\frac{1}{2}$, or 1 is a good beginning for fraction number sense. It begins to focus on the size of fractions in an important yet simple manner. The next activity also helps students reflect on fraction size.

ACTIVITY 9.7

About How Much?

Draw a picture like one of those in Figure 9.12 (or prepare some ahead of time for the overhead). Have each student write down a fraction that he or

(continued)

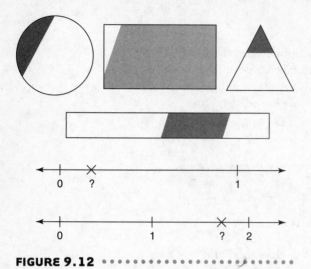

FIGURE 9.12

About how much? Name a fraction for each drawing, and explain why you chose that fraction.

she thinks is a good estimate of the amount shown (or the indicated mark on the number line). Listen without judgment to the ideas of several students and discuss with them why any particular estimate might be a good one. There is no single correct answer, but estimates should be "in the ballpark." If children have difficulty coming up with an estimate, ask if they think the amount is closer to 0, $\frac{1}{2}$, or 1.

Thinking About Which Is More

The ability to tell which of two fractions is greater is another aspect of number sense with fractions. That ability is built around concepts of fractions, not on an algorithmic skill or symbolic tricks.

Concepts, Not Rules

Children have a tremendously strong mind-set about numbers that causes them difficulties with the relative size of fractions. In their experience, larger numbers mean "more." The tendency is to transfer this whole-number concept to fractions: Seven is more than four, so sevenths should be bigger than fourths. The inverse relationship between number of parts and size of parts cannot be told but must be a creation of each student's own thought process.

ACTIVITY 9.8

Ordering Unit Fractions

List a set of unit fractions such as $\frac{1}{3}$, $\frac{1}{8}$, $\frac{1}{5}$, and $\frac{1}{10}$. Ask children to put the fractions in order from least to most. Challenge children to defend the way they ordered the fractions. The first few times you do this activity, have them explain their ideas by using models.

This idea is so basic to the understanding of fractions that arbitrary rules ("Larger bottom numbers mean smaller fractions") are not only inappropriate but dangerous. Come back to this basic idea periodically. Children will seem to understand one day and revert to their more comfortable ideas about big numbers a day or two later. Repeat Activity 9.8 with all numerators equal to 4. See how students ideas change.

You have probably learned rules or algorithms for comparing two fractions. The usual approach is to find a common denominator. This rule can be effective in getting correct answers but requires no thought about the size of the fractions. If children are taught the common denominator rule before they have had the opportunity to think about the relative size of various fractions, there is little chance that they will develop any familiarity with or number sense about fraction size. Comparison activities (which fraction is more?) can play a significant role in helping children develop concepts of relative fraction sizes. But keep in mind that reflective thought is the goal, not an algorithmic method of choosing the correct answer.

STOP Before reading further, try the following exercise. Assume for a moment that you know nothing about equivalent fractions or common denominators or cross-multiplication. Assume that you are a student who was never taught these procedures. Now examine the pairs of fractions in Figure 9.13 and select the larger of each pair. Write down or explain one or more reasons for your choice in each case.

Which fraction in each pair is greater?
Give one or more reasons. Try not to use drawings or models. Do not use common denominators or cross-multiplication. Rely on concepts.

A. $\frac{4}{5}$ or $\frac{4}{9}$ G. $\frac{7}{12}$ or $\frac{5}{12}$

B. $\frac{4}{7}$ or $\frac{5}{7}$ H. $\frac{3}{5}$ or $\frac{3}{7}$

C. $\frac{3}{8}$ or $\frac{4}{10}$ I. $\frac{5}{8}$ or $\frac{6}{10}$

D. $\frac{5}{3}$ or $\frac{5}{8}$ J. $\frac{9}{8}$ or $\frac{4}{3}$

E. $\frac{3}{4}$ or $\frac{9}{10}$ K. $\frac{4}{6}$ or $\frac{7}{12}$

F. $\frac{3}{8}$ or $\frac{4}{7}$ L. $\frac{8}{9}$ or $\frac{7}{8}$

FIGURE 9.13 •

Comparing fractions using concepts.

Conceptual Thought Patterns for Comparison

The first two comparison schemes listed here rely on the meanings of the top and bottom numbers in fractions and on the relative sizes of unit fractional parts. The third and fourth ideas use the additional ideas of 0, $\frac{1}{2}$, and 1 as convenient anchors or benchmarks for thinking about the size of fractions.

1. *More of the same-size parts.* To compare $\frac{3}{8}$ and $\frac{5}{8}$, it is easy to think about having 3 of something and also 5 of the same thing. It is common for children to choose $\frac{5}{8}$ as larger simply because 5 is more than 3 and the other numbers are the same. Right choice, wrong reason. Comparing $\frac{3}{8}$ and $\frac{5}{8}$ should be like comparing 3 apples and 5 apples.

2. *Same number of parts but parts of different sizes.* Consider the case of $\frac{3}{4}$ and $\frac{3}{7}$. If a whole is divided into 7 parts, the parts will certainly be smaller than if divided into only 4 parts. Many children will select $\frac{3}{7}$ as larger because 7 is more than 4 and the top numbers are the same. That approach yields correct choices when the parts are the same size, but it causes problems in this case. This is like comparing 3 apples with 3 melons. You have the same number of things, but melons are larger.

3. *More and less than one-half or one whole.* The fraction pairs $\frac{3}{7}$ versus $\frac{5}{8}$ and $\frac{5}{4}$ versus $\frac{7}{8}$ do not lend themselves to either of the previous thought processes. In the first pair, $\frac{3}{7}$ is less than half of the number of sevenths needed to make a whole, and so $\frac{3}{7}$ is less than a half. Similarly, $\frac{5}{8}$ is more than a half. Therefore, $\frac{5}{8}$ is the larger fraction. The second pair is determined by noting that one fraction is less than 1 and the other is greater than 1.

4. *Distance from one-half or one whole.* Why is $\frac{9}{10}$ greater than $\frac{3}{4}$? Not because the 9 and 10 are big numbers, although you will find that to be a common student response. Each is one fractional part away from one whole, and tenths are smaller than fourths. Similarly, notice that $\frac{5}{8}$ is smaller than $\frac{4}{6}$ because it is only one-eighth more than a half, while $\frac{4}{6}$ is a sixth more than a half. Can you use this basic idea to compare $\frac{3}{5}$ and $\frac{5}{9}$? (*Hint:* Each is half of a fractional part more than $\frac{1}{2}$.) Also try $\frac{5}{7}$ and $\frac{7}{9}$.

How did your reasons for choosing fractions in Figure 9.13 compare to these ideas? It is important that you are comfortable with these informal comparison strategies as a major component of your own number sense as well as for helping children develop theirs.

Tasks you design for your students should assist them in developing these and possibly other methods of comparing two fractions. It is important that the ideas come from your students and their discussions. To teach "the four ways to compare fractions" would be adding four more mysterious rules and would be defeating for many students.

ACTIVITY 9.9

Choose, Explain, Test

Present two or three pairs of fractions to students. The students' task is to decide which fraction is greater (choose), to explain why they think this is so (explain), and then to test their choice using any model that they wish to use. They should write a description of how they made their test and whether or not it agreed with their choice. If their choice was incorrect, they should try to say what they would change in their thinking. In the student explanations, rule out drawing as an option. Explain that it is difficult to draw fraction pictures accurately and, for this activity, pictures may cause them to make mistakes.

Rather than directly teach the different possible methods for comparing fractions, select pairs that will likely elicit desired comparison strategies. On one day, for example, you might have two pairs with the same denominators and one with the same numerators. On another day, you might pick fraction pairs in which each fraction is exactly one part away from a whole. Try to build strategies over several days by the appropriate choice of fraction pairs.

The use of a model in Activity 9.9 is an important part of students' development of strategies as long as the model is helping students create the strategy. However, after several experiences, change the activity so that the testing portion with a model is omitted. Place greater emphasis on students' reasoning. If class discussions yield different choices, allow students to use their own arguments for their choices in order to make a decision about which fraction is greater.

The next activity extends the comparison task a bit more.

ACTIVITY 9.10

Line 'Em Up

Select four or five fractions for students to put in order from least to most. Have them indicate approximately where each fraction belongs on a number line labeled only with the points 0, $\frac{1}{2}$, and 1. Students should include a description of how they decided on the order for the fractions. To place the fractions on the number line, students must also make estimates of fraction size in addition to simply ordering the fractions.

Including Equivalent Fractions

The discussion to this point has somewhat artificially ignored the idea that students might use equivalent fraction concepts in making comparisons. Equivalent fraction concepts are such an important idea that we have devoted a separate section to the development of that idea. However, equivalent fraction concepts need not be put off until last and certainly should be allowed in the discussions of which fraction is more.

Smith (2002) thinks that it is essential that the comparison question is asked as follows: "Which of the following two (or more) fractions is greater, *or are they equal*?" (p. 9, emphasis added). He points out that this question leaves open the possibility that two fractions that may look different can, in fact, be equal. Be absolutely certain to revisit the comparison activities and include pairs such as $\frac{8}{12}$ and $\frac{2}{3}$ in which the fractions are equal but do not appear to be. Also include fractions that are not in lowest terms.

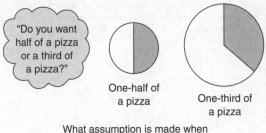

What assumption is made when answering this question?

FIGURE 9.14 ● ● ● ● ● ● ● ● ● ● ● ● ● ● ● ●

The "pizza fallacy."

Only One Size for the Whole

A key idea about fractions that students must come to understand is that a fraction does not say anything about the size of the whole or the size of the parts. A fraction tells us only about the *relationship* *between* the part and the whole. Consider the following situation.

Mark is offered the choice of a third of a pizza or a half of a pizza. Since he is hungry and likes pizza, he chooses the half. His friend Jane gets a third of a pizza but ends up with more than Mark. How can that be? Figure 9.14 illustrates how Mark got misdirected in his choice. The point of the "pizza fallacy" is that whenever two or more fractions are discussed in the same context, the correct assumption (the one Mark made in choosing a half of the pizza) is that the fractions are all parts of the same size whole.

Comparisons with any model can be made only if both fractions are parts of the same whole. For example, $\frac{2}{3}$ of a light green strip cannot be compared to $\frac{2}{3}$ of an orange strip.

Estimation

Early in this chapter we said that computation with fractions should probably be held off until grade 4 or later. Having said that, consider the following: For addition and subtraction of fractions, a surprising number of problems found on standardized tests can be solved with simple number sense without knowledge of an algorithm. For example, $\frac{3}{4} + \frac{1}{2}$ requires only that students can think of $\frac{3}{4}$ as $\frac{1}{2}$ and $\frac{1}{4}$ more or, alternatively, think of $\frac{1}{2}$ as $\frac{1}{4}$ and $\frac{1}{4}$. This sort of thinking is a result of a focus on fraction meanings, not on algorithms.

The development of fraction number sense, even at grade 3, should certainly involve estimation of sums and differences of fractions. Estimation focuses on the size of fractions and encourages students to use a variety of strategies.

The following activity can be used as a regular short warm-up for any fraction lesson.

ACTIVITY 9.11

First Estimates

Tell students that they are going to estimate a sum or difference of two fractions. They are to decide only if the exact answer is more or less than one. On the overhead projector show, for no more than about 10 seconds, a fraction addition or subtraction problem involving two proper fractions. Keep all denominators to 12 or less. Students write down on paper their choice of more or less than one. Do several problems in a row. Then return to each problem and discuss how students decided on their estimate.

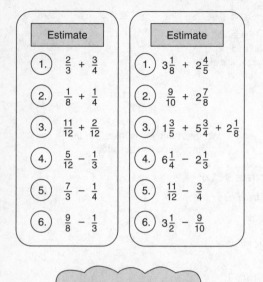

Estimate	
1.	$\frac{2}{3} + \frac{3}{4}$
2.	$\frac{1}{8} + \frac{1}{4}$
3.	$\frac{11}{12} + \frac{2}{12}$
4.	$\frac{5}{12} - \frac{1}{3}$
5.	$\frac{7}{3} - \frac{1}{4}$
6.	$\frac{9}{8} - \frac{1}{3}$

Estimate	
1.	$3\frac{1}{8} + 2\frac{4}{5}$
2.	$\frac{9}{10} + 2\frac{7}{8}$
3.	$1\frac{3}{5} + 5\frac{3}{4} + 2\frac{1}{8}$
4.	$6\frac{1}{4} - 2\frac{1}{3}$
5.	$\frac{11}{12} - \frac{3}{4}$
6.	$3\frac{1}{2} - \frac{9}{10}$

Number your papers 1 to 6. Write only answers.

Estimate!
Use whole numbers and easy fractions.

FIGURE 9.15 • • • • • • • • • • • • • • • • •

Fraction estimation drill.

Restricting Activity 9.11 to proper fractions keeps the difficulty to a minimum. When students are ready for a tougher challenge, choose from the following variations:

- Use fractions that are less than one. Estimate to the nearest half (0, $\frac{1}{2}$, 1, 1$\frac{1}{2}$, 2).
- Use both proper and mixed fractions. Estimate to the nearest half.
- Use proper and mixed fractions. Estimate the best answer you can.

In the discussions following these estimation exercises, ask students if they think that the exact answer is more or less than the estimate that they gave. What is their reasoning?

Figure 9.15 shows both an early and a later set of sums and differences that might be used in a "First Estimates" activity.

STOP **Test your own estimation skills with the sample problems in Figure 9.15. Look at each computation for only about 10 seconds and write down an estimate. After writing down all six of your estimates, look at the problems and decide if your estimate is higher or lower than the actual computation. Don't guess! Have a good reason.**

In most cases students' estimates should not be much more than $\frac{1}{2}$ away from the exact sum or difference.

Equivalent-Fraction Concepts

STOP **How do you know that $\frac{4}{6} = \frac{2}{3}$? Before reading further, think of at least two different explanations.**

Concepts Versus Rules

Here are some possible answers to the question just posed:

1. They are the same because you can reduce $\frac{4}{6}$ and get $\frac{2}{3}$.
2. If you have a set of 6 things and you take 4 of them, that would be $\frac{4}{6}$. But you can make the 6 into groups of 2. So then there would be 3 groups, and the 4 would be 2 groups out of the 3 groups. That means it's $\frac{2}{3}$.

3. If you start with $\frac{2}{3}$, you can multiply the top and the bottom numbers by 2, and that will give you $\frac{4}{6}$, so they are equal.
4. If you had a square cut into 3 parts and you shaded 2, that would be $\frac{2}{3}$ shaded. If you cut all 3 of these parts in half, that would be 4 parts shaded and 6 parts in all. That's $\frac{4}{6}$, and it would be the same amount.

All of these answers are correct. But let's think about what they tell us. Responses 2 and 4 are very conceptual, although not very efficient. The procedural responses, 1 and 3, are quite efficient but indicate no conceptual knowledge. All students should eventually be able to write an equivalent fraction for a given fraction. At the same time, the rules should never be taught or used until the students understand what the result means. Consider how different the algorithm and the concept appear to be.

Concept: Two fractions are equivalent if they are representations for the same amount or quantity—if they are the same number.

Algorithm: To get an equivalent fraction, multiply (or divide) the top and bottom numbers by the same nonzero number.

In a problem-based classroom, students can develop an understanding of equivalent fractions and also develop from that understanding a conceptually based algorithm. As with most algorithms, a serious instructional error is to rush too quickly to the rule. Be patient! Intuitive methods are always best at first.

Equivalent-Fraction Concepts

The general approach to helping students create an understanding of equivalent fractions is to have them use models to find different names for a fraction. Consider that this is the first time in their experience that a fixed quantity can have multiple names (actually an infinite number). The following activities are possible starting places.

ACTIVITY 9.12

Different Fillers

Using circular pie pieces, prepare a worksheet with two or at most three outlines of different fractions. Do not limit yourself to unit fractions. For example, you might draw an outline for $\frac{2}{3}$, $\frac{1}{2}$, and $\frac{3}{4}$. The students' task is to use their own fraction pieces to find as many single-fraction names for the region as possible. After completing the three examples, have students write about the ideas or patterns they may have noticed in finding the names. Follow the activity with a class discussion.

BLM 33

In the class discussion following the "Different Fillers" activity, a good question to ask involves what names could be found if students had any size pieces that they wanted. For example, ask students "What names could you find if we had sixteenths in our fraction kit? What names could you find if you could have any piece at all?" The idea is to push beyond filling in the region in a pure trial-and-error approach.

The following activity is just a variation of "Different Fillers." Instead of a manipulative model, the task is constructed on grid paper.

ACTIVITY 9.13

Dot Paper Equivalencies

Create a worksheet using a portion of a rectangular dot grid paper. (These can be found in the Blackline Masters.) On the grid, draw a rectangle and

(continued)

EXPANDED LESSON

(pages 273–274)
A complete lesson plan based on "Dot Paper Equivalencies" can be found at the end of this chapter.

Filling in regions with fraction pieces

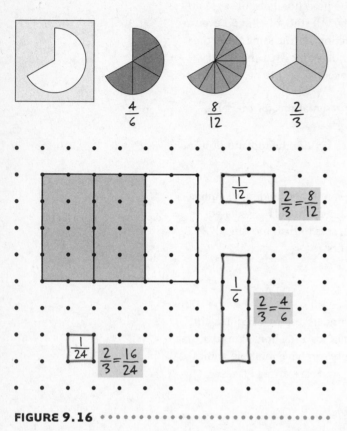

FIGURE 9.16

Area models for equivalent fractions.

Fraction strips

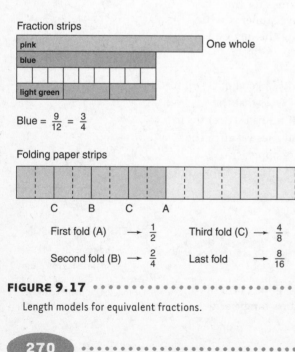

FIGURE 9.17

Length models for equivalent fractions.

designate it as one whole. Lightly shade a fractional part of the region within the whole. The task is to use different parts of the whole determined by the grid to find names for the part. Figure 9.16 includes an example. Students should draw a picture of the unit fractional part that they use for each fraction name. The larger the size of the whole, the more names the activity will generate.

The "Dot Paper Equivalencies" activity is a form of what Lamon (2002) calls "unitizing," that is, given a quantity, finding different ways to chunk the quantity into parts in order to name it.

Length models can be used to create activities similar to the "Different Fillers" task. For example, as shown in Figure 9.17, rods or strips can be used to designate both a whole and a part. Students use smaller rods to find fraction names for the given part. To have larger wholes and, thus, more possible parts, use a train of two or three rods for the whole and the part. Folding paper strips is another method of creating fraction names. In the example shown in Figure 9.17, one-half is subdivided by successive folding in half. Other folds would produce other names and these possibilities should be discussed if no one tries to fold the strip in an odd number of parts.

The following activity is also a unitizing activity in which students look for different units or chunks of the whole in order to name a part of the whole in different ways. This activity is significant because it utilizes a set model.

ACTIVITY 9.14

Group the Counters, Find the Names

Have students set out a specific number of counters in two colors—for example, 24 counters, 16 of them red and 8 yellow. The 24 make up the whole. The task is to group the counters into different fractional parts of the whole and use the parts to create fraction names for the red and the yellow counters. In Figure 9.18, 24 counters are arranged in different array patterns. You might want to suggest arrays or allow students to arrange them in any way they wish. Students should record their different groupings and explain how they found the fraction names.

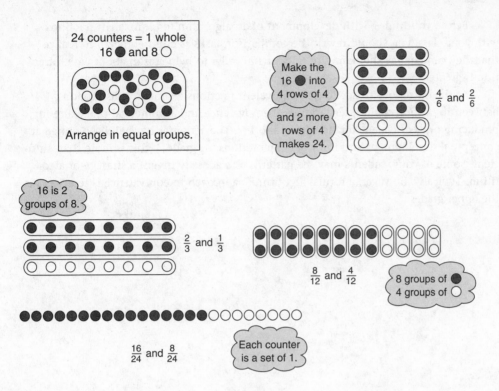

FIGURE 9.18 • • • • • • • • • •

Set models for equivalent fractions.

In Lamon's version of the last activity, she prompts students with questions such as, "If we make groups of four, what part of the set is red?" For our example in Figure 9.18, groups of four counters, the black portion is named $\frac{4}{6}$.

In the activities so far, there has only been a hint of a rule for finding equivalent fractions. The following activity moves a bit closer but should still be done before development of a rule.

ACTIVITY 9.15

Missing-Number Equivalencies

Give students an equation expressing an equivalence between two fractions but with one of the numbers missing. Here are four different examples:

$$\frac{5}{3} = \frac{\square}{6} \qquad \frac{2}{3} = \frac{6}{\square} \qquad \frac{8}{12} = \frac{\square}{3} \qquad \frac{9}{12} = \frac{3}{\square}$$

The missing number can be either a numerator or a denominator. Furthermore, the missing number can either be larger or smaller than the corresponding part of the equivalent fraction. (All four of these possibilities are represented in the examples.) The task is to find the missing number and to explain your solution.

When doing "Missing-Number Equivalencies" you may want to specify a particular model, such as sets or pie pieces. Alternatively, you can allow students to select whatever methods they wish to solve these problems. One or two equivalencies followed by a discussion is sufficient for a good lesson. This activity is surprisingly challenging, especially if students are required to use a set model.

Before continuing with development of an algorithm for equivalent fractions with your class, you should revisit the comparison tasks as children begin to realize that they can change the names of fractions in order to help reason about which fraction is greater.

At the outset of this section on equivalent fractions we made a distinction between the conceptual understanding of equivalence and a numerical procedure for producing one equivalent fraction from another. The activities have all been aimed at conceptual development and informal explorations. At grade 3, this is more than sufficient. Some of your students may see patterns and actually invent a strategy or algorithm. Typically, however, a formal algorithmic approach to equivalence is reserved for the upper grades.

Chapter 9   EARLY FRACTION CONCEPTS

EXPANDED LESSON

Dot Paper Equivalencies

Based on: Activity 9.13, p. 269

GRADE LEVEL: Third or fourth grade.

MATHEMATICS GOALS
- To develop a conceptual understanding of equivalent fractions; the same quantity can have different fraction names.
- To look for patterns in equivalent fractions.

THINKING ABOUT THE STUDENTS
Students should have a good understanding of what the top and bottom numbers (numerator and denominator) in a fraction stand for. Although this is an early activity in developing equivalent fraction concepts, it is probably not the best first activity. "Different Fillers" (Activity 9.12) is a better first activity for equivalent fractions.

MATERIALS PREPARATION
- A transparency of a centimeter dot grid (Blackline Master 31).
- Copies of the "Fraction Names" worksheet for each student (Blackline Master L-5) plus a transparency for use in the AFTER portion of the lesson.

....

lesson

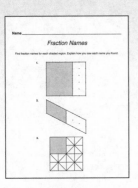

BLM L-5

BEFORE

Begin with a Simpler Version of the Task
- On the dot transparency outline a 3 by 3 rectangle and shade in $\frac{2}{3}$ of it as shown here.

- Tell this story: *Two students looked at this picture. Each saw a different fraction. Kyle saw $\frac{6}{9}$, but Terri said she saw $\frac{2}{3}$.* Ask: *How can they see the same drawing and yet each see different fractions? Which one is right? Why?*
- Have students come to the front of the class and offer explanations for how Kyle saw the picture and how Terri saw it. When students in the class agree on and also understand a correct explanation, draw the corresponding unit fraction to aid in understanding. For example, you can explain: *Terri saw a row of three squares as $\frac{1}{3}$.* (Draw a row of 3 squares to the side of the rectangle.) *If a row of 3 squares is $\frac{1}{3}$, then there are two rows of three squares shaded. Therefore, the shaded portion is $\frac{2}{3}$.* Similarly, be sure that students see that one square is $\frac{1}{9}$ of the whole. *Since there are 6 squares shaded, the shaded part is $\frac{6}{9}$.*

The Task
- For each outlined region on the worksheet, find as many fraction names as possible.

Establish Expectations
- For each fraction name, students draw a picture of a fractional part and use words to tell how they found that fraction name for the shaded portion.

DURING
- For students who are having difficulty getting started, draw a fractional part for them. For example, for 1, draw a two-square rectangle. Ask: *How many rectangles like this make up the whole?* Try not to give more assistance than is absolutely necessary to get students on track.
- Students who do not seem to understand counting the fractional parts may need more development of the meaning of top and bottom numbers.
- For students who seem to have finished quickly, make sure first that their explanations reflect their capabilities. Also, consider challenging them to find even more names. In number 2, for example, a small triangle can be used as a unit to produce $\frac{12}{24}$.

....

273

AFTER

- Use a transparency of the worksheet to help students share their ideas. For each drawing on the worksheet, first make a list of all of the fraction names that students have found for the shaded region. Record these on the board without comment even if some are incorrect. Then have students explain how they got the fractions. Let one student explain one fraction, not all of them. Be sure students all agree and understand. For some explanations, other students may have used a differently shaped unit fraction. For example, in the first drawing, four squares make $\frac{1}{6}$ and can be used to name the shaded region as $\frac{4}{6}$. Some students may have used a column of four squares and others a 2-by-2 arrangement of four squares. Although completely the same, students should be allowed to discuss this.

- The first region can be named $\frac{2}{3}$, $\frac{4}{6}$, $\frac{8}{12}$, and $\frac{16}{24}$. Of course, a 1-by-1 square could be halved to produce $\frac{32}{48}$. Also, note that three squares is $\frac{1}{8}$ of the whole. Can the shaded region be named with eighths? Yes! The shaded region contains $5\frac{1}{3}$ eighths; $5\frac{1}{3}$ in the numerator. It is unlikely that students will think of this.

- The second region can be named $\frac{1}{2}$, $\frac{2}{4}$, $\frac{3}{6}$, and $\frac{6}{12}$. If a small triangle is used, it can be seen as $\frac{12}{24}$. If a trapezoid of three triangles is used, it is $\frac{4}{8}$. Students may divide it up in other ways as well.

- The last region also has lots of names from $\frac{1}{4}$ to $\frac{8}{32}$.

- If time permits, you may want to focus attention on all of the names for one region and discuss any patterns that students may observe.

ASSESSMENT NOTES

- The issue of greatest concern will be the students who, even after marking off an appropriate unit fraction, cannot correctly name the shaded portion. For example, in the third figure, if the full shaded region is used as the unit (fourths), some students may write $\frac{1}{3}$ (1 region to 3 regions) or in other ways still not know how to name the fraction. These students will need further foundational work with fraction concepts.

- Do not be concerned if students do not find all of the fraction names that are possible. The goal is not to exhaust the possibilities but to develop the understanding that a given quantity can have multiple names.

- For students who seem to find this activity easy, see if they can generate other fraction names for these regions by looking at the fractions they have already found and seeing if they can discover a rule for generating more.

- For students who have had serious difficulty with this lesson, you will want to explore their understanding of what the numerator and denominator mean—the denominator tells us what type of fractional part is being used to name the fraction, and the numerator counts how many of these fractional parts are being considered. The parts-and-whole tasks (see pp. 260–261) are appropriate.

- Even if students showed understanding with this lesson, it is important to explore the same concept with a set model as in Activity 9.14, "Group the Counters, Find the Names." Activity 9.15 can then be explored with students being permitted to use a model of their choice.

next steps

ALGEBRAIC REASONING

*P*rinciples and Standards for School Mathematics (NCTM, 2000) lists algebra as one of the five content strands for pre-K–12 mathematics. Today, most states also have an algebra component to their curricula. Rather than the algebra you may remember from your high school days, the algebra intended for K–8 focuses on patterns, relationships and functions, and the use of various representations—symbolic, numeric, and graphic—to help make sense of all sorts of mathematical situations. As students become comfortable with these ideas and methods of representation, they will begin to utilize them in nearly all of mathematics, not just in a study of algebraic ideas.

It is common today to hear or read about *algebraic reasoning* or *algebraic thinking.* This involves the way a student uses the content of algebra—patterns, representations, and functions—in generalizing and formalizing regularity in all aspects of mathematics. Activities aimed at the goal of algebraic thinking should begin in kindergarten and continue to develop across the years, and not just in algebra lessons but to some extent in all of the other strands of mathematics.

This chapter focuses on the content of algebra: pattern and regularity, representation and symbolism, and relationships and functions.

big ideas

1 Logical patterns exist and are a regular occurrence in mathematics. They can be recognized, extended, and generalized with both words and symbols. The same pattern can be found in many different forms. Patterns are found in physical and geometric situations as well as in numbers.

2 A variety of representations such as diagrams, number lines, charts, and graphs can be used to illustrate mathematical situations and relationships. These representations help in conceptualizing ideas and in solving problems.

3 Symbolism, especially that involving equations and variables, is used to express generalizations of patterns and relationships.

4 Variables are symbols that take the place of numbers or ranges of numbers. They have different meanings depending on whether they are being used as representations of quantities that vary or change, representations of specific unknown values, or placeholders in a generalized expression or formula.

5 Equations and inequalities are used to express relationships between two quantities. Symbolism on either side of an equation or inequality represents a quantity. Thus, $3 + 8$ and $5n + 2$ are both expressions for numbers, not something "to do."

6 Functions are a special type of relationship or rule that uniquely associate members of one set with members of another set. For example, *one-more-than* is a functional relationship on the set of all numbers. It associates the number 3 with 4 and the number 2386 with 2387. Another example of a function is the rule that associates any polygon with the number of vertices of that polygon.

Repeating Patterns

Identifying and extending patterns is an important process in algebraic thinking. Simple repetitive patterns can and should be explored as early as kindergarten.

Using Materials in Patterning

When possible, patterning activities should involve some form of physical materials. This is especially true of repeating patterns in grades K–3. When patterns are built with materials, children are able to test the extension of a pattern and make changes without fear of being wrong.

Many kindergarten and first-grade textbooks have pages where students are given a pattern such as a string of colored beads. The task may be to color the last bead or two in the string. There are two differences between this and the same activity done with actual materials. First, by coloring on the page, the activity takes on an aura of right versus wrong. If a mistake is made, correction on the page is difficult and can cause feelings of inadequacy. Materials allow a trial-and-error approach to be used. Second, pattern activities on worksheets prevent children from extending patterns beyond the few spaces provided by the page. Most children enjoy using materials such as colored blocks, buttons, and connecting cubes to extend their patterns well beyond the printed page. Children are frequently observed continuing a pattern with materials halfway across the classroom floor.

Repeating-Pattern Activities

The concept of a repeating pattern and how a pattern is extended or continued can be introduced to the full class in several ways. One possibility is to draw simple shape patterns on the board and extend them in a class discussion. Oral patterns can be joined in by all children. For example, "do, mi, mi, do, mi, mi, . . ." is a simple singing pattern. Up, down, and sideways arm positions provide three elements with which to make patterns: up, side, side, down, up, side, side, down, ... From these ideas, the youngest children learn quickly the concept of patterns. Children can explore patterns with all sorts of materials. Pattern elements might be pictures from a circus unit, symbols related to a holiday, sponge- painted designs, letters of the alphabet, blocks from the block corner, and so on. It is especially useful to integrate pattern activities with other activities in your school day.

ACTIVITY 10.1

Pattern Strips

Students can work independently or in groups of two or three to extend patterns made from simple materials: buttons, colored blocks, connecting cubes, toothpicks, geometric shapes—items you can gather easily. For each set of materials, draw two or three complete repetitions of a pattern on strips of tagboard about 5 cm by 30 cm. The students' task is to use actual materials, copy the pattern shown, and extend it as far as they wish. Figure 10.1 illustrates possible patterns for a variety of materials. Make 10 to 15 different pattern strips for each set of materials. With six to eight sets, your entire class can work at the same time in small groups working with different patterns and different materials.

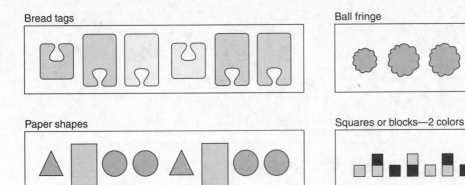

Bread tags

Ball fringe

Paper shapes

Squares or blocks—2 colors

Pattern blocks

Keys

Toothpicks

FIGURE 10.1 •

Examples of pattern cards drawn on tagboard. Each pattern repeats completely and does not split in the middle of a core.

The *core* of a repeating pattern is the shortest string of elements that repeats. Notice in Figure 10.1 that the core is always fully repeated and never only partially shown. If the core of a pattern is –oo, a card might have –oo–oo (two repetitions of the core), but it would be ambiguous if the card showed –oo–oo– or –oo–.

A significant step forward mathematically is to see that two patterns constructed with different materials are actually the same pattern. For example, the first pattern in Figure 10.1 and the first pattern in Figure 10.2 can both be "read" A-B-B-A-B-B-, and the pattern below those in both figures is A-B-C-C-A-B-C-C-. Translating two or more essentially alike patterns to a common format helps children to go beyond the materials making up the pattern and to see the fundamental mathematical structure involved. Using some form of symbolism (in this case the alphabet) to represent the structure of a pattern is a beginning of algebraic reasoning.

The following activities reflect this powerful algebraic concept of repeating patterns.

ACTIVITY 10.2

Pattern Match

Using the chalkboard or overhead projector, show six or seven patterns with different materials or pictures. Teach students to use an A, B, C method of reading a pattern. Half of the class can close their eyes while the other half uses the A, B, C scheme to read a pattern that you point to. After hearing the pattern, the students who had their eyes closed examine the patterns and try to decide which pattern was read. If two of the patterns in the list have the same structure, the discussion can be very interesting.

FIGURE 10.2 ·······

More examples of repeating patterns.

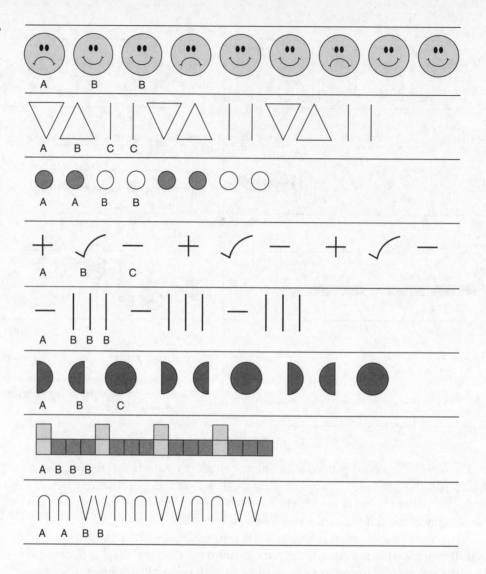

The following independent activity involves translation of a pattern from one medium to another, which is another way of helping students separate the relationship in a pattern from the materials used to build it.

ACTIVITY 10.3

Same Pattern, Different Stuff

Have students make a pattern with one set of materials given a pattern strip showing a different set. This activity can easily be set up by simply switching the pattern strips from one set of materials to another. A similar idea is to mix up the pattern strips for four or five different sets of materials and have students find strips that have the same pattern. To test if two patterns are the same, children can translate each of the strips into a third set of materials or can write down the A, B, C pattern for each.

Many teachers have their students make up patterns and then have other students extend them. Although this is an opportunity for creative work, having students make up patterns is a limited learning experience because no new ideas are explored. Rather, students have a tendency to create long "complicated" patterns and then have difficulty identifying the core of their pattern.

Extensions and Challenges

The activities described so far are not uncommon in the K–1 curriculum. However, students in grades 2 and 3 should also have experiences with repeating patterns. There are several ways that repeat patterns can be made quite challenging and profitable beyond the first grade.

The challenge in the next activity is a forerunner to looking at the function aspect of patterns.

ACTIVITY 10.4

Predict Down the Line

For most repeating patterns, the elements of the pattern can be numbered 1, 2, 3, and so on. Provide students with a pattern to extend. Before students begin to extend the pattern, have them predict exactly what element will be in the number 15 position or the number 27 position. Students should be required to provide a reason for their prediction, preferably in writing. Students should then extend the pattern as before and check their prediction. If their prediction is incorrect, have them examine their reasoning and try to figure out why the prediction was off.

The prediction activity may be quite challenging before the second grade. Eventually, students will figure out that the length of the core of the pattern plays a significant role. If you ask for a prediction of the hundredth element or even the three-hundredth element, students will not be able to check the prediction by extending the pattern. Verification focuses on the rationale for the prediction. Students may need to use a calculator to skip-count or multiply. But it is always the reasoning that is most important.

A variation of the prediction activity adds yet another challenge. Suppose that you are working with a red-blue-blue-red-blue-blue pattern made of blocks. Instead of asking what will be in position 38, ask in what position will the 38th blue block be? What color will come after it? Notice that it is more difficult to locate the position of an element that repeats in the pattern. The same question is more difficult for this pattern: blue-blue-blue-red.

Typically we think of repeating patterns extending in a line. Figure 10.3 illustrates how repeat patterns can be positioned on a grid. Notice that the size of the grid affects how the pattern appears. It is interesting to observe how the pattern elements tend to make diagonal or column patterns. As illustrated with the following activity, patterns on a grid give rise to new questions that can be asked.

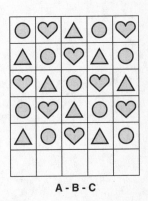

A - B - C   A - A - B - C   A - B - C

FIGURE 10.3

Repeat patterns can be transferred or built on a grid. In the examples shown, the patterns begin in the upper left corners and go left to right, beginning each new line on the left.

Grid Patterns

Provide students with centimeter grid paper. On the paper they can mark off grids that are the width that they want to use: 3, 4, 5, or 6 squares wide. As an initial introduction to patterns on these grids, have them record an A-B-B-C pattern on a 3-square-wide grid. They can use crayons and make colored dots or circles to record the patterns. Discuss what they see after recording five or six rows in the grid. Next have them record the same pattern on a 4-square-wide grid. They will notice that the colors all line up in columns. What would happen with an A-B-C pattern? Suggest five or six different patterns for students to explore on the grid paper in any way that they wish. Have them write about what they have discovered.

As described, "Grid Patterns" is only the introduction to patterns on a grid. Once students are familiar with the results of placing patterns on a grid, try some of the following challenges. Begin by giving them a pattern to use, such as A-A-B-C.

- What grid sizes will result in a pattern of columns of colors?

- In a 3-grid, what rows will be the same as the first row? How did you decide? Answer the same question for a 5-grid.

- On what size grids will the B color make a diagonal from left to right? Right to left?

- What will be in the 15th row of a 3-grid? What will be in the 15th row of a 5-grid? The 100th row?

- What patterns happen in the columns? How will the column patterns change if you change the grid size?

You may find additional challenges to pose. The interesting feature is the interaction between the length of the core of the pattern and the width of the grids. All students will be able to answer most of these questions by simply making the grids and filling them in. Some may be able to use the numbers involved to offer a more sophisticated explanation.

Assessment Note

Although we have been talking only about repeating patterns, the discussion has included a wide range of problem difficulty. Kindergarten and first-grade children should be able to copy a given pattern and extend it using the same materials. By late first or second grade it is reasonable that students should be able to translate patterns using letters and should be able to match one pattern with an equivalent one. Identification of the core of a pattern is not always easy for students at this level, but most second-grade students should be able to do this. Assessing these skills is simply a matter of observation while students are doing the related tasks.

Tasks that require numeric reasoning are considerably more difficult. "Predict Down the Line" will be challenging for second graders but is certainly appropriate for third-grade students. Second-grade students may also have difficulty with predicting how patterns are going to look on a grid (columns or diagonals). These challenges allow you to extend pattern activities for all of your students before going to the next step of growing patterns.

Growing Patterns

By third grade, students can begin to explore patterns that involve a progression from step to step. In technical terms, these are called *sequences;* we will simply call them *growing patterns.*

Figure 10.4 illustrates some growing patterns that can be built with various materials or drawn on grids. The patterns consist of a series of separate steps, with each new step related to the previous one according to the pattern.

The first thing to do with growing patterns is to get students comfortable building them and talking about how they can be extended. Building the patterns with physical materials such as tiles, counters, or flat toothpicks allows students to make changes if necessary and to build on to one step to make a new step. It is also more fun! Some growing patterns get quite large quickly and can require more materials than you have. One solution to this dilemma is to have students make a step with materials and then draw it on grid paper. In this way, they will only need enough materials to make one step at a time.

The following activity will introduce growing patterns to your students.

ACTIVITY 10.6

Extend and Explain

Show students the first three or four steps of a pattern. Provide them with appropriate materials and grid paper, have them extend the patterns recording each step, and explain why their extension indeed follows the pattern.

FIGURE 10.4 • • • • • • • •

Growing patterns with materials or drawings.

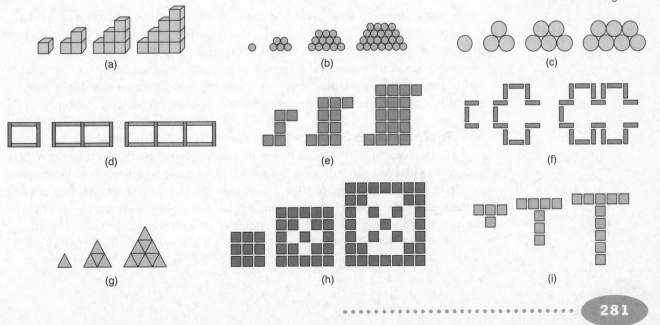

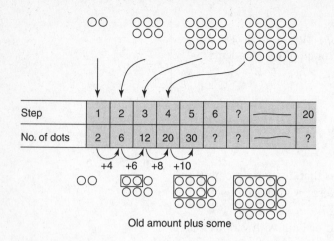

Old amount plus some

FIGURE 10.5 •

A table records a number for each step. It is useful to try to see how each new step is built on the preceding step.

When discussing a pattern, students should try to determine how each step in the pattern differs from the preceding step. If each new step can be built by adding on to or changing the previous step, the discussion should include how this can be done. For example, each stairstep in Figure 10.4a can be made by adding a column of blocks to the preceding stairsteps. In contrast, the square pattern of tiles (Figure 10.4h) involves a form of expansion rather than adding on.

Growing patterns also have a numeric component, the number of objects in each step. As shown in Figure 10.5, a table can be made for any growing pattern. One row of the table or chart is always the number of steps, and the other is for recording how many objects are in that step. Frequently, a pattern grows so quickly and requires so many blocks or spaces to draw it that it is only reasonable to build or draw the first five or six steps. This leads to the following activity.

ACTIVITY 10.7

Predict How Many

Have students begin to extend a growing pattern you provide. They should also make a table showing how many items are needed to make each step of the pattern. The task is to predict the number of items in the tenth or fifteenth step of the pattern. Predictions should also be accompanied by an explanation.

Activity 10.7 is a natural progression from the earlier prediction activities with repeating patterns.

Searching for Relationships

Once a table or chart is developed, students have two representations of the pattern: the one created with the drawing or materials and the numeric version that is in the table. When looking for relationships, some students will focus on the table and others will focus on the physical pattern. It is important for students to see that whatever relationships they discover, they exist in both forms. So if a relationship is found in a table, challenge students to see how that plays out in the physical version.

Patterns from Step to Step: Recursive Relationships

For most students, it is easier to see the patterns from one step to the next. When you have a chart constructed, the differences from one step to the next can be written next to or below it, as in Figure 10.5. In that example, the number in each step can be determined from the previous step by adding successive even numbers. The description that tells how a pattern changes from step to step is known as a *recursive relationship*.

Whenever there is a pattern in the table, see if students can find that same pattern in the physical version. In Figure 10.5, notice that in each step, the previous step

has been outlined. That lets you examine the amount added and see how it creates the pattern of adding on even numbers. The picture or physical pattern and the table should be as closely connected as possible.

Patterns from Step Number to Step: Functional Relationships

The recursive step-to-step pattern is almost certainly the first that your students will observe. However, to find the table entry for the hundredth step, the only way a recursive pattern can help is to find all of the prior 99 entries in the table. If a rule or relationship can be discovered that connects the number of objects in a step to the number of the step, any table entry can be determined without building or calculating all of the intermediate entries. A rule that determines the number of elements in a step from the step number is an example of a *functional relationship*.

It is not reasonable to expect third-grade students to discover functional relationships. There is plenty of time for that in the next several years. At this level, it is appropriate only that you, as the teacher, are aware of the concept of function that is implicit in the growing patterns that your students are exploring. You may even have some students who could be profitably challenged to determine the hundredth entry in a table without having to find all of the entries that precede it.

Graphing the Patterns

So far, growing patterns are represented by the physical materials or drawings and by a chart. We also know that a symbolic rule or functional representation is possible. A graph of the data from the growing pattern adds another way of seeing these data. A graph is a significant form of representation in mathematics. The growing patterns are a good opportunity to expose students to this powerful way to see a relationship.

Before making a graph, students should extend a growing pattern and make a table of values, as discussed previously. Even if the physical pattern could not be created for more than five or six steps, students should use the recursive pattern to find at least the first ten entries. It is not the procedure for making graphs that is important but seeing the result and understanding what it represents. In fact, you may have a simple graphing program on your computer that will plot the points for the students. Figure 10.6 shows a growing pattern of dots forming rectangles. The table and graph were made with a simple spreadsheet.

Perhaps the easiest way for students to make a graph is to use centimeter grid paper. Show them how to number each line along the bottom of the graph to correspond to the step numbers. If the numbers in the table are greater than 20, help them use a multiple of 2 or 5 for each square along the vertical axis. After showing students how to plot a few pairs from the table, they should be able to finish the graph.

In the pattern shown in Figure 10.6, notice that the recursive pattern is constant. That is, the change from each step to the next is always 4; four additional dots are added at each step. When the recursive pattern is constant as in this example, the points in the graph will be in a straight line. If the recursive pattern changes from one step to another, the dots in the graph will form a curved line. (When the graph is curved, the functional rule or relationship is generally even more difficult to discover than for straight lines.)

FIGURE 10.6 ●●●●●●●

A growing figure, a table, and a graph: three representations of the same relationship. The table and graph were created in a simple spreadsheet designed for young students (E-Tools, Scott Foresman, 2004).

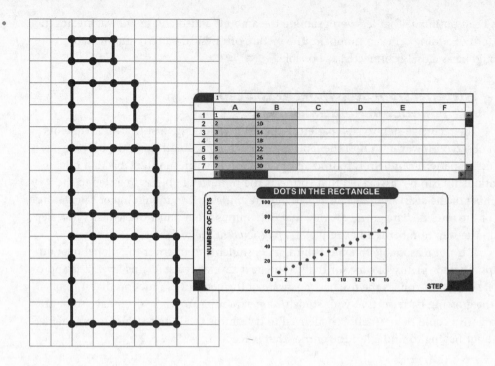

Assessment Note

Late second or third grade is just the beginning stage of working with growing patterns. At this level you should be satisfied if students can build successive steps of a growing pattern and can explain in words how it is growing. Remember that when the next step can be built on the previous one, the pattern will be easier for students to see and extend.

It is important to connect the numbers in the tables or charts that students build with the actual patterns. After students have constructed a chart for their pattern, select different numbers in the chart and ask them to explain where these numbers came from. Include the step number in this discussion as well.

If you have students who are especially capable, challenge them by having them try to find a general rule for the growing pattern. This is the rule that tells how many elements are in each step of the pattern by simply knowing what the step number is. For example, in the dotted rectangle pattern (Figure 10.6), the number of dots used in each step is $4 \times N + 2$ or four times the step number plus two more.

Patterns with Numbers

The patterns discussed so far, repeating and growing patterns, are far from the only patterns in mathematics. Our number system is full of wonderful patterns. Numbers not only offer children an opportunity to explore patterns but also to learn to expect, see, and use patterns in all of mathematics.

Number Patterns

The simplest form of a number pattern is a string of numbers that follows some rule for determining how the string continues.

ACTIVITY 10.8

What's Next and Why?

Show students five or six numbers from a number pattern. The task for students is to extend the pattern for several more numbers and to explain the rule for generating the pattern. The difficulty of the task depends on the number pattern and the familiarity of students with searching for patterns. Here is a short list of patterns, some easy enough for kindergarten.

1, 2, 1, 2, 1, 2, . . .	a simple alternating scheme
1, 2, 2, 3, 3, 3, . . .	each digit repeats according to its value
5, 1, 5, 2, 5, 3, . . .	the counting sequence interspersed with 5s
2, 4, 6, 8, 10, . . .	even numbers—skip counting by 2
1, 2, 4, 5, 7, 8, 10, . . .	two counts, then skip one
1, 2, 4, 8, 16, . . .	double the previous number
2, 5, 11, 23, . . .	double the previous number and add 1
1, 2, 4, 7, 11, 16, . . .	successively increase the skip count
1, 4, 9, 16, 25, . . .	squares: $1^2, 2^2, 3^2, . . .$
0, 1, 5, 14, 30, . . .	add the next square number
2, 2, 4, 6, 10, 16, . . .	add the preceding two numbers

Most of the preceding examples also have variations you can try. Make up your own or challenge students to make up their own number pattern rules.

Skip counts by 2, 5, and 10 are part of most K–2 curricula. However, skip counting can be an excellent source of patterns and can help students begin to do some serious reasoning about numbers.

The calculator can skip count by any amount beginning anywhere. For example, to count by 3s, enter [0] [+] [3] [=]. (The 0 isn't necessary but is a good idea with young children.) Successive presses of the [=] key will count on from 3 by 3s. To skip count by 3s from a different number, say 16, simply press [1] [6] [+] [3] and continue pressing the [=] key. What is happening is that the calculator "remembers" the last operation, in this case "+3" and adds that to whatever is currently in the window whenever the [=] key is pressed. The [=] will continue to have this effect until an operation key is pressed.

ACTIVITY 10.9

Calculator Skip Counting

If you've not done so, teach students how to make their calculators count by 2s. When the children are able to do this without pressing a new operation key—which is what they have a tendency to do—show them how to change the beginning number. For example, press [5] [+] [2] [=], [=], [=], ... They can return to beginning the count at 5 (or any other number) by pressing 5 and continuing to press [=].

(continued)

Now challenge students working in pairs to say the next number before they press the ▣ key. Have them hold their finger over the ▣ button and say the next skip count, press the ▣ to confirm or correct, and then continue, always trying to say the next count before pressing the key.

As students skip count on the calculator, discuss the patterns that they see. For example, when counting by 2s starting with 0, they see numbers ending in 0, 2, 4, 6, and 8, and then that pattern repeats. Note how this same sequence appears if you begin with any even number, such as 34 (although the sequence begins with 4 instead of 0). If counting by 2s beginning with 1, the numbers are odd: 1, 3, 5, 7, and 9.

When students have become comfortable skip counting by small numbers, suggest that they try a "big" number. Begin by suggesting counting by 20 or 50. These large numbers will seem very difficult to students, who will then be surprised to recognize familiar patterns in the tens and hundreds places. Continue as appropriate with challenges to count by 25 or by 30 or 40. Other good skip-count numbers are 9, 11, 12, 15, or 21.

The next activity encourages students to be even more analytic about these patterns.

ACTIVITY 10.10

Start and Jump Numbers

To begin this activity, have students make a list of numbers beginning with 3 and skip counting by 5. The 3 is called the "start number" and 5 is the "jump number." It is helpful to make the list in a vertical column as in Figure 10.7. The task is to examine the list of numbers and find as many patterns as possible. Ideas should be shared with others in the class. Students should be sure that all suggested patterns really exist.

When students have found patterns for this first list, suggest that they change the start number and see how the patterns change. Different groups can explore different start numbers.

Next, make changes in the jump numbers. Jump-number changes will cause the patterns to change much more radically than a change in the start numbers.

FIGURE 10.7 • • • • • •

Start with a number and list the numbers that occur by skip counting according to the "jump" number. How are the patterns for the same jump numbers alike? How are they different?

Start with 3 Jump by 5s	Start with 6 Jump by 5s	Start with 5 Jump by 4s	Start with 3 Jump by 4s	Start with 2 Jump by 3
3	6	5	3	2
8	11	9	7	5
13	16	13	11	8
18	21	17	15	11
23	26	21	19	14
28	31	25	23	17
33	36	29	27	20
38	41	33	31	23
43	46	37	35	26
48	51	41	39	29
53	56	45	43	32
...	...	...	...	...

With a jump number of 5 you should see the following:

- There is at least one alternating pattern.

- There is an odd/even pattern.

- There is a pattern in the tens place as well as in the ones place. When the list goes over 100, you can think of each digit separately (1 hundred, 1 ten, 3 ones), in which case the pattern is starting over. However, you can also think of 113 as 11 tens ("eleventy-three"), in which case the pattern is continuing. Both interpretations are correct.

- Try adding the digits. For a start of 3 and a jump of 5, the numbers are 3, 8, 4, 9, 5, 10, 6, 11, 7, 12, 8, ... Examine every other number in this list. What is the sum for 113? It can either be 5 or 14 (thinking of 113 as 11 tens and 3 ones).

With a jump number of 5, the ones-place pattern repeats every two jumps—the core has a length of 2. When you change the jump numbers, you will probably change the length of this core. The core for jumps of 4, 6, and 8 all have a length of 5. Explore how these patterns are alike and different when each starts with the same number. What happens if you change the start number from one even number to another even number? Is there still a pattern when you add the digits?

With a jump number of 3, the core length is 10. If you put the ten numbers in a circle as in Figure 10.8, students can see how the order for these ten digits is the same regardless of the starting number. Try putting the ending digits in order for the shorter patterns or for other jump numbers.

Some students will want to explore these patterns even further. For example, there is no reason that jump numbers must be restricted to single digits. Calculators can be used to explore jumps by larger numbers so that tedious adding is not required.

Patterns on the Hundreds Chart

In Chapter 2, students are encouraged to look for patterns on the hundreds chart, primarily because the structure found in the chart can aid in learning to count and eventually develop ten-structured thinking. (See Activity 2.29 on p. 57.) Additional patterns can be explored beyond the simple ideas mentioned there.

FIGURE 10.8 • • • • • • •

For jumps of 3, this cycle of digits will occur in the ones place. The start number determines where the cycle begins.

ACTIVITY 10.11

Start and Jump on the Hundreds Chart

After students have explored the patterns in Activity 10.10, have them color the start-and-jump sequences on printed hundreds charts (Blackline Masters). Every skip-count number pattern will make a visual pattern on the hundreds chart.

(continued)

BLM 10

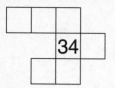

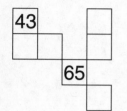

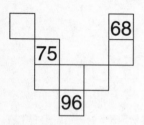

FIGURE 10.9 • • • • • •

"Fractured Chart Pieces" are partial grids from a hundreds chart. Students fill in the missing numbers. Worksheets can be sketched by hand. With more numbers in the piece, students get additional clues to check the numbers they provide. Some students may need to see a hundreds chart to complete the pieces.

Questions that students can explore include:

- How do patterns change when only the start number changes?
- How are the diagonal patterns alike and different for jumps of 4, 6, and 8?
- Which skip counts make diagonal patterns and which make column patterns?
- Pick any number between 1 and 100. How can you tell if your pattern will land on that number?

Even if students are unable to articulate the interesting patterns that they observe, coloring the different patterns—one pattern per chart—is interesting and pleasing in itself.

For students still developing their understanding of the structure of the numbers 1 to 100, the following activity can help.

ACTIVITY 10.12

Fractured Chart Pieces

Prepare worksheets similar to those shown in Figure 10.9. Each collection of squares represents a portion of the hundreds chart. Technically, it is sufficient to provide only one number in a piece and the remaining numbers can be filled in. Some children may benefit by having two or even three numbers filled in. To make the task accessible to all children, a hundreds chart can be made available to those who need assistance.

Some may wish to argue that "Fractured Chart Pieces" is more about numeration than algebra. However, because algebra is about looking for pattern and regularity in all of mathematics, it is appropriate to encourage algebraic thinking embedded in numeration activities and in all aspects of the mathematics curriculum.

Assessment Note

As your students work on the number patterns and other activities discussed in this chapter, try not to think about the activities in terms of mastery. It is not reasonable at any grade level to say "my students have mastered number patterns." There are number patterns appropriate for kindergarten and others that will challenge capable high school students. (Those we've included are about right for the K–3 child.) Instead, look for how individual students are able to reason with the patterns you explore. Ideas about place value are included in many of the pattern ideas we've just discussed. If a student is having difficulty with skip counts beyond 20, or with "Fractured Chart Pieces," you should probably be examining his or her understanding of place-value concepts.

For students whose number concepts are still developing, encourage them to use a hundreds chart or number line to keep track of patterns and counting. Use "Calculator Skip Counting" (Activity 10.9) as a one-on-one assessment. First check skip counts by 2s, 5s, and 10s, starting with 0. Then see if they can count by these numbers starting at a number other than zero. Do students actually count from one number to the next, or can they "jump" to the next number? For a second- or third-grade child, it is especially important to be able to quickly skip count by 10 beginning with any number. A hundreds chart is the best tool for remediation.

Patterns with Operations

Interesting and useful patterns can be found in the operations on numbers as well as patterns made with numbers. The following tasks are each in the form of explorations. That is, students are asked to explore a situation and see what they can find out about that situation. What is alike? What is different? How do things change?

ACTIVITY 10.13

How Many Ways?

Select a number that students are working on, such as 8. The task is to explore how many different ways there are to add two numbers to make 8. Students should use numbers, words, and pictures to show what they have found out. If students think they have solved this problem for 8, have them try a different number.

Many students will approach "How Many Ways?" in a seemingly haphazard fashion, writing down all of the sums they can think of in any order. Other students will try to make an orderly list such as 1 + 7, 2 + 6, 3 + 5, 4 + 4. They often forget the combinations with 0. There will most certainly be a discussion about the "turnaround" combinations or commutative pairs. That is, is 2 + 6 different than 6 + 2? Students should decide how they think the combinations should be counted. The most interesting generalization will appear if the commutative pairs are counted separately. In that case, there is always one more combination than the number itself. Eight has nine combinations.

ACTIVITY 10.14

One Up and One Down: Addition

Have students select a number, such as 7, and add it to itself. The task is to find out what happens to the sum if you make one of the 7s one greater and the other one less (8 + 6). Does this work with other numbers? Does it only work if you start with a number plus itself? Can you explain why it works? What else can you find out?

EXPANDED LESSON

(pages 308–309)
A complete lesson plan based on "One Up and One Down: Addition" can be found at the end of this chapter.

At the adult level, "One Up and One Down" is rather trivial. However, it is a significant task for first- and second-grade students and perhaps even for late kindergarten. Some students may wonder if it works for "really big numbers." Suggest they test their ideas with a calculator. It is also useful to explore the idea of *two* up and *two* down, and so on. Of course, the results are the same as long as the same amount is added and subtracted from each number. Notice that the result of this exploration can be useful when learning basic facts (6 + 8 is the same as 7 + 7 or double 7). Students may want to know if the one-up/one-down idea works for subtraction. Of course, it does not. But there is an important pattern to discover: If both numbers change in the same direction, up or down, the result is the same. Knowing this allows us to change 12 – 8 to 10 – 6, or 83 – 48 to 85 – 50. That is, some differences that may seem difficult to remember or compute can be changed to ones that are easy to do.

The next activity extends the one-up/one-down idea to multiplication.

One Up and One Down: Multiplication

Show students that when you begin with 7 × 7 = 49 and then raise one factor and lower the other, each by one, the product is one less than the original: 8 × 6 = 48. Their task is to explore this for other numbers multiplied by themselves (squares). To help with their exploration, suggest that they cut out a square array from grid paper. How can they change the square array into the new rectangle using scissors and tape? Students should use words, pictures, and numbers to tell what they have found out. Encourage students to explore similar situations and see what patterns they can discover.

You might want to play around with the last activity yourself. The results are quite interesting and not nearly as obvious as those for addition. In the multiplication version, the new product will be one less if the original product is a square—a number multiplied by itself. Figure 10.10 illustrates how an array changes in the case of a square. When the original factors are not alike (increase the larger number and decrease the smaller), the difference can be related to the difference in the original factors.

Earlier, we explored the hundreds chart for patterns resulting from skip counting. There are other interesting patterns hiding in the hundreds chart that can be discovered with operations.

Diagonal Sums

Have students select any four numbers in the hundreds chart that form a square. Add the two numbers on each diagonal as in the example shown here.

Have students explore other diagonal sums on the chart. Expand their search to diagonals of any rectangle. For example, the numbers 15, 19, 75, and 79 form four corners of a rectangle. The sums 15 + 79 and 19 + 75 are equal. Challenge students who are able to see if they can figure out why this is so. (See Figure 10.11.)

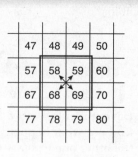

FIGURE 10.10 • • • • • •

What happens when you begin with a number times itself and then make one factor one greater and the other factor one less?

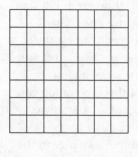

7 × 7 = 49

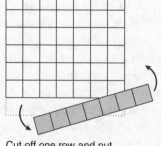

Cut off one row and put it on the side.

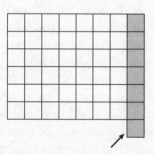

6 × 8 = 48
There will always be one unused square.

After finding that the diagonal sums are alike, a natural question to ask is: What about the differences in diagonal corners?

> **STOP**
>
> Exploring differences on the hundreds chart is certainly within reach of second- and third-grade students, but the generalizations are not as obvious as they are with addition. The two diagonal differences will always differ by some amount. How much they differ can be predicted by knowing only the top two numbers in the rectangle, regardless of the choice of the two bottom numbers.
>
> Stop to figure this out yourself.

If you explore the diagonal differences, you will find that they differ by twice the distance between the top two numbers. If the top numbers are 16 and 19 (three apart), the diagonal differences will differ by 2 × 3, or 6. To confirm this try 56 and 59 as the bottom numbers: 59 − 16 = 43; 56 − 19 = 37. The difference between 43 and 37 is 6.

Interested students may also want to examine multiplication patterns using a calculator. Again, there are patterns to be found, but they are perhaps more obscure. The difference between the larger and smaller diagonal products will be the same for all rectangles on the chart that have the same dimensions, regardless of orientations. Check these two rectangles as an example: 23, 27, 43, 47 and 56, 58, 96, 98. The first is a 4 × 2 rectangle and the second a 2 × 4 rectangle. The diagonal products in each differ by 80.

Finally, all of the patterns found through addition, subtraction, or multiplication remain even if the rectangles are "tilted," with sides not parallel to the chart. (The numbers 33, 15, 77, and 59 form a rectangle that is "tilted.")

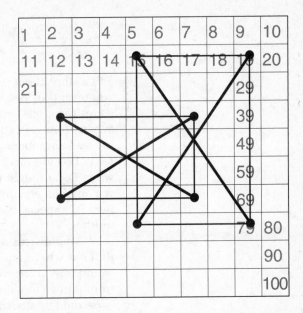

FIGURE 10.11 •

Diagonals on a hundreds chart. For any four numbers forming a rectangular arrangement on the hundreds chart, the sum of the corner numbers on one diagonal equals the sum of the corner numbers on the other diagonal. There is also a pattern for the differences of these same numbers and for the products.

Odd and Even Numbers

The categorization of numbers as odd or even is an important regularity in our number system. All too often students are simply told that the even numbers are those that end in 0, 2, 4, 6, or 8 and odd numbers are those that end in 1, 3, 5, 7, or 9. While of course this is true, it is only an attribute of even and odd numbers rather than a definition that explains what *even* or *not even* (i.e., *odd*) really means. The next two activities provide students with conceptual ideas of even and odd numbers without forcing definitions. In fact, as a result of either one of these activities, students should be able to classify numbers into the categories that we call odd and even. After they have conceptualized these classes of numbers, the appropriate labels of *odd* and *even* can be applied.

Fair Shares for Two

Tell a story about two twin sisters (or brothers). The twins always shared whatever they had equally. If they found some pretty seashells, they would count them out and share them so that each had the same number of shells. When Mom gave them cookies for lunch, they would be sure that each got the same number of cookies. Sometimes they were not able to share things fairly because there would be something left over. This happened once when Dad brought them five marbles. (Discuss why they could not share five marbles equally.) Whenever there was a leftover, the twins put the extra item in a special box of "leftovers" that they decided to keep for their baby brother.

After discussing the way that the twins shared things, ask children to find out what numbers of things they could share fairly and what numbers would have a leftover when they shared them. Assign three or four numbers from 6 to 40 to pairs of students. The task is to decide which of their numbers could be shared and which would have a leftover. Provide counters to help them in their decision. Collect the information and make lists of numbers that can be shared and those that will have a leftover. Examine the lists as a class and ask for observations. Select numbers not in the list and ask if students can tell which list they belong in and why they think so.

The critical portion of the last activity is the discussion. Based on this activity, *an even number is an amount that can be made of two equal parts with no leftovers. An odd number is one that is not even or cannot be made of two equal parts*. The number endings of 0, 2, 4, 6 and 8 are only an interesting and useful pattern or observation and should not be used as the definition of an even number.

The next activity develops the same concept but this time in a visual manner.

BLM 43

Bumpy or Not Bumpy

Duplicate the Blackline Master of "two-column cards" for each student. Have students cut them out and keep them in an envelope. Explain how each piece (except the single square) is made of two columns of squares. Have students work in pairs or small groups to see how many things they can find to tell about the pieces. (For example: There is a piece for each number 1 to 10. Some are like rectangles. Some have a square sticking out.) For those who might need a start, suggest that they put the pieces in order from one square to ten. You might have students sort their pieces into two sets. It is very likely that some group will sort the pieces as shown in Figure 10.12. (If no one sorts the pieces this way, do so on the overhead and ask what rule you are using to sort them.) Refer to the two groups

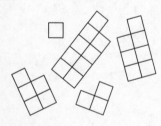

FIGURE 10.12 •

Two-column pieces separated into "bumpy" and "not bumpy" pieces. Note that these are also odd and even numbers. Why? Try making new two-column cards using any two of the cards. What can you discover about adding bumpy and not bumpy cards (odd and even numbers)?

of pieces as "bumpy" numbers and "not bumpy" numbers (or whatever labels your students prefer to use).

Next, assign groups of students three or four numbers between 11 and 40 or 50 and have them decide whether two-column cards for these numbers would be bumpy or not bumpy. They can use any method to decide. Have them use words and pictures to explain their conclusions.

As in "Fair Shares for Two" students can eventually see that bumpy numbers end in 1, 3, 5, 7, or 9 and even numbers in 0, 2, 4, 6, or 8. Explain that these are actually called *odd* and *even* numbers.

As a wonderful follow-up exploration to "Bumpy or Not Bumpy," ask students what kind of piece they get when two pieces in the set are added together. The two pieces must make a new two-column piece. It is fairly easy to conclude that evens plus evens and odds plus odds will always produce evens, whereas an odd plus an even will be odd. Students may enjoy examining this result with very big numbers using a calculator.

If you do both the "Fair Shares for Two" and the "Bumpy or Not Bumpy" activities, students can see how the two ideas are really the same. The squares in an even two-column strip can clearly be shared fairly, one column per person. A bumpy strip would have an extra square.

Representing Ideas

Representation is one of the five process standards in the NCTM *Principles and Standards* document. When we talk of representing ideas, we refer to external things that we can see, such as drawings, graphs, numbers and equations, and manipulative models. If these things are to be representative of students' ideas, students must have those ideas before a representation will have any meaning for them. Meanings do not *come from* the representations. You cannot represent an idea you have not yet formed.

In this section we discuss some types of symbolic representations and drawings that students can learn to use to help them solve problems and communicate their ideas. However, as the *Standards* authors caution, we must not make these or other representations become an end in themselves.

> *Representations should be treated as essential elements in supporting students' understanding of mathematical concepts and relationships: in communicating mathematical approaches, arguments, and understandings to one's self and to others; in recognizing connections among related mathematical concepts; and in applying mathematics to realistic problem situations through modeling. (NCTM, 2000, p. 67)*

Chapter 1 described models for mathematical ideas as tools for learning. The reference was primarily to manipulative materials, representations such as base-ten blocks, or counters. However, the term *model* was used to expand the notion of representation beyond physical materials to include any external representation onto which a concept can be imposed. This includes student drawings and symbolism. (See Figure 1.6, p. 10.)

The Algebra standard in *Principles and Standards* also calls for students to "represent mathematical situations" and to use representations to "understand quantitative relationships." And so, once again, we see that algebra is not always a separate strand of the curriculum but is found whenever students are trying to represent quantitative relationships throughout the curriculum.

Drawings and Diagrams for Story Problems

Diezmann and English (2001) found that students need to be taught how to draw different types of diagrams and how to use them. Second-grade students working in pairs were encouraged to "draw pictures" to help solve the following problem:

....

How many legs and tails are there with five cows and four chickens? (Adapted from a task by Burns and Tank, 1988.)

....

In Figure 10.13 Michael and Paul drew detailed pictures of five cows and one of the four chickens (lower right). The tedium required by their explicit renditions of the animals prevented them from completing the task. Their drawing may have solved the problem eventually but they could benefit from learning an efficient method of representation. Many students interpret "draw a picture to help solve the problem" to mean that a realistic picture is to be drawn—not necessarily one that has something to do with the numbers in the problem.

Eli and Kara also drew detailed pictures complete with a fence and feeding trough. Here, the drawing gave them the correct numbers (their error is in adding), although they were more interested in drawing than solving the problem. Shanna and Cally were much closer to a truly symbolic representation. One child drew the "legs" and was content to make groupings of four (cows) and two (chickens). Her partner drew realistic tails. These students had also used counters to solve the problem. It is not clear which representation was most useful for them. Kellen and Kevin were given some teacher guidance that helped them see that realistic drawings were not necessary. They still felt the need to label these pictures and they forgot the tails for the chickens.

These students illustrate the point that without some form of instruction, most students will interpret the instruction to draw a picture to mean "draw a realistic picture." For many problems, this poses a seemingly insurmountable task. For example, students may protest, "I don't know how to draw a kangaroo!" The drawing by Kellen and Kevin gives us a hint. Teachers can model appropriate drawings or make useful suggestions. Students also need to have words like *diagram* or *drawing* explained to them.

Let's explore another story problem.

....

Grace has a piggy bank. Today, Grandpa gave her 6 pennies to put in her bank. When she dumped out her bank, she had 18 pennies. How many pennies did she have before today?

....

Two generic types of drawings can be suggested for this and many similar problems. The first drawing is essentially a number line, and the other is some form of a part-whole drawing. (See Figure 10.14 on p. 296.) In these examples, the unknown amount is shown because the students have used the drawing to find the solutions.

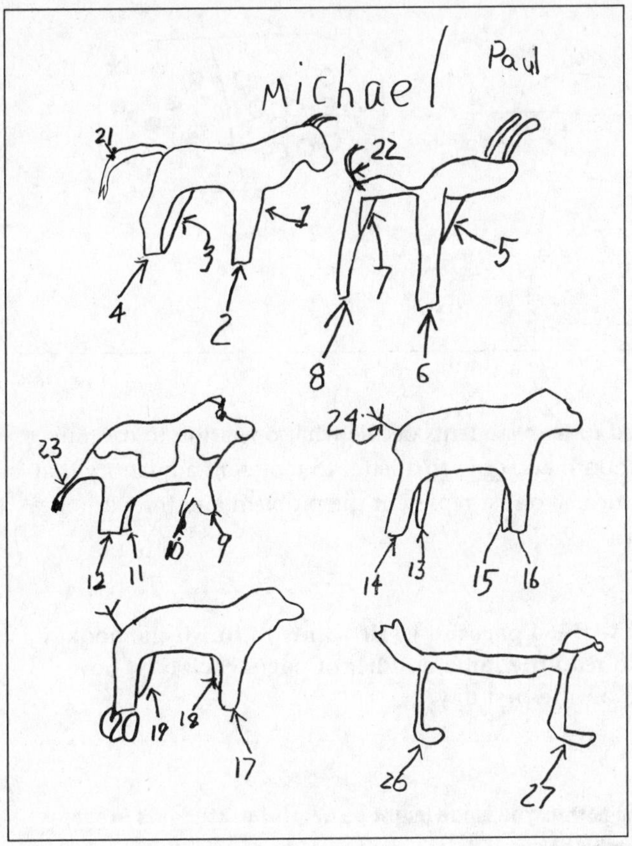
Michael / Paul
21
22
1
3
5
4
2
7
8
6
23
24
12
11
10
9
14
13
15
16
20
19
18
17
26
27

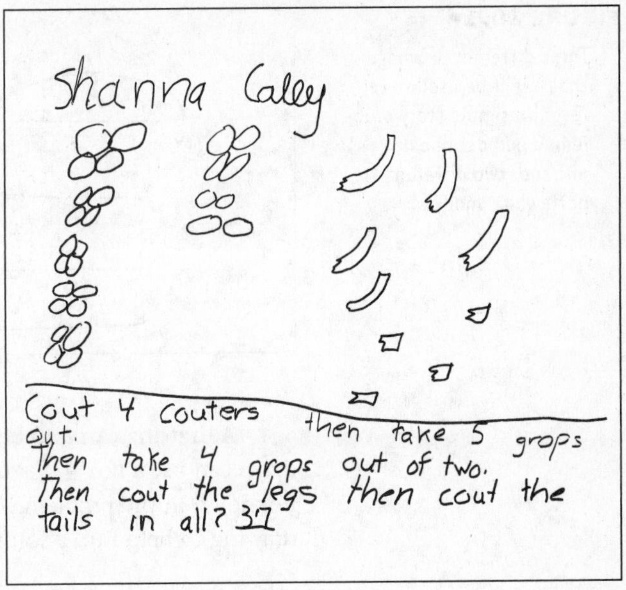
Shanna Caley
Cout 4 couters out then take 5 grops
then take 4 grops out of two.
Then cout the legs then cout the
tails in all? 37

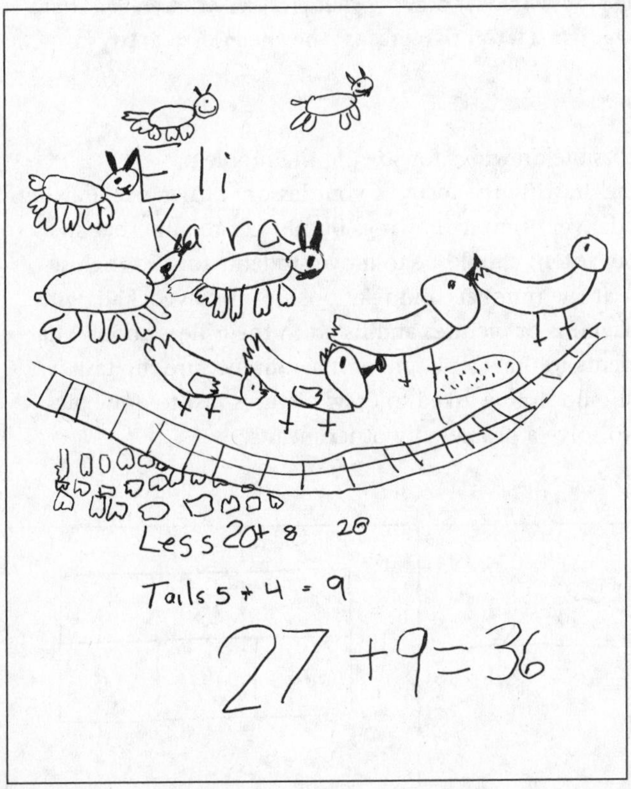
Eli
Kara
Legs 20+8 28
Tails 5+4 = 9
27+9=36

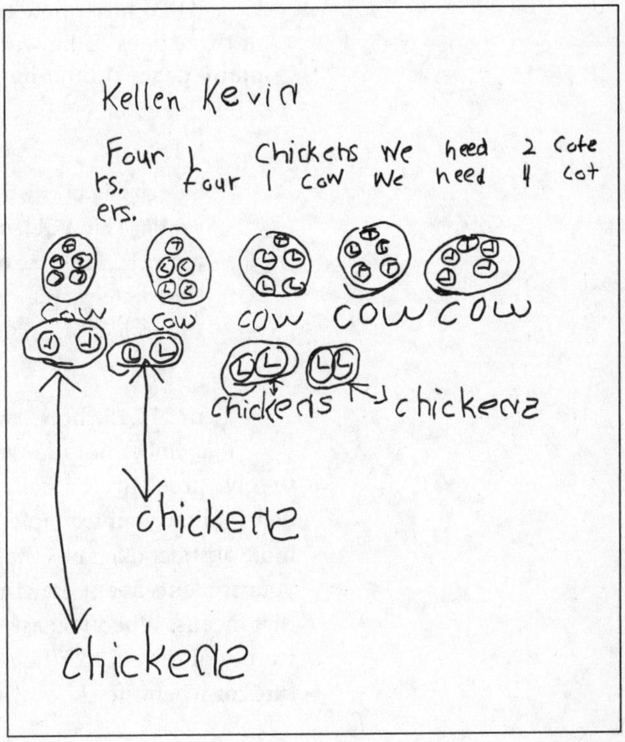
Kellen Kevin
Four legs chickens we need 2 Cote
Four legs 1 cow we need 4 cot
cow
cow
cow
cowcow
chickens
chickenz
chickenz
chickenz

FIGURE 10.13

Second-grade students are told to draw a picture to help solve the problem: five cows and four chickens. How many legs and tails?

FIGURE 10.14 • • • • • •

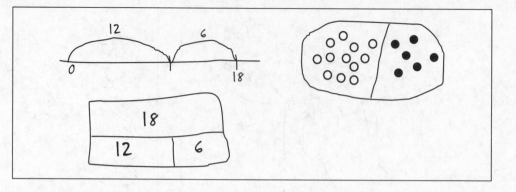

A drawing can also be used to help students decide what operation to use. Students can use a box (☐), a question mark, or even a letter to represent a quantity that is unknown in the problem. The idea is to first represent the problem and then use the drawing to help find a solution.

> Allen has a new book with 54 pages in it. He wants to finish the book in three days. If he wants to read the same number of pages each day, how many pages should he read on the first day?

STOP Sketch one or two drawings that you think might be helpful to students in representing this problem. Remember, you do not want them to draw details, just the essential features of the problem. After drawing your picture, write an equation that matches your picture. Use a letter to represent the unknown quantity in the problem.

Figure 10.15 shows two possible drawings for solving the problem.

Remember not to make the drawing the focus of your lesson; rather, use drawings to solve problems. Casually model very simple drawings but do not require that students follow your examples. Your intent should be to move students toward the use of more abstract diagrams that get at the numbers and relationships involved. Talk with your students about drawing diagrams or pictures and listen to their ideas about what that means. When you ask students to draw a picture or diagram, be sure the task is worthy of the effort. Students should not be asked to draw pictures just to draw pictures or when they know how to solve a problem by other means.

FIGURE 10.15 • • • • • •

Drawings can also incorporate unknown amounts. Then the drawing doesn't solve the problem but helps students understand what operation to use.

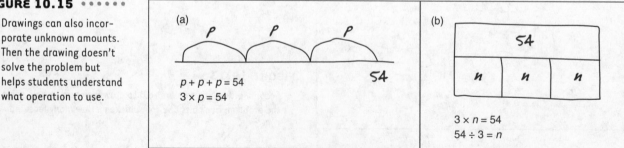

Students who typically have difficulty solving verbal problems can benefit most from learning to draw pictures to represent their ideas. In a one-on-one setting, ask the student if she could draw a diagram of the problem you have presented. First, you want to know if the student has any idea what you mean by "diagram" or "picture" of the problem. If a student tries to draw a realistic picture, you know that some instruction in the meaning of a diagram or a drawing is called for.

Some students will be able to make a drawing but fail to capture the correct or complete mathematics in their drawing. They may draw errors or leave out information. These students require time to explain how their diagram shows what the problem is about. They have probably rushed to make a drawing and have lost sight of the details. Relating the diagram to the problem can help.

Variables and Equations

We teach students to write equations as early as kindergarten, and they continue to experience equations in every subsequent grade. In the preceding section we saw variables used within simple drawings and in equations. Variables and equations are powerful tools in representing mathematical ideas and the primary grades are not too early to begin using them. However, many misconceptions often develop in these early years that unfortunately stay with students into later years. It is important for teachers to have a complete and accurate understanding of variables and equations so that we can help students construct appropriate ideas.

Variables

A *variable* is a symbol that can stand for any one of a set of numbers or other objects. This simple-sounding definition has a variety of interpretations, depending on how variables are used.

At least three different uses of variables have been identified. As the use of the variable changes, the meaning of the variable changes accordingly.

1. *As a specific unknown.* This is the most common use of variables in the primary grades. When students or textbooks use a box in an equation, such as in $8 + \square = 12$, the box represents a specific value that makes the equation true. This is the same meaning of *variable* that students encounter in later years when they are given an equation such as $3x + 2 = 4x - 1$ and are asked to solve for x.
2. *As a pattern generalizer.* When we state general patterns or rules of arithmetic, it is enormously economical to use variables. These are statements that are true for all numbers. For example, $a \times b = b \times a$ is the statement of the commutative property for multiplication. At the primary level, the properties of our number system are the patterns in which students are likely to see this use of variables.
3. *As quantities that vary in joint variation.* *Joint variation* occurs when change in one variable determines a change in another. Although $A = L \times W$ may be seen as a formula, it actually describes a relationship between three different variables.

As the values of L and W change, the value of A changes accordingly. A study of joint variation gives rise to the concept of function. As we will see, the primary level is not too early to begin an exploration of this important algebraic idea.

There certainly is no need for primary students to know or recognize the distinctions among these three uses of variables in algebraic reasoning. As noted, young students will most likely experience variables as specific unknowns more than other uses. It is useful for them to think of variables as numbers that can be operated on and manipulated like other numbers. The box that they see in an equation is not an answer space but a yet-to-be-determined number. They write a number in the box to show what the box represents.

One occasion when students may explore this concept is when they are writing equations for story problems. For example: *If Yolanda has 12 cards and Karl has 5, write an equation that tells how many more cards Yolanda has.* Some students might write 12 − 5 = □ while others may write 5 + □ = 12. The latter equation can be interpreted as "Karl's 5 cards plus some more cards are the same as Yolanda's 12 cards." When students are encouraged to write equations with a space for the unknown quantity, different equations will often occur. The variable allows students to focus on the structure of the equations rather than on the answer.

The following activity illustrates how an unknown can be manipulated or treated just like a number.

ACTIVITY 10.19

Number Tricks

Have students do the following sequence of operations:

Write down any number.
Add to it the number that comes after it.
Add 9.
Divide by 2.
Subtract the number you started with.

Now you can magically read their minds. Everyone ends up with 5!

The task is to see if students can discover how the trick works. Suggest that instead of using a specific number to begin with, they draw a shape like a box or triangle or a letter of the alphabet. The letter or shape represents a number, but even they do not need to know what the number is. Then do each step using that shape: □ + (□ + 1) is the sum of the original number plus the number that comes after it. Adding 9 gives □ + □ + 1 + 9 or 2□ + 10. Dividing this by 2 leaves only the box plus 5 or □ + 5. When you subtract the number you began with (□), only 5 remains.

There are endless trick sequences like the one in the last activity. Here are two more:

- Pick a number between 1 and 9, multiply by 5, add 3, multiply by 2, add another number between 1 and 9, subtract 6. What do you see?

- Pick a number, multiply by 6, add 12, take half of the result, subtract 6, divide by 3. What happens?

These tricks can profitably be explored with models by using a box or a block for the unknown and simple counters to represent numbers. Figure 10.16 shows how the first of the two preceding tricks might be modeled. Notice how place-value understanding is involved.

Equations and Inequalities

In the expression $3B + 7 = B - C$, the equal sign means that the quantity on the left *is the same as* the quantity on the right. To understand expressions in this way, students must interpret simple arithmetic expressions such as $3 + 5$ or 4×17 as *single quantities*.

Unfortunately, students tend to look on expressions such as $3 + 5$ and 4×17 as commands or things to do. The = tells you to add, and students think of *add* as a verb or an operator button, like pressing ▣ on a calculator. As students read left to right in an equation, the = tells them, "Now give the answer." Because of this "get an answer" view of operations and equal signs, students fail to think of $5 + 2$ as another way to write 7.

A Balance Pan Approach to Equality

The following activities are ways to help students with the basic concepts needed to understand equations.

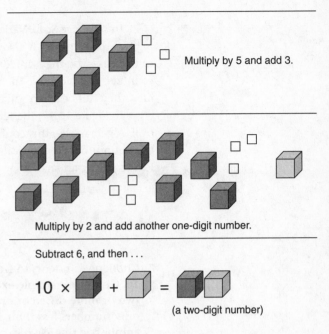

 Pick a number between 1 and 9.

Multiply by 5 and add 3.

Multiply by 2 and add another one-digit number.

Subtract 6, and then . . .

$$10 \times \blacksquare + \square = \blacksquare\square$$
(a two-digit number)

FIGURE 10.16 ●

Number tricks can be modeled using a block or a box for the unknown. Additional numbers are shown with counters or base-ten pieces.

ACTIVITY 10.20

Balance Scale Variables

Each student will need a worksheet similar to the one shown in Figure 10.17 as well as about 20 counters that can be placed on the shapes (representing variables) in the balance pans. Color tiles work well. The task is to place a total of 18 tiles on the pans so that the scale balances. Like shapes must have the same number of tiles because in any equation all like variables have the same value. When one solution has been found, students should try to find additional solutions. Help students record their solutions in a chart with a column for each shape. Two solutions to the scale in Figure 10.17 are shown here. After students have found as many solutions as possible with

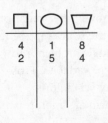

□	○	⊔
4	1	8
2	5	4

(continued)

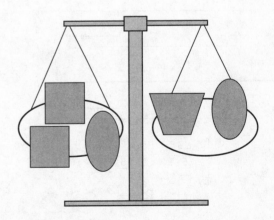

FIGURE 10.17 ● ● ● ● ● ● ● ● ● ● ● ● ● ● ● ● ● ● ●

A simple scale drawn on a worksheet contains variables on each pan. Students stack counters on the shapes to make the scale balance. Like shapes must have the same number of counters.

18 tiles, have them balance the scale with 12 or 20 tiles. (Why can't the scale be balanced using 15 tiles?) Other scales can be created using only two shapes or different combinations of three shapes.

In "Balance Scale Variables," children begin to understand the concept of equating two quantities. It is also interesting that there are multiple solutions, and students can discuss why they think they have found them all. Notice that a shape can have no counters, in which case the value of that variable is zero. Once students have the basic idea, they can begin to solve balance problems such as this without the use of counters.

In Figure 10.17, the left side of the scale represents the sum of two squares and an oval. Algebraically, this could be $2A + B$. The purpose of the next activity is to develop the notion that an expression such as $3 + 4$ or 2×7 is actually a quantity, not a problem requiring an answer.

ACTIVITY 10.21

Names for Numbers

Challenge students to find different ways to express a particular number, say, 10. Give a few simple examples, such as $5 + 5$ or $12 - 2$. Encourage the use of two or more different operations. "How many names for 8 can you find using only numbers less than 10 and at least three operations?" In your discussion, emphasize that each expression is a way of representing or writing a number.

Notice that there are no equal signs used in Activity 10.21. The next activity develops the concept of the equal sign. It begins with numbers only but can be quickly extended to include variables.

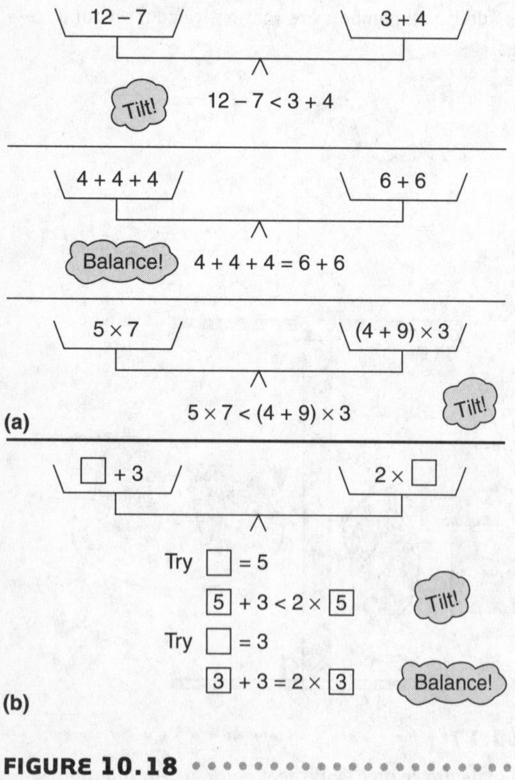

ACTIVITY 10.22

Tilt or Balance

On the board, draw a simple two-pan balance. In each pan, write a numeric expression and ask which pan will go down or whether the two will balance (see Figure 10.18). Challenge students to write expressions for each side of the scale to make it balance. For each, write a corresponding equation to illustrate the meaning of =. Note that when the scale "tilts," either a "greater than" or "less than" symbol (> or <) is used.

After a short time, add variables to the two-pan balance activity as shown in Figure 10.18b.

In Figure 10.19, a series of examples shows other variations of scale problems. As before, each shape on the scales represents a different value. Two or more scales for a single problem provide different information about the shapes or variables. Problems of this type can be adjusted in difficulty for children throughout first to eighth grades. Those shown are appropriate

$12 - 7$ $3 + 4$

Tilt! $12 - 7 < 3 + 4$

$4 + 4 + 4$ $6 + 6$

Balance! $4 + 4 + 4 = 6 + 6$

5×7 $(4 + 9) \times 3$

(a) $5 \times 7 < (4 + 9) \times 3$ Tilt!

$\square + 3$ $2 \times \square$

Try $\square = 5$

$\boxed{5} + 3 < 2 \times \boxed{5}$ Tilt!

Try $\square = 3$

$\boxed{3} + 3 = 2 \times \boxed{3}$ Balance!

(b)

FIGURE 10.18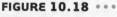

Using expressions and variables in equations and inequalities. The two-pan balance helps develop the meaning of =, <, and >.

FIGURE 10.19 ● ● ● ● ● ●

Examples of problems
with multiple scales
(equations).

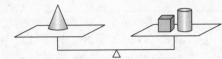

Which shape weighs the most? Explain.

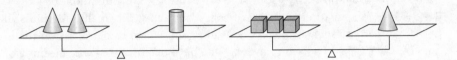

Which shape weighs the most? Explain.
Which shape weighs the least? Explain.

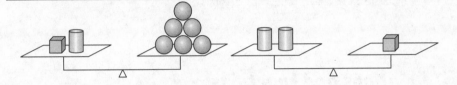

What will balance two spheres? Explain.

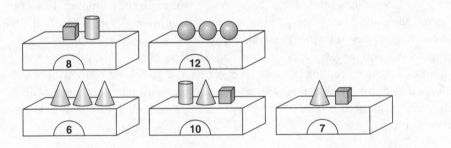

How much does each shape weigh? Explain.

for primary students. (Books with similar tasks are available. For example, see Greenes & Findell, 1999.)

When no numbers are involved, as in the top three examples of Figure 10.19, students can find combinations of numbers for the shapes that make all of the balances balance. If an arbitrary value is given to one of the shapes, then values for the other shapes can be found accordingly.

The scale problems (with a number for each scale) are to be solved for a unique value for each shape. There are often several paths to finding a solution.

STOP **How would you solve the last problem in Figure 10.19? Can you solve it in two ways?**

You (and students) can tell if you are correct by checking your solutions with the original scale positions. Believe it or not, you have just solved a series of simultaneous equations, a skill generally left to a formal algebra class. Try making up your own scale problems. It is easier than you think. Start by giving values to two or three shapes. Place shapes in groups and add the values. These are the numbers on the scales. (Be sure your problems can be solved.)

Assessment Note

Relations and Functions

In the everyday world of children, all sorts of things exist in relationship to other things. John is *taller than* Mark. Mom takes a *longer time* to do the shopping than Aunt Gretchen. "Taller than" and "longer time" are relationships. Five is *more than* four. Five is also *two less than* seven. "More than" and "two less than" are also examples of relationships. As we will see later, a function is a special kind of relationship.

Part of algebraic thinking involves recognizing and describing relationships and functions. It also involves learning different ways to represent relations and functions. Different representations offer different ways to think about relationships so as to better understand them.

Relations

A *relation* is simply a correspondence between two sets of things. The correspondence can be between all sorts of things. The time of day, the height of a bean plant, the number of blocks in the block castle, or simply numbers are all examples of things on which or between which correspondences or relationships can be described. Sometimes the two sets are the same or are similar. This bean plant is more wilted than that bean plant (plants related to plants). At other times the relationship is between different things. Bobby's favorite color is red (students to colors).

At the earliest grades children can become aware of relationships and begin to articulate or describe them in a variety of ways. When relationships are described on a single set, such as the students in the classroom, one good way to represent the relationship is with arrows. In Figure 10.20a, the arrows show the relationship "longer name." Sue's dot in the diagram points to both Lucy's and Robert's and "says" *your name is longer than mine*. For many relationships there is an opposite or *inverse* relationship. In this case, the opposite of *longer than* is *shorter than*. The same arrow diagram can utilize two different arrows at the same time. On the board, use colored chalk to distinguish the arrows. Students use crayons on their papers. The diagram should tell what each color arrow stands for.

Once students are familiar with how an arrow diagram works, they are ready for the following activity.

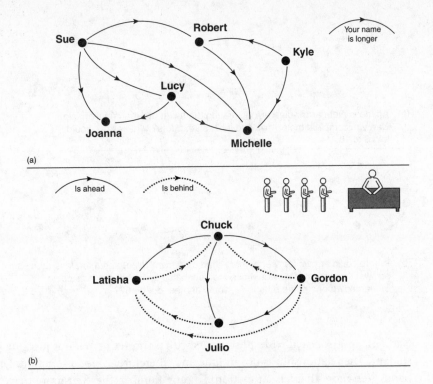

FIGURE 10.20 ● ● ● ● ● ●

Arrow diagrams can be used to show relationships. In these diagrams more arrows can be drawn with the information that is already in the diagram. Can you identify the children in the line?

(a)

Is ahead   Is behind

(b)

ACTIVITY 10.23

Incomplete Diagrams

Prepare on the board or on paper an arrow diagram that is incomplete. Discuss with the students what they think the arrows in the diagram represent. Explain that some arrows were left off the diagram. Their task is to finish the diagram by adding all the arrows that are possible. Figure 10.20b is an example of an incomplete diagram, showing how four children are lined up at the desk. As students complete the diagram, see if they can tell who is first, second, third, and fourth in line.

In both diagrams in Figure 10.20, each dot is related to every other dot, and the result is a lot of arrows. In Figure 10.21a, the arrows each represent *two-more-than*. In this case, each dot can have at most one arrow coming from it.

As a further variation of "Incomplete Diagrams," draw an arrow diagram with the arrow identified but none of the dots labeled, as shown in Figure 10.21b. Students can be asked questions such as: "If this dot is 42, what would the other dots be?" "Where could we draw plus 20 arrows?" "Where could you draw a minus 30 arrow?" Of course, the questions will vary with the diagram you suggest. Similarly, you can have students create their own "mystery diagrams" with unlabeled dots, unlabeled arrows, or both. The creators of the mystery diagrams should be able to complete them or explain them in some way.

Functions

A *function* is a special type of relationship in which each element is *uniquely* associated with another element. For example, in the relationship "has-longer-name,"

RELATIONS AND FUNCTIONS

FIGURE 10.21 •••••••••

Incomplete arrow diagrams.

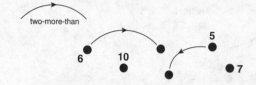

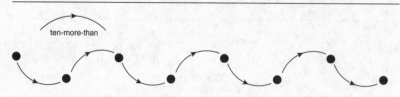

(a) An incomplete arrow diagram illustrating the two-more-than relationship. Can you complete the arrows and label all the dots? What arrow would join 6 to 10?

(b) Where could arrows for twenty-more-than be drawn? What about ten-less-than arrows? How many dots would need to be labeled so that all the dots could be named? If one of the dots is 42, could another dot be 57?

Nathanial is associated with *all* students with a shorter name, not just one particular student. The relationship is not unique and, therefore, is not a function. On the other hand, "ten-more-than" is a function. For any number, the "ten-more-than" rule associates a unique number. It is not at all necessary for young children to be able to distinguish between functions and nonfunction relationships, but it is useful for you to be aware of the distinction.

Functions can be represented in a variety of very useful ways. Arrow diagrams such as those that have just been discussed are one way, but that approach is only useful for a small number of elements. Charts or tables, function "machines," equations, and graphs are typical methods of illustrating functions, and each is accessible to the primary-aged child.

Function Machines

The next activity is a method of introducing function machines. From that representation, we can help students develop other ways to explore functions.

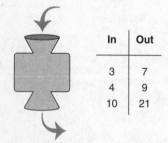

In	Out
3	7
4	9
10	21

FIGURE 10.22 ••••••••

A simple function machine is used to play "Guess My Rule." Students suggest input numbers and the operator records the output value.

ACTIVITY 10.24

Guess My Rule

Draw a simple in–out "machine" on the board, as shown in Figure 10.22. The machine "operator" knows the secret that is stored in the machine. For example, a rule might be *double the input number and add 1.* Students try to guess the rule by putting numbers into the machine and observing what comes out. A list of in–out pairs are kept on the board. Students who think they have guessed the rule raise their hands. As more numbers are put into the machine, those students who think they know the rule tell what comes out. Continue until most have guessed the rule.

"Guess My Rule" can be played with the whole class, or students can play in small groups, perhaps as a station activity. Provide a collection of rules on cards.

Include at least two examples so that the machine operator is sure to understand the rule. The guesses can be kept in a chart on paper that all players can see. Eventually students can make up their own rules to try to stump their classmates.

Charts or Tables

The charts used to keep track of the in–out numbers for the function machines are themselves a form of representation of functions. A chart can be in either vertical or horizontal form. (See Figure 10.23.) Although the format itself is not important, note that a chart or table can represent a function by itself. For example, an incomplete chart can be used as a variation of "Guess My Rule." Students examine the entries that are already in the chart and try to determine what the missing entries are.

Equations

The function rules we have discussed so far have been described with words. It is important for students to begin to use variables for the rules so that they can be expressed with equations. Suppose that the rule for a machine is "Add the number to itself and subtract 1." Use a box ($\square$) to represent the input number and a triangle ($\triangle$) for the output number. The task is to write an equation that relates these two. In this case the equation would be $\triangle = \square + \square - 1$ or $\triangle = 2 \times \square - 1$.

Graphs

Even students in the second and third grades can begin to plot points on a grid. A reasonable approach is to first create a chart or table with six to ten entries. Select one column to be the horizontal axis (usually the input number from a function machine) and the other to be the vertical axis. At this level, it is likely that all values will be positive. Make graphs on a sheet of centimeter grid paper and use the bottom and left sides as the axes for a graph. Figure 10.24 shows the graph of $\triangle = 2 \times \square - 1$. Have students connect the dots. They should notice that some graphs form straight lines and others make curves. For example, the graph for $\triangle = \square \times \square$ will be a curve. After connecting the dots from the values in their charts, students should use the graph to find other values not in the chart. Figure 10.24 illustrates this process. They should check to see that these values also make the equations true. The graphs may also suggest the exploration of numbers less than zero.

In your discussion with students, it is important to help them see that the equation, the chart, and the graph are all ways of "seeing" the function. The equation is the

In	3	8	1	4	10	6	0	5	20	100
Out	5	15	1	7	19	11	−1	9	39	199

FIGURE 10.23 •

A chart in horizontal form is just as good as one in vertical form. Notice that the input numbers need not be in any order. It is the relationship between the input and output that creates the pattern, not the order that the numbers are entered. If 6 is input into this rule, 11 will be the result, no matter what was put in previously.

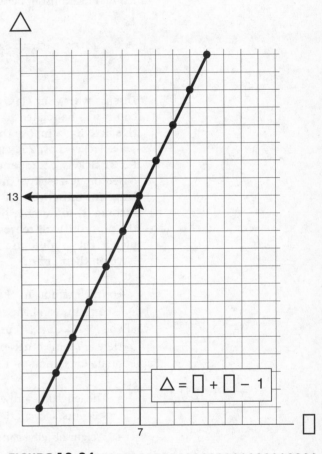

$$\triangle = \square + \square - 1$$

FIGURE 10.24 •

Students can plot simple equations or the results of function machines on centimeter grid paper and connect the points. The arrows illustrate how an input of 7 is connected by the graph to an output of 13.

RELATIONS AND FUNCTIONS

best form to see exactly what the rule is. The chart best tells the values of different input–output pairings. The graph gives us a visual picture that indicates (in this case) that the output values get larger as the input values get larger. Furthermore, this rule ($\triangle = \square + \square - 1$) has a graph or picture representation that is a straight line.

Real-World Functions

It is not too early in the second and third grades to begin finding functions in the real world. It is because the real world is so full of related factors that the idea of function is so important. As just one example, if candy bars cost 50¢ each, then there is a functional relationship between the number of candy bars purchased and the total cost.

ACTIVITY 10.25

Real Functions

Discuss with your class a real situation in which the value of one measure or count will be related to another measure or count. A list of examples follows this activity. Suppose the situation is the total sales of tickets to the class play. Tickets cost 25¢ each. If 20 tickets are sold, the income will be $5.00, for 21 tickets, $5.25, and so on. The task is to create a chart and a graph based on at least five different values for the number of tickets. As a challenge for those who are ready, see if they can find an equation that relates income (I) to number of tickets (N). For young students, the equation will be the most difficult representation of the function. Once the graph is completed, they should use it to determine the income for values they did not have on their chart.

For the example in "Real-World Functions," the graph will be a straight line and, if done correctly, can be used to predict other values not in the chart. The equation would be $I = N \times 25¢$. (To use 25¢ or $0.25 or simply 25 is of minimal importance.)

Here are some other examples of real-world situations that give rise to functions appropriate for second- or third-grade students.

- The length of a row of students holding arms outstretched. Input: number of students. Output: length of the row.

- Weight of jellybeans. Input: multiples of 10 jellybeans. Output: weight.

- Height of liquid in a bottle determined by the number of units poured in. The input unit could be a small container such as a medicine cup, or use milliliters or ounces. The experiment is most interesting if the bottle has an irregular shape that will cause the graph to curve. Input: number of small containers of water poured into bottle. Output: height of liquid.

- Height of bean plants compared to the days since they sprouted. Input: days. Output: height.

- The number of pendulum swings in 15 seconds dependent on the length of the pendulum. Suspend a tennis ball or other suitable weight from a string. Start with a length of 2 feet measured to the bottom of the ball. Change the string in 6-inch increments and repeat the experiment. The graph for this experiment will be a curve. Input: length of pendulum. Output: number of swings in 15 seconds.

- Distance a toy car will roll down a ramp depending on the height of the ramp. Use a board about 3 feet long. Raise one end 5 cm. Place a toy car at the top and let it roll. Measure the distance from the bottom of the ramp to the place where it started. You may want to repeat each trial several times to get a good reading. Raise the ramp in 5-cm increments. Input: height of ramp. Output: distance from bottom of ramp.

- Distance a wad of paper can be thrown. Start with a 2-square-inch piece of plain paper (not heavy). Have five students throw the paper from behind a line and measure the distance it can be thrown. Use the median distance in the chart. Repeat with larger pieces of paper in increments of 2 square inches. The distance will increase for a while and then eventually level off. Input: square inches of paper. Output: distance thrown.

Clearly some of these real-world experiments will not produce perfectly straight lines or even smooth curves. For example, the paper-throwing task will have quite erratic data, but there will be a trend. For these situations, an equation is not at all possible. When the numbers come from computation rather than from an experiment, an equation is more likely. For example, in most any cost versus quantity situation, students should be able to see how an equation could work. Consider the task of creating a tower of 1-inch cubes. The tower is made on a 2-by-3-inch base of six cubes. As the height of the tower changes from 1 inch to 10 inches, the volume of the tower will increase in 6-cubic-inch increments. The equation would be $V = H \times 6$ and the graph will be a straight line.

When the points on the graph form an approximate straight line, discuss with your students how a straight line that comes close to the dots may be a good approximation of the real situation. The line can be used to predict the outcomes of trials not yet conducted.

RELATIONS AND FUNCTIONS

EXPANDED LESSON

One Up and One Down: Addition

Based On: Activity 10.14, p. 289

GRADE LEVEL: Late kindergarten, first grade, or second grade.

MATHEMATICS GOALS
- To discover and explore number patterns within the context of addition.
- To help understand how complementary changes in two addends leave the sum unchanged.

THINKING ABOUT THE STUDENTS
Students need not know their addition combinations to engage in this lesson. However, they should have been exposed to the plus and equal sign and understand how an addition equation is a representation of two parts of a whole.

MATERIALS AND PREPARATION
- Students should have access to simple counters, pencil, and paper.
- Optional: In late first or second grade, students should have access to calculators.

lesson

BEFORE

Introduction to the Task
- Explain this problem: *The other day, a friend of mine was thinking about adding 7 + 7.* (Write 7 + 7 on the board.) *She wondered what would happen if she made the first 7 one more and the second 7 one less.* With students' help, write this new sum, 8 + 6, on the board. Have students complete each equation.

Brainstorm
- Ask: *Why do you think the answers are the same?* Have students offer their ideas. Ask: *Do you think this will work if we started with 5 + 5 or 8 + 8?* Discuss this briefly.

The Task
- (For kindergarten and early first grade): The task is to use counters and try to figure out why 7 + 7 and 8 + 6 have the same answers. Then try another sum, like 5 + 5, and see if it works for that sum also.
- (For late first grade and second grade): The task is to use counters and try to figure out why 7 + 7 and 8 + 6 have the same answers. Will it work for any double (like 5 + 5, 6 + 6, 8 + 8, and so on)? What if the two numbers you begin with are not the same?

Establish Expectations
- Students should use pictures, numbers, and words to show their thinking. If someone picks up the papers, they should be able to understand what students' ideas are. (Optional: You may want to have students work in pairs. Work could be shown on large newsprint to be shared with the class.)

DURING

- Some students may use their counters and complete each sum independently without relating one to the other. Ask these students to show you 7 + 7 with counters. Be sure that there are two separate piles of seven and not a single pile of 14. Ask: *How could you change these piles to show 8 + 6?* Whatever your hint, avoid simply showing students how to move a counter from one part of the sum to the other. Always try first to listen to the ideas that students have.

- Encourage students to get their ideas on paper for the 7 + 7 case before they explore further.
- How much you push students to explore further depends on the abilities and maturity of the students. In the lower grades, you might remind them to try another double such as 5 + 5 and see if the same thing works there. Older students can be challenged with more open-ended explorations, such as: *Does it always work? Do you have to start with a double? What if you change the numbers by 2 or some other number? What about really big numbers like 87 + 87?* (For large numbers, students should be encouraged to use calculators, even if they cannot compute the sums by hand.)
- For those students who may find this exploration rather easy, challenge them to see how this might work for subtraction.

AFTER

- Select students to share their ideas. Perhaps call first on students who have struggled and need to be encouraged. Although it is good for students to see the more sophisticated ideas, it is important to also focus on emerging ideas as well. For each student who shares, encourage students to ask questions or to offer additional ideas.
- Some students may have difficulty articulating their ideas. Suggest that they use counters on the overhead or magnetic counters on the board so that they can show students their thinking.
- Ask students how this idea could help them if they forgot how much 5 + 7 was. (5 + 7 will be the same as 6 + 6. Similarly, 6 + 8 is double 7, and so on.)

ASSESSMENT NOTES

- Especially for very young students, be aware of students who do not have a clear connection between a model for addition—especially a part-part-whole model—and the symbolic equation that represents this. Many students learn only to use counters to get answers but do not see the counters as a way to show what the equation means.
- Students who shove counters together and begin counting at once to solve an addition equation are the most likely to have difficulty with this activity.
- A few students will see this activity as rather simple. These students have a good understanding of what addition means.

- For students who experienced difficulty with this activity, try activities in which students begin with a fixed number of counters and attempt to make all possible combinations of two quantities to make that total. If for each combination, they are to write a corresponding addition equation, they will be helped to make the connection between the model and the equation. If they are given no more counters than the whole, as they explore each new combination, it will be necessary to take counters from one part and put them with the other. In so doing, the relationships found in this activity may be clearer. You should be more concerned with connections between a model and the equation than with success in this lesson.

- One good follow-up to this lesson is to explore the same idea with subtraction. In that case, the pattern is to raise or lower both numbers in the same direction to keep the result the same. (If you add or subtract from the whole and do the same with one of the parts, the other part will stay fixed.) The subtraction relationship is very valuable with mental mathematics and invented strategies. For example, 83 – 38 is the same as 85 – 40 (both numbers increased by 2).

next steps

HELPING CHILDREN USE DATA

ata, especially in the form of various types of graphs, play a significant role in the information we receive every day in newspapers, magazines, and on television. It is certainly reasonable to expect students to develop an understanding of graphs and how graphs depict information. All states include some form of graphing and data analysis in their standards for nearly every grade.

At the K–3 level, students can begin this understanding by learning how data can be categorized and displayed in various graphical forms. The focus of the explorations at this and every grade level should be on using data and graphs to answer questions. This means that the emphasis should be on ways to present data and how to interpret data in the context of real questions. We should minimize time spent teaching students tedious techniques of graph making.

big ideas

1 A collection of objects with various attributes can be classified or sorted in different ways. A single object can belong to more than one class. Classification is the first step in the organization of data.

2 Data are gathered and organized in order to answer questions about the populations from which the data come. With data from only a sample of the population, inferences are made about the population.

3 Different types of graphs and other data organizations provide different information about the data and, hence, the population from which the data were taken. For example, a cluster graph can help with seeing subdivisions of data. A bar graph provides quantitative comparisons among the classes. A line graph is used to show changes across time or other variables with a numeric ordering.

Gathering Data to Answer Questions

The first goal in the Data Analysis and Probability standard of *Principles and Standards* says that students should "formulate questions that can be addressed with data and collect, organize, and display relevant data to answer them" (NCTM, 2000, p. 48). Notice that data collection should be for a purpose, to answer a question, just as in the real world. At all grades, the analysis of data should have the agenda of adding information about some aspect of our world. This is what political pollsters, advertising agencies, market researchers, census takers, wildlife managers, and hosts of others do: gather data to answer questions. Avoid gathering data for the purpose of making a graph. Gather data to help answer a question of interest.

When students formulate the questions they want to ask, the data they gather become more and more meaningful. How they organize the data and the techniques for analyzing them have a purpose. For example, one class of students gathered data concerning which cafeteria foods were most often thrown in the garbage. As a result of these efforts, certain items were removed from the regular menu. The activity illustrated to students the power of organized data, and it helped them get food that they liked better.

Ideas for Questions and Data

Often the need to gather data will come from the class naturally in the course of discussion or from questions arising in other content areas. Science, of course, is full of measurements and thus abounds in data requiring analysis. Social studies is also full of opportunities to pose questions requiring data analysis. The next few sections suggest some additional ideas.

Classroom Questions

Young children can learn about themselves, their families and pets, the animals in their neighborhood, measures such as arm span or time to get to school, their likes and dislikes, and so on. At the K–2 level, the easiest questions to deal with are those that can be answered by each class member's contributing one piece of data. When there are lots of possibilities, suggest that students restrict the number of choices. Here are a few ideas:

- *Favorites:* TV show, fruit, season of the year, color, football team, pet, ice cream flavor
- *Numbers:* Number of pets, sisters, or brothers; hours watching TV or hours of sleep; birthdays (month or day of month); bedtime
- *Measures:* Height, arm span, area of foot, long-jump distance, letters in name, time to button a sweater, daily temperature, weather, shadow length, rainfall

Beyond the Classroom

The questions in the previous section are designed for students to contribute data about themselves. This is appropriate for younger children who are interested in learning who they are as a class and how each fits into the class as an individual. Eventually, you will sense that your students are ready to gather data for which they need to go outside the class or at least ask questions about things beyond the classroom.

Discussions about communities provide a good way to integrate social studies and mathematics. As you study the neighborhood in which students live, many questions arise:

- Counts of restaurants or stores (number of various burger franchises or convenience stores).
- Number of police officers, firefighters, nurses, doctors, elected officials, and other similar data can most likely be found on websites of local institutions.

If the information is not immediately available, this is a good chance to write a letter of request, even if it is just an e-mail.

- Types of businesses that are in the community. Students can solicit information from their parents, or a survey of the newspaper may be used.

The newspaper itself suggests all sorts of data-related questions. For example, how many full-page ads occur on different days of the week? What types of stories are on the front page? Which comics are really for kids and which are not?

Science is another area in which questions can be asked and data gathered. Students might collect leaves, rocks, or even insects from their own backyards. These objects can then be classified in various ways, creating categories for graphing. Experiments provide another type of question. How many times do different types of balls bounce when each is dropped from the same height? How many days does it take for different types of bean, squash, and pea seeds to germinate when kept in moist paper towels?

Comparisons

Another type of progression from the questions children ask about themselves is to consider if they as a class are alike or different from other groups. Do the fifth-grade students spend the same amount of time watching TV or like the same foods as we do? How much taller are students in the next grade or two grades ahead of us? Comparisons can also be made between your own class and selected groups of adults to which the students have access such as parents or faculty.

To expand your students' perspective, you might explore ways that your class can compare themselves or their data with similar classes in your school district, other places in the state, other states, or perhaps even in a foreign country. With the Internet making communication so quick and easy, any connection you may have with teachers in other cities, states, or countries can open up not just a source of interesting data but also a way for your children to see beyond their own localities.

Other Sources of Information

Gathering data can mean using data that have been collected by others. For example, newspapers, almanacs, sports record books, maps, and various government publications are sources of data that may be used to answer student questions. Students may be interested in facts about another country as a result of a social studies unit. Olympic records in various events over the years or data related to space flight are other examples of topics around which student questions may be formulated. For these and hundreds of other questions, data can be found on the World Wide Web. Here are three websites with a lot of interesting data.

U.S. Census Data (www.census.gov): This website contains copious statistical information by state, county, or voting district.

The World Fact Book (www.odci.gov/cia/publications/factbook/index.html): This website provides demographic information for every nation in the world, including population, age distributions, death and birth rates, and information on the economy, government, transportation, and geography. Maps are included as well.

Internet Movie Database (www.imdb.com): This website offers information about movies of all genres.

Classification and Data Analysis

Classification involves making decisions about how to categorize things. This basic activity is fundamental to data analysis. In order to formulate questions and decide how to represent data that have been gathered, decisions must be made about how things might be categorized. Farm animals, for example, might be grouped by number of legs; by type of product they provide; by those that work, provide food, or are pets; by size or color; by the type of food they eat; and so on. Each of these groupings is based on a different attribute of the animals.

Young children need experiences with categorizing things in different ways in order to learn to make sense of real-world data. Attribute activities are explicitly designed to develop this flexible reasoning about the characteristics of data.

Attribute Materials

Attribute materials are sets of objects that lend themselves to being sorted and classified in different ways. *Unstructured* attribute materials include such things as seashells, leaves, the children themselves, or the set of the children's shoes. The *attributes* are the ways that the materials can be sorted. For example, hair color, height, and gender are attributes of children. Each attribute has a number of different *values:* for example, blond, brown, or red (for the attribute of hair color); tall or short (for height); male or female (for gender).

A *structured* set of attribute pieces has exactly one piece for every possible combination of values for each attribute. For example, several commercial sets of plastic attribute materials have four attributes: color (red, yellow, blue), shape (circle, triangle, rectangle, square, hexagon), size (big, little), and thickness (thick, thin). The specific values, number of values, or number of attributes that a set may have is not important. Two teacher-made sets of structured attribute pieces are illustrated in Figure 11.1. A large version of the attribute shapes can easily be cut from poster board. Make the large shapes approximately 1 foot across and the small shapes about 4 or 5 inches across. The 16 Woozle cards can be duplicated on two sheets of paper. Students color and cut them out to use at their desks.

The value of using structured attribute materials is that the attributes and values are clearly identified and easily described by students. There is no confusion about what values a particular piece possesses, so you can focus your attention on the reasoning skills that the activities are meant to serve.

BLM 44

Activities with Attribute Materials

Most attribute activities are best done with young children sitting on the floor in a large circle where all can see and have access to the materials. All activities should be conducted in an easygoing manner that encourages risk taking, clear thinking, attentiveness, and discussion of ideas.

Most of the activities here will be described using the geometric shapes in Figure 11.1. However, each could be done with any structured set, and some could be done with nonstructured materials.

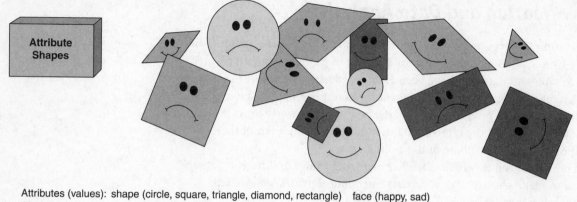

Attribute Shapes

Attributes (values): shape (circle, square, triangle, diamond, rectangle)   face (happy, sad)
60 pieces   color (red, yellow, blue)   size (big, little)

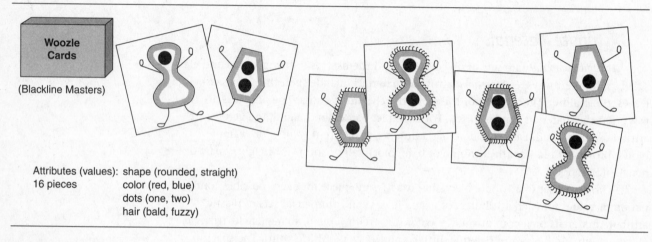

Woozle Cards

(Blackline Masters)

Attributes (values): shape (rounded, straight)
16 pieces   color (red, blue)
                     dots (one, two)
                     hair (bald, fuzzy)

FIGURE 11.1 • • • • • • •

Three teacher-made attribute sets. Attribute shapes are made in large sizes from poster board and laminated. Woozle cards can be duplicated on card stock, quickly colored in two colors, laminated, and cut into cards (see Blackline Masters).

Learning Classification Schemes

Several attribute activities involve using overlapping loops, each containing a designated class of materials such as pieces that are "red" or "not square." Loops can be made of yarn or drawn on large sheets of paper. When two loops overlap, the area that is inside both loops is for the pieces that have both properties. Children as young as kindergarten can have fun with simple loop activities. With the use of words such as *and, or,* and *not,* the loop activities become quite challenging.

Before children can use loops in a problem-solving activity, the scheme itself must be understood. A good way to accomplish this is to do a few activities that involve the loops. Children find these interesting and fun. After several days of working with these initial activities, you can move on to problem-solving activities involving the same formats.

ACTIVITY 11.1

The First Loops

Give children two large loops of yarn or string. Direct them to put all the red pieces inside one string and all triangles inside the other. Let the children try to resolve the difficulty of what to do with the red triangles. When the notion of overlapping the strings to create an area common to both loops is clear, more challenging activities can be explored.

Later, "strings" or loops can be drawn on poster board or on large sheets of paper. If you happen to have a magnetic blackboard, try using small magnets on the backs of the pieces, and conduct full-class activities with the pieces on the board. Students can come to the board to place or arrange pieces inside loops drawn on the board with colored chalk.

Each loop can be given a label indicating a particular attribute. As shown in Figure 11.2, the labels need not be restricted to single attributes. Affix or draw labels on each loop and have students take turns placing pieces in the appropriate regions. If a piece does not fit in any region, it is placed outside of all of the loops.

It is important to introduce labels for negative attributes such as "not red" or "not small." Also important is the use of *and* and *or* connectives, as in "red and square" or "big or happy." This use of *and, or,* and *not* significantly widens children's classification schemes. It also will cause young children considerable difficulty as they attempt to place pieces in the correct regions of the loop diagrams.

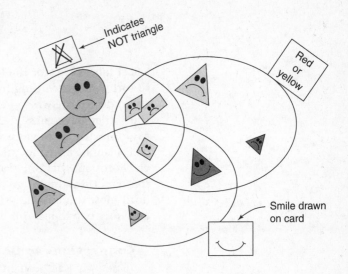

FIGURE 11.2 •

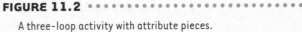
A three-loop activity with attribute pieces.

Classification Problems

The activities described so far have students attempting to classify materials according to *our* schemes—the teacher creates a classification, and the children fit pieces into it. All that is required in these activities is an understanding of the loop method of classification and the ability to discriminate the attributes. Very limited logical reasoning or problem solving is involved. A more significant activity is to infer how things have been classified when the scheme is not clearly articulated. The following activities require students to make and test conjectures about how things are being classified. These activities more directly prepare students to analyze their world, formulate questions, and do data analysis.

> **ACTIVITY 11.2**
>
> ## Guess My Rule
>
> For this activity, try using students instead of shapes as attribute "pieces." Decide on an attribute of your students such as "blue jeans" or "stripes on clothing" but do not tell your rule to the class. Silently look at one child at a time and move the child to the left or right according to this attribute rule. After a number of students have been sorted, have the next child come up and ask students to predict which group he or she belongs in. Before the rule is articulated, continue the activity for a while so that others in the class will have an opportunity to determine the rule. This same activity can be done with virtually any materials that can be sorted. When unstructured materials such as students, students' shoes, shells, or buttons are used, the classifications may be quite obscure, providing an interesting challenge.

ACTIVITY 11.3

Hidden Labels

Select label cards for the loops of string and place the cards face down. Begin to sort pieces according to the turned-down labels. As you sort, have students try to determine what the labels are for each of the loops. Let students who think they have guessed the labels try to place a piece in the proper loop but avoid having them guess the labels aloud. Students who think they know the labels can be asked to "play teacher" and respond to the guesses of the others. Point out that one way to test an idea about the labels is to select pieces that you think might go in a particular section. Do not turn the cards up until most students have figured out the rule. With simple, one-value labels and only two loops, this activity can easily be played in kindergarten.

Connections to Data Analysis

"Guess My Rule" can and should be repeated with real-world materials connected to students' current explorations. For example, if you were doing a unit on animals in the backyard, you can use pictures of animals. The loops used with the attribute materials provide a first form of data presentation. The class can "graph" data about themselves by placing information in loops with labels. A graph of "Our Pets" might consist of a picture of each student's pet or favorite stuffed animal (in lieu of a pet) and be affixed to a wall display showing how the pets were classified. Different classifications would produce different graphs. For example, the graphs could show pets by the number of legs; by fur, feathers, or scales; by how long they have been with the family; and so on. Remember that it is the students who should decide on the classification schemes to use. Remember also that data should help us answer questions. "What kinds of things would you like to know about our animals?"

Numerous resource books contain exciting and challenging activities involving attribute materials. These are aimed primarily at logical reasoning and less at the skills of classification. These logic activities were first made popular in the 1960s and 1970s. The idea was that young children would learn reasoning skills by playing these games. But reasoning should not be a strand of the curriculum. Rather, it should pervade all of the mathematics that occurs in the classroom. Furthermore, research has not supported the hoped-for claims of logic activities. They have persisted in the early childhood curriculum primarily because they are fun and involve thinking. No harm is done by these activities, but they do not really fit into any of the content strands of the curriculum.

Assessment Note

The ability to classify is an important skill for early data analysis even though it may not appear on your district curriculum guide. You can assess your students' ability to classify by observing them in small groups or listening to students as they participate in full-class discussions. What should you be looking for? Here are some suggestions:

- Are students able to place items into categories once they have been formed? Do they explain reasons for placing items in a category?
- Do students contribute to ideas for classification schemes?

- Do students understand that different classification schemes will result in a different organization of the items being sorted? For example, if student names are sorted by number of letters, they can also be sorted by which part of the alphabet they begin with—first half or second half. These two schemes would result in different sortings.
- Do students correctly use an overlapping category—items that belong to two different groups at the same time?
- Can students correctly use logical connectors *and* and *or* and the adjective *not* when creating classifications?

As you discuss a particular classification, ask students to justify their placement of items. Requiring students to explain their reasoning will provide you with much more information than if you simply accept answers or act as the authority figure in the class.

Technology Note

A popular program that encourages creation of classification schemes and using loop diagrams is *Tabletop, Jr.* (Brøderbund, 1995b). This program can be used by individuals or the full class. The program provides a wide variety of objects that can each be constructed with varying attributes. Various sorting choices are available, including the loop diagrams seen here. Objects can also be sorted according to a hidden rule specified by a user, a computer version of "Guess My Rule" with a lot of variation. Picture graphs can be constructed with the objects providing a direct link to data graphing.

Graphical Representations

How data are organized should be directly related to the question that caused you to collect the data in the first place. For example, suppose that students want to know how many pockets they have on their clothing, an idea suggested by Marilyn Burns (1996). Each student in the room counts his or her pockets and the data are collected.

If your second-grade class had collected these data, what are some ways that you might suggest they organize and graph them? Is one of your ideas better than others for answering the question about how many pockets? Think about this before reading on.

If a large bar graph is made with a bar for every student, that will certainly tell how many pockets each student has. However, is it the best way to answer the question? If the data were categorized by number of pockets, then a graph showing the number of students with two pockets, three pockets, and so on will easily show which number of pockets is most common and how the number of pockets varies across the class.

Students should be involved in deciding how they want to represent their data. However, children with little experience with the various methods of picturing data will not be aware of the many options that are available. Sometimes you can suggest a new way of displaying data and have children learn to construct that type of graph or chart. Once they have made the display, they can discuss its value. Did this graph (or chart or picture) tell about our data in a clear way? Compared to other ways of displaying data, how is this better?

The emphasis or goal of this instruction should be to help children see that graphs and charts tell about information, that different types of representations tell different things about the same data. The value of having students actually construct their own graphs is not so much that they learn the techniques but that they are personally invested in the data and that they learn how a graph conveys information. Once a graph is constructed, the most important activity is discussing what it tells the people who see it, especially those who were not involved in making the graph. Discussions about graphs of real data that the children have themselves been involved in gathering will help them interpret other graphs and charts that they see in newspapers and on TV.

What we should *not* do is get overly anxious about the tedious details of graph construction. The issues of analysis and communication are your agendas and are much more important than the technique! In the real world, technology will take care of details of graph construction.

There are two equally good possibilities you may consider when planning to have your students construct graphs or charts. First, you can simply encourage students to do their best and make, by hand, charts and graphs that make sense to them and that they feel communicate the information they wish to convey. This is not to say that children do not need guidance. They should have seen and been involved in group constructions of various types of graphs and charts. This provides them with some ideas from which to choose for their own graphs. This informal approach may be best with younger students because they will be more personally invested in their work and not distracted by the techniques of technology. Care should be taken not to worry about fancy labeling or nice, neat pictures. The intent is to get the students involved in communicating a message about their data.

The second option is to use technology. The computer has provided us with many tools for constructing simple yet powerful representations. With the help of technology, it is possible to construct several different pictures of the same data with very little effort. The discussion can then focus on the message or information that each format provides. Students can make their own selections of various graphs and can justify their choice based on their own intended purposes. As just one example, Figure 11.3 shows four graphs produced by *The Graph Club* (Tom Snyder, 1993). When two or more graphs are being created from the same data, it is possible to see all graphs change accordingly. How does a pie graph show information differently than a picture graph?

Cluster Graphs

As mentioned earlier in the discussion of attribute materials, a simple form of graph is a natural result of a classification activity. A *cluster graph* is nothing more than two or more labeled loops in which students write or place items that they have classified. For example, suppose students have been asked to tell about different types of bugs and insects that they see in their backyards. After listing and describing the different bugs, students can draw pictures of the bugs on large index cards. They can then be

FIGURE 11.3 •••••••••••

Four graphs produced with *Graph Club* software.

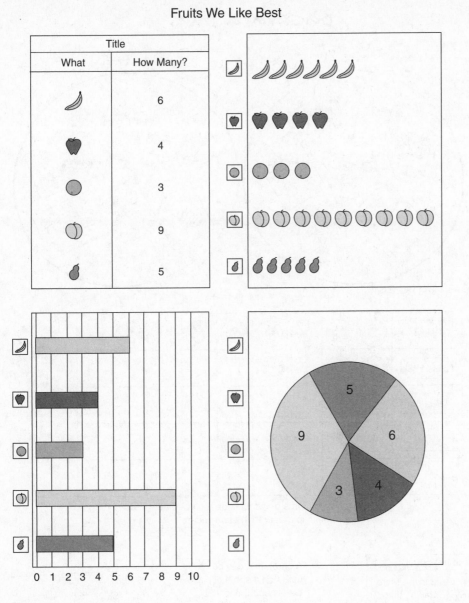

Fruits We Like Best

challenged to think of different ways to sort the bugs. The question they are answering is "What kinds of bugs do we have in our backyards?" Figure 11.4 shows one possibility for a cluster graph that would help to answer this question. Other students may want to sort the bugs in different ways (e.g., where they are found, color, number of legs). The resulting collection of cluster graphs would tell the students a lot about the bugs in their backyards.

Bar Graphs

Bar graphs and tally charts are among the first ways to group and present data and are especially useful in grades K–3. At this early level, bar graphs should be made so that each bar consists of countable parts such as squares, objects, tallies, or pictures of objects. No numeric scale is necessary. Graphs should be simple and quickly constructed.

FIGURE 11.4 ● ● ● ● ● ● ●

A cluster graph is a good first graph for young students. It is especially useful for situations in which classification of data is part of the activity. For one set of data (in this case, bugs found in the backyard) two or more different cluster graphs provide even more information. Some cluster graphs may have overlapping loops.

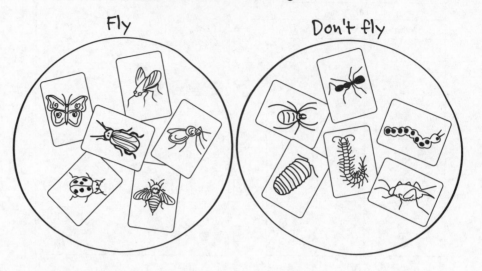

Backyard Bugs

Fly

Don't fly

FIGURE 11.5 ● ● ● ● ● ● ●

Some ideas for quick graphs that can be used again and again.

Bus 417	☺	☺	☺	☺	☺	☺	☺	☺	
Bus 206	☺	☺	☺	☺					
Bus 63	☺	☺							
Walk	☺	☺	☺	☺	☺				

Clip paper pictures or symbols on a chart that has a paper clip prepared in each square.

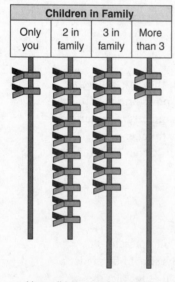

Children in Family			
Only you	2 in family	3 in family	More than 3

Hang ribbons, and students clip on pinch-style clothespins

A graph mat can be made on a sheet of plastic about 8 to 10 feet long and used on the floor. Make 5 or 6 columns with 12 to 15 squares in each column. Students place real objects in the columns to show the number of each.

Figure 11.5 illustrates a few techniques that can be used to make a graph quickly with the whole class.

A "real graph" uses the actual objects being graphed. Examples include types of shoes, seashells, and books. Each item can be placed in a square so that comparisons and counts are easily made.

Picture graphs use a drawing of some sort that represents what is being graphed. Students can make their own drawings, or you can duplicate drawings to be colored or cut out to suit particular needs.

Symbolic graphs use something like squares, blocks, tallies, or Xs to represent the things being counted in the graph. An easy idea is to use sticky notes as elements of a graph. These can be stuck directly to the chalkboard or other chart and rearranged if needed.

To make a quick graph of class data, follow these steps:

1. Decide on what groups of data will make up the different bars. It is good to have two to six different bars in a graph.
2. Have each participant prepare a contribution to the graph before you begin. For real or picture graphs, the object or picture should be ready to be placed on the graph. For symbolic graphs, students should write down or mark their choice.
3. Have students, in small groups, quickly place or mark their entry on the graph. A graph mat can be placed on the floor, or a chart can be prepared on the wall or chalkboard. If tape or pins are to be used, have these items ready.

A class of 25 to 30 students can make a graph in less than 10 minutes, leaving ample time to use it for questions and observations.

Once a graph has been constructed, engage the class in a discussion of what information the graph tells or conveys. "What can you tell about our class by looking at this shoe graph?" Graphs convey factual information (more people wear sneakers than any other kind of shoe) and also provide opportunities to make inferences that are not directly observable in the graph (kids in this class do not like to wear leather shoes). The difference between actual facts and inferences is an important idea in graph construction and is also an important idea in science.

As children begin to see different types of graphs, they can begin to make their own graphs of information gathered independently or by a group. A simple way to move graphing from the entire class to a small group is to assign different data collection tasks to different groups of children. The task is to gather the data and decide on and make a graph that displays as clearly as possible the information found. The expanded lesson for this chapter illustrates having students develop a question, gather data, and construct a graph.

EXPANDED LESSON

(pages 329–330)
This chapter's Expanded Lesson illustrates having students develop a question, gather data, and construct a graph.

Continuous Data Graphs

Bar graphs or picture graphs are useful for illustrating categories of data that have no numeric ordering—for example, colors or TV shows. When data are grouped along a continuous scale, they should be ordered along a number line. Examples of such information include temperatures that occur over time, height or weight over age, and percentages of test takers scoring in different intervals along the scale of possible scores.

GRAPHICAL REPRESENTATIONS

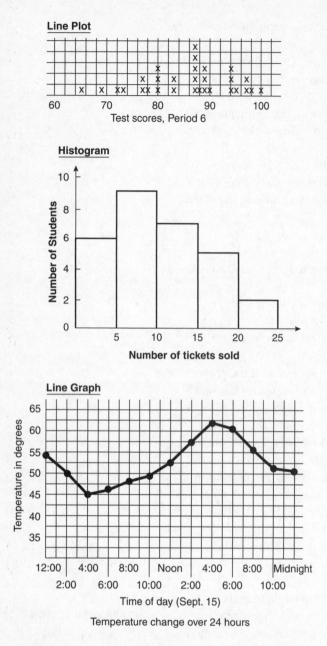

Line Plot

Test scores, Period 6

Histogram

Number of Students

Number of tickets sold

Line Graph

Temperature in degrees

Time of day (Sept. 15)

Temperature change over 24 hours

FIGURE 11.6

Three approaches to graphing data over continuous intervals. Notice that the horizontal scale must show some progression and is not just a grouping, as in a bar graph.

Line Plots

Line plots are useful *counts* of things along a numeric scale. To make a line plot, a number line is drawn and an X is made above the corresponding value on the line for every corresponding data element. One advantage of a line plot is that every piece of data is shown on the graph. It is also a very easy type of graph for students to make. It is essentially a bar graph with a potential bar for every possible value. A simple example is shown in Figure 11.6.

Histograms

A *histogram* is a form of bar graph in which the categories are consecutive equal intervals along a numeric scale. The height or length of each bar is determined by the number of data elements falling into that particular interval. Histograms are not difficult in concept but can cause problems for the students constructing them. What is the appropriate interval to use for the bar width? What is a good scale to use for the height of the bars? That all of the data must be grouped and counted within each interval causes further difficulty. Unless your district curriculum specifically indicates an understanding of histograms, it is reasonable to skip over this type of graph before fourth grade or even above. By middle school, students will have access to graphing calculators that make histogram construction rather easy.

Line Graphs

A *line graph* is used when there is a numeric value associated with equally spaced points along a continuous number scale. Points are plotted to represent two related pieces of data, and a line is drawn to connect the points. For example, a line graph might be used to show how the length of a flagpole shadow changed from one hour to the next during the day. The horizontal scale would be time, and the vertical scale would be the length of the shadow. Points can be plotted and straight lines drawn connecting them. In the example of the shadow, a shadow did exist at all times, but its length did not jump or drop from one plotted value to the other. It changed continuously as suggested by the graph. See the example in Figure 11.6.

A common error that students make is to use a line graph when the data are not distributed across a continuous scale. For example, a graph showing how tall the students in a group are is best shown with a bar graph, one bar for each student. It does not make sense to list the names of students (or the names of TV shows or the colors in the crayon box) along a scale because there is no natural ordering. With a bar graph, it

Chapter 11 HELPING CHILDREN USE DATA

does not make any difference which bar is first, second, or third.

Line graphs and line plots do show trends or tendencies that cannot be shown with bar graphs, and students should be encouraged to use them when they are appropriate. Furthermore, most computer graphing programs will produce a line graph relating two sets of numeric data. Consider the following fun exercise experiment:

When you give the signal, the full class begins to hop on one foot. Count off the number of seconds that elapse in five-second intervals. As students stop or stumble, they remember the last number you called. Now make a chart as shown in Figure 11.7 showing how long students were able to hop. This example illustrates the value of line graphs for showing trends. Had the same data been entered into a spreadsheet for children, the same graph could be produced easily.

Seconds	5	10	15	20	25	30	35	40	45	50	55	60
Still hopping	25	25	23	22	19	15	10	7	6	5	4	2

Circle Graphs

Typically, we think of circle graphs as showing percentages and, as such, these would probably not be appropriate for primary students. However, notice in Figure 11.3 that the circle graph only indicates the number of data points (in that case, students) in each of five categories. Many simple graphing programs will create a similar graph. An understanding of percentages is not required when the computer creates the graph.

Notice also that the circle graph shows information that is not easily available from the other graphs. For example, the peach and pear categories account for a bit more than half of the class, while the apple and orange groups are about one-fourth of the class. These fractional part ideas are quite appropriate at the primary level, even before students are able to make fractional estimates. As fraction concepts are developed in the third grade, making circle graphs is a good way to integrate different aspects of your curriculum.

If students are making comparisons between their class and another class or perhaps to the entire grade level, the circle graph may be one of their best tools. A circle graph for each of two groups of different size can show proportional subsets of the total. Imagine if the same data in Figure 11.3 had been gathered from the entire grade level of 128 students. Bar graphs would not be very useful. However, a circle graph for your class and one for the full grade can easily be compared.

Easily Made Circle Graphs

For students in grades 2 or 3 wishing to make circle graphs, a computer graphing program is strongly recommended and has been noted. Several such programs exist. (See Figure 11.3 for an example.) However, there are two techniques that students can use to create a circle graph that will help them understand what these graphs represent.

FIGURE 11.7 •

Line graph made from data in the table. Students tried to see how long they could hop on one foot. The graph shows that as the time increased fewer and fewer students remained hopping.

GRAPHICAL REPRESENTATIONS

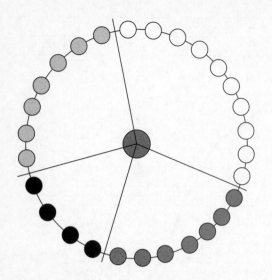

FIGURE 11.8 •••••••••••••••••••••••

A human circle graph: Students are arranged in a circle, with string stretched between them to show the divisions.

Circle graphs of the students in your room can be made quickly and quite dramatically. Suppose, for example, that each student picked his or her favorite school subject: reading, mathematics, science, or social studies. Line up all of the students in the room so that students selecting the same subject are together. Now form the entire group into a circle of students. Tape the ends of four long strings to the floor in the center of the circle and extend them to the circle at each point where the subjects change. Voilà! A very nice circle graph with no measuring and no percentages. See Figure 11.8.

Another easy approach to circle graphs is similar to the human circle graph. Begin by having students make a bar graph of the data. Once complete, cut out the bars themselves, and tape them together end to end. Next, tape the two ends together to form a circle. Estimate where the center of the circle is, draw lines to the points where different bars meet, and trace around the full loop. These two informal techniques along with a computer graphing program bring the circle graph appropriately into the primary grades.

Assessment Note ──────────────────────

As you evaluate students in the area of graphing, it is important not to pay too much attention to the skills of constructing a graph. It is more important to think about the choice of graphs that the students make to help answer their questions or complete their projects. Your goal is for students to understand that a graph helps answer a question and provides a picture of the data. Different graphs tell us different things about the data. If you make all of the decisions about what type of graphs to make, how they should be labeled and constructed, all that students are doing is following your directions. Students who are simply not good at graphic arts are likely to do poorly even though they may have exceptional understanding of what their graph shows and why they chose to make that particular type.

Students should write about their graphs, explaining what the graph tells and why they selected that type of graph to illustrate the data. Use this information for your assessment.

Describing a Set of Data

The various types of graphs we have discussed can be used to help answer the question that caused the data to be collected in the first place. The bar graph, for example, can clearly show the category that is the largest and the one that is the smallest, as well as tell exactly how large each category is. A graph provides a visual image of the data that cannot be captured in other forms.

Initially, students' focus will be on answers that come from a portion of the graph. Only one bar is necessary to tell which team sold the most candy. Two bars can be used to say how much more the red team sold than the blue team. An individual student may wish to see where his or her data point falls in the full graph. However, much more can be said about a set of data than about these individual questions. The idea is to consider the data set as a whole. One simple concept concerns the *shape of data,* a sense of how the data are spread or grouped. Another idea is to introduce simple *statistics,* numbers or measures of the data as a whole set. Although not typical in the K–3 curriculum, students at this level can begin to think about these ideas in an informal manner.

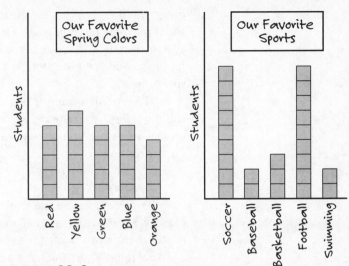

FIGURE 11.9

Two bar graphs for 25 students. The shapes of the data in these two graphs are quite different. One is spread evenly whereas the other has two high values and three low values.

The Shape of Data

Consider the two graphs in Figure 11.9, showing data that have been gathered from a class of 25 students. In the Favorite Spring Color graph, the students are roughly distributed even though there is a most favored color. In the Favorite Sports graph, two sports received most of the votes from the class and the remainder of the class is somewhat spread among the other three.

Whenever there are two or more graphs of the same type, it is worth talking with students about the overall look of the graphs—how they are alike and how they are different. Some graphs have lots of highs and lows. Others are somewhat spread out. Some graphs have most of the data in one or two categories.

When the data are depicted on a number line, such as in a line plot or histogram, the idea of data that are spread out or grouped together takes on a numeric meaning as well. For example, in a measure of the heights of boys and girls in inches, we might notice that the girls' heights are spread over a wider range than the boys'. The boys' heights may cluster around a particular height.

These informal observations about a set of data require no particular skill other than observation. At the same time they help students begin to see how a data set can be used to describe a group from which it is drawn using more global descriptors.

Descriptive Statistics

Numeric descriptions or measures of data generally apply when the individual data points are numbers rather than counts or tallies. For example, students' height, distance each can throw the playground ball, and the time required to run a lap on the playground are all numeric data. In the elementary grades, two measures of data are generally discussed: *range* and *average.*

Range

The *range* is simply the distance between the highest and the lowest data values or the difference between these values. Students can calculate the range by subtraction or by simple counting. Even if the term *range* is not used, students can talk about the difference between the top and bottom data points. For example, suppose a single lap around the playground track is timed for the second- and third-grade students. In general, the times will likely be faster for the third graders. However, the range of times may be about the same for each grade. Or the second graders may have some very slow runners as well as some who are nearly as fast as the fastest third graders. In that case, the range for the second-grade students would be quite large—their data would be much more spread out.

The range is a number or a statistic. It tells how much the data are spread out without telling what the top and bottom numbers are. When looking at two line plots on the same scale, you can see which set of data has the greater range—which is the most spread out.

Average

We sometimes use the term *average* loosely, without a real number in mind such as in "she is about average height" or "the average student will miss two or three days of school this year." More precise use of the term is found in discussions of "the average daily rainfall" or "the test average in my class." In either case, an average is a single number or measure that in some way describes or is representative of the full collection. To say the average student height in the room is 4 feet 5 inches means that, in some way, that height represents all of the students even though there may be quite a range of heights.

To be precise, an average is a *measure of central tendency,* and there are three such measures: the *mean, median,* and *mode.* The *mode* is the value that occurs most frequently in the data set. Of these three types of averages, the mode is the least useful and could perhaps be ignored completely. Consider the following set of numbers:

$$1, 1, 3, 5, 6, 7, 8, 9$$

The mode of this set is 1 and is not a very good representative of the set. If the 8 were a 9, there would be two modes. If a 1 were changed to a 2, there would be no mode at all.

The *median* is the middle value when the data are placed in order. Half of all values lie at or above the median and half below. For the eight numbers just listed, the median is between the 5 and 6, or $5\frac{1}{2}$. The median is easier to understand and compute than the mean and is a quite reasonable statistic for young students to use. It is easy for children to understand "the middle of the data."

The *mean* is the statistic that is often meant when someone refers to the "average." It is also referred to as the *arithmetic mean.* The mean is computed by adding all of the numbers in the set and dividing this sum by the number of elements added. For the small set of eight numbers we have been using, the mean is $40 \div 8$ or 5. For small sets of data, the median is usually a more stable and meaningful measure of the data center. For larger data sets the mean is also stable and is the measure most often used for this purpose by statisticians.

Understanding Average

With children below grade 4 it would be a mistake to spend time teaching how to compute these different averages without some appreciation for why someone would do that. The concept of a single number in some way representing all of the numbers in the set is a bit difficult. However, as already noted, it is quite reasonable to talk about the "middle" number or the "middle of the data" (even when the middle is not a data point). This is a good way to introduce the idea of a single measure representing the data. The term *median* can be applied once students understand what is meant by the middle of the data.

If you want to explore the notion of mean with young students, a good introductory concept is one of leveling off the data.

Suppose that the average number of family members for the students in your class is 5. One way to interpret this is to think about distributing the entire collection of moms, dads, sisters, and brothers to each of the students so that each would have a "family" of the same size. To say that you have an average of 93 for the four tests in your class is like spreading the total of all of your points evenly across the four tests. It is as if each student had the same family size and each test score were the same, but the totals matched the actual distributions. This concept of the mean is easy to understand and explain and has the added benefit that it leads directly to the method for computing the mean.

ACTIVITY 11.4

Leveling the Bars

Have students make a bar graph of some data using plastic connecting cubes such as Unifix. Choose a situation with 5 or 6 bars with no more than 10 or 12 cubes in each. For example, the graph in Figure 11.10 shows prices for six toys. The task for students is to use the graph itself to determine what the price would be if all of the toys were the same price, assuming that the total for all the toys remained the same. Students will use various techniques to rearrange the cubes in the graph but will eventually create six equal bars, possibly with some leftovers that could mentally be distributed in fractional amounts. (In the example, the total number of cubes is a multiple of six.) Do not tell students they are finding the average or mean, only that they are to find equal-length bars.

Explain to students that the size of the leveled bars is the *mean* of the data—the amount that each item would cost if all items cost the same amount but the total of the prices remained fixed.

Follow "Leveling the Bars" with the next activity to help students develop an algorithm for finding the mean.

ACTIVITY 11.5

The Mean Foot

Pose the following question: What is the mean length of our feet in inches? Have each student cut a strip of adding machine tape that matches the length of his or her foot. Students record their

(continued)

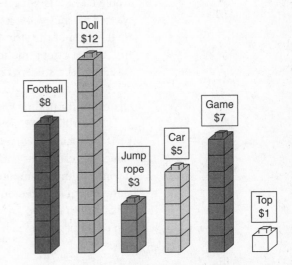

Bar graph made with plastic snap cubes

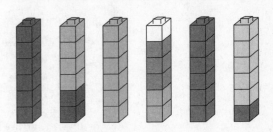

The same cubes rearranged into equal stacks.
Their height is the <u>mean</u> value of the bars above.

FIGURE 11.10 • • • • • • • • • • • • • • • • •

Understanding the mean as a leveling of the data.

names and the length of their feet in inches on the strips. Suggest that before finding a mean for the class, you will first get means for smaller groups. Put students into groups of four, six, or eight students. (Groups of five or seven will prove to be problematic.) In each group, have the students tape their foot strips end to end. The task for each group is to come up with a method of finding the mean without using any of the lengths written on the strips. They can only use the combined strip. Each group will share their method with the class. From this work, they will devise a method for determining the mean for the whole class.

> **STOP** Before reading on, what is a method that the students could use in "The Mean Foot"?

To evenly distribute the inches for each student's foot among the members of the group, they can fold the strip into equal parts so that there are as many sections as students in the group. Then they can measure the length of any one part.

How can you find the mean for the whole class? Suppose there are 23 students in the class. Using the strips already taped together, make one very long strip for the whole class. It is not reasonable to fold this long strip into 23 equal sections. But if you wanted to know how long the resulting strip would be, how could that be done? The total length of the strip is the sum of the lengths of the 23 individual foot strips. To find the length of one section if the strip were actually folded in 23 parts, simply divide by 23. In fact, students can mark off "mean feet" along the strip. There should be very close to 23 equal-length "feet." This dramatically illustrates the usual add-up-and-divide algorithm for finding the mean.

Regardless of how you approach the ideas of mean, median, and possibly mode, keep the focus on what these numbers represent—different ways to determine a single value that can represent or be used in place of a full set of data. Do not spend time having children compute these statistics for lots of different data sets. Little is to be gained from such tedious exercises. Rather, discuss what can and can't be told about a set of data if all you know is the range and either the mean or the median. Students can easily begin to see that while these measures are helpful, they really don't tell the full story.

Assessment Note

Just as with the assessment of graphing, your focus on students' work with mean, median, and range should be on the interpretation of these numbers rather than exercises to compute them. In subsequent years students will have ample opportunity to use calculators and computers to do the computations for them. What is most important is for students to offer their understanding of what the numbers mean. By way of example, you can have students write a short paragraph explaining what the mean of their data tells them and what it does not tell them.

EXPANDED LESSON

Using Data to Answer Our Questions

GRADE LEVEL: First through third grades.

MATHEMATICS GOALS
- To learn how different graphing techniques are used to answer questions about a population.
- To learn how to use data to create graphs.

THINKING ABOUT THE STUDENTS
- This lesson assumes that students have had experiences with several different types of graphs, at least cluster graphs and some form of bar graph. Bar graphs may be picture graphs, real graphs, or simple bar graphs of columns or rows of squares. Tallies or numbers may also

have been used to represent data. Students may have access to and have used a computer program that will produce graphs. Most such programs include circle graphs as an option. If that is the case, the computer should be available as an option in this lesson.

MATERIALS AND PREPARATION
- Students should have ready access to large pieces of paper such as chart paper. Paper with a large grid, such as a 1-cm grid should also be available. (See BLM 31.) Because the lesson allows students to make their own choices about graphing techniques, these materials simply need to be available to students.

....

lesson

This lesson may require several days to complete. It is more of a project than a typical problem-solving lesson. Nonetheless, a problem spirit should be employed in each of three phases of the lesson: (1) What question do we want to answer, and how will we collect the data? (2) What type of graph should we use to answer our question? (3) How do our graphs answer the question? For young students, these issues will need to be addressed separately and perhaps on different days. Here they are presented as two tasks with the third phase dealt with in the AFTER portion of the second task.

BEFORE (1)

The First Task
- Decide on a question you would like to answer and how you will gather data to answer it.

  How you guide this discussion will vary with the age of your students and perhaps their recent experiences, such as a field trip or unit of study in science, or a book that has been read to the class. Regardless, the first problem is to decide: What do we want to know or learn? Consider such ideas as favorites (books, food, etc.), nature or science (weather, what lives in our yards), comparisons (something about your class as compared with another class, children compared to adults), measures (heights, arm spans), how many (pets, hours watching TV, minutes spent brushing teeth), and so on.

  After focusing attention on a general topic, brainstorm ideas about what students want to know. It would be useful to have different groups explore different aspects of the same broad topic. For kindergarten, the class will need to work jointly on a topic.

  Once a question or questions are determined, talk about how information (data) can be gathered. If a survey is required, you will probably need to help formulate one to three questions that have simple responses—not full sentences or explanations. What is important is that students are personally invested in the decisions.

BLM 31

DURING (1)

- Set students to gathering the data. If the collection involves getting data from home or from another class, you will need to help students be very organized about doing this so that real data are available when you need it.
- Monitor the data collection to be sure it is being gathered in a useful manner.

AFTER (1)

- When the data have been collected, briefly discuss what data the class, groups, or individuals have gathered. At this point, a new problem develops as follows.

BEFORE (2)

The Second Task

- Decide on a type of graph to make with the data that will help answer your question. Make the graph.

Brainstorm

- Engage the class in thinking about the various types of graphs that they know how to make and ask for ideas that match a type of graph with the question to be answered and the data gathered. You may need to remind students about techniques they have seen or that are available on the computer.

Establish Expectations

- Show students the types of materials available to them (including the computer if appropriate). They are to select a type of graph, use the data they have collected, and create a presentation of the data in a way that they believe answers the question. Students will work best in groups of two or three, even if multiple groups are working on the same data and question.

DURING (2)

- Be sure students are profitably working. Do not worry excessively with details or precision. If the bars in a graph do not represent the quantities, help students use squares or other methods. However, even if the graph is not exactly accurate, as long as it approximately represents the data and will not distort conclusions, it should be left alone.
- Encourage students to add words to their posters or presentations to tell what the graph stands for.

AFTER (2)

- Have groups display their graphs. Take turns having students explain their graphs and how the graph answers their question. Ask the other students if they agree that the graph shows the answer to the question. There may be some discussion about which graphs best answered the question and why. (Note that this means the best *type* of graph for the data and the question.)
- Ask students if they can answer other questions using the graphs or what else the graphs show.

....

- Continued work with data analysis is a matter of practice. Lessons such as this one can and should be repeated several times during the year. If new graphing techniques are introduced, such as continuous data graphs or circle graphs, that is a good time to repeat a project such as this one.

- Appropriate accomplishment in this area should be viewed as an awareness of graphical options and the ability to get information from a graph.

EARLY EXPERIENCES WITH PROBABILITY CONCEPTS

Chapter 12

Young children's concept of the likelihood of a future event is often bewildering to adults. Children can be absolutely convinced that the next roll of the die will be a three "because I just know it's going to happen" or "because three is my lucky number." Consider how engrossing the pre-K or kindergarten child finds a game of chance such as Old Maid or Candyland. These games of pure chance have become timeless because children do not comprehend that random chance makes each player equally likely to win. Rather, winning makes them proud of the accomplishment.

More realistic concepts of chance will require considerable development before children are ready to construct formal ideas about the probability of a future event. This development best occurs as children consider and discuss with their peers the outcomes of a wide variety of probabilistic situations. Simply telling students how probability works will be completely useless. Probability instruction at the K–3 level involves confronting students with the outcomes of simple experiments and games and discussing the reasons for these outcomes. During these early years, our goal should be to develop in students an intuitive understanding of chance that will be a firm foundation for the more precise ideas that will be developed in grades 4 through 6.

big ideas

1 Chance has no memory. For repeated trials of a simple experiment (e.g., tossing a coin), the outcomes of prior trials have no impact on the next. The chance occurrence of six heads in a row has no effect on getting a head on the next toss of the coin. That chance is still 50-50.

2 The occurrence of a future event can be characterized along a continuum from impossible to certain.

3 The *probability of an event* is a number between 0 and 1 that is a measure of the chance that a given event will occur. A probability of 0 indicates impossibility and that of 1 indicates certainty. A probability of $\frac{1}{2}$ indicates an even chance of the event occurring.

4 The relative frequency of outcomes of an event (*experimental probability*) can be used as an estimate of the exact probability of an event. The larger the number of trials, the better the estimate will be. The results for a small number of trials may be quite different than those experienced in the long run.

5 For some events, the exact probability can be determined by an analysis of the event itself. A probability determined in this manner is called a *theoretical probability*.

Probability on a Continuum

The big ideas you just read can provide a fairly good sense of how you might expect to develop students' ideas about probability. An understanding that chance has no memory can only come with experience and through discussion with peers. Many adults still do not believe this. For example, many select lottery numbers because they have not come up recently. However, this is a critical idea if children are going to abandon their naïve ideas about chance and become more analytical in examining outcomes.

The most important big idea at the primary level is the second one: Not all events occur with equal likelihood. Even knowing the likelihood of an event does not predict its occurrence in the short run. However, if we know the likelihood or probability of two events, we can compare the chance of one event to the other.

From Impossible to Certain

Remember that young children have strong beliefs about chance or luck. If red is their favorite color, they may strongly believe red will turn up when they spin a red/blue spinner, even if only a small portion of the spinner is red. To change these early misconceptions, a good place to begin is with the extremes of the continuum. The following activity is designed for that purpose. In preparation for this activity, have a discussion of the words *impossible* and *certain*. Certain is the harder of these words for children. It means "absolutely for sure." It is the exact opposite of impossible.

ACTIVITY 12.1

Is It Likely?

Ask students to judge various events as *certain, impossible,* or *possible* ("might happen"). Consider these examples:

- It will rain tomorrow.
- Drop a rock in water and it will sink.
- Trees will talk to us in the afternoon.
- The sun will rise tomorrow morning.
- Three students will be absent tomorrow.
- George will go to bed before 8:30 tonight.
- You will have two birthdays this year.

Have children describe or make up events that are certain, impossible, or possible. For each event, they should justify their estimate of likelihood.

As you discuss events that are either certain or impossible, be sure to pay attention to those events that are possible but not certain. The key idea to developing chance or probability on a continuum is to help children see that some of these possible events are more likely or less likely than others. You might get picked to be the line leader today. There is a better chance that you will be near the front of the line and an even better chance that you will not be last.

The use of random devices that can be analyzed (e.g., spinners, number cubes, coins to toss, colored cubes drawn from a bag) can help students make predictions about the likelihood of an event. The following activity or variations of it should be repeated often using the same random devices and also with a variety of devices.

Race to the Top

Two players take turns spinning a spinner with two outcomes. Each game requires a simple recording sheet with ten rows or spaces. Figure 12.1 shows a sheet for a two-color spinner. In the simplest version of the game, use only one spinner: one-fourth red and three-fourths blue. Before playing, each student predicts which color will win, red or blue. (Note that it is *color* that wins, not a player!) After each spin, an X is drawn in the appropriate column. Play continues until one color reaches the top of the chart.

Students should play "Race to the Top" several times. After all students have played, ask "Which color won the most times? Why do you think so? If you play again, what color do you think will win?"

Repeat "Race to the Top" using a variety of spinners. Notice that both equal spinners—each color having the same total area—and not equal spinners can be made using either two regions or more than two regions as shown here. If a spinner has three colors, the game sheet should have three columns.

As a random device, spinners have the advantage that students can see the relative portion of the whole given to each color or outcome. The other advantage is that spinner faces can easily be made to adjust the chances of different outcomes. Transparent plastic spinners can be purchased that have no partitions. Paper spinner faces that suit your current needs are taped to the bottom of these spinners and can be changed later. Transparent spinners can also be used on the overhead projector. Use an overhead pen to mark the sections. There are also several methods that can be used to make a spinner. One is shown in Figure 12.2.

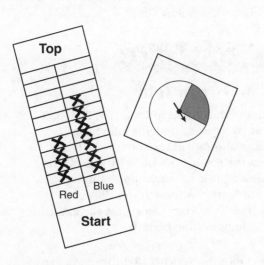

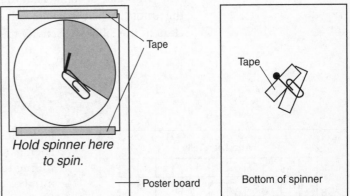

Hold spinner here to spin.

Tape

Poster board

Tape

Bottom of spinner

Draw spinner faces and duplicate them so that you can easily make lots of spinners. Cut these out and tape to poster board. Students can color the sections of the spinner. Make a small hole in the spinner center. Unbend one end of a sturdy paper clip and poke this upward from the bottom of the spinner. Tape the paper clip to the back leaving a paper clip post sticking up in the center of the spinner. To use the spinner, students put another paper clip on the post to act as the pointer. Hold the spinner flat to spin fairly. Spinner faces can be changed easily.

FIGURE 12.1 • • • • • • • • • • • • • • • • • •

Students take turns spinning a spinner and recording the result. The first color to reach the top is the winner. The same game can be played with other random devices.

FIGURE 12.2 •

An easy way to make a spinner.

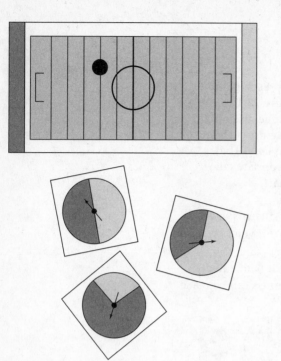

FIGURE 12.3 ● ● ● ● ● ● ● ● ● ● ● ● ● ● ●

A simple game of chance played with different spinners helps young children with basic concepts of chance.

Play "Race to the Top" with other devices. Put 4 red dots and 2 blue dots on the sides of a wooden cube to create a different red/blue device. Similarly, use opaque bags with 8 red and 2 blue tiles or some other ratio of red to blue. Students draw a tile from the bag. Be sure that students return the tiles to the bag after each draw.

In the following game, students select the spinner of their choice on each turn.

ACTIVITY 12.3

Spinner Hockey

Using a game board like the one shown in Figure 12.3, each of two players selects a goal. A marker (the puck) is placed in the center of the board. On their turn, players announce which color they think will come up next. Then they select any of the three spinners. If the announced color comes up, the puck is moved one space toward their goal. If not, it moves one space toward the opponent's goal. Play continues until a player gets the puck in the goal.

"Spinner Hockey" is an opportunity for students to play a game of chance in which they can influence the results. However, many students will still be strongly guided by their belief in luck. Students may pick different colors on different turns because of subjective reasons. ("The other color just came up." "Red comes up more than blue.") The most important thing to watch for is the choice of spinner. Do they select a spinner that is most favorable to the color? They may simply pick one that is their lucky spinner.

The value of spinners in these activities is that students can readily see the size of the regions. When there are only two outcomes, the choices are simple and reasonably clear. In the following activity the favored outcome is not as clear.

ACTIVITY 12.4

Add Then Tally

Make number cubes with sides as follows 1, 1, 2, 3, 3, 3. Each game requires two cubes. Students take turns rolling the two cubes and record the sum of the two numbers. To record the results, run off tally sheets with five rows of ten squares, one for each sum 2 through 6. (See Figure 12.4.) Students continue to roll the cubes until one of the rows is full. They can repeat the game on a new tally sheet as long as time permits.

It is important to talk with students after they have played "Add Then Tally." Which numbers "won" the most and the least often? If they were to play again, which number would they pick to win and why?

Add Then Tally

2										
3										
4										
5										
6										

FIGURE 12.4 ● ● ● ● ● ● ● ● ● ● ● ● ● ● ● ● ● ● ●

A recording sheet for "Add Then Tally."

With these number cubes, a sum of 4 is the most likely. Sums of 2 or 3 are the least likely. However, because young students will almost certainly not analyze the possible outcomes, their predictions for future games will tell you a lot about their probabilistic reasoning. Students who observe that 4 comes up a lot and, therefore, is the best choice to win have abandoned earlier subjective ideas about luck or of chance having a memory.

Assessment Note

Remember that students' ideas about chance must develop from experience. An explanation from a teacher will likely provide only superficial understanding. It is important to have discussions with students after playing each of these simple games. During the discussions, your task is to elicit their ideas, not to explain or offer judgment. The main idea that you are looking for is a growth from a belief in pure chance or luck to one in which students begin to understand that some results are clearly more or less likely to happen than others regardless of luck or favorite colors. When you sense that this sort of growth has taken place, a significant milestone has been reached and you will know that your students are ready to move on and begin to refine their ideas of chance a bit more.

The Probability Continuum

Your goal for the activities in the previous section was for students to discover that some outcomes are more likely than others. The phrases "more likely" and "less likely" should be used whenever there is an opportunity.

To begin refining this concept, introduce the idea of a continuum of likelihood between impossible and certain. Draw a long line on the board. Label the left end "Impossible" and the right end "Certain." Write "Chances of Spinning Blue" above the line. Call this a "probability line" or a "chance line." Next, show students a spinner that is all white. "What is the chance of spinning blue with this spinner?" Indicate the left end of the probability line as showing this chance. Repeat with an all blue spinner, indicating the right end, labeled Certain. Next, show a spinner that is half blue and half white. "What is the chance of spinning blue with this spinner?" The discussion should develop a consensus that it is about *equally likely* that blue will come up as not blue. Place a mark exactly in the center of the line to indicate this chance. Some students may know other words to describe this such as "50 percent chance" or "even chances."

Repeat the preceding discussion with a spinner that is less than $\frac{1}{4}$ blue and with one that is nearly all blue. Ask students where they would put a mark on the line to indicate the chance of spinning blue for each of these. These marks should be close to the ends of the line. (See Figure 12.5.) To review these ideas, show the spinners one at a time and ask which marks represent the chance of getting blue for that spinner.

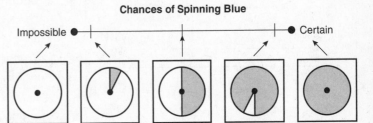

FIGURE 12.5 •

The probability line or "chance line." Use these spinner faces to help students see how chance can be at different places on a continuum between impossible and certain.

In the next activity students design random devices that they think will create chances for various designated positions on the probability line. The activity suggests that students use a bag of colored tiles or cubes, which is a bit different than the spinners. Even if the idea of drawing tiles from a bag seems new to your students, do not provide additional hints to help them with their reasoning.

ACTIVITY 12.5

Design a Bag

[Note that students must be introduced to the idea of a probability line as described in the paragraphs preceding this activity.]

Provide pairs of students with a copy of a worksheet similar to that shown in Figure 12.6. This can be hand sketched. Be sure there are 12 squares drawn on the bag. On the board mark a place on a probability line at roughly the 20 percent position. Of course, you are not using percent language with the children. Students are to mark this position on their worksheet probability lines. Alternatively, you could mark the worksheets before making copies. Students should color the square indicated by "Color" at the top of the page. Explain that they are going to decide what color tiles should be put in bags of 12 total tiles so that the chance of drawing this designated color is about the same as the chance indicated on the probability line. Before students begin to design their bags, ask for ideas about what colors of tiles might be put in the bag if the mark were very close to the middle of the line. Show how the real bags will be filled based on the design on the page. Demonstrate with tiles, a bag, and a completed worksheet. Emphasize that the tiles will be shaken up so that which particular squares on the bag design are colored makes no difference.

At the bottom of each sheet (and on the reverse if needed), students explain why they chose their tiles. Give them an example: *We put in 8 red and 4 of other colors because* _____.

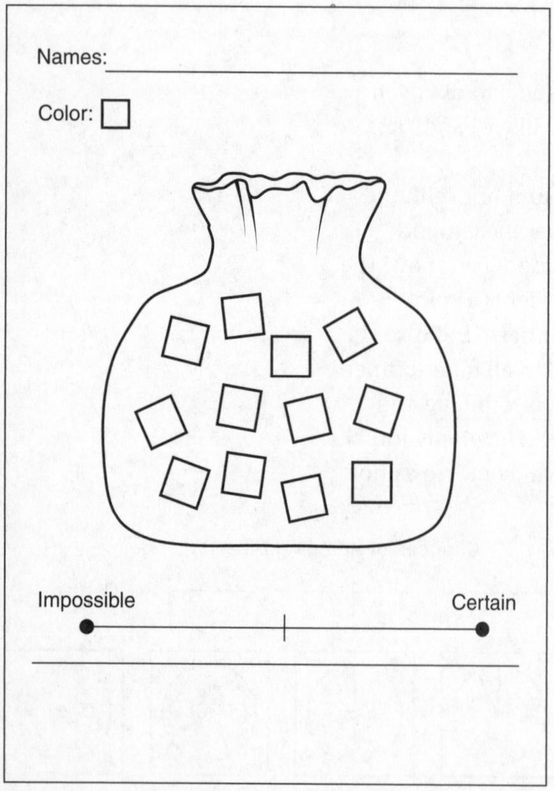

The "Design a Bag" activity provides useful information about how your students conceive of chance as appearing on a continuum. More importantly, however, you should follow up "Design a Bag" with the following related activity.

FIGURE 12.6 •

A possible recording sheet for the "Design a Bag" activity. Students mark a point on the line between impossible and certain. Then they color the tiles in the bag to create a mix that will produce the estimated chance of the designated color being drawn.

ACTIVITY 12.6

Testing Bag Designs

Collect and display the designs made by the students in "Design a Bag." Discuss the ideas that students had for the number of designated colors to put in the bag. (Expect some variation.) Some students may think that the colors used for the other tiles make a difference, and this point should be discussed. Do not provide your opinion or comment on these ideas. Select a bag design that most students seem to agree on for the 20 percent mark. Distribute lunch bags and tiles or cubes to pairs of students to fill as suggested. Once filled, students shake the bag and draw out one tile. Tally marks are used to record a Yes (for the designated color) or No for any other color. This is repeated at least ten times. Be sure that students replace each tile after it is drawn.

Discuss with the class how their respective experiments turned out. Did it turn out the way they expected? With the small number of trials, there will be groups that get rather unexpected results.

Next, make a large bar graph or tally graph of the data from all of the groups together. This should show many more No's than Yes's. Here the discussion can help students see that if the experiment is repeated a lot of times, it is clearer that the chances are about as predicted.

The dual activities of "Design a Bag" and "Testing Bag Designs" can and should be repeated for two or three other marks on the probability line. Try marks at about $\frac{1}{3}$, $\frac{1}{2}$, and $\frac{3}{4}$. You may want to assign a different mark to different groups so that a discussion can include comparisons of different designs and outcomes. To compare results it is useful if the total number of trials for each design is about the same.

"Design a Bag" and "Testing Bag Designs" are important activities. Because no numbers are used for the probabilities, there are no "right" answers. The small group testing of a design shows students that chance is not an absolute predictor in the short run. The group graphs may help students with the difficult concept that the chance tends to approach what is expected in the long run. However, this latter idea involves comparing ratios in the small trials with ratios in large numbers using the accumulated data. Do not be surprised or concerned if students do not see this as clearly as you might hope.

As another variation of "Design a Bag" have students design a spinner instead of a bag of tiles. This will allow you to revisit the concept at a later time without being repetitious.

Sample Spaces and Probability

So far in this chapter, activities have been designed to explore the basic idea that some events may be more or less likely than others. Furthermore, students have attempted to locate the likelihood of an event along a continuum from impossible to certain. A next step is to identify all of the possible outcomes of an experiment and consider their relative chances of occurring.

The *sample space* for an experiment or chance situation is the set of all possible outcomes for that experiment. For example, if a bag contains two red, three yellow, and five blue tiles, the sample space consists of all ten tiles. The *event* of drawing a yellow tile has three elements in the sample space and the event of drawing a blue tile has five elements in the sample space. For rolling a single number cube, the sample space always consists of the numbers 1 to 6. However, we might define several different events that split up the sample space in different ways. For example, rolling either an odd or an even number splits the sample space into two equal parts. Rolling either 5 or more or less than 5 splits the sample space into two unequal parts. When rolling a number cube, each number from 1 to 6 has an equal chance of occurring. Therefore, the chances of rolling an odd or an even number are equal. However, the chance of rolling a 5 or 6 is less than the chance of rolling a number less than 5.

One-Stage Experiments

For primary students, begin with experiments that require only a single device such as a number cube, a spinner, or drawing a tile from a bag. These can be referred to as *one-stage* experiments because there is only one activity to determine an outcome.

The activities in this section will help children learn to identify all of the possible outcomes of a simple experiment and consider the relative chances of events that make up these outcomes.

ACTIVITY 12.7

Six Chips

This two-player game requires one number cube. Each player needs a game board such as the one shown here and six counters or chips that will fit in the columns of the game board.

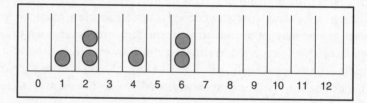

Before beginning play, each player places six chips on his or her columns of the game board. The chips can be placed in any of the 13 columns. More than one chip may be placed in a column if desired. For example, a player may choose to place three chips in the 5 column, two in the 3 column, and one in the 6 column. After placing their chips, the players roll to see who goes first. A turn consists of rolling the number cube one time. If the result indicates a column in which the player has chips, one chip is removed from that column. Then it is the other player's turn. Play continues in this manner until one player has removed all six counters from his or her board.

After students have had several chances to play the game, discuss where they placed their chips and why. Which numbers are possible? Which are impossible? Why did you put your chips on the board the way you did? Do you think there is a best way to place your chips so that you will have a better chance of winning?

One value of the "Six Chips" game is to see if students understand what outcomes are possible even though the outcomes on a single number cube seem rather straightforward. The board includes numbers that are impossible to roll (0, and 7 through 12). Watch for students who place chips on these numbers but allow them to continue to play the game without interference.

Sometimes students are so influenced by their belief in luck that certain outcomes of an experiment may not seem possible even when they clearly are (Jones, Langrall, & Thornton, 1999). When students leave a column blank in "Six Chips," it is not clear if they understand that a column left blank is possible or if they simply believe it is not likely to come up. Discussion is important. In the next activity, the task is to identify all possible outcomes.

EXPANDED LESSON
(pages 348–349)
A complete lesson plan based on "Create a Game" can be found at the end of this chapter.

ACTIVITY 12.8

Create a Game

Two students are given a bag with different colored tiles. For example, the bag might have six red, two green, one yellow, and three blue tiles. The task is to separate the possible outcomes into two lists, one for each of the two players. For example, Player A might be assigned red tiles and Player B green, yellow, and blue. This should be recorded. The players take turns drawing a tile from the bag and then replacing it. When players draw a tile of their color, they win one counter. If it is not their color, the opponent wins a counter. Start with ten counters. Players take turns drawing and replacing tiles until all ten counters have been won.

Repeat the activity with different tile combinations so that you can observe how students divide the events and on what basis. Try situations such as two red, three blue, and seven yellow, where there is no possible way to create a fair game. Will these bother students? What do they believe about their chances of winning? For a two-three-five bag of tiles, will students separate the three colors to create a fair game? Allow students to replay the game with the same tiles but with a change of how the colors are divided.

Instead of drawing tiles from a bag, try playing "Create a Game" with different spinners. Provide a variety of spinner faces and see how students divide up the possible outcomes. Some examples are shown here but do not feel restricted to these.

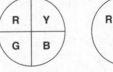

Assessment Note

In "Create a Game" watch for students who omit an outcome from the two lists. Allow them to play the game anyway. When the omitted outcome occurs in the game, listen to how students handle the situation. Remember, you want them to realize that all outcomes are possible, even those that have small chances.

The other thing to watch for in "Create a Game" is the manner in which the outcomes are sorted between the two players. Do they seem to understand the relative chances of each and try to make the game fair, or do luck and "favorite colors" influence decisions?

Two-Stage Experiments

Flipping a penny is a one-stage experiment, and the sample space has only two elements: heads and tails. Flipping two pennies is a two-stage experiment. What is the sample space for two coins?

For a one-coin toss, you would confidently predict that about half of the trials
would result in heads and half tails. For tossing two coins, it is quite common for people to observe that there are three outcomes: both heads, both tails, and one of each; so
they predict that a head–tail combination will occur about one-third of the time. (What
did you predict?) After conducting the experiment, they are surprised to find that the
head–tail combination occurs about *half* of the time. To understand the results it is useful to reexamine the sample space.

Although both coins are pennies, they are different coins. We could identify
them as the first and the second penny. They could be tossed by two different people
or in sequence. There is only one way that two heads can occur and one way that two
tails could occur. But one head and one tail can occur in two ways:
first coin heads—second coin tails and first coin tails—second coin
heads. The sample space has four—not three—equally likely outcomes: HH, HT, TH, and TT. The event of a head and a tail makes
up two of the four outcomes.

Rolling two dice and adding the two results is also a two-
stage experiment, even though the two dice may be rolled at the
same time. (Think about a red die and a green die.) The sample
space really has 36 outcomes, not just the sums 2 through 12. Figure 12.7 shows the results of a large number of dice rolls recorded
in two ways—first by the sum and second by the result of each die.

Two-stage experiments are appropriate for second- and third-
grade students to use in their explorations of probability. However,
an accurate analysis by students of all of the elements of the sample space (as in Figure 12.7) is not very likely without some guidance. What is more important than explaining to students how to
interpret these two-stage sample spaces is to always allow ample
time for students to explore experiments and to think about why
the results turned out as they did. An experimental approach—
actually conducting experiments and looking at the outcomes—is
important for a number of reasons.

- It is significantly more intuitive. Results generally make
  more sense to students than an abstract rule.

- It diminishes guessing at probabilities. Initial estimates of
  probabilities can and should be made on the basis of
  experimental results.

- It provides a background for examining the theoretical
  model. When you begin to sense that a head–tail combination occurs about half of the time rather than a third of
  the time, the explanation seems more reasonable.

- It helps students see how the ratio of a particular outcome
  to the total number of trials gets closer to a fixed number

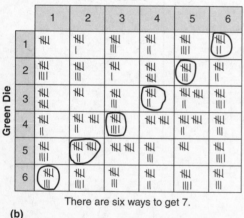

(a)

(b)

There are six ways to get 7.

FIGURE 12.7

Tallies can account only for the total (a) or keep
track of the individual dice (b).

Chapter 12 EARLY EXPERIENCES WITH PROBABILITY CONCEPTS

as the number of trials increases. (The way that results converge in the long run is explored in the next section of the chapter.)

- It is a lot more fun and interesting! Searching for the explanation is challenging, especially when the result is different than expected.

Activities 12.9 and 12.10 each involve two-stage experiments. For most students, the results of their experiments will be different from their initial expectations. Refrain from explaining the sample spaces. Rather, encourage students to accumulate results from an even larger number of trials. If you have students who you think may be able to construct the sample spaces for these experiments, by all means challenge them to do so.

ACTIVITY 12.9

Twelve Chips

This game for two players is just like "Six Chips" (Activity 12.7) but is played with two number cubes instead of one. Students need not have played "Six Chips" first. As in "Six Chips," each player needs a game board with 13 numbered columns (0 to 12) and 12 chips that can be placed in the columns. Before beginning play, each player places his or her 12 chips on the columns of the game board. These can be placed in any of the 13 columns. More than one chip may be placed in a column if desired. Some students may even wish to put all of their chips in one column, although spreading them out from 2 to 12 is the most common approach among young students. After placing their chips, the players roll to see who goes first. A turn consists of rolling the two number cubes one time and adding the two numbers that come up. If the result indicates a column in which the player has a chip, one chip is removed from that column. After one roll, it is the other player's turn. Play continues in this manner until one player has removed all 12 chips from his or her board.

After students have had several chances to play the game, discuss where they placed their chips and why. Which numbers are possible (2 to 12)? Which are impossible (0 and 1)? Do some numbers come up more often than others (yes)? Why do you think that happens?

Allow students ample opportunities to play "Twelve Chips." See if students have noticed that some numbers seem to come up more often than others. Many students will notice that 2 and 12 are "hard to get." Exploring that observation may lead to students noticing that there is only one way to get each of these numbers. A natural question then is "How many ways are there of getting other numbers?" Students may not think about the fact that a 2 and a 5, for example, can happen two different ways. You might increase the likelihood of this observation by having students use two different colors of number cubes. In any event, at this level it is not important that students completely analyze this sample space.

ACTIVITY 12.10

Match

In this game for two players, tiles or cubes of two different colors are placed in a bag. Before playing, one player is selected to be Match and the other is

(continued)

Not Match. Each player reaches into the bag and draws out one tile. If the two players' tiles match in color, Match scores a point. If they are different colors, Not Match scores a point. The tiles are then returned to the bag for the next turn. The player with the most points after 12 turns wins.

Match should be played often with different combinations of tiles. Begin with two tiles of two colors (e.g., two red and two yellow). Then let students try other combinations of two colors, but use no more than six total chips.

The important question to ask about the "Match" activity is this: Is this game fair? That is, does each player have the same chance of winning? For the 2-and-2 version (two chips of each color), students may be surprised to find that Not Match seems to win more often than Match. This version of "Match" will, in the long run, favor Not Match twice as often. Many students will attribute this result to luck but others may want to find a way to make the game fair by changing the tiles in the bag. Still others may want to discover why the game seems to be fair for some combinations and not for others.

This is a good example of allowing students to explore a problem to an extent compatible with their interest and ability. At one level, students will enjoy playing the game and perhaps trying out different combinations of colors. At the other extreme, students will be eager to find a logical explanation for the results.

 Before reading on, see if you can determine all of the elements of the sample space for the situation with two tiles of each color and explain why Not Match will win more often. As a hint, the sample space has 12 elements, each of which is equally likely.

Possible results for first draw.   Possible results for second draw.

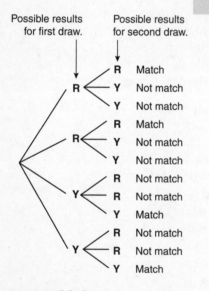

FIGURE 12.8 • • • • • • • • • • • •

This is a tree diagram analysis of drawing two successive chips from a bag with two red and two yellow chips. Each complete branch shows one outcome in the sample space. There are 12 branches each resulting in a Match (both chips same color) or a Not Match (different colors).

For those students who are interested in why the "Match" activity is not fair for the 2-and-2 version, a good suggestion is to introduce a tree diagram as shown in Figure 12.8. The first branches of the tree show all of the ways that the first tile can be drawn. The second branches show the ways that the second tile can be drawn. Note that the second branches depend on what was drawn first. If a red chip is drawn first, then there is only one way—one red chip—that the second player has to get a match and two ways two yellow chips to get a not match.

A tree diagram is a good method for young students to analyze two-stage experiments as long as there are not too many outcomes for each stage. In the 2-and-2 version there are four outcomes for the first stage and three outcomes for the second. This produces a total of 12 (4 × 3) outcomes for the combined experiment. If there are six tiles in the bag, there will be 6 × 5 or 30 elements in the sample space. This is about as large a tree diagram as is reasonable to draw.

In "Match" the outcome of the second stage or second tile drawn depends on the outcome of the first. These are called *dependent* events. But when two number cubes are thrown, the result of each cube is independent of the other. These are known as *independent* events. Even if students played "Match" by themselves, drawing two tiles at once, the results remain the same as if drawing one tile and then drawing a second. However, if the first tile is returned to the bag before the second tile is drawn, then the two draws are independent of each other; the contents of the bag are the same for each

Chapter 12 EARLY EXPERIENCES WITH PROBABILITY CONCEPTS

draw. The results of "Match" are much more predictable for the replacement version because any bag with the same number of tiles of each color will be a fair game. Other combinations will not be fair. (Can you tell why?)

Tree diagrams should only be used when the outcomes of the experiments are equally likely. For example, consider the two-stage experiment of spinning this spinner and tossing a coin. If you draw a tree for which the first branch represents the result of the spinner and the second branch represents the result of the coin toss, the branch for red is twice as likely as the branch for yellow or blue. In this case you could make two branches for red and the diagram would be correct. In the upper grades students will learn to assign probabilities to each segment of a tree diagram and multiply these to obtain probabilities for each complete branch.

Short-Run versus Long-Run Results

You may have noticed that in none of the activities so far have we asked students to determine the probability of an event. Rather, we have had students place events on a continuum from impossible to certain and compare the likelihood of one event with another. Before explaining why the activities to this point have not required a computation of probabilities, let's discuss two different ways that probabilities can be determined.

Experimental Probability and Theoretical Probability

Suppose that you have conducted the experiment of tossing a coin 100 times. In your experiment, heads came up 56 times and tails 44 times. The relative frequency of heads for your experiment is $\frac{56}{100}$. The *relative frequency* of an event is

$$\frac{\text{The number of observed occurrences of the event}}{\text{The total number of trials}}$$

If you toss the coin another 100 times, the relative frequency may even drop below $\frac{1}{2}$, perhaps to $\frac{93}{200}$. If you toss it 1000 times, you would expect that the relative frequency would be very close to $\frac{1}{2}$, although you might be surprised if it was exactly $\frac{500}{1000}$. The fractions $\frac{56}{100}$, $\frac{93}{200}$, and $\frac{489}{1000}$ can be compared as ratios of a part to the whole although each of the wholes is different (100, 200, and 1000). Note that the number of heads for each successive fraction is further from one-half (4, 7, 11). However, the corresponding ratios are closer to one-half (56%, 46.5%, 48.9%).

The relative frequency of an event is also called the *experimental probability* of the event. The more trials that are conducted, the more confident we can be that the relative frequency or experimental probability is close to the actual probability for that event. Conversely, if the experimental probability is based on only a small number of trials, we should not be very confident that this ratio is close to the actual probability.

For some experiments or situations, it may seem that the probability is obvious and that there is no need to conduct the experiment a large number of times. We are completely confident that the probability of tossing a fair coin and getting a head is $\frac{1}{2}$. This probability can be referred to as the theoretical probability. The *theoretical probability of an event* is the proportion of the sample space that is defined by the event. The theoretical probability is determined by an analysis of the event itself without any reference to experiments that may have been conducted. When all of the events of the sample space are equally likely, we can define the theoretical probability as

$$\frac{\text{The number of outcomes in the event}}{\text{Number of outcomes in the sample space}}$$

We can also determine the theoretical probability for some experiments that do not have equally likely outcomes, such as a spinner that is half red and one-fourth each green and yellow. This is because we can measure the proportion of the spinner for each color.

But spinners, dice, and tiles in a bag are only used to develop ideas about probability. In the real world, probability is often used to express the likelihood of situations such as the chance of a tornado, the rise of the stock market, or the number of hours a lightbulb will burn. For "muddy" events such as these, experiments are typically run a large number of times and the relative frequency or experimental probability of the event is used as an estimate of the actual probability.

These definitions (relative frequency and experimental probability) involve ratios. The ratio for 10 trials is compared to that for 100 trials and for 100,000 trials. The comparison of ratios for different-sized wholes (here the number of trials) requires proportional reasoning—an idea that research has indicated is not at all easy for young students. Typically, it is developed in the middle school years and only then with appropriate meaningful experiences. In contrast, fraction concepts in the primary grades are based on the idea of a single whole or *one*—one circle, one candy bar, one segment, or one unit on the number line.

Comparing Results as Numbers Increase

A visual comparison may help young students understand how the relative frequency of an event gets closer to a fixed probability as the number of trials gets very large. The next two activities are designed to help students with this difficult idea.

BLM 45

ACTIVITY 12.11

Checking the Theory

Make a transparency of Blackline Master 45. Provide pairs of students with a spinner face that is half red and half blue. Discuss the chances of spinning blue. After this discussion, students should agree that the chance of blue is one-half. Mark the $\frac{1}{2}$ point on the Impossible–Certain continuum and draw a vertical line down through all of the lines below this point. Then have each pair of students spin their spinner one time. Make a tally chart for Red and Blue results and tally these first spins. Collect the results of additional spins until you have a total of 20 spins. Mark the result of the 20 spins on the second line. For example, if there are 13 Blue and 7 Red, place a mark at about 13 on the 0-to-20 number line. If the result of these 20 spins was not exactly 10 and 10, discuss possible reasons why this may be so.

Now have student pairs each spin their spinners ten more times. Collect these results and add them to the tallies for the first 20 spins. Your total should be a multiple of ten. Mark the total in the right-hand box of the third line and indicate the number of Blue spins on the line as before. Repeat this at least two more times, continuing to add the results of new spins to the previous results. Each time, enter the total in the right-hand box to create a new number line but with the same length as before. If possible, try to get the total number of spins to be at least 1000.

The successive number lines used in "Checking the Theory" each have the same length and each represent the total number of trials. When the results are plotted on any one number line, the position shows the fraction of the total spins as a visual portion of the whole line. If you try to be fairly accurate with your marks (perhaps measuring with a centimeter ruler), successive marks will almost certainly get closer and closer to the $\frac{1}{2}$ line you drew earlier down the page. Note that 240 Blue spins out of 500 is 48 percent, or very close to one-half. This is so even though there are 20 more Red spins (260) than Blue. To be that close with only 100 spins, the results would need to be 48 and 52. For even larger numbers, the marks should be extremely close to the line you have drawn. If you draw much longer lines—say 2 meters each—on the board, the results of "Checking the Theory" will be more dramatic. It will be clearer that the ratios are closing in on one-half.

Many of your students will not fully understand the ratio concept involved in the successive number lines. However, they should be able to see that as the number of trials increases, the results shift much less or get very close to the theoretical probability of one-half.

A spinner is suggested for "Checking the Theory" because it is the easiest method for determining the theoretical probability. However, spinners sometimes are less than accurate due to spinning techniques, bent spinners, and so on. The same experiment can and should be conducted with other devices. For example, bags with two each of four colors could be used with the probability of each color marked on each line. Rolling a number cube with the event being an odd number is also a good idea.

The following activity is similar to "Checking the Theory" except that the theoretical probability cannot be determined.

ACTIVITY 12.12

Experimental Probability

The purpose of this activity is to estimate the probability of an event in which the theoretical probability cannot be determined. Students will gather data on how often you can expect a dropped thumb tack to land with the point straight up. Each pair of students will need five thumbtacks and a small box with a cover or lid. All the tacks in the room must be the same.

Use the same Blackline Master as you used for Activity 12.11. Demonstrate the two possibilities for a tack to land on a flat surface. After exploring their own tacks briefly, let students decide about where on the top line of the worksheet they think the probability of point up should fall. Next, have four students shake their boxes of tacks and report the number of point-up results. Tally these as in the previous activity and mark the corresponding point on the 0-to-20 line. Have students get data for ten more tacks—two

(continued)

tosses of five tacks. Tally and record on the third number line. Continue to gather data on more and more tacks, recording accumulated data on successive lines.

It should not take too long to get 1000 total tosses. At this point, discuss with students where they think the correct probability mark on the top line should be and why. Draw a vertical line from this point through the other number lines. The marks near the bottom of the page should be very close to this line.

The difference between Activities 12.11 and 12.12 is the ability to determine a theoretical probability. In the first of these activities, the observed results are compared to the expected result. In the second, the results of more and more trials should converge or get closer to a single value, which is an estimate of the actual probability. Once again, your students may not understand the ratio concept but should be able to see the results visually.

If your students have at least some informal experience with percentages, you may want to help them with a numeric probability in those terms. After each gathering of data, compute the percentage of point-up results by dividing by the total number of tosses. Record this percentage next to each number line marking.

Instead of tossing thumb tacks, you might want to explore "Experimental Probability" by experimenting with the ways that these items land when tossed: small plastic portion cups or medicine cups (side, open end up, upside down), plastic spoons (bowl up, bowl down), or marshmallows (side or end). (Note that large marshmallows produce different results from small marshmallows.)

This approach of repeating an experiment a large number of times can be applied to other situations. For example, students can open phone books to any page, randomly point to a name on the page, and count the number of letters in the last name. What is the probability of a name having five or fewer letters?

Discuss with students how this method could be used with events that happen over time but are difficult to recreate in the classroom. For example, what is the chance of getting hit by lightning? What is the chance of having to stop at the next stoplight? What is the chance of the phone ringing during dinner? In all of these cases, data can be collected over a long period of time by observing what happens rather than by conducting experiments. The point of this discussion is to bring the science of probability into the real world.

Assessment Note

By late second grade or certainly third grade, an important idea you want to develop is that of long-run results being better predictors of probabilities than short-run results. However, it is difficult to ask questions about this idea without students playing "guess what the teacher wants you to say." Instead, pose the following situation and have students write about their ideas.

> *Margaret spun the spinner ten times. Blue turned up on three spins. Red turned up on seven spins. Margaret says that there is a 3 in 10 chance of spinning blue. Carla then spun the same spinner 100 times. Carla recorded 53 spins of blue and 47 spins of red. Carla says that the chance of spinning blue on this spinner is about even.*

Who do you think is more likely to be correct: Margaret or Carla? Explain. Draw a spinner that you think they may have been using.

In the students' responses, look for evidence that they know that even ten spins is not very good evidence of the probability and that 100 spins tells us more about the chances.

Recall that the first big idea in the chapter was this: Chance has no memory. Toward the end of your probability unit, you may want to see if students have developed this idea to any extent although the activities explored have not explicitly addressed this idea. Have students either write about or discuss the following:

Duane has a lucky coin that he has tossed many times. He is sure that it is a fair coin—that there is an even chance of heads or tails. Duane tosses his coin six times and heads come up six times in a row. Duane is sure that the next toss will be tails because he has never been able to toss heads seven times in a row. What do you think the chances are of Duane tossing heads on the next toss? Explain your answer.

In this case you are looking for the idea that each toss of the coin is independent of prior tosses. As noted earlier, however, do not be surprised if students are as convinced as Duane is about the next toss being tails. As noted, many adults would agree with Duane as well even though they would be in error.

EXPANDED LESSON

Create a Game
Based on: Activity 12.8, p. 339

GRADE LEVEL: Second or third grade.

MATHEMATICS GOALS
- To develop the ability to analyze a one-stage experiment and identify all possible outcomes—the sample space.
- To explore informally the probability of an event in a one-stage experiment when all of the outcomes are equally likely.
- To contrast the concept of chance or luck with that of probability.

THINKING ABOUT THE STUDENTS
- Although students need not have a firm understanding of probability, they should have been exposed to the

basic idea that the outcome of an experiment can lie at different points along the probability continuum from impossible to certain.

MATERIALS AND PREPARATION
- Each pair of students will need a paper lunch bag or the equivalent and a collection of colored chips or cubes of four colors. Color Tiles or Unifix cubes are suggested. Another option is to cut up squares of colored poster board.

lesson

BEFORE

Begin with a Simpler Version of the Task
- Discuss children's favorite games. Ask: *Have you ever wondered how games are created? Today we are going to make up our own games.* Explain that the game will consist of putting tiles (or whatever is to be used) in a bag and taking turns drawing out a tile. Each player will be given a color. The person whose color is drawn gets a point. After ten draws, the game is over.
- Say: *Suppose we wanted to put in two colors of tiles, red and blue. We want four tiles in the bag. How many of each tile should we put in?* Accept whatever ideas the class agrees on. Play the game quickly between two halves of the class. Be sure to return the tile to the bag after each draw. Make a big point of this so that students will not forget to return the tiles to the bag when they play. Ask if they think this is a good game or not. Is it fair? Why?
- Now suggest putting in five tiles and three different colors. How would they design the game for two players? One player has to get a point with each draw. Give students a moment to design a game with five tiles and three colors. Have students share their ideas. For different ideas, ask which side they think will win or is it even—a fair game. Of course, there is no way to create a fair game with five tiles. Do not explain this to the students! It is not necessary to play this game.

The Task
- Design a game with 6 red, 1 yellow, 2 green, and 3 blue tiles. Make a list of colors for each player. The tiles are drawn one at a time and returned to the bag. By playing the game to ten points, decide if your game is fair or not.
- Repeat the same task for a bag with 2 red, 3 blue, and 7 yellow tiles.

Establish Expectations
- Students are to make a list of the colors for each player and then play the game. Ten total points is a full game. Have them play the game two times without changing the color list.
- Next they decide if the game is fair or not fair to both players. They should explain their reasoning on their papers and be prepared to discuss this with the class.

- Students then design a new game with the second set of colors (write these on the board). For this new game, they again play the game, decide if it is fair, and explain why.

DURING

- Be sure that students are playing the game correctly and following the rules they have established.
- After a team has played two times, be sure that they first write down their ideas about the game before designing a second game.
- Listen to the ideas that students use in deciding if the game is fair or not. With only 10 points in a game, it is possible that the score will produce a winner even if the game is designed fairly. For the second set of tiles, a truly fair game is impossible. Listen to see if students realize that before they play. Do they still believe in what they thought after the game has been played? Listening to these discussions will give you insights into students' understanding of luck versus probability.

AFTER

- Have groups share their designs, explain their thinking about the fairness of the game, and how the game turned out. When there are discrepancies between their thinking about the design and the results, confront this. *You thought the game was fair but Sandra won both times. Why do you think that happened? If you play a lot of times, who do you think will win the most times?* Engage the class in this discussion of game designs, luck, probability, and short- and long-term results. Rather than describe probabilities with fractions, use language like this: *Player A can win with 6 of the 12 tiles and Player B can win with 6 of the tiles.*
- In the first set of tiles, a fair game design will result in one player with only one color and the other player with three colors, 6 red versus 1 yellow, 2 green, and 3 blue. Some students may focus on the number of colors rather than the number of tiles for each color.
- Repeat the discussion for the second set of tiles in which a truly fair game is impossible. Even with a 5 to 7 ratio, however, the player with fewer chances to win may still win.

ASSESSMENT NOTES

- Pay attention to students who seem to believe more in chance or luck than in observable probabilities. This is a main idea that you want to develop at this point in their understanding of probability.
- If students are leaving colors out of the game, they do not have a good understanding of sample space.
- Try to decide how well your students are able to determine the probabilities of the outcomes in these games. Students who correctly analyze these games—who can tell if a game is fair or not and who can design fair and unfair games—are ready to progress further.

- If you have a significant number of students who seem to believe more in luck than in an analysis of the game, then additional activities such as games should be explored. Use games that are clearly biased. It is also important to look at results of a lot of trials. Pooling data across the class can help.
- If students do not include all of the colors or show other signs of not understanding sample space, this is not a big concern. However, you should discuss the idea that when there is an experiment, all possible things that can happen have to be considered.
- If your class seems to understand this activity, you might want to explore a two-stage experiment next. Activity 12.9, "Twelve Chips," is a fun game and can be explored by students in free time once they have learned how to play.

next steps

APPENDIX A

PRINCIPLES AND STANDARDS FOR SCHOOL MATHEMATICS

Content Standards and Grade Level Expectations

NUMBER AND OPERATIONS

STANDARD

Instructional programs from prekindergarten through grade 12 should enable all students to—

Understand numbers, ways of representing numbers, relationships among numbers, and number systems

Understand meanings of operations and how they relate to one another

Compute fluently and make reasonable estimates

PRE-K–2

Expectations

In prekindergarten through grade 2 all students should—

- count with understanding and recognize "how many" in sets of objects;
- use multiple models to develop initial understandings of place value and the base-ten number system;
- develop understanding of the relative position and magnitude of whole numbers and of ordinal and cardinal numbers and their connections;
- develop a sense of whole numbers and represent and use them in flexible ways, including relating, composing, and decomposing numbers;
- connect number words and numerals to the quantities they represent, using various physical models and representations;
- understand and represent commonly used fractions, such as $\frac{1}{4}$, $\frac{1}{3}$, and $\frac{1}{2}$.

- understand various meanings of addition and subtraction of whole numbers and the relationship between the two operations;
- understand the effects of adding and subtracting whole numbers;
- understand situations that entail multiplication and division, such as equal groupings of objects and sharing equally.

- develop and use strategies for whole-number computations, with a focus on addition and subtraction;
- develop fluency with basic number combinations for addition and subtraction;
- use a variety of methods and tools to compute, including objects, mental computation, estimation, paper and pencil, and calculators.

GRADES 3–5

Expectations

In grades 3–5 all students should—

- understand the place-value structure of the base-ten number system and be able to represent and compare whole numbers and decimals;
- recognize equivalent representations for the same number and generate them by decomposing and composing numbers;
- develop understanding of fractions as parts of unit wholes, as parts of a collection, as locations on number lines, and as divisions of whole numbers;
- use models, benchmarks, and equivalent forms to judge the size of fractions;
- recognize and generate equivalent forms of commonly used fractions, decimals, and percents;
- explore numbers less than 0 by extending the number line and through familiar applications;
- describe classes of numbers according to characteristics such as the nature of their factors.

- understand various meanings of multiplication and division;
- understand the effects of multiplying and dividing whole numbers;
- identify and use relationships between operations, such as division as the inverse of multiplication, to solve problems;
- understand and use properties of operations, such as the distributivity of multiplication over addition.

- develop fluency with basic number combinations for multiplication and division and use these combinations to mentally compute related problems, such as 30×50;
- develop fluency in adding, subtracting, multiplying, and dividing whole numbers;
- develop and use strategies to estimate the results of whole-number computations and to judge the reasonableness of such results;
- develop and use strategies to estimate computations involving fractions and decimals in situations relevant to students' experience;
- use visual models, benchmarks, and equivalent forms to add and subtract commonly used fractions and decimals;
- select appropriate methods and tools for computing with whole numbers from among mental computation, estimation, calculators, and paper and pencil according to the context and nature of the computation and use the selected method or tool.

NUMBER AND OPERATIONS

STANDARD

Instructional programs from prekindergarten through grade 12 should enable all students to—

Understand numbers, ways of representing numbers, relationships among numbers, and number systems

Understand meanings of operations and how they relate to one another

Compute fluently and make reasonable estimates

GRADES 6–8

Expectations

In grades 6–8 all students should—

- work flexibly with fractions, decimals, and percents to solve problems;
- compare and order fractions, decimals, and percents efficiently and find their approximate locations on a number line;
- develop meaning for percents greater than 100 and less than 1;
- understand and use ratios and proportions to represent quantitative relationships;
- develop an understanding of large numbers and recognize and appropriately use exponential, scientific, and calculator notation;
- use factors, multiples, prime factorization, and relatively prime numbers to solve problems;
- develop meaning for integers and represent and compare quantities with them.

- understand the meaning and effects of arithmetic operations with fractions, decimals, and integers;
- use the associative and commutative properties of addition and multiplication and the distributive property of multiplication over addition to simplify computations with integers, fractions, and decimals;
- understand and use the inverse relationships of addition and subtraction, multiplication and division, and squaring and finding square roots to simplify computations and solve problems.

- select appropriate methods and tools for computing with fractions and decimals from among mental computation, estimation, calculators or computers, and paper and pencil, depending on the situation, and apply the selected methods;
- develop and analyze algorithms for computing with fractions, decimals, and integers and develop fluency in their use;
- develop and use strategies to estimate the results of rational-number computations and judge the reasonableness of the results;
- develop, analyze, and explain methods for solving problems involving proportions, such as scaling and finding equivalent ratios.

GRADES 9–12

Expectations

In grades 9–12 all students should—

- develop a deeper understanding of very large and very small numbers and of various representations of them;
- compare and contrast the properties of numbers and number systems, including the rational and real numbers, and understand complex numbers as solutions to quadratic equations that do not have real solutions;
- understand vectors and matrices as systems that have some of the properties of the real-number system;
- use number-theory arguments to justify relationships involving whole numbers.

- judge the effects of such operations as multiplication, division, and computing powers and roots on the magnitudes of quantities;
- develop an understanding of properties of, and representations for, the addition and multiplication of vectors and matrices;
- develop an understanding of permutations and combinations as counting techniques.

- develop fluency in operations with real numbers, vectors, and matrices, using mental computation or paper-and-pencil calculations for simple cases and technology for more-complicated cases;
- judge the reasonableness of numerical computations and their results.

ALGEBRA

STANDARD

Instructional programs from prekindergarten through grade 12 should enable all students to—

Understand patterns, relations, and functions

Represent and analyze mathematical situations and structures using algebraic symbols

Use mathematical models to represent and understand quantitative relationships

Analyze change in various contexts

PRE-K–2

Expectations

In prekindergarten through grade 2 all students should—

- sort, classify, and order objects by size, number, and other properties;
- recognize, describe, and extend patterns such as sequences of sounds and shapes or simple numeric patterns and translate from one representation to another;
- analyze how both repeating and growing patterns are generated.

- illustrate general principles and properties of operations, such as commutativity, using specific numbers;
- use concrete, pictorial, and verbal representations to develop an understanding of invented and conventional symbolic notations.

- model situations that involve the addition and subtraction of whole numbers, using objects, pictures, and symbols.

- describe qualitative change, such as a student's growing taller;
- describe quantitative change, such as a student's growing two inches in one year.

GRADES 3–5

Expectations

In grades 3–5 all students should—

- describe, extend, and make generalizations about geometric and numeric patterns;
- represent and analyze patterns and functions, using words, tables, and graphs.

- identify such properties as commutativity, associativity, and distributivity and use them to compute with whole numbers;
- represent the idea of a variable as an unknown quantity using a letter or a symbol;
- express mathematical relationships using equations.

- model problem situations with objects and use representations such as graphs, tables, and equations to draw conclusions.

- investigate how a change in one variable relates to a change in a second variable;
- identify and describe situations with constant or varying rates of change and compare them.

ALGEBRA

STANDARD

Instructional programs from prekindergarten through grade 12 should enable all students to—

Understand patterns, relations, and functions

Represent and analyze mathematical situations and structures using algebraic symbols

Use mathematical models to represent and understand quantitative relationships

Analyze change in various contexts

GRADES 6–8

Expectations

In grades 6–8 all students should—

- represent, analyze, and generalize a variety of patterns with tables, graphs, words, and, when possible, symbolic rules;
- relate and compare different forms of representation for a relationship;
- identify functions as linear or nonlinear and contrast their properties from tables, graphs, or equations.

- develop an initial conceptual understanding of different uses of variables;
- explore relationships between symbolic expressions and graphs of lines, paying particular attention to the meaning of intercept and slope;
- use symbolic algebra to represent situations and to solve problems, especially those that involve linear relationships;
- recognize and generate equivalent forms for simple algebraic expressions and solve linear equations.

- model and solve contextualized problems using various representations, such as graphs, tables, and equations.

- use graphs to analyze the nature of changes in quantities in linear relationships.

GRADES 9–12

Expectations

In grades 9–12 all students should—

- generalize patterns using explicitly defined and recursively defined functions;
- understand relations and functions and select, convert flexibly among, and use various representations for them;
- analyze functions of one variable by investigating rates of change, intercepts, zeros, asymptotes, and local and global behavior;
- understand and perform transformations such as arithmetically combining, composing, and inverting commonly used functions, using technology to perform such operations on more-complicated symbolic expressions;
- understand and compare the properties of classes of functions, including exponential, polynomial, rational, logarithmic, and periodic functions;
- interpret representations of functions of two variables.

- understand the meaning of equivalent forms of expressions, equations, inequalities, and relations;
- write equivalent forms of equations, inequalities, and systems of equations and solve them with fluency—mentally or with paper and pencil in simple cases and using technology in all cases;
- use symbolic algebra to represent and explain mathematical relationships;
- use a variety of symbolic representations, including recursive and parametric equations, for functions and relations;
- judge the meaning, utility, and reasonableness of the results of symbol manipulations, including those carried out by technology.

- identify essential quantitative relationships in a situation and determine the class or classes of functions that might model the relationships;
- use symbolic expressions, including iterative and recursive forms, to represent relationships arising from various contexts;
- draw reasonable conclusions about a situation being modeled.

- approximate and interpret rates of change from graphical and numerical data.

GEOMETRY

STANDARD

Instructional programs from prekindergarten through grade 12 should enable all students to—

Analyze characteristics and properties of two- and three-dimensional geometric shapes and develop mathematical arguments about geometric relationships

Specify locations and describe spatial relationships using coordinate geometry and other representational systems

Apply transformations and use symmetry to analyze mathematical situations

Use visualization, spatial reasoning, and geometric modeling to solve problems

PRE-K–2

Expectations

In prekindergarten through grade 2 all students should—

- recognize, name, build, draw, compare, and sort two- and three-dimensional shapes;
- describe attributes and parts of two- and three-dimensional shapes;
- investigate and predict the results of putting together and taking apart two- and three-dimensional shapes.

- describe, name, and interpret relative positions in space and apply ideas about relative position;
- describe, name, and interpret direction and distance in navigating space and apply ideas about direction and distance;
- find and name locations with simple relationships such as "near to" and in coordinate systems such as maps.

- recognize and apply slides, flips, and turns;
- recognize and create shapes that have symmetry.

- create mental images of geometric shapes using spatial memory and spatial visualization;
- recognize and represent shapes from different perspectives;
- relate ideas in geometry to ideas in number and measurement;
- recognize geometric shapes and structures in the environment and specify their location.

GRADES 3–5

Expectations

In grades 3–5 all students should—

- identify, compare, and analyze attributes of two- and three-dimensional shapes and develop vocabulary to describe the attributes;
- classify two- and three-dimensional shapes according to their properties and develop definitions of classes of shapes such as triangles and pyramids;
- investigate, describe, and reason about the results of subdividing, combining, and transforming shapes;
- explore congruence and similarity;
- make and test conjectures about geometric properties and relationships and develop logical arguments to justify conclusions.

- describe location and movement using common language and geometric vocabulary;
- make and use coordinate systems to specify locations and to describe paths;
- find the distance between points along horizontal and vertical lines of a coordinate system.

- predict and describe the results of sliding, flipping, and turning two-dimensional shapes;
- describe a motion or a series of motions that will show that two shapes are congruent;
- identify and describe line and rotational symmetry in two- and three-dimensional shapes and designs.

- build and draw geometric objects;
- create and describe mental images of objects, patterns, and paths;
- identify and build a three-dimensional object from two-dimensional representations of that object;
- identify and build a two-dimensional representation of a three-dimensional object;
- use geometric models to solve problems in other areas of mathematics, such as number and measurement;
- recognize geometric ideas and relationships and apply them to other disciplines and to problems that arise in the classroom or in everyday life.

GEOMETRY

STANDARD

Instructional programs from prekindergarten through grade 12 should enable all students to—

Analyze characteristics and properties of two- and three-dimensional geometric shapes and develop mathematical arguments about geometric relationships

Specify locations and describe spatial relationships using coordinate geometry and other representational systems

Apply transformations and use symmetry to analyze mathematical situations

Use visualization, spatial reasoning, and geometric modeling to solve problems

GRADES 6–8

Expectations

In grades 6–8 all students should—

- precisely describe, classify, and understand relationships among types of two- and three-dimensional objects using their defining properties;
- understand relationships among the angles, side lengths, perimeters, areas, and volumes of similar objects;
- create and critique inductive and deductive arguments concerning geometric ideas and relationships, such as congruence, similarity, and the Pythagorean relationship.

- use coordinate geometry to represent and examine the properties of geometric shapes;
- use coordinate geometry to examine special geometric shapes, such as regular polygons or those with pairs of parallel or perpendicular sides.

- describe sizes, positions, and orientations of shapes under informal transformations such as flips, turns, slides, and scaling;
- examine the congruence, similarity, and line or rotational symmetry of objects using transformations.

- draw geometric objects with specified properties, such as side lengths or angle measures;
- use two-dimensional representations of three-dimensional objects to visualize and solve problems such as those involving surface area and volume;
- use visual tools such as networks to represent and solve problems;
- use geometric models to represent and explain numerical and algebraic relationships;
- recognize and apply geometric ideas and relationships in areas outside the mathematics classroom, such as art, science, and everyday life.

GRADES 9–12

Expectations

In grades 9–12 all students should—

- analyze properties and determine attributes of two- and three-dimensional objects;
- explore relationships (including congruence and similarity) among classes of two- and three-dimensional geometric objects, make and test conjectures about them, and solve problems involving them;
- establish the validity of geometric conjectures using deduction, prove theorems, and critique arguments made by others;
- use trigonometric relationships to determine lengths and angle measures.

- use Cartesian coordinates and other coordinate systems, such as navigational, polar, or spherical systems, to analyze geometric situations;
- investigate conjectures and solve problems involving two- and three-dimensional objects represented with Cartesian coordinates.

- understand and represent translations, reflections, rotations, and dilations of objects in the plane by using sketches, coordinates, vectors, function notation, and matrices;
- use various representations to help understand the effects of simple transformations and their compositions.

- draw and construct representations of two- and three-dimensional geometric objects using a variety of tools;
- visualize three-dimensional objects from different perspectives and analyze their cross sections;
- use vertex-edge graphs to model and solve problems;
- use geometric models to gain insights into, and answer questions in, other areas of mathematics;
- use geometric ideas to solve problems in, and gain insights into, other disciplines and other areas of interest such as art and architecture.

MEASUREMENT

STANDARD

Instructional programs from prekindergarten through grade 12 should enable all students to—

Understand measurable attributes of objects and the units, systems, and processes of measurement

Apply appropriate techniques, tools, and formulas to determine measurements

PRE-K–2

Expectations

In prekindergarten through grade 2 all students should—

- recognize the attributes of length, volume, weight, area, and time;
- compare and order objects according to these attributes;
- understand how to measure using nonstandard and standard units;
- select an appropriate unit and tool for the attribute being measured.

- measure with multiple copies of units of the same size, such as paper clips laid end to end;
- use repetition of a single unit to measure something larger than the unit, for instance, measuring the length of a room with a single meterstick;
- use tools to measure;
- develop common referents for measures to make comparisons and estimates.

GRADES 3–5

Expectations

In grades 3–5 all students should—

- understand such attributes as length, area, weight, volume, and size of angle and select the appropriate type of unit for measuring each attribute;
- understand the need for measuring with standard units and become familiar with standard units in the customary and metric systems;
- carry out simple unit conversions, such as from centimeters to meters, within a system of measurement;
- understand that measurements are approximations and understand how differences in units affect precision;
- explore what happens to measurements of a two-dimensional shape such as its perimeter and area when the shape is changed in some way.

- develop strategies for estimating the perimeters, areas, and volumes of irregular shapes;
- select and apply appropriate standard units and tools to measure length, area, volume, weight, time, temperature, and the size of angles;
- select and use benchmarks to estimate measurements;
- develop, understand, and use formulas to find the area of rectangles and related triangles and parallelograms;
- develop strategies to determine the surface areas and volumes of rectangular solids.

MEASUREMENT

STANDARD

Instructional programs from prekindergarten through grade 12 should enable all students to—

Understand measurable attributes of objects and the units, systems, and processes of measurement

Apply appropriate techniques, tools, and formulas to determine measurements

GRADES 6–8

Expectations

In grades 6–8 all students should—

- understand both metric and customary systems of measurement;
- understand relationships among units and convert from one unit to another within the same system;
- understand, select, and use units of appropriate size and type to measure angles, perimeter, area, surface area, and volume.

- use common benchmarks to select appropriate methods for estimating measurements;
- select and apply techniques and tools to accurately find length, area, volume, and angle measures to appropriate levels of precision;
- develop and use formulas to determine the circumference of circles and the area of triangles, parallelograms, trapezoids, and circles and develop strategies to find the area of more-complex shapes;
- develop strategies to determine the surface area and volume of selected prisms, pyramids, and cylinders;
- solve problems involving scale factors, using ratio and proportion;
- solve simple problems involving rates and derived measurements for such attributes as velocity and density.

GRADES 9–12

Expectations

In grades 9–12 all students should—

- make decisions about units and scales that are appropriate for problem situations involving measurement.

- analyze precision, accuracy, and approximate error in measurement situations;
- understand and use formulas for the area, surface area, and volume of geometric figures, including cones, spheres, and cylinders;
- apply informal concepts of successive approximation, upper and lower bounds, and limit in measurement situations;
- use unit analysis to check measurement computations.

DATA ANALYSIS AND PROBABILITY

STANDARD

Instructional programs from prekindergarten through grade 12 should enable all students to—

Formulate questions that can be addressed with data and collect, organize, and display relevant data to answer them

Select and use appropriate statistical methods to analyze data

Develop and evaluate inferences and predictions that are based on data

Understand and apply basic concepts of probability

PRE-K–2

Expectations

In prekindergarten through grade 2 all students should—

- pose questions and gather data about themselves and their surroundings;
- sort and classify objects according to their attributes and organize data about the objects;
- represent data using concrete objects, pictures, and graphs.

- describe parts of the data and the set of data as a whole to determine what the data show.

- discuss events related to students' experiences as likely or unlikely.

GRADES 3–5

Expectations

In grades 3–5 all students should—

- design investigations to address a question and consider how data-collection methods affect the nature of the data set;
- collect data using observations, surveys, and experiments;
- represent data using tables and graphs such as line plots, bar graphs, and line graphs;
- recognize the differences in representing categorical and numerical data.

- describe the shape and important features of a set of data and compare related data sets, with an emphasis on how the data are distributed;
- use measures of center, focusing on the median, and understand what each does and does not indicate about the data set;
- compare different representations of the same data and evaluate how well each representation shows important aspects of the data.

- propose and justify conclusions and predictions that are based on data and design studies to further investigate the conclusions or predictions.

- describe events as likely or unlikely and discuss the degree of likelihood using such words as certain, equally likely, and impossible;
- predict the probability of outcomes of simple experiments and test the predictions;
- understand that the measure of the likelihood of an event can be represented by a number from 0 to 1.

DATA ANALYSIS AND PROBABILITY

STANDARD

Instructional programs from prekindergarten through grade 12 should enable all students to—

Formulate questions that can be addressed with data and collect, organize, and display relevant data to answer them

Select and use appropriate statistical methods to analyze data

Develop and evaluate inferences and predictions that are based on data

Understand and apply basic concepts of probability

GRADES 6–8

Expectations

In grades 6–8 all students should—

- formulate questions, design studies, and collect data about a characteristic shared by two populations or different characteristics within one population;
- select, create, and use appropriate graphical representations of data, including histograms, box plots, and scatterplots.

- find, use, and interpret measures of center and spread, including mean and interquartile range;
- discuss and understand the correspondence between data sets and their graphical representations, especially histograms, stem-and-leaf plots, box plots, and scatterplots.

- use observations about differences between two or more samples to make conjectures about the populations from which the samples were taken;
- make conjectures about possible relationships between two characteristics of a sample on the basis of scatterplots of the data and approximate lines of fit;
- use conjectures to formulate new questions and plan new studies to answer them.

- understand and use appropriate terminology to describe complementary and mutually exclusive events;
- use proportionality and a basic understanding of probability to make and test conjectures about the results of experiments and simulations;
- compute probabilities for simple compound events, using such methods as organized lists, tree diagrams, and area models.

GRADES 9–12

Expectations

In grades 9–12 all students should—

- understand the differences among various kinds of studies and which types of inferences can legitimately be drawn from each;
- know the characteristics of well-designed studies, including the role of randomization in surveys and experiments;
- understand the meaning of measurement data and categorical data, of univariate and bivariate data, and of the term variable;
- understand histograms, parallel box plots, and scatterplots and use them to display data;
- compute basic statistics and understand the distinction between a statistic and a parameter.

- for univariate measurement data, be able to display the distribution, describe its shape, and select and calculate summary statistics;
- for bivariate measurement data, be able to display a scatterplot, describe its shape, and determine regression coefficients, regression equations, and correlation coefficients using technological tools;
- display and discuss bivariate data where at least one variable is categorical;
- recognize how linear transformations of univariate data affect shape, center, and spread;
- identify trends in bivariate data and find functions that model the data or transform the data so that they can be modeled.

- use simulations to explore the variability of sample statistics from a known population and to construct sampling distributions;
- understand how sample statistics reflect the values of population parameters and use sampling distributions as the basis for informal inference;
- evaluate published reports that are based on data by examining the design of the study, the appropriateness of the data analysis, and the validity of conclusions;
- understand how basic statistical techniques are used to monitor process characteristics in the workplace.

- understand the concepts of sample space and probability distribution and construct sample spaces and distributions in simple cases;
- use simulations to construct empirical probability distributions;
- compute and interpret the expected value of random variables in simple cases;
- understand the concepts of conditional probability and independent events;
- understand how to compute the probability of a compound event.

APPENDIX B

A GUIDE TO THE BLACKLINE MASTERS

This appendix contains thumbnails of all of the Blackline Masters that are referenced throughout the book. Those introduced in the Expanded Lessons appear at the end and are numbered separately. Go to the Companion Website at www.ablongman.com/vandewalleseries to download full-sized Blackline Masters.

Tips for the Use of the Blackline Masters

When a blackline is to be used either as a workmat for children or will be cut apart into smaller pieces, the best advice is to duplicate the master on card stock. Card stock (also known as index stock) is heavy paper that comes in a variety of colors and can be found at copy or office supply stores.

Workmats such as the ten-frame mat and the place-value mat are best if not laminated. Lamination makes the mats slippery so that counters slide around or off.

With materials that require cutting into smaller pieces, we suggest that you laminate the card stock before you cut out the pieces. This will preserve the materials for several years and save valuable time in the future. Here are some additional, specific instructions for certain masters.

- Dot Cards (BLMs 3–8): Make each set of six pages a different color. Otherwise, it is difficult to tell to which set a stray card belongs.

- Little Ten-Frames (BLMs 17 and 18): Make the full ten-frames on one-color card stock and the less-than-ten sheet on another. One set consists of the ten cards of each type, cut from a strip of ten on the master.

- Assorted Shapes (BLMs 20–26): Make each set of 7 pages a different color. Otherwise, it is very difficult to tell to which set a stray shape belongs.

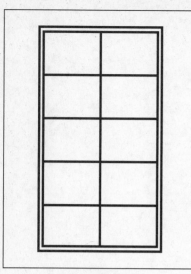

BLM 1
Ten-frame

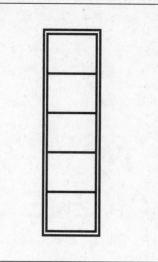

BLM 2
Five-frame

BLM 3
Dot cards

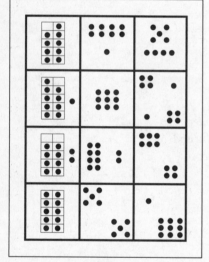

BLM 4
Dot cards

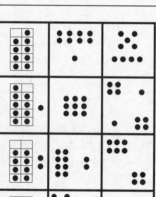
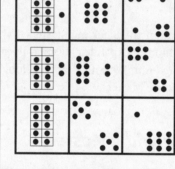

BLM 5
Dot cards

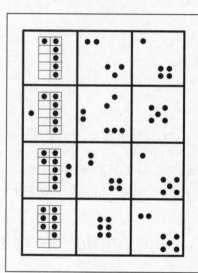

BLM 6
Dot cards

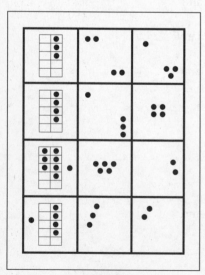

BLM 7
Dot cards

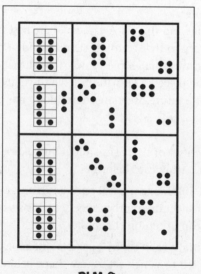

BLM 8
Dot cards

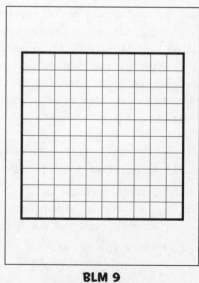

BLM 9
Blank hundreds chart
(10 × 10 square)

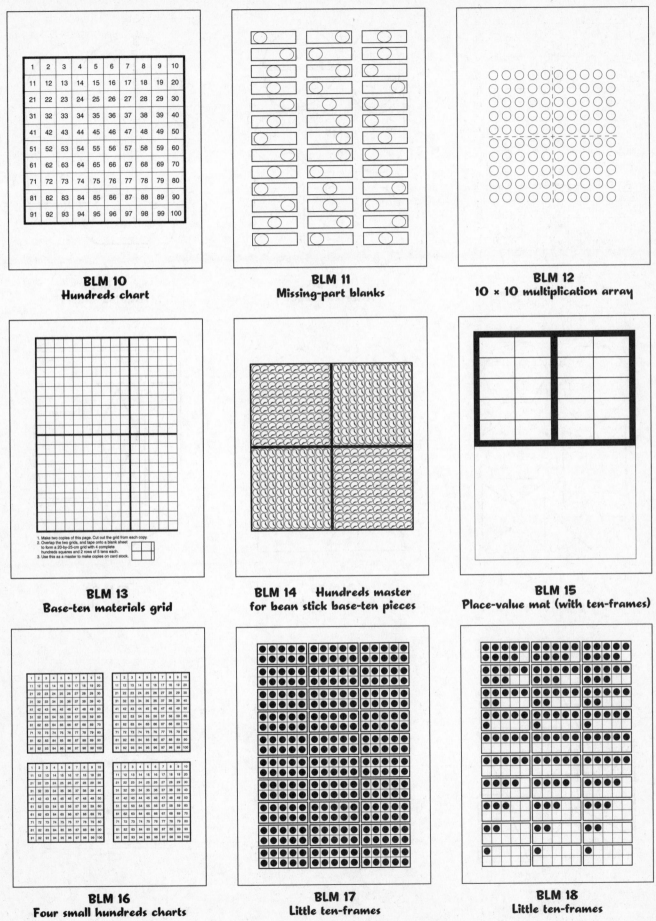

BLM 10
Hundreds chart

BLM 11
Missing-part blanks

BLM 12
10 × 10 multiplication array

BLM 13
Base-ten materials grid

BLM 14   Hundreds master
for bean stick base-ten pieces

BLM 15
Place-value mat (with ten-frames)

BLM 16
Four small hundreds charts

BLM 17
Little ten-frames

BLM 18
Little ten-frames

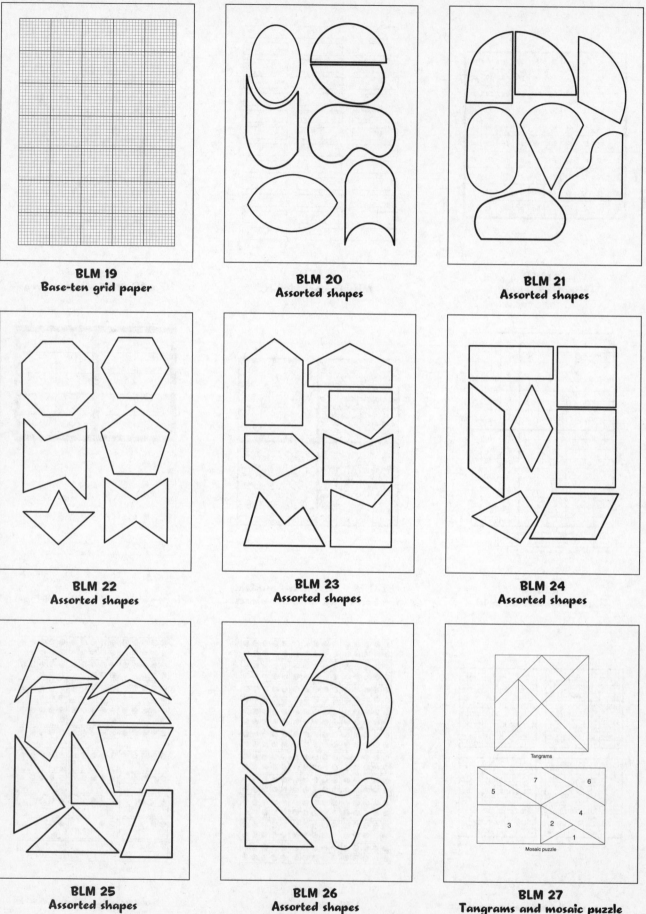

BLM 19
Base-ten grid paper

BLM 20
Assorted shapes

BLM 21
Assorted shapes

BLM 22
Assorted shapes

BLM 23
Assorted shapes

BLM 24
Assorted shapes

BLM 25
Assorted shapes

BLM 26
Assorted shapes

BLM 27
Tangrams and mosaic puzzle

Tangrams

Mosaic puzzle

5 7 6 4 3 2 1

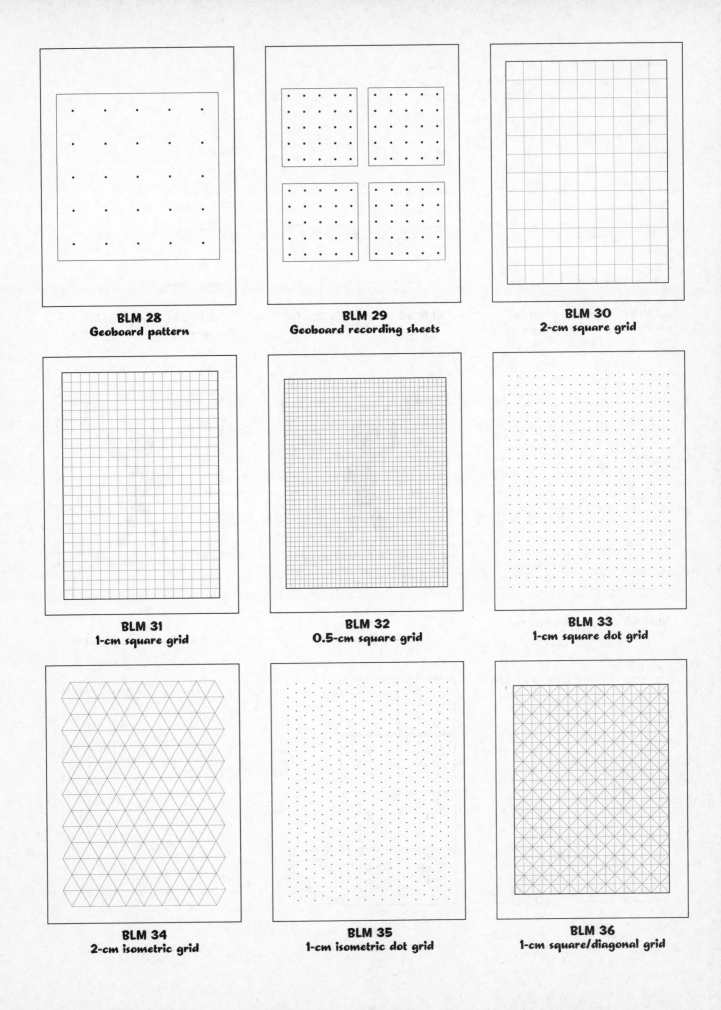

BLM 28
Geoboard pattern

BLM 29
Geoboard recording sheets

BLM 30
2-cm square grid

BLM 31
1-cm square grid

BLM 32
0.5-cm square grid

BLM 33
1-cm square dot grid

BLM 34
2-cm isometric grid

BLM 35
1-cm isometric dot grid

BLM 36
1-cm square/diagonal grid

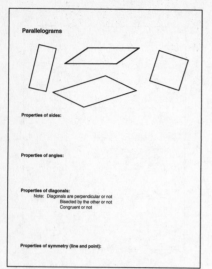

Parallelograms

Properties of sides:

Properties of angles:

Properties of diagonals:
 Note: Diagonals are perpendicular or not
 Bisected by the other or not
 Congruent or not

Properties of symmetry (line and point):

BLM 37   Property lists for quadrilaterals (parallelograms)

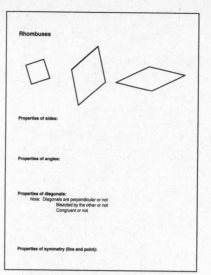

Rhombuses

Properties of sides:

Properties of angles:

Properties of diagonals:
 Note: Diagonals are perpendicular or not
 Bisected by the other or not
 Congruent or not

Properties of symmetry (line and point):

BLM 38   Property lists for quadrilaterals (rhombuses)

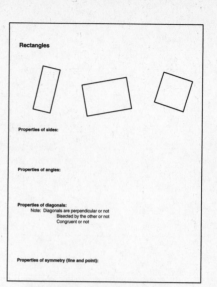

Rectangles

Properties of sides:

Properties of angles:

Properties of diagonals:
 Note: Diagonals are perpendicular or not
 Bisected by the other or not
 Congruent or not

Properties of symmetry (line and point):

BLM 39   Property lists for quadrilaterals (rectangles)

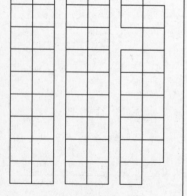

Squares

Properties of sides:

Properties of angles:

Properties of diagonals:
 Note: Diagonals are perpendicular or not
 Bisected by the other or not
 Congruent or not

Properties of symmetry (line and point):

BLM 40   Property lists for quadrilaterals (squares)

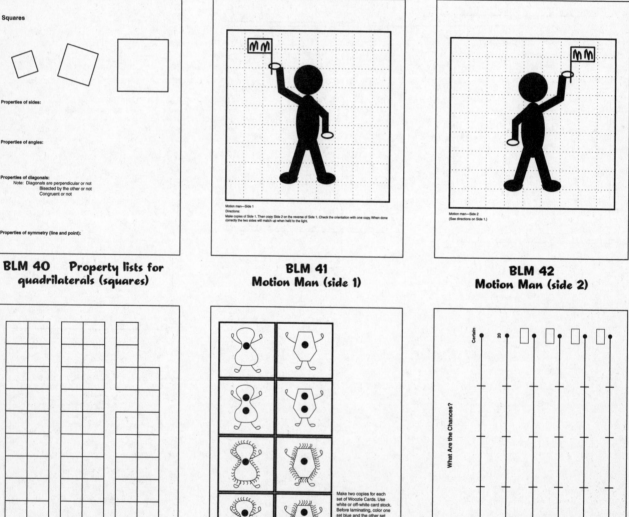

Motion man—Side 1
Directions:
Make copies of Side 1. Then copy Side 2 on the reverse of Side 1. Check the orientation with one copy. When done correctly the two sides will match up when held to the light.

**BLM 41
Motion Man (side 1)**

Motion man—Side 2
(See directions on Side 1.)

**BLM 42
Motion Man (side 2)**

**BLM 43
Two column cards**

Make two copies for each set of Woozle Cards. Use white or off-white card stock. Before laminating, color one set blue and the other set red. Trace around the inside of each Woozle with a marker, leaving the rest of the creature white. Coloring the entire Woozle may obscure the dots.

**BLM 44
Woozle Cards**

What Are the Chances?

Certain

Impossible

**BLM 45
What are the chances?**

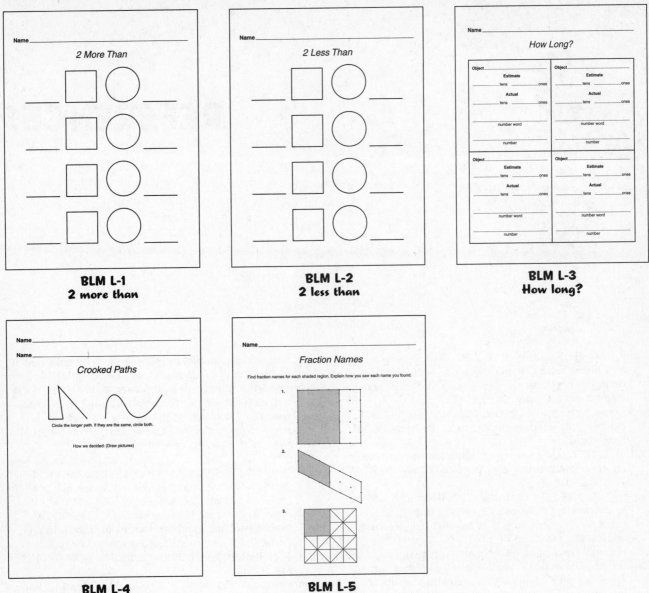

BLM L-1
2 more than

BLM L-2
2 less than

BLM L-3
How long?

BLM L-4
Crooked paths

BLM L-5
Fraction names

REFERENCES

Ashcraft, M. H., & Christy, K. S. (1995). The frequency of arithmetic facts in elementary texts: Addition and multiplication in grades 1–6. *Journal for Research in Mathematics Education, 26*, 396–421.

Backhouse, J., Haggarty, L., Pirie, S., & Stratton, J. (1992). *Improving the learning of mathematics.* Portsmouth, NH: Heinemann.

Ball, D. L. (1992). Magical hopes: Manipulatives and the reform of math education. *American Educator 16*(2), 14–18, 46–47.

Barrett, J. E., Jones, G., Thornton, C., & Dickson, S. (2003). Understanding children's developing strategies and concepts of length. In D. H. Clements (Ed.), *Learning and teaching measurement* (pp. 17–30). Reston, VA: National Council of Teachers of Mathematics.

Battista, M. C. (1999). The mathematical miseducation of America's youth: Ignoring research and scientific study in education. *Phi Delta Kappan, 80*, 424–433.

Broderbund. (1995b). *Tabletop, Jr.* Novato, CA: Author.

Burger, W. F. (1985). Geometry. *Arithmetic Teacher, 32*(6), 52–56.

Burns, M. (1996). *50 problem-solving lessons: Grades 1–6.* White Plains, NY: Cuisenaire (distributor).

Burns, M. (2000). *About teaching mathematics: A K–8 resource* (2nd ed.). Sausalito, CA: Math Solutions Publications.

Burns, M., & Tank, B. (1988). *A collection of math lessons from grades 1 through 3.* Sausalito, CA: Math Solutions.

Campbell, P. B. (1995). Redefining the "girl problem in mathematics." In W. G. Secada, E. Fennema, & L. B. Adajian (Eds.), *New directions for equity in mathematics education* (pp. 225–241). New York: Cambridge University Press.

Campbell, P. F. (1996). Empowering children and teachers in the elementary mathematics classrooms of urban schools. *Urban Education, 30*, 449–475.

Campbell, P. F. (1997, April). Children's invented algorithms: Their meaning and place in instruction. Presented at the annual meeting of the National Council of Teachers of Mathematics, Minneapolis, MN.

Campbell, P. F., Rowan, T. E., & Suarez, A. R. (1998). What criteria for student-invented algorithms? In L. J. Morrow (Ed.), *The teaching and learning of algorithms in school mathematics* (pp. 49–55). Reston, VA: National Council of Teachers of Mathematics.

Carpenter, T. P., Ansell, E., Franke, M. L., Fennema, E., & Weisbeck, L. (1993). A study of kindergarten children's problem-solving processes. *Journal for Research in Mathematics Education, 24*, 428–441.

Carpenter, T. P., Carey, D. A., & Kouba, V. L. (1990). A problem-solving approach to the operations. In J. N. Payne (Ed.), *Mathematics for the young child* (pp. 111–131). Reston, VA: National Council of Teachers of Mathematics.

Carpenter, T. P., Fennema, E., Franke, M. L., Levi, L., & Empson, S. B. (1999). *Children's mathematics: Cognitively guided instruction.* Portsmouth, NH: Heinemann.

Carpenter, T. P., Franke, M. L., Jacobs, V. R., Fennema, E., & Empson, S. B. (1998). A longitudinal study of invention and understanding in children's multidigit addition and subtraction. *Journal for Research in Mathematics Education, 29*, 3–20.

Carpenter, T. P., & Moser, J. M. (1983). The acquisition of addition and subtraction concepts. In R. A. Lesh & M. Landau (Eds.), *Acquisition of mathematics concepts and processes* (pp. 7–44). Orlando, FL: Academic Press.

Carroll, W. M. (1996). Use of invented algorithms by second graders in a reform mathematics curriculum. *Journal of Mathematical Behaviour, 15*, 137–150.

Carroll, W. M., & Porter, D. (1997). Invented strategies can develop meaningful mathematical procedures. *Teaching Children Mathematics, 3*, 370–374.

Chambers, D. (1996). Direct modeling and invented procedures: Building on students' informal strategies. *Teaching Children Mathematics, 3*, 92–95.

Clements, D. H., & Battista, M. T. (1990). Constructivist learning and teaching. *Arithmetic Teacher, 38*(1), 34–35.

Clements, D. H., & Battista, M. T. (1992). Geometry and spatial reasoning. In D. A. Grouws (Ed.), *Handbook of research on mathematics teaching and learning* (pp. 420–464). Old Tappan, NJ: Macmillan.

Clements, D. H., & Sarama, J. (1995). *Shapes—Mathematical Thinking.* Highgate Springs, VT: Logo Computer Systems Inc. (LCSI).

Cobb, P. (1996). Where is the mind? A coordination of sociocultural and cognitive constructivist perspectives. In C. T. Fosnot (Ed.), *Constructivism: Theory, perspectives, and practice* (pp. 34–52). New York: Teachers College Press.

Cochran, L. (1991). The art of the universe. *Journal of Mathematical Behavior, 10,* 213–214.

Davis, R. B. (1986). *Learning mathematics: The cognitive science approach to mathematics education.* Norwood, NJ: Ablex.

Dietzman, C. M., & English, L. D. (2001). Promoting the use of diagrams as tools for thinking. In A. A. Cuoco (Ed.), *The roles of representation in school mathematics* (pp. 77–89). Reston, VA: National Council of Teachers of Mathematics.

Empson, S. B. (2002). Organizing diversity in early fraction thinking. In Litwiller, B. (Ed.), *Making sense of fractions, ratios, and proportions* (pp. 29–40). Reston, VA: National Council of Teachers of Mathematics.

Fennema, E., Carpenter, T., Levi, L., Franke, M. L., & Empson, S. (1997). *Cognitively guided instruction: Professional development in primary mathematics.* Madison, WI: Wisconsin Center for Education Research.

Fosnot, C. T., & Dolk, M. (2001). *Young mathematicians at work: Constructing number sense, addition, and subtraction.* Portsmouth, NH: Heinemann.

Fuson, K. C., Wearne, D., Hiebert, J. C., Murray, H. G., Human, P. G., Olivier, A. I., Carpenter, T. P., & Fennema, E. (1997). Childrens' conceptual structures for multidigit numbers and methods of multidigit addition and subtraction. *Journal for Research in School Mathematics, 28,* 130–162.

Fuys, D., Geddes, D., & Tischler, R. (1988). The van Hiele model of thinking in geometry among adolescents. *Journal for Research in Mathematics Education Monograph, 3.*

Geddes, D., & Fortunato, I. (1993). Geometry: Research and classroom activities. In D. T. Owens (Ed.), *Research ideas for the classroom: Middle grades mathematics* (pp. 199–222). New York: Macmillan.

Greenes, C., & Findell, C. (1999). *Groundworks: Algebraic thinking.* Chicago: Creative Publications.

Greer, B. (1992). Multiplication and division as models of situations. In D. A. Grouws (Ed.), *Handbook of research on mathematics teaching and learning* (pp. 276–295). Old Tappan, NJ: Macmillan.

Gutstein, E., & Romberg, T. A. (1995). Teaching children to add and subtract. *Journal of Mathematical Behavior, 14,* 283–324.

Hiebert, J. (1990). The role of routine procedures in the development of mathematical competence. In T. J.

Cooney (Ed.), *Teaching and learning mathematics in the 1990s* (pp. 31–40). Reston, VA: National Council of Teachers of Mathematics.

Hiebert, J., & Carpenter, T. P. (1992). Learning and teaching with understanding. In D. A. Grouws (Ed.), *Handbook of research on mathematics teaching and learning* (pp. 65–97). Old Tappan, NJ: Macmillan.

Hiebert, J., Carpenter, T. P., Fennema, E., Fuson, K., Human, P., Murray, H., Olivier, A., & Wearne, D. (1996). Problem solving as a basis for reform in curriculum and instruction: The case of mathematics. *Educational Researcher, 25* (May), 12–21.

Hiebert, J., Carpenter, T. P., Fennema, E., Fuson, K., Wearne, D., Murray, H., Olivier, A., & Human, P. (1997). *Making sense: Teaching and learning mathematics with understanding.* Portsmouth, NH: Heinemann.

Hiebert, J., & Wearne, D. (1996). Instruction, understanding, and skill in multidigit addition and subtraction. *Cognition and Instruction, 14,* 251–283.

Hoffer, A. R. (1983). van Hiele–based research. In R. A. Lesh & M. Landau (Eds.), *Acquisition of mathematics concepts and processes* (pp. 205–227). Orlando, FL: Academic Press.

Hoffer, A. R., & Hoffer, S. A. K. (1992). Ratios and proportional thinking. In T. R. Post (Ed.), *Teaching mathematics in grades K–8: Research-based methods* (2nd ed.) (pp. 303–330). Needham Heights, MA: Allyn & Bacon.

Huinker, D. (1998). Letting fraction algorithms emerge through problem solving. In L. J. Morrow (Ed.), *The teaching and learning of algorithms in school mathematics* (pp. 170–182). Reston, VA: National Council of Teachers of Mathematics.

Janvier, C. (Ed.). (1987). *Problems of representation in the teaching and learning of mathematics.* Hillsdale, NJ: Erlbaum.

Jones, G. A., Thornton, C. A., Langrall, C. W., & Tarr, J. E. (1999). Understanding students' probabilistic reasoning. In L. V. Stiff (Ed.), *Developing mathematical thinking in grades K–12* (pp. 146–155). Reston, VA: National Council of Teachers of Mathematics.

Kamii, C. K. (1985). *Young children reinvent arithmetic.* New York: Teachers College Press.

Kamii, C. K. (1989). *Young children continue to reinvent arithmetic: 2nd grade.* New York: Teachers College Press.

Kamii, C. K., & Dominick, A. (1997). To teach or not to teach the algorithms. *Journal of Mathematical Behavior, 16,* 51–62.

Kamii, C. K., & Dominick, A. (1998). The harmful effects of algorithms in grades 1–4. In L. J. Morrow (Ed.), *The teaching and learning of algorithms in school mathematics* (pp. 130–140). Reston, VA: National Council of Teachers of Mathematics.

Kamii, C., & Long, K. (2003). The measurement of time: Transitivity, unit iteration, and the conservation of speed. In D. H. Clements (Ed.), *Learning and teaching measurement* (pp. 168–179). Reston, VA: National Council of Teachers of Mathematics.

Kenney, P. A., & Kouba, V. L. (1997). What do students know about measurement? In P. A. Kenney & E. Silver (Eds.), *Results from the sixth mathematics assessment of*

the national assessment of educational progress (pp. 141–163). Reston, VA: National Council of Teachers of Mathematics.

Kulm, G. (1994). *Mathematics and assessment: What works in the classroom.* San Francisco: Jossey-Bass.

Labinowicz, E. (1985). *Learning from children: New beginnings for teaching numerical thinking.* Menlo Park, CA: AWL Supplemental.

Labinowicz, E. (1987). Assessing for learning: The interview method. *Arithmetic Teacher, 35*(3), 22–24.

Lamon, S. J. (1996). The development of unitizing: Its role in children's partitioning strategies. *Journal for Research in Mathematics Education, 27,* 170–193.

Lesh, R. A., Post, T. R., & Behr, M. J. (1987). Representations and translations among representations in mathematics learning and problem solving. In C. Janvier (Ed.), *Problems of representation in the teaching and learning of mathematics* (pp. 33–40). Hillsdale, NJ: Erlbaum.

Liedtke, W. (1988). Diagnosis in mathematics: The advantages of an interview. *Arithmetic Teacher, 36*(3), 26–29.

Lindquist, M. M. (1987). Problem solving with five easy pieces. In J. M. Hill (Ed.), *Geometry for grades K–6: Readings from the Arithmetic Teacher* (pp. 152–156). Reston, VA: National Council of Teachers of Mathematics.

Mack, N. K. (2001). Building on informal knowledge through instruction in a complex content domain: Partitioning, units, and understanding multiplication of fractions. *Journal for Research in Mathematics Education, 32,* 267–295.

Martin, G., & Strutchens, M. E. (2000). Geometry and measurement. In E. A. Silver & P. A. Kenney (Eds.), *Results from the seventh mathematics assessment of the National Assessment of Educational Progress* (pp. 193–234). Reston, VA: National Council of Teachers of Mathematics.

Mokros, J., Russell, S. J., & Economopoulos, K. (1995). *Beyond arithmetic: Changing mathematics in the elementary classroom.* Palo Alto, CA: Dale Seymour Publications.

National Council of Teachers of Mathematics. (1989). *Curriculum and evaluation standards for school mathematics.* Reston, VA: Author.

National Council of Teachers of Mathematics. (1995). *Assessment standards for school mathematics.* Reston, VA: Author.

National Council of Teachers of Mathematics. (2000). *Principles and standards for school mathematics.* Reston, VA: Author.

O'Brien, T. C. (1999). Parrot math. *Phi Delta Kappan, 80,* 434–438.

Post, T. R., Wachsmuth, I., Lesh, R. A., & Behr, M. J. (1985). Order and equivalence of rational numbers: A cognitive analysis. *Journal for Research in Mathematics Education, 16,* 18–36.

Pothier, Y., & Sawada, D. (1983). Partitioning: The emergence of rational number ideas in young children.

Journal for Research in Mathematics Education, 14, 307–317.

Rathmell, E. C., Leutzinger, L. P., & Gabriele, A. (2000). *Thinking with numbers.* Cedar Falls, IA: Thinking With Numbers.

Reys, B. J., & Reys, R. E. (1995). Japanese mathematics education: What makes it work. *Teaching Children Mathematics, 1,* 474–475.

Ross, S. H. (1986). *The development of children's place-value numeration concepts in grades two through five.* Presented at the annual meeting of the American Educational Research Association, San Francisco. (ERIC Document Reproduction Service No. ED 2773 482)

Ross, S. H. (1989). Parts, wholes, and place value: A developmental perspective. *Arithmetic Teacher, 36*(6), 47–51.

Rowan, T. E., & Bourne, B. (1994). *Thinking like mathematicians: Putting the K–4 standards into practice.* Portsmouth, NH: Heinemann.

Scheer, J. K. (1980). The etiquette of diagnosis. *Arithmetic Teacher, 27*(9), 18–19.

Schroeder, T. L., & Lester, F. K., Jr. (1989). Developing understanding in mathematics via problem solving. In P. R. Trafton (Ed.), *New directions for elementary school mathematics* (pp. 31–42). Reston, VA: National Council of Teachers of Mathematics.

Schwartz, S. L. (1996). Hidden messages in teacher talk: Praise and empowerment. *Teaching Children Mathematics, 2,* 396–401.

Silver, E. A., & Stein, M. K. (1996). The QUASAR project: The "revolution of the possible" in mathematics instructional reform in urban middle schools. *Urban Education, 30,* 476–521.

Smith, J. P., III. (2002). The development of students' knowledge of fractions and ratios. In B. Litwiller, (Ed.), *Making sense of fractions, ratios, and proportions* (pp. 3–17). Reston, VA: National Council of Teachers of Mathematics.

Sunburst Communications. (1995). *Shape up.* Pleasantville, NY: Author.

Thompson, P. W. (1994). Concrete materials and teaching for mathematical understanding. *Arithmetic Teacher, 41,* 556–558.

Tom Snyder Productions. (1993). *The graph club* [Computer Software]. Watertown, MA: Author.

Tzur, R. (1999). An integrated study of children's construction of improper fractions and the teacher's role in promoting learning. *Journal for Research in Mathematics Education, 30,* 390–416.

van Hiele, P. M. (1999). Developing geometric thinking through activities that begin with play. *Teaching Children Mathematics, 5,* 310–316.

Wood, T., & Turner-Vorbeck, T. (2001). Extending the conception of mathematics teaching. In T. Wood, B. S. Nelson, & J. Warfield (Eds.), *Beyond classical pedagogy: Teaching elementary school mathematics* (pp. 185–208). Mahwah, NJ: Lawrence Erlbaum.

INDEX